M000020874

THE PERILS OF THE ONE

THE PERILS OF THE ONE

STATHIS GOURGOURIS

Columbia University Press
New York

Columbia University Press
Publishers Since 1893
New York   Chichester, West Sussex
cup.columbia.edu

Library of Congress Cataloging-in-Publication Data
Names: Gourgouris, Stathis, 1958– author.
Title: The perils of the one / Stathis Gourgouris.
Description: New York : Columbia University Press, 2019. |
Includes bibliographical references and index.
Identifiers: LCCN 2018050155 | ISBN 9780231192880 (cloth : alk. paper) |
ISBN 9780231550024 (ebook)
Subjects: LCSH: Transcendence (Philosophy) | Critical theory. |
Political science—Philosophy. | Said, Edward W.
Classification: LCC BD362 .G68 2019 | DDC 199/.495—dc23
LC record available at https://lccn.loc.gov/2018050155

Columbia University Press books are printed
on permanent and durable acid-free paper.
Printed in the United States of America

Cover image: Painting from the Tomb of the Diver from the southern
cemetery at Paestum, 480-470 BC (fresco), Etruscan (5th century BC) /
Museo Archeologico Nazionale di Paestum, Capaccio, Salerno, Campania,
Italy / Bridgeman Images

for Neni, always

CONTENTS

PREFACE

For a long time now, I've come to terms with the fact that books write themselves—and not just books, all compositions. I don't mean to subjectify the object. I am just pointing to what, in my experience at least, seems unavoidable. Compositions emerge from some irreducible improvisation, even if they're never actualized and remain just flashes of thought. What enables them to be constituted is a specific time and space that they come to occupy uniquely. This space-time dimension belongs to them fully and may be thought of as the fold within which they are generated. Of course, once actualized, fully composed, and objectified, they belong to the space-time of history, within which they may continue to live or die, freed not only from the author's intentions but from their own parameters of composition.

Composite projects and artworks, series or suites, exhibitions or installations, collections of poetry—indeed, all multiple iterations within a specific formal or thematic rubric—dramatize this contingent space-time even further. The uniqueness of each part is implicated in a nexus that exceeds it without abolishing it. *The Perils of the One* likewise belongs to a nexus I have titled "lessons in secular criticism," but it is hardly situated in a sequence. It bears both an inaugural mark and the mark of consequence.

The still ongoing "lessons in secular criticism" project—a third book, titled *Nothing Sacred*, is nearly completed—has followed a long and circuitous trajectory, very much on track with the immanent and improvisational nature of its name. As secular criticism is foremost a practice and not a theory, whatever elements may figure as its theoretical principles at different points in time cannot hold on to the primacy of concept that would characterize a systematic work. Whatever may be the conceptual sovereignty of such theoretical vantage points in their own time, it is always provisional. It comes and goes, sometimes like the tide (where a certain repetition itself holds theoretical sway), but other times by way of what all sovereignty inevitably faces: vanishing with the same groundbreaking force that it had once emerged.

In this trajectory, the "Thinking Out Loud Lectures in Philosophy and Society" that I gave at the Sydney State Library, which then formed the backbone of *Lessons in Secular Criticism* (2013), signify all at once the distillation, culmination, and general framework of the entire fifteen-year-long research project. In comparison, *The Perils of the One* includes some of the earliest and most formative material of the project. For example, the first version of "The Lesson of Pierre Clastres" was created back in 1999, while in fact I was in the midst of writing *Does Literature Think?* Indeed, at that time, I had very much considered the essay on Clastres to belong to those studies in mythographic thinking, and surely in its present form it serves as a sort of bridge document, testifying to the endemic connection between the secular criticism project and the epistemology of literature project. The same can be said of the discussion of Karlheinz Stockhausen's notorious remarks about 9/11 or of Sigmund Freud's mythistorical fictions of Moses, to take opening and closing examples among multiple such moments and figures strewn throughout the book. The intersections between these two projects are tangible. The radical creative capacities of mythic and poietic thinking are constitutive of the secular imagination, as well as necessary to any sort of critical encounter with social reality that does not compromise its political significance.

From this standpoint, all the work I have ever done, in all its range of forms and perspectives, historical or philosophical, artistic or performative, consists of nothing more than an attempt to negotiate the encounter between the poetic and the political. *Poiēsis* and *krisis* are practices that are enmeshed in my mind. One can never make a judgment without creating a form. And no created form exists in some pure aesthetic plenitude, transcendentally immune from the politics of its own emergence. We can choose to separate, to isolate—perhaps with the provisional advantage of gaining a certain perspective—but this too is a critical decision, a judgment, and it bears a politics, no matter if we choose to ignore the fact of this politics, and it bears a form, no matter if we can't quite conceive or concede this form's existence. Secular criticism is the sort of practice that first and foremost acknowledges the worldliness of all creation and resists the presumption that critique is impartial.

***

The term *secular criticism* belongs to Edward Said and I deploy it very much in his spirit, even if not quite in his language, as a kind of open-ended interrogative encounter with the world that not only disdains but uncompromisingly subverts, battles, and outdoes any sort of transcendentalist resolution of social and historical problems. The task of secular criticism is to confront social-historical situations where authority is assumed to emerge from *elsewhere*—and to do so from within those situations. This is why it is not a theory but a practice. This is also why, as a practice, it is always involved, in one form or another, in a deconstruction of transcendence. The fact that I begin the book with an essay called "Transformation, Not Transcendence," which is an examination of Edward Said's overall epistemology, is hardly incidental.

This deconstruction of transcendence is not merely formal; it engages a specific politics—as does all deconstruction worthy of its name, whether acknowledged or not. In other words, I am not merely interested in a philosophical critique of transcendence in favor of, say, a philosophy of immanence (even if I have been personally partial to immanent criticism since my earliest studies of Adorno). Rather, I conduct a critique of the *politics of transcendence* as this is manifested in a broad range of historical instances and theoretical languages, always careful to remain attentive to the historical and geographical specifics but impervious to those commands that aim at the construction of specific identities. This process is inevitably long and circuitous. Said often reminds us that secular interpretation requires a certain historical slowness, as opposed to the ahistorical speed scale of identity-making and identity politics, religious or secular regardless.

By contesting a politics of transcendence in favor of a politics of transformation, I not only mean to engage with occasions where a religious imaginary exhaustively occupies the domain of the political (even if these are increasingly prevalent in our time), but equally the less apparent secularist metaphysics of so-called Western democracies. The latter is a misnomer all around, not only by the political-philosophical standards of democracy but also by the geocultural standards that continue to confine societies of global immigration and contentious cultural differences to the vacuous toponym of "the West." Whether it faces the legacy of Kantian transcendentalist morality or the indomitable (pseudo) rationalism of market economics and technocracy, secular criticism proceeds along the same interrogative path as when it faces any politics of faith. If one is to engage responsibly in this sort of Saidian practice, the task of secular criticism would spare none of its critical capacity in the face of uninterrogated secularist mentalities, which exhibit the same faith in an origin of authority believed to transcend their social-historical boundaries as do the religious faithful in their ubiquitous divinity. The trajectory of the institutional politics of secularism since Said's writings in the 1980s has not altered the landscape of his argument. On the contrary, it registers the superlative confirmation of his argument, evident most of all in the way that Said's writing is often ignored or disparaged by the avatars of academic anti-secularism. In the end, an essential political and epistemological point is evaded: the critique of religion and the critique of secularism are actually the same work—the work of secular criticism.

Moreover, a critique of the politics of transcendence does not mean adopting a self-referential framework, where, for example, the social is explored in terms of society, the historical in terms of history, etc.—a framework, in other words, presumed to be closed and bound by its own repetition, tautologically immanent in that sense. On the contrary, such critique opens up spaces where no interrogation of the social, the historical, the political—indeed, I would add, the anthropological—can take place without confronting the enigma of social-imaginary institution: namely, the psychohistorical process by which societies produce and reproduce themselves and their others, their identities and their alterities.

This process is always *in excess* of whatever already exists, whatever is already instituted, even if, as is most often the case, this excess is duly occluded and erased from memory. In other words, social-imaginary institution isn't a process of mere social reproduction, no matter what contortions in the collective unconscious are always needed to ensure simple reproduction. The enigma of social-imaginary institution is, in another language, the enigma of discontinuity in history. From this standpoint, the question raised by the task of secular criticism can be rephrased: Can we conceive the political as a realm of society's self-critical interrogation of its destiny and not reduce it to the schema of power becoming external to society, independent of society? Or, from another angle, can we envision the social-historical realm without necessarily falling back on some specific framework of social organization or discipline, without having to translate the terms of the social-historical to the classic relation between command and obedience?

***

Here, it is necessary to interject an elaboration on how I use the term *transcendence* in light also of various criticisms raised to my use of it in *Lessons in Secular Criticism*. I understand the concern behind the charge that I may be violating a core principle of philosophy by erasing the difference between the transcendent and the transcendental. There is no secret, I am certainly not a Kantian and I cast doubt on the presumption that this difference is a core principle of philosophy. I don't recognize the Kantian difference in the same way I don't recognize Heidegger's ontological difference. In fact, the two are kin frameworks. Kant names as transcendent those principles that exceed experience, and this is necessary to him in order to posit an impartial, categorical ethics—a *transcendental* ethics that is based on a priori principles even if these principles are nominally worldly. It's certainly not clear to me what exactly exceeds experience, if our notion of experience is not reduced to the scientifically empirical or even more to some sort of subjective psychology but covers a range of social-historical material that cannot be determined or limited a priori. Instead, the a priori determination of principles that stand on their own terms is precisely the mark of authority presumed-to-be elsewhere, which, as I said earlier, secular criticism relentlessly confronts.

The fact that this *a priori* and *elsewhere* are conceivable—or, more accurately, determinable—by the faculty of reason means nothing to me. Reason does not exist as such—any more than Being exists as such. Both are phantasms created by the human animal as aspects of its specific mode of living/being-in-the-world. They are sublime phantasms, they may even have become existentially necessary phantasms, but as phantasms they are themselves subject to the interminable (and indeterminable) range of subjective experience: the interminable and indeterminable variations of the interplay between life and death. But this is not the place to consume ourselves in this debate.

The most legitimate objection is the one which rightfully protests that without the possibility of exceeding one's situation no change is possible. It is not clear to me, however, that to exceed your situation presupposes a verifiable existing standpoint already assumed to be beyond your situation. Here, basic Aristotle is useful: the elemental notion that to change means at the very least to move. I take this notion as a point of departure without consenting to Aristotelian entelechy, to what he sees as the teleological necessity embedded in every being. We are not concerned here with ends, embedded or otherwise. To move elsewhere than where you are (situated) does not mean to move forward or backward, better or worse. It just means to alter your position.

One can object that this means no alteration, but mere variation. Yet, I don't think the notion of variation can measure up to or sustain its meaning against the notion of excess—of exceeding one's situation. Variation remains within the playfield of the situation. It confirms its reference frame by confining difference to the realm of identity, even if identity may be thought to be pluralized by its variation. In any case, a transcendent standpoint (at least in Kantian terms) requires an understanding of something beyond mere variation.

So, the big question becomes how to measure the production of difference versus the production of otherness in relation to a situation. While variation is a matter of difference, radical alteration means the production of otherness. The wager for me is how this production of otherness can take place without presupposing a transcendent standpoint that enables it—even *in potentia*—and at the same time without producing (performing) a semblance or assumption of a transcendent point as a result: that is, neither a transcendental end point (*telos*) of alteration nor a transcendent point as a priori *archē* (enabling potential) of alteration.

We have to be able to imagine—and give language to—the possibility that one can exceed one's situation from within the terms of that situation by altering the terms of that situation. This does not mean that this is the work of the mind—of the intellectual will or any other such trope (reason or imagination) that would confine us within the well-known Enlightenment/Romanticism nexus of the "external" self-sufficient subject. There are plenty of "internal/objective" factors that can activate the potential in any situation to unravel within its own terms and thus to be altered and to exceed—if you will, transcend—itself.

Of course, it's perfectly understandable why human beings desire to imagine self-sufficient transcendent/transcendental spaces, or even the idea of transcendence as something in itself, as independent of situation and action. But this isn't to say that human beings *must* do so in order to change, in order to exceed their situation. Nor is it to say that, once they change or exceed their situation, they *must* attribute this fact to a transcendental process.

The greatest obstacle in this discussion is, of course, the problem of change—radical change. I'm not interested in the rationalist-objectivist desire or need for the transcendent point to serve as external point of evaluation, judgment, or critique. I don't believe that such a point is sustainable in the same way that I don't believe perfect impartiality in judgment is sustainable. In order, however, not to get mired in subjectivist self-enclosure, we have to give ground to the situation as fact, as a mark in space, however determinable or not. How this mark in space is altered—how it moves or how we move from it—has to account also for how we move by means of it, how we exceed it by means of it, or how we make it exceed itself from within it. Otherwise, we wade in subjectivist enclosure, which would encompass even the most indeterminate transcendent/transcendental standpoint.

The question that haunts this whole issue is, how can anything be altered if in fact it resides all within itself? Much of this I have answered in the essay "Confronting Heteronomy" in *Lessons in Secular Criticism*. Surely, an amoeba as an entity all-within-itself cannot radically alter itself. It is altered by some wholly other externality: a counter-organism, a drug, a poisonous environment. From that standpoint, transcendence is nothing else but a name for the abyss that signifies the otherness of existence—indeed, a name that occludes (and occults) the otherness of existence as if it is a thing, a something that can be handled. But single-cell organisms aside, the symbiotic complexity of life does not allow such easy designations of externality, where a name, a sacred name or a sacred space, can be invented to seal the abyss. And even so, why should such projections of altering externality, however ambiguous and complex and whatever may be their names, necessarily mark a transcendent horizon? Can we retain a radical notion of existential otherness without imputing transcendence to it? That's the profound wager of secular criticism.

***

In the end, the problem of transcendence per se is secondary relative to my concern with how transcendence seems unavoidably imagined as a unitary horizon. However inventively conceivable or vaguely determinable, an Elsewhere is never plural. In fact, no transcendentalized authority can be plural, even if its subjectivity is presumed to be plural. We need not elaborate here on the obvious problem with political notions such as "the people" or, in the Spinoza-derived idiom, "the multitude"; their revolutionary transcendentalism abolishes their subjective plurality. But this is the case also when the subject does indeed remain plural. For instance, insofar as they became a transcendental authority, "the workers" were reduced either to "the proletariat" or, in more guarded but nonetheless still monological fashion, to "the workers' movement."

I mention outright these political terms—and without in fact dwelling on the more obvious ones: the state, the nation, the community, and the like—so as not to begin where one conventionally considers secular criticism to begin: the critique of religion. There is no doubt, of course, that a great part of this book addresses monotheistic transcendentalism in this regard. All theistic religions have some form of transcendentalism in common, but monotheistic religions, no matter whether they enact heterogeneous or differential rituals of devotion to divinity, posit a framework of authority that not only emerges from elsewhere but determines this elsewhere to be *monological*—or, to use a language of Latin derivation, unique, unitary, and, insofar as it produces a speech, universal. In this specific sense, the general aim of this framework of lessons is to address the perils of *monological* thinking in the entire range from monotheism to universalism in both "East" and "West."

Universalism is not just the prerogative of Christianity; in Christianity it's just explicitly professed. It exists in all three religions of the Book, as the characterization itself suggests. The divine text's purchase of the truth is not just one's own, the truth of the faithful; it's the one-and-only truth of the universe. The singularity of the perspective—the exclusivity, the exceptionalism, whether of "the chosen people" or the authentic faith that produces infidels everywhere—does not alleviate the totalizing power of this truth. In a strange way, this one-and-only truth is not an end but a means, a perfect and total instrument. By means of it, appalling (even if sublime) ends are achieved. That's the essence of fundamentalist logic, which is not exclusive to religion but would include militant universalism and its zealots—all zealots, regardless: "their actions may be appalling, but their quotations are perfect."[1]

"Monotheism" is recognized as a name in the discourse of religion, but it interests me as a political term. In this respect, it belongs together with a whole a set of such *monological* notions, starting with Odo Marquard's incisive notion of "monomythical thinking" and extending to other kin figures such as "mononatural" (Bruno Latour), "monolatry" and "monohumanism" (Peter Sloterdijk), "monocentrism" (Edward Said), "monolingualism" (Jacques Derrida), and "monovalence" (Peter Sloterdijk, Jean-Luc Nancy). These terms play specific roles in their own discourses but they converge on political grounds. They point to discourses that are *monarchical* in the strict sense of the word: discourses that are authorized by a singular *archē*—simultaneously a single point of origin and a core or primary principle—and produce in turn situations that make such singular *archē* meaningful in ever-renewable ways.

The political stakes of this process are so elementary that it seems scandalous to me that they are not being confronted in their terms, spawning instead an inordinate variety of discursive inventions—languages, concepts, frames of knowledge—that make sure this recognition will never happen. Theological frames are supremely deceptive in this regard, especially as Carl Schmitt's notorious axiom—"all significant concepts of the modern theory of the state are secularized theological concepts"—is nowadays treated by the academy as self-evident fact. Political theology may be one of the most deceptive discourses of our time, and the fact that it remains so uninterrogated while at the same time being relentlessly discussed is a perfect symptom of its deceptiveness. Paraphrasing Schmitt, but against this debilitating frame, the premise of this book is to test the grounds of a counter-proposition: namely, that *all significant concepts of the modern theory of the state are residual monarchical concepts*.

The book is not, of course, focused on theories of the state per se. After all, as a social-imaginary institution, the state is but a symptom of the basic heteronomous division in society along the lines of command and obedience. And one of the core forces driving this text is a repudiation of command/obedience structures. In many ways, a position against command and obedience is situated against presumptions of liberal subjectivity where the range of becoming/being a subject is framed along the lines of domination and resistance, whether in terms of relations to power in the everyday (capitalist) world, or in terms of what is internally constructed in the psychic space of desire (or even consciousness) that is essential to the formation of self and encounter with the other. So, even when engaged with problems of sovereignty or the state per se, this book is not an exercise in political philosophy, strictly speaking. It is closer to an exercise in philosophical anthropology, even if unorthodox in relation to the discipline, and with specific forays into psychohistorical inquiry. Thus, even when large questions of social-imaginary institution are examined in various cultural and historical instances, the book persistently returns, even if not always explicitly, to the question of the subject, which after all epitomizes psychosocial formation. The question of the One and the question of the subject are entwined—in the obvious sense that pertains to the core of the problem of autonomy, but also in the less evident sense that makes the encounter with oneness a problem from the standpoint of singularity or, as Derrida often argued, iterability. In this respect, I have learned a great deal from Samuel Weber's incisive considerations of singularity in its various discourses. As he says bluntly, singularity is always an uncanny experience—using the translation of Freud's *unheimlich* into French as *inquiétant*, but mining from the word its colloquial use as well: disquieting, disruptive of stability, disturbing.[2]

Weber's reading is correct, for singularity can never quite be assimilated into the order of things; it cannot be mathematized. This is why singularity cannot find safety under the sign of the One. It exceeds even the safety of concept, since the singular cannot be located in the range between difference and repetition. Even gravitational singularity in physics, which is presumed by mathematical projection, is tantamount to the dissolution of physics as we know it, where infinity and the single point become one and the same, therefore none, neither point nor infinity as we know them conceptually. In essence, singularity does not exist; conceptual language cannot convey it, since every utterance that calls it forth plunges it into the realm of identity/difference and makes it vanish. No doubt, we do have a *sense* of the thing that cannot ever be reiterated—even its phantom, as trace of its appearance, betrays it—but this sense belongs to the realm of intuition. Singularity cannot be conceptualized or analyzed. It can be known, but only in the sense of being grasped as imagined—apprehended, not comprehended, in a single moment before it vanishes. It's true, as Weber points out, that the singular provokes repetition at the very same time that it resists it (305), but this too is no more than a trick of language and its psychosocial consequences: the desire to make connections between a beginning and an end. The key question that emerges is, what compels us to trace repetition to a singular moment of emergence, an *archē*? Or even more, what compels us to determine that this trajectory, this narrative unfolding from beginning to end, this reiteration of moments between the One and the Multiple, constitutes an Elsewhere, parallel to the singularity that refuses to be connected to anything?

***

Insofar as singularity cannot be ultimately mathematized, it refuses the logical framework of the One—and the All, which is the most deceptive conceptual victory of the One. As opposed to oneness, "singularity perturbs and fragments the economy of self (*soi*)" (*Inquiétantes singularités*, 195) where *soi*, in French, is a linguistic category that carries none of the humanist/subjectivist elements of "self," which are unavoidable in English. We need to keep this linguistic character in mind whenever in the text we encounter the prefix "self-," which I use persistently and in a number of ways that are crucial to the argument: self-critique, self-determination, self-interrogation, self-limitation, self-authorization, self-alteration, and so on. Self-alteration especially—to which a whole essay is specifically devoted—is the core element in the elaboration of autonomy, which runs in the background of the entire book and in the series of lessons in secular criticism generally.

In my terms, autonomy is neither primary nor foundational, and it is as foreign as can be imagined to the Kantian use (whether we deem it transcendentalist or not). Autonomy is not a ground, except nominally in a specific utterance. And this is because autonomy equals self-alteration. The terms imply each other and are intertwined. Autonomy is not a state (of being), but a process (of coming to being from non-being and back again). It is not a state, but a flow—of becoming other. This is why autonomy does not mean autarky (self-sufficiency), as is often thought to mean, and this is also why it is not exclusionary because it has no limits—except for the ones that it places provisionally on itself before the abyssal absence of limits that it cannot overcome. Autonomy's difference from heteronomy at this literal level consists in the fact that, while in heteronomy the other is the subject of the law (the other who establishes and executes the law), in autonomy the other resides within the process itself, within the otherness created by giving—and in the very moment of giving—oneself the law.

Of course, in real social-historical terms this is always the case regardless. From the general standpoint of social-imaginary institution, no law is created by an other. All societies create their own law(s). Heteronomy occurs because the otherness produced at the very moment of the creation of the law—the *archē* of autonomy—is transferred either to the law itself (both sacred and secular) or to an extra-social source of authority that is thereby abstracted from the process of societal institution. This too can be either sacred (God or the Book) or secular (the Monarch or the Constitution)—same difference, as the fabulous American saying goes.

It makes sense that this otherness in autonomy often goes unconfronted or is repressed. It is literally unbearable, for what conceptual framework in traditional Western metaphysics can handle the self-as-other? We encounter it in psychoanalysis, of course, but psychoanalytic thinking is hardly likely to ever be the framework on which societies institute themselves. But in addition to psychoanalysis and a modern tradition of nonidentitarian thinking that extends from Adorno to Said, what enabled me most to unlock traditional notions of autonomy so as to entwine it with self-alteration was the long-term engagement of feminist thinking with the problem of sexual difference. For, in the most elementary terms of the argument in this book, sexual difference is the insurmountable division of the One.

In the essay on self-alteration and sexual difference, which thinks together the psychoanalytic work of Cornelius Castoriadis with the philosophical work of Judith Butler and Luce Irigaray, as well as in the last section in the essay on Clastres, where I account for Nicole Loraux's critique, I sought specifically to unwind the many tropes by which sexual difference troubles identity and dislocates the power of the One. In another language, we might say that sexual difference incapacitates the law of genre, not because it abolishes the general in favor of the particular—as it's often, rather lazily, made to do in social reality—but because it disrupts the coincidence of the general with the particular (the simultaneity of Man with human, human with person, sex with gender, and so on). In this specific sense, it is unfortunate that the politics of sexual difference has often been forced into the politics of identity, which unavoidably obeys the law of genre even when it claims not to. The same can be said of the also rather lazy presumption that transgendering or transsexual practices abolish sexual difference. Especially when this presumption is deployed in the service of a politics of identity, when it makes itself into an identity, the transgender or transsexual position exemplifies the law of genre. It makes a general category out of its professed non-category, not to mention that, in its almost ontological claims (even if radically contrarian), it undercuts the profoundly subversive tradition of transvestism, whose inveterate performativity de facto disarticulates investment in identity. On the contrary, when they refuse identity, both transsexual and transgender positions actually dramatize the terrain of sexual difference as quintessentially disruptive of monological or monovalent thinking, which includes the explicitly non-binary and relational elements these positions put into action.[3]

Without making a direct connection, in several instances and in different registers in the book I have sought to expose how the logic of identity is a perfect actualization of heteronomy, much as, in reverse, autonomy implies self-alteration. Identitarian thinking always obeys the logic of the One, and this is hardly a phenomenon of modernity, as my close readings of Early Christian theology (the Apostle Paul or Saint Gregory Nazianzus) or, in counterposition, Renaissance anti-Christian and anti-monarchical thinking (Etienne de La Boétie's notion of "voluntary servitude") elaborate. What I mean to say is that the logic of identity bears a monovalent ontology regardless of its historical situation. To quote Peter Sloterdijk indicatively: "Monovalence of speech about what is means: the things that are said to be actually are, and if they're said they are not, they are not; nor are they anything other than what they are. Hence, they share in being, both in the fact *that* and the act of *what* and *how*. Hence, they can best be expressed in tautologies" (*God's Zeal*, 92).

The broad historical range of the material treated here, often in juxtapositions that defy the strict demands of history as a discipline, can also be seen as a gesture of resisting or evading the logic of identity that lies at the core of monarchical/monovalent thinking. This is also the case with the rather uncoordinated entwinement of a range of discourses and disciplinary languages (philosophy, political theory, literary and art criticism, feminism, anthropology, psychoanalysis, theology, biography, and history as such), which is less a decision to engage in "interdisciplinarity" and more symptomatic of the object that provokes the inquiry and the mode of thinking that the writing seeks to discover in the process.

In saying this, I still defend my choice of insisting on the term *lessons*, which pertains to the overall project. The didactic tenet of this word is commensurable with the interrogative character of secular criticism. The point is to elucidate instances of critique and certain thinking practices of question that exemplify Said's calling for secular criticism and its precarious encounter with the worldly, even if in a manner he would not necessarily have adopted. Following this line, the point becomes to map a trajectory of experimentation with various methods of thinking against transcendence—indeed, going so far as to transform terms and modes of thinking so that transcendentalist solutions to historical problems are shown to be ultimately unfeasible.

But I would add that the overall impetus of these essays, of these lessons, is to showcase a gallery of exemplary didactic instances by certain thinkers who, whatever might be their recognized expertise (and sometimes even despite their intentions), ultimately foster and practice *auto-didacticism*, a sort of self-teaching position that encapsulates the risk of experimental thinking by undoing, in the practice itself, the external authority of a Master Other, the authority of heteronomous knowledge that transcendentalist thinking confirms and perpetuates. Often, I choose to realize this—I mean in a theatrical sense, to stage it—by engaging in rather uncanny juxtapositions, which are neither historically justified (say, the juxtaposition of Amazonian Indians with ancient Athenians) nor epistemologically conventional (the Trinity as monarchy or monotheism as a political problem). This risk exemplifies the task of the essay as a genre—as an altogether idiomatic and perhaps even paradoxical form of writing that proceeds "methodically unmethodically," as Adorno put it with uncanny precision.

For the same reason, the essays are not made to mask their occasions or grounds of emergence, which is also to say, their improvisational character, even if they are revisited and reconfigured in time as a result of new situations that arise in order to produce new frameworks of question. In the long time it has taken me to bring this project to completion, one advantage has been to weave together the radically contingent points of departure (which I have tried, as much as I can, to keep intact, or at least recognizable in their terms) with the retrospective re-evaluation of a problem or reconfiguration of the initial impetus. In musical terms, I have allowed improvisations to become compositions in the same way that I have allowed myself to sustain each essay as a compositional space where new improvisations—provoked by new events or new encounters—might unfold. Much like the process of literally forming and conducting a lesson, this book has grown in directions I had initially never considered possible and in terrains I came to discover, as this process was for me as well a matter of learning.

In the last instance, the historical ground that permeates these essays, both in the singular space-time of their emergence and in the plurality of spaces and temporalities that the essays themselves create in the process of being written and in the encounter with one another, is the world as it was marked by a specific trajectory from the events of 9/11 to the ensuing global financial crisis and the deadly radiation they produced. Without meaning to reduce this space-time complexity to one or two moments, I am acknowledging the fact that these singular events—themselves, no doubt, symptoms of long-term, developed, and embedded social-historical situations on a global scale—produced new epistemological conditions and different insurrectionary mentalities around the world, whose structures and connections we are still struggling to clarify. The sheer fact of continuous war that has irreparably damaged societies and annihilated populations, redrafted borders and identities, deracinated practices and beliefs, regenerated old hatreds and generated new ones, and most of all inspired catastrophic and apocalyptic visions that ultimately deprive societies of self-critical consciousness cannot be dismissed as some sideline show that goes on while we (academics, scholars, researchers, scientists, writers, or artists) continue to "just do our work" unaffected. Without being objects of pure determination by history as if we are products of some historical assembly line, we nonetheless never work in a formal vacuum. So, even if we look backward into the depths of time or forward to what we can't quite yet envision, we are doing no more than trying to understand where we are. This too is a core aspect in the practice of secular criticism and indeed of the essay as a form of writing that best encapsulates the pedagogy of this practice.

ACKNOWLEDGMENTS

Given the importance of contingent points of emergence and reconsideration, which always, as in every lesson, happen in public, I record here the occasions of presentation or publication that formed and enabled each essay to exist in a variety of forms over time until they came to be finalized in this book's folds, with my profound gratitude to all those who extended to me their generosity and hospitality in numerous ways.

"Transformation, Not Transcendence" was initially commissioned by Aamir Mufti for a special issue on "Critical Secularisms" in *boundary* 2, where an early version was first published (31, no. 2 [Summer 2004]). "The Late Style of Edward Said," which I include here as appendix to the original essay, was commissioned by Ferial Ghazoul for the Egyptian journal *Alif* and was republished in his volume *Edward Said and Critical Decolonization* (American University of Cairo Press, 2007). The fact that Edward Said read and discussed with me the first manuscript of this essay concerning his work, while he was in Cambridge in 2003 just a few months before his death, is a gift I treasure beyond account. The final essay in this book remains haunted by it.

"The Lesson of Pierre Clastres" was initially presented at the American Anthropological Association meetings in Chicago (1999), at the invitation of Neni Panourgia, and subsequently as the keynote lecture for the Belgrade Circle conference "The Duty of Collective Memory" (2004), at the invitation of Obrad Savić. The fact that no part of it was ever published or presented anywhere else over all these years makes this essay unique as a kind of personal laboratory of my thinking over a long time of evaluation and reconsideration. Of all the work here, this has benefited the most from my teaching Clastres's work in several pedagogical contexts and at different universities. It is indeed a lesson in more ways than one.

"On Self-Alteration" owes itself initially to the invitation by Athena Athanasiou and Elena Tzelepis to think about the problem of sexual difference for a volume on the work of Luce Irigaray (*Rewriting Difference: Luce Irigaray and "the Greeks,"* SUNY Press, 2010). Other parts of the essay were published in the Australian online journal *Parrhesia* (9 [Spring 2010]), for which I thank Arne de Boever, and in the volume *Creation, Rationality, and Autonomy* (Malmö, Sweden: NSU Press, 2013), for which I thank Ingerid Straume.

"Žižek's Realism" was initially commissioned as part of the DVD release of the film *Slavoj Žižek: The Reality of the Virtual*, produced by Ben Wright and Olive Films, 2007. "Recoil from the Real?—Žižek Out of Athens," which I include here as an appendix, with significant additions and reworkings, was published in *Psychoanalysis, Culture, and Society* (16, no. 3 [September 2011]) at the request of Dušan Bjelić.

"Paul's Greek" was initially written in Los Angeles in 2006 at the request of Hent de Vries and Ward Blanton, after conversations with both of them, which were instrumental for what eventually became their volume *Paul and the Philosophers* (Fordham University Press, 2014). I dedicate this final version to the memory of Helen Tartar. She and I worked (and fought) over the argument's various excesses with tenacity—it was, alas, our last editorial collaboration.

"Every Religion Is Idolatry," which is by far the longest essay in the book, has had equally long-term, circuitous, and multiple fragmentary histories of presentation and publication. Different parts were presented in turn at the Hannah Arendt Symposium, New School of Social Research (2011), as part of "Thinking Out Loud: Sydney Lectures in Philosophy and Society" at the Sydney State Library in Australia (2012), at Northwestern University (2013), at Birkbeck College, London (2014), and as the Annual "Constellations" lecture in New York (2015). Various small fragments of it were published in the journals *Social Research* (80, no. 1 [Spring 2013]), *boundary 2* 40, no. 1 [Spring 2013]), and *Constellations* (23, no. 2 [June 2016]). For the opportunity of all these occasions, I thank Richard Bernstein, Paul Bové, Jean Cohen, Costas Douzinas, Andreas Kalyvas, Aamir Mufti, Folahan Olowoyeye, and Dimitris Vardoulakis. This is the first occasion where, in lieu of published and unpublished fragments, this complex historical and philosophical argument is articulated in its full-fledged baroque architecture.

As with everything I write, my close friends and students are present all over this book. Their arguments and questions, or sometimes just simply their patience as interlocutors, kept these texts open and alive and turned them into paths of discovery. My gratitude to them is beyond measure.

But for the overall impetus of the project and the source of persistence in pursuing it through so many distractions and contingencies, I must invoke the bright, even if sad, memory of my two most significant intellectual mentors, Cornelius Castoriadis (Constantinople 1922–Paris 1997) and Edward W. Said (Jerusalem 1935–New York 2003), in whose exilic sensibility the worldliness of human lives meant everything and unworldly constructions were irrelevant. I hope that I have been worthy of their lessons.

Galaxidi, June 2018

THE PERILS OF THE ONE

CHAPTER 1

TRANSFORMATION, NOT TRANSCENDENCE

This essay belongs to a trail of meditations on the secular imagination, by which I mean, very broadly, humanity's capacity (occasional though it is) to conceptualize its existence in the absence of external and transcendental authority, and thus to exercise its radical potential for transforming the conditions of its existence in full cognizance of its historical character. Obviously, this demands an interrogation as to what constitutes the historical subject—the subject of history as well as, of course, the subject in history—and would thus require equally an investigation of subjectivity's psychic dimensions. (Hence, the simultaneous interest in the politics of sublimation, though on this occasion this will be broached only tangentially.) The central figure here is the project of Edward Said, as indicative of an intransigent intellectual position that seeks the critique and transformation of existing conditions—and this holds true equally in matters of aesthetic form (literature, music) and social-political action (the Palestinian question)—without submitting to the allure of otherworldly or transcendent solutions. The motif of transformation against the grain of transcendence is the core element in Said's conceptual framework. It reaches beyond mere opposition between the secular and the religious to another configuration that strips away from the religious (and indeed from metaphysics itself) an assumed imperviousness to the political, so that perhaps we may speak of Said's work, rather dramatically, as an exfoliation of the repressed politics of transcendence.[1]

If Said's core understanding of these elements tends to elude the majority of critics in favor of discussing his other, more explicitly political, aspects, the events and aftermath of 9/11 underscore evermore profoundly the urgency of what he calls secular criticism. The present historical moment, I believe, marks a watershed for a range of positions (often held with dire political consequences) on the relation between religion and politics, which I draw here in the broadest sense to include our elemental decisions as to what constitutes our encounter, as historical subjects, with the world. Hence the impression of real methodological and epistemological confusion over the global significance of the events of 9/11, particularly as revealed by certain voices in—let us say, for the sake of argument—the "secular Left," who are so conscious of the historical ground slipping into uncharted waters that they fall either into silence or into thoughtless declaration.

It is difficult not to acknowledge that the continuous and yet still indeterminable unfolding of this historical moment has produced a sense of being suspended before a confounding crossroads of histories made and unmade, known and to be known. In full recognition of this sense of suspension, I begin by considering a curious incident that emerged alongside the initial ripple effects of 9/11 as an allegorical instance of the wider psychosymbolic dimensions framing the events. Placing oneself within these dimensions makes imperative precisely the mode of interrogation needed to break down the deadly social-historical logic that produced these events in the first place and yet continues to be strengthened by their occurrence: namely, a mode of interrogation that begins with the question "how can the secular be philosophically articulated apart from its traditional opposition to the religious?"—the very interrogation that Said's thought carries out so incisively.[2]

Stockhausen's Attack

On Wednesday, September 19, 2001, in the back pages of one of the *New York Times* sections, a tiny unsigned article was introduced by the astonishing headline "Attacks Called Great Art." What followed was a hastily and scantily reported news item that hardly justified the stunning claim. It reported that Karlheinz Stockhausen, the leading figure in contemporary music at the time, described the September 11 attacks as "the greatest work of art ever," going on to reproduce a relatively long and awkward quotation by the composer himself: "What happened there—they all have to rearrange their brains now—is the greatest work of art ever. That characters can bring about in one act what we in music cannot dream of, that people practice madly for ten years, completely, fanatically, for a concert and then die. That is the greatest work of art for the whole cosmos. I could not do that. Against that, we, composers, are nothing." Then the article concluded with a quizzical statement, which really belongs to the world of a novel, not a news report: "Mr. Stockhausen was reported to have left Hamburg in distress."

This last sentence, I suppose, refers to the immediate consequences that the composer's statements provoked, though this short article barely touched on them. Apparently, the scandalous remarks were made during a press conference that Stockhausen had given in Hamburg, on the occasion of a performance of his recent work in a yearly festival, which this year carried the title *Welt-Raum*, a theme whose multiple significations become all the more pertinent at this juncture. The scandalous remarks prompted a scandalous response and the performance was summarily canceled by the city's culture commissioner. The significance of this scandal in German (and, more generally, European) circles, both at the state level and in the cultural community ranks, was obviously deemed not newsworthy to this *New York Times* correspondent. Neither was, apparently, the labyrinthine process of correcting this apparent misquotation in the original German press report, nor was the laborious story of how the city of Hamburg dealt with the event. It is likely that the whole lot was considered irrelevant because it pertained to the complex relation between public funding and art production one finds in Germany but, of course, would never find in the United States in a million years.

I shall lay aside the sequence of these events and their significance for Germany, for the European framework of cultural production, and, surely, for Stockhausen himself, all of which is exceedingly fascinating as a national-historical document. I shall also lay aside, however, for reasons that will become apparent as we go, the problem emerging from the fact that the remarks I just quoted are in effect a misquotation—apparently, a deliberate act by a hostile reporter. Indeed, I would insist that the trouble with word accuracy is merely symptomatic of the entire problem, because, even though Stockhausen was certainly misquoted (as taped transcripts reveal), the gist of his thinking was curiously preserved. It almost seems as if the hostile reporter was so caught up in Stockhausen's logic that he could not but reveal its inner fold in misquoting him. So, any turning to Stockhausen's actual, accurate comments would best be conducted not in the spirit of correction but in the spirit of enhancement. Examining the composer's response to the misquotation indeed enhances the overarching problematic of both his thinking and the grim historical events he addresses.[3]

Arguably, the most likely reaction to hearing that Stockhausen called the horrific acts of 9/11 "the greatest work of art ever" is to consider it yet another instance of the extreme aesthetization of violence that decidedly characterizes the fascist tradition. Hence the anxious response of the German authorities, which are as attuned to refined fascist overtones as they are astutely committed to the continuation of German aesthetic expression. That Hitlerian fascism conceptualized war and violence in the purest aesthetic terms is indisputable in retrospect, and German intellectual and artistic minds, from Walter Benjamin and Theodor Adorno to Heiner Müller and Hans-Jürgen Syberberg, have gone a long way, ultimately by negative ritualization, to isolate and disintegrate the phenomenon's many insidious folds. That Stockhausen's universe bears real affinity to this latter against-the-grain tendency does not necessarily preclude it from falling into this sort of problematic aesthetization; this is in itself indicative of the extremely complex and contradictory conditions of German modernity since the late eighteenth century, of which I have spoken extensively elsewhere.[4] To put it bluntly (and to allude to what lies ahead), negative ritualization of fascist aestheticism better deploys the most inventive antitranscendentalist imagination if it is to guard itself against the danger of reproducing the forces of the object it aims to disintegrate.

Yet, if we merely remain at this level—the suspicion that Stockhausen's aestheticism is cryptofascist—we shall miss the profound inroads opened by his remarks, misquoted though they were. Let us play a devilish game, for a moment, and take seriously the comments I quoted from the *New York Times*. If we don't merely settle into thinking of art as personal expression within the canonically bounded domain of the aesthetic, and we ascribe to art an active involvement (however difficult to define precisely) in the transformation of social conditions—which I hardly mean in the lazy Marxist sense of carrying out the order of political economy into the cultural battlefield—then we better be ready to come to terms with art as a realm in which humanity exercises its utmost creative/destructive potential, and not in the so-called (since Hegel) "world of the spirit" but in the world itself. At its best, this exercise takes place within—and *takes on* as a challenge—the entirety of society's imaginary significations: its foundational images and symbols, its implicit or explicit assertions and preconceptions, its basic organizational principles, whatever a community takes for granted and reproduces thoughtlessly.

To speak of society's *poiēsis* is to speak of society's self-alteration: of nothing less than the capacity of society to alter the terms and conditions of its very being. This involves a profoundly radical gesture of transforming terms and conditions, where the creative force can never be philosophically disentangled from the destructive force. Opting out of art as purely bounded within the aesthetic, we thus lend to the *poiētic* an overarching scope, relevant to the broadest range of human creativity, which opens the way for a better understanding of the interwoven condition of the poetic with the political beyond the traditional (and often mechanical) infusion of art with a didactic moral imperative. From this standpoint, the conventional reading of the aesthetization of the political as characteristic of fascism does not hold its ground. On the contrary, only if one effaces the basic dialectical entwinement of the poetic with the political at all levels of human/social activity does one practice a fascist aesthetization of politics, whose unacknowledged content, after all, is to depoliticize society, indeed to *anaesthetize* society to politics.

Stockhausen claims that in order to comprehend what happened on 9/11 we have to rearrange—to reset, as he actually said—the wiring of our brains. So, instead of rejecting his alleged aesthetization of these events, let us take it as a point of departure. In aesthetics, praxis entails a composition, a creative/destructive refiguration of present and imagined elements so that presumably a new relationality emerges. Oftentimes, if the composition demands a truly radical refiguration, this praxis signals a rupture with instituted meaning that throws everything into a whirlwind. The aesthetics of modernity has always yearned for the one composition that would signify in all senses the end of composition—because it would exceed all possible points of reception and interpretation, including the point of its creation. To practice fanatically for years for one act and then die in executing it encapsulates the aesthetic essence of the sublime performance: the performance that exceeds both the agency and the temporality of its praxis. Such performance also requires the obliteration of its identity, which I take to mean the ensemble of traces that makes a subject's and an object's historical existence decipherable. *Identicide* is in this sense the supreme logic of Mallarmé's project, to speak of a celebrated instance of impossible (and, from a certain point of view, self-destructive) aesthetics.

No doubt, as the history of modern aesthetics suggests, this sublime yearning is also associated with failure; its power is predicated on the knowledge that it will remain forever immaterial. Mallarmé's *Livre* owes its conceptual existence and creative drive to the impossibility of its actualization. Any evidence that the sublime praxis of *identicide* in art is actualized in history profoundly disturbs the autonomy of the aesthetic, as if in a perverse sense it reminds us that the aesthetics of the sublime (from Kant onward) is actually terrified of history, terrified of history's outmaneuverable contingency, which is by definition impervious to excess, indeed impervious to the sublime. Whatever his immersion into pure aesthetics, Stockhausen cannot but bow before history, concluding his remarks with the desperate admission that, in the foreground of the 9/11 events, "we, composers, are nothing."

Whether accurately rendered or not, this statement is entirely sincere. But what makes it dramatic is what underlies it, namely, the composer's intractably gothic and otherworldly conceptualization of his work and the world, which makes it all the more susceptible to the aesthetic allure of the literally spectacular signature of the attacks on the World Trade Center. Its susceptibility is due to two factors: On the one hand, Stockhausen's work has been characterized since the beginning by relentless commitment to the technology of sound as the medium for the invocation of the transcendental, an attitude bearing the precarious duplicity of conceiving technology itself as an immaterial, transcendental language: as *sound* pure and simple, devoid of any instrumentality.

From the sumptuous *Gesang der Jünglinge* (1955), in which real voices are combined with electronically produced vocal sounds so that all distinction between the "natural" and the "technological" is blurred, producing a rather uncanny choral effect, to the inimitable (and, from a certain conventional standpoint, insufferable) *Helicopter String Quartet* (1993), in which the string players perform each in his own helicopter, with the sound of the rotor blades providing the consistent rhythmic backdrop to a barrage of disembodied *glissandi*, Stockhausen has sought not merely to enlist technology's aid in musical composition but much more: to render possible, audible, by virtue of composition, the sound of technology as such, in an intransigent gesture of making the Kantian object speak its own uninstrumentalized language.

On the other hand, however, Stockhausen's aesthetic and psychic universe, which arguably culminates in the ultra-Wagnerian gesture of his magna opera *Licht*—an impossible work, whose composition was virtually interminable and whose performance (if ever actualized in full) lasts seven days according to the seven days of Creation in *Genesis*—suggests a rather traditional expression of transcendence. Constructed entirely along biblical motifs, whereby the archangels Michael and Lucifer are locked into the originary and definitive battle between Good and Evil, this work is profoundly religious. And though Lucifer here is drawn in Miltonian fashion through and through—as literally the heroic bearer of light who seeks to destroy Light—the mythological conceptualization of this work is hardly emancipatory. The opera merely serves to confirm, beyond any of his other works, Stockhausen's aesthetic cosmos, which hinges on articulating the material power of technology as consubstantial with metaphysical excess, precisely the deadly combination of the 9/11 events.

From this standpoint, it hardly matters that Stockhausen attributed the assessment of 9/11 as the "greatest work of art ever" not in fact to his person but to the Luciferian protagonist of his opera. This character figures, in the composer's mind, as a veritable spiritual force. As he put it in the corrective statement he issued to the press three days after the notorious remark:

> At the press conference in Hamburg, I was asked if Michael, Eve, and Lucifer were historical figures of the past and I answered that they exist now, for example Lucifer in New York. In my work, I have defined Lucifer as the cosmic spirit of rebellion, of anarchy. He uses his high degree of intelligence to destroy creation. He does not know love. After further questions about the events in America, I said that such a plan appeared to be Lucifer's greatest work of art. Of course, I used the designation "work of art" to mean the work of destruction personified in Lucifer. . . . I cannot find a fitting name for such a "satanic composition."[5]

Stockhausen's aesthetic principles dictate that Lucifer is a mythic figure with historical presence: the presence of destruction that has disengaged itself from its dialectical entwinement with creation. Stockhausen might be said to have responded to the events as if he were William Blake.[6] There is indeed something hallucinatory about his response, although, unlike Blake, his hallucinations show disdain for the materiality of myth in favor of the mystifying incorporeality of metaphysics. There is a bottom line that Stockhausen's own attempt to modify and clarify his reported comments cannot efface: namely, his aesthetics is religious in essence. And thus, like Mallarmé and perhaps Wagner (who is obviously the Oedipal father figure to be outdone), Stockhausen aspires to an aesthetics that, although it claims to hold a hand over history, is actually anesthetized to historical materiality, if only because it cannot comprehend the enormous and undeconstructible significance of humanity's finitude. In his case, the recognition that the artistic sublime is doomed to failure ("we, composers, are nothing") resounds in the backdrop of the terrifying failure of history itself: the annihilation of the world in the name of religious transcendence of the world.

But this resonance reveals yet one more twist in this circuitous story, which is worth considering. Stockhausen's commentary on the events of 9/11, which flash on his horizon as the hallucinatory translation of his religious aestheticism into historical reality, leans directly against the nominal religious-terrorist logic behind the events. In outrageously aestheticizing an event whose horror defies measure, Stockhausen unwittingly serves to plunge the declared transcendentalist ideology of its perpetrators back into the pool of historical finitude to which they belong. An act of avowed religious martyrdom is irreparably damaged by being construed as artwork, once we hold on to the profound entwinement of the poetic with the political. It cannot extricate itself from the worldly universe within which it is executed; moreover, the worldliness of its terms of execution surpasses whatever might be the alleged transcendental intention. In a way that arguably pushes all our experiential buttons, the fact that this horrifying event exists by virtue of its spectacularization enables us to counteract its proclaimed logic: to see it, first and foremost, as a political act that deserves a political response.

But here Stockhausen's art actually falls short. At this specific historical juncture, a political response cannot rely on the allegorical terms of the archaic religious battle between Good and Evil, Michael and Lucifer, because these are precisely the terms of "God Bless America" and "fundamentalist Islam" (or "Holy Islam" and "America as Satan"—the four terms bear *exactly* the same content). Such allegory may be said to fail even as evidence of the presumed utopian function of art, speaking aesthetically, because its unwitting proximity to history dramatically unveils an otherwise occluded aspect of utopian art: namely, certain utopian visions of art often harness, for their own alleged gain, the transcendentalist element of religion. But ultimately, such allegory fails because history has rendered it too proximate to the literal plane. It is rather rare that the literal can achieve such spectacular actualization of the psychosymbolic elements that animate it, but this may be the crux of what brought the events of 9/11 so perilously close to a pure aesthetic realm, a peril that Stockhausen's remarks (accurate or inaccurate, regardless) splendorously evoke.[7]

Contrapuntal Reading

The Stockhausen incident may have been otherwise trivial, if its peculiar (and rather incidental) logic didn't ultimately echo, as Edward Said would understand it, the *contrapuntal* nature of the aesthetics-religion equation. Understanding the contrapuntal nature of complicity between events and things, concepts and beliefs, may be the most succinct task of secular criticism, as Said encapsulates it in his *Culture and Imperialism* project, beyond the actual texts and details taken up in the book. In an idiosyncratic and surely ingenious way, Said creates a unique methodology by proceeding from a Gramscian sense of spatial complexity (a sense of asymmetrical, multilateral, geographical relation) to a musicological sense of *co-incidentally* entwined figures that testify to a polyphonic simultaneity understood as *internal* to the object of inquiry. In other words, a contrapuntal reading does not seek a presumed order of things that might arise from various external forces bearing upon the object, nor does it settle for an interpretive framework that privileges singular identities emerging from an otherwise assumed and unexamined totality. Rather, it perceives both singularities and external forces as internal instances within a complex orchestration, where they might be privileged provisionally and always in distinctive relation, indeed accented by this provisional distinction, which itself then becomes internal to the dynamic, and so on.

Said's sense of contrapuntal reading has both a spatial and a temporal component. His keen geographical mind, refined by his early perception that Antonio Gramsci's thought introduced into the Marxist dialectical tradition the primacy of the concept of territory and inevitably sharpened by his own exilic existence as a dispossessed Palestinian, enables him to appreciate and gauge precisely the multiversality of a situation, a political event, a text, an artwork. At the same time, his acknowledged allegiance to Georg Lukács and his groundbreaking understanding of the reification of consciousness—the cornerstone of so-called Western Marxism—remain at the core of his constant reminder that the force of *identity* (as a concept, form, psychic state, mode of thinking) must be battled and resisted at all costs. Resistance to identity means profound alertness to history, to the temporal fluidity and multiplicity we inhabit in our being in the world. The temporal and the spatial—or as Said prefers, the historical and the geographical—are thus distinguished by a shared multidimensional configuration, and the Saidian methodology, throughout its complex and multivalent trajectory over the years, settles for nothing less.

The musicological expression that Said lends to this methodology harkens back to his deep-seated veneration for Theodor Adorno, whose remarkable intellectual edifice, Said argues, must be read primarily as the multifaceted work of a musical sensibility. Indeed, in Adorno, Said's own personal investment in the figures of displacement (the intellectual as an exile) and nonidentity (the thinker as a performative subjectivity) finds precise and elaborated resonance. This triptych of intellectual figures might well serve as a referential network for those primary significations animating the language of secular criticism. This does not mean that the three thinkers form a nucleus of influence, from which then Said's thought can merely be derived. They belong to a group of twentieth-century figures with whom Said remains consistently in dialogue (such as Erich Auerbach, C. L. R. James, Frantz Fanon, Michel Foucault, and Glenn Gould), but they are distinct insofar as they preside over the *methodological* coordinates of the task of secular criticism, which Said's work conducts in such uncompromising fashion.

Let us consider some of Said's own descriptions—so as not to say, definitions—of the task of secular criticism:

> The secular intellectual works to show the absence of divine originality and, on the other side, the complex presence of historical actuality. The conversion of the absence of religion into the presence of actuality is secular interpretation.[8]

> A secular attitude warns us to beware of transforming the complexities of many-stranded history into one large figure, or of elevating particular moments or monuments into universals . . . Secular transgression chiefly involves moving from one domain to another, the testing and challenging of limits, the mixing and intermingling of heterogeneities, cutting across expectations, providing unforeseen pleasures, discovering experiences.[9]

> If secular criticism deals with local and worldly situations and is constitutively opposed to the production of massive, hermetic systems, then it must follow that the essay—a comparatively short, investigative, radically skeptical form—is the principal way in which to write criticism.[10]

Right off, one perceives two elemental figures that animate the conceptual framework of these statements. First, an unequivocal sense of mobility characterizes Said's encounter with the realm of objective phenomena: not only the worldly realm as such, the order of things, but also the less tangible but equally objective realm of concepts, ideas, desires, affects. This sense of mobility, of restlessly moving from object to object, of denying the stability of any presumable ground, produces an equivalent philosophical sense of mobility regarding the subject-object relation as such—indeed, a condition of mobility that is just as much a condition of mutability, particularly as it pertains to forms. This leads to the second elemental figure in this framework: namely, the consistent characteristic of what Said calls in multiple contexts *elaboration*, a working upon the plasticity (mutability) of form that denies the frequent theoretical compulsion to engulf matters in impermeable and lasting structures. Converting thus "the absence of religion into the presence of actuality," which is admittedly an abstract statement, can be read as the epitome of the critical secular attitude, not merely because it recognizes the concealed void of religion (which arguably exists in order to fill the void of existence) but because, more importantly, it describes a transformative process whereby the metaphysical void is elaborated as an actual condition in the world with definitive consequences. This elaboration presupposes that form is both material force and mutable ground and that one's engagement with it is the most tangible confirmation of one's significance as historical subject.

Said's essentially modernist outlook, in matters of both literature and music, exemplifies this understanding of elaboration as transformation and transgression, as he says in the statements earlier. The epistemic *co-incidence* of transformation and transgression is crucial in determining the meaning of the secular—a term that is, in turn, not locked into an a priori signifying framework, given once and for all (even if in a figure of opposition to a rival signifying term: presumably, the religious), but points instead to an attitude, perhaps we might even say a method, which is experimental at the core. The meaning of secular in the term *secular criticism* does not designate an ensemble of properties—to be therefore enacted in the critical practice—but characterizes the substance of the critical act itself. This is, in my opinion, the profound gesture in Aamir Mufti's reverse formulation of "critical secularism," to which my essay also belongs.[11] The etymological ground of criticism—the Greek notion of *krisis* means not merely judgment or decision, but also distinction, investigation, interrogation, interpretation, all under the rubric of a performative mind—underlines this elaborative, contingent, mutable, non-systemic, experimental nature of critique.

This is why Said will explicitly select the essay as the form of writing that *formally* exemplifies critique: the kind of provisional and interrogative trial of bringing together *contrapuntally* the contentious but intertwined aspects of human activity, of history. And though the very notion of elaboration grasps precisely the meaning of *essai* as Montaigne initially conceived it, it is the intransigent manner of Adorno—which Said characterizes indicatively as "dogged stubbornness"—that animates his distinct use of the form. It is important to remember that Adorno explicitly names the essay as the critical form par excellence because it is formally bound to its own self-reflection on every turn. This doesn't just take place at the level of argumentation—in other words, it is not merely a conceptual self-reflection—but, more importantly, at the level of signification, of language itself. Thus, Adorno claims, the essay is marked by a resistance to "the ambitious transcendence of language beyond its meaning," which is the characteristic element of systematic philosophy, whereby language consists of "words [that] tremble as though possessed, while remaining secretive about what possesses them."[12] Adorno is making here a cryptic reference to Heidegger, but the comment reaches beyond the specific insinuation. It links self-reflection, and indeed critique, with resistance against transcendence, with exposing the tendency of a certain language to render itself sacred and to do so, moreover, by veiling the mode of its own sacralization. Adorno sees the essay as a form of praxis that belongs to what he calls "emancipated intellect," which he characterizes variably as homeless, mobile, experimental, heretic, unbinding, nonidentitarian (all these are his terms). The essay is a form that recognizes the force of contingency and finitude in history and, hence, the importance of elaborating a kind of thinking process that does not owe itself to (or is not *possessed* by) any preconceived or predetermined principles, forging instead its own way through a problem on the terrain that the problem itself constitutes each time anew. This is what Adorno means when he says, "[the essay] proceeds, so to speak, methodically unmethodically."[13]

The idea that unmethod is the formal method of the essay isn't some sort of sophistic cleverness. It provides actually an opening to thinking about method much more rigorously than merely defining (if not in fact confirming, codifying) a writer's or a text's retrospectively predictable ways and modes of operation. Although Adorno doesn't quite say it, his sense of method in the essay is linked to its performativity. When Said oftentimes focuses on musical performance in the midst of discussions of literature, philosophy, or politics, he is shifting our attention to an ephemeral and finite figure of humanity's imprint on the world in order precisely to *dispossess* those discourses of their reverential hold on their own certainty. Thinking from the standpoint of performativity means breaching the structure of an immovable core of identity. It is a transgressive act. And the transgression in this sense becomes tangible in the manner in which ideas, concepts, thoughts, art forms, textual figures, and so on break open the presumable closure of their existence and become entwined with the fluidity of social-historical forms and events. "The transgressive element in music is its nomadic ability to attach itself to, and become part of, social formations,"[14] says Said, and I suggest we take this further than the specifically musical—or rather, expand the musical reference to include the broader consequences of Said's notion of "performance as an extreme occasion"—in order to underline the precarious relation of critique with the experimental, which is always connected, in some way or other, to the profoundly social-historical sense of the experiential. Grasping the matter in this way is confirmed by the fact that historical experience can never be retrieved intact but only through its experimental transmutation into form (in essence, its transformation). This is one of the central aspects of modernist thinking and applies distinctly to

Said's own attempts both to record his memoirs and to articulate the significance of his right to return to Palestine.

Before we take this up, however, I want to consider the way in which Said broaches dialogically a kind of pedagogy of performativity in his celebrated discussions with Daniel Barenboim. A good part of their conversation is taken up with an attempt to articulate the relation between performance and interpretation. Both Said and Barenboim focus on performance in the musical domain, while Said returns repeatedly to interpretation as a figure that pertains to the act of reading, constituted primarily by the experience of reading literature. In this respect, the meaning of performance (and, more broadly, the implicit significance of performativity as a particular quality) partakes strongly of the language of music, which leads Barenboim in fact to certain astute remarks on the phenomenology of sound, the profound dialectical relation of music to silence, and music's defiance of the physical laws of nature. Surely, one can argue that interpretation in music (by an orchestra conductor or an instrumentalist) is inevitably subsumed to the discourse of performance and that the most crucial questions pertain to the domain that Barenboim rightly emphasizes: namely, using Said's language, the profound materiality of sound in its extreme relation to the occasion of its emergence—space, time, body.

Yet, insightful though it is, this side of the argument unwittingly casts its shadow over a whole range of other instances, like the very act of reading texts, where grasping the precise nature of interpretive performance itself is at stake. Although reading belongs to a literary universe where orality is no longer primary and is thus unavoidably individualized and silent, its constitutive performativity does not cease—Flaubert's self-consciousness epitomizes this relation. It may become less tangible, it may become implicated in the technological capacity for repetition, for returning to a printed text whose words on the page do not change, but there is no convincing epistemological ground on which to argue that each occasion of reading, even the same text by the same person, loses hereby its occasionality, its singular, ephemeral, contingent relation to the act of reading. And though the bodily dimension of reading a text is rather elusive compared to the musical and theatrical arts (which confront directly the physical laws of nature, as Barenboim formulates it), it does not mean that the corporeality of reading, the actual sensation of engagement and apprehension in the occasion of reading, isn't a presence to be reckoned with in assessing the experience of interpretation. I would signify this experience as essentially performative. The limit point between interpretation and performance is not determinable with any certainty; in the ancient use of *hermēneia*, to interpret means literally to perform.

I insist on this point because it is crucial to Said's understanding of the secular. Said never hesitates to remind us that the critical faculty (for him linked directly to the interpretive condition) requires a gesture of transgression against one's identity—more precisely, a displacement of identity so as to position oneself in or *as* a certain "otherness." Addressing Barenboim, Said says: "In your work as a performer, Daniel, and in my work as an interpreter—an interpreter of literature and literary criticism—one has to accept the idea that one is putting one's own identity aside in order to explore the 'other.' "[15] Exploring this other should not be understood here as the gesture of an empirical desire to enter unknown, strange territory, if only because the elementary sense of explorer, in its traditional meaning, requires an intact sense of self: an integral subject that pursues a presumably discoverable object. However, Said seems to demand a radical *disintegration* of the self (much in the way that Adorno would use the term), producing a self-induced condition of homelessness within one's own subjectivity. This kind of deconstitution of the subject is achieved by positing an otherness at the core of one's identity in the act of interpretation, which is tantamount, in the sort of language familiar to us from the theater, to an act of impersonation, of taking on the attributes of an other.[16] Thus, the requisite gesture for the interpreter and the performer—here Said brings the two together—is self-alteration, the elemental meaning of the radical critical faculty, a poetically transformative, revolutionary gesture in the best sense. The vocabulary of secular criticism is all over this gesture—mobility, mutability, displacement, nonidentity, transgression, transformation—and this gesture is exemplary in its performativity.

Performative Self-Deconstitution

Nowhere does Said exercise this performative deconstitution of the subject more acutely than in his meditation on the significance of his own name that opens his memoir *Out of Place*. It is essential to quote at length:

> All families invent their parents and children, give them a story, character, fate, and even a language. There was always something wrong with how I was invented and meant to fit in with the world of my parents and four sisters. Whether this was because I constantly misread my part or because of some deep flaw in my being I could not tell for most of my early life. Sometimes I was intransigent, and proud of it. At other times I seemed to myself to be nearly devoid of any character at all, timid, uncertain, without will. Yet the overriding sensation I had was of always being out of place. Thus, it took me about fifty years to become accustomed to, or, more exactly, to feel comfortable with, "Edward," a foolishly English name yoked forcibly to the unmistakably Arabic family name Said. True my mother told me that I had been named Edward after the Prince of Wales, who cut so fine a figure in 1935, the year of my birth, and Said was the name of various uncles and cousins. But the

> rationale of my name broke down when I discovered no grandparents called Said and when I tried to connect my fancy English name with its Arabic partner. For years, and depending on the exact circumstances, I would rush past "Edward" and emphasize "Said"; at other times I would do the reverse, or connect these two to each other so quickly that neither would be clear. The one thing I could not tolerate, but very often would have to endure, was the disbelieving, and hence, undermining, reaction: Edward? Said?[17]

For any student of literature, the literariness of this passage is striking. There is a Proustian self-irony, the consciousness of how perilous it is to apply oneself to the task of self-representation in writing, but there is also a daring clarity about the theatricality of self-fashioning—familial invention, (mis)reading one's part in the drama of life, attempting to fit into a character, a kind of Brechtian *Verfremdungseffekt* on the utterance of the name(s) "Edward" "Said"—all of which defies any sort of propriety in the gesture of autobiographical self-reference. The literary effect consists in the double gesture of simultaneously foregrounding the principle of fictionalization present in any process of fashioning an identity with an unabashedly genuine staging of the process of being named.

Thus, the author Edward Said begins to take on the genre of memoir by instantly dismantling whatever metaphysical qualities traditionally authorize the proper name. His first "autobiographical" gesture is to cast the authorial personality in uncertain light, to problematize the otherwise assumed seamlessness of self-recognition across space and time by staging a contradictory situation of othering oneself. A phrase from Proust comes to mind that encapsulates this contradictory aspect of recognition: "For to 'recognize' someone and, *a fortiori*, having failed to recognize someone to learn his identity, is to predicate two contradictory things of a single subject, it is to admit that what was here, the person whom one remembers, no longer exists, and also that what is now here is a person whom one did not know to exist."[18] Said's self-referential point of departure is to immerse the name into the flux of historical contingency, so as to set up an interpretive mode that is radically skeptical toward the minutest tendency to grant the principle of identity a natural and transparent authority. It is not only that Edward Said is out of place, that his story and the story of his people (his family, of course, but, by inference, the Palestinian people themselves) is a story of displacement; it is that *identity itself is out of place*.

But in the incisive irony of the passage one also reads a certain urgency, perhaps even a compulsion, to register the epistemic significance of this inaugural placelessness, as well as the history of social and cultural displacement that inevitably expands its meaning. Said has alluded elsewhere, in reference to what animated his theoretical study on beginnings in the 1970s, to just this sense of inaugural self-authorization in the absence of even the most elemental authorities, such as home, family, religion, nation, language: "This was then my autobiographical impetus [in writing *Beginnings*], to rethink the whole question of what it means to start again, to begin. It involved acts of choice, acts of designation, rather than things coming from heaven. That is why the emphasis on the secular is so great, as far as I'm concerned. It is a congeries of things, a number of things, working at the same time."[19] Much like his sense of contrapuntal thinking, thinking in secular terms for Said involves an irreducible plurality at the core of signification, even the inaugural signification of one's own being. This plurality is marked by both contestation and entwinement; Said isn't content merely to posit a fragmented self, as is often nowadays fetishized. He has a definite grasp of the authorial "I." Authors of all kinds, including composers of music and artwork, occupy a central position in his referential network. But they are never impervious to the worldly conditions that permeate them. On the contrary, an author's relative autonomy is predicated on recognizing the contingent nature of his or her authorization and on sustaining an oppositional stance in respect to the dominant terms of authority all around.

Standing along with Adorno in tireless resistance to the forced reconciliation of the subject-object antinomy in the world, Said remains vigilant against the tendency of thinkers to be co-opted by enveloping structures of ideas, systems, beliefs, and even political alliances. Even though he generally distances himself from psychoanalytic frameworks of explanation, he accentuates the radical importance of subjectivity in the worldly domain. He has never hesitated publicly to affirm the significance of personal pleasure in the things one chooses to engage above and beyond the commitment to respond politically to those social and historical exigencies that permeate one's daily existence. He often speaks of literature and music, of reading, listening, and, of course, writing, as something profoundly motivated by a not quite analyzable sense of personal pleasure—an unadulterated instance of *plaisir du texte*, to use a now forgotten term of Roland Barthes. This is a crucial dimension of secular subjectivity, for which objects that merit one's psychic investment (sublimation) do not provide the certainty and safety of permanence or transcendence. Sublimation—a concept entirely absent from Said's vocabulary—is hardly a psychogenetic condition, emerging from the innermost needs of an impermeable subjectivity, but a condition that says as much about the society that makes it possible as about the individual who is produced by it. In other words, sublimation has a politics; the objects in which one invests are always indicative of a particular socialization, never neutral or singular. Said's memoir provides, perhaps unwittingly, a chronicle of a specific politics of sublimation in the very same gesture in which it provides, altogether consciously, a chronicle of a lost world, a lost social-historical experience.

Oftentimes in interviews, which constitute for Said a veritable genre of developing orally and improvisationally the interrogative composition he attributes to essay writing, Said seizes on a detail that unlocks the methodological underpinnings of a project. Consider his elaboration on the impetus for writing his memoir:

> I have resisted the use of the word "autobiography." I call it a memoir because I don't try to account for a public trajectory. I felt that I had something to understand about a peculiar past. . . . We had an extremely strange—because my father sort of invented it—a very strange, constructed life. . . . I think probably the main thread of the memoir is to trace the effects of this sort of imprisoning or limiting life that I had as a child, perhaps because my family felt they had to protect me.[20]

The intriguing thing in this rumination isn't so much the final qualifying phrase as to whether a sense of limitation might be due to parental overprotectiveness (which returns us rather to a recognizable literary *tropos*), but the immediately prior part of the sentence that ties the writing of a memoir to threading together a way out of the perceived labyrinth of a constructed and constrained childhood. The stated intention, an *authorial* intention, is to weave the strands of memory so as to ponder the enigma of a particular childhood in a distinctly traceable, though actually now perished, social world: in other words, a particular sublimation that is, no doubt, also a cultural-historical experience which exceeds its avowed uniqueness. Said's indefatigable resistance in his subsequent public trajectory to any sort of structure that limits life could be interpreted as the response to this childhood experience and, in effect, the extension of this initial sublimation. But this would be just a psychoanalytic explanation. What is more important is the expressed intention to achieve some sort of commensurable relation between the odd familial experience and the altogether pervasive social-historical drama that surrounds it and, indeed at times, remains shielded by it: Palestinian victimization and exile.

The phrase "I felt I had something to understand about a peculiar past" resonates entirely, *contrapuntally*, with other such phrases spoken in other instances and perhaps with other things in mind, but still hanging in irredeemable suspension, perfectly clear yet inscrutable in their own isolation: "My own past is irrecoverable . . . I don't really belong anywhere, but I've resolved that that's the way it is."[21] Or: "What return does mean to me is return to oneself, a return to history, so that we understand exactly what happened, why it happened, and who we are."[22] The relation between the "I" and the "we" here is a matter of *co-incidence*; the two subjects are entirely consubstantial in their antithesis. The homeless "I" may be settled in its irrecoverable condition, but this is precisely what enables it to articulate the necessity of achieving a home for the exiled and disenfranchised community. Said has often been maligned for this dialectical position, which is the envy of many who do not dare the risk of being committed to personal homelessness and yet, simultaneously, to political community. Regarding the memoir specifically, the charges of elitism or narcissism from various quarters of both American and Arab cultural-intellectual terrains dovetail perfectly with slanderous attempts by Zionist propagandists to discredit Said's claim to familial and territorial connection to his native Palestine. In all cases, of course, a profound disdain, even contempt, is reserved for what remains defiantly personal in the worldly encounter with the other, even though in fact, contrary to conventional wisdom, it is precisely this radically personal imaginary that fuels one's unwavering commitment to communal affairs, one's responsibility toward the polis.

The Politics of Placeless Coexistence

Throughout his activist trajectory on behalf of the Palestinian cause, Said remained consistently vehement in his critique of both nativism and separatism. He always made a point of reiterating Fanon's crucial lesson that all nativism signals the victory of the colonial/imperial project (or, in a Saidian language, confirms the domination of Orientalism) by bearing out to its end point the fetishist logic of identity, singularity, and abolition of the other. In the same way, he rejected all separatist discourses as epitomes of nationalism, as politics of exclusion, dispossession, deterritorialization. For this reason Said insisted that the grave task of resolving what he called the "sublime conflict" between Israel and Palestine cannot be conducted under a politics of partition. Partition, he reminds us, has been the legacy of British colonialism since the Lausanne Treaty, which separated Greek and Turkish populations, and it has left an indelible inaugural mark on the Palestinian conflict, much as it has done on the ongoing conflicts in India or Cyprus. In this respect, from *The Question of Palestine* onward, Said advocated, both politically and theoretically, that the coexistence of the two peoples had become historically insurmountable.

In an interview I conducted with him in 1990 for a Greek journal, Said responded skeptically to a deliberately provocative question about a future Palestinian national history inevitably embracing the typical identitarian ideology of ancestry and ascendancy, claiming instead that what made Palestinian history and society different was the impossibility of disengagement from its adversarial other.[23] The force of identitarian principles that fuels the writing of national history, he argued, is in this case disrupted by an antagonistic entwinement between two ongoing complicitous histories that can be neither ignored nor dissolved. Some years later, Said wrote a bold article in the *New York Times Magazine* that elaborated on the one-state solution as the only historically possible outcome short of total annihilation of both cultures. This drew support from certain Israelis but was disparagingly rejected by many American Jewish commentators. Drawing on the region's centuries-old (though now severely damaged) tradition of multiethnic and multicultural coexistence, which he then grafted onto a theoretical privileging of civil society over religious-nationalist community, Said put forth the thesis that "there can be no reconciliation unless both peoples, two communities of suffering, resolve that their existence is a secular fact, and that it has to be dealt with as such."[24]

This activist theoretical and political trajectory, which is made possible by virtue of an intellectual mind that rejects totalizing and transcendentalist figures, has never been quite appreciated in these terms. On the contrary, the secular vision is summarily discredited, arguably because its historical power is tangible and perfectly real. When Zionist critics assail Said for being "the professor of terror," one gets the impression that they do so because they desire to silence a Palestinian voice that articulates the profound historical reality of such coexistence.[25] Although nowadays, in the context of such extreme adherence to nationalist/religious dogmatism on both sides, this position seems utopian, the actual historical reality to which it focuses our attention is ultimately more threatening to the militarist position of the Israeli state apparatus than scores of suicide bombers, precisely because it casts an insurmountable shadow over the Zionist dream-wish to do away with the Palestinian factor altogether, so as to clear out the territories for the unimpeded establishment of *Eretz Israel*.

Said had trained his eye on this annihilating logic since the seminal essay "Zionism from the Standpoint of Its Victims" (1979), in which he argued that, even at the simplest discursive level, the nationalist dream of Zionism was predicated on a vision of a pristine, uninhabited land inherited from time immemorial by ancestral privilege. It was thus inevitable that the foundation of the Israeli state in the wake of the Holocaust and the brutal militarization of the Zionist dream would spin forth a logic of unacknowledged but tacitly justified and altogether totalizing victimization and ultimately annihilation of the other. "We are the victims of the victims," Said repeatedly declared. This phrase is formidable in its utter simplicity because it exposes the unsayable belief that occupies the imaginary core of post-Holocaust Zionism: namely, "we are the last, the ultimate victims." From a psychoanalytic point of view, this unutterable conviction is drawn from the same compulsion toward a monopoly of signification that animates the inaugural imaginary signifier of Hebrew ancestry: "we are God's chosen people." The monopoly of victimization is, in other words, "religious" in essence. I mean this not in the sense of emerging out of a specific theological dogma (and thus pertaining to Judaism's religious practice), but rather in the same way that nationalism is proximate to religion, insofar as it obliterates the multivalent and contentious worldliness within which it exists. In this respect, to echo both Bruce Robbins's and Aamir Mufti's positions, Said's secular critique of Zionism (and, one must add, equally of Islamic fundamentalism or pan-Arabism) is predicated on a configuration of the secular in opposition, not to the religious, but to the nationalist.

This is exactly why the Zionist response to Said's secular criticism has been so enraged. When Said was first slandered as a promulgator of terrorism, it was in response to the use of the term *secular criticism* in *The World, the Text, and the Critic*, where the term bears an explicit literary meaning. Said's use of the secular was linked by a certain writer in the American Jewish Committee to Yasir Arafat's mandate for Palestine as a secular democratic state.[26] I would argue, again with a certain psychoanalytic slant, that there is real substance to this otherwise absurd and boneheaded syllogism. Said's critical secularism threatens Zionism to its core. No monolithic identitarian principle, which is essentially theologically grounded (and here certain Islamist positions mirror Zionist ones in ways that neither would ever tolerate), can withstand the exfoliation of the identity principle that Said's critical secularism takes as a point of departure. The denouncement of the secular as terrorist marks an instance where, like the Stockhausen incident at the outset, a fraudulent logic exposes the inner verity of the matter, in this case the accuser being driven by genuine, though unconscious, fear that his position will be exposed for what it is: "National identity becomes not only a fetish, but is also turned into a kind of idol, in a Baconian sense—an idol of the cave, and of the tribe. That produces, pulls along with it, the rise of what I would call a kind of desperate religious sentiment."[27]

Because it is conducted as a critical secular project, Said's uncompromising critique of Zionism has stayed explicitly clear from any of the discursive traps that mirror the adversary's tactics. Hence his insistence against any notion of de-Zionization, any sort of annihilating gesture in return. He was so deeply involved in the experience of communal erasure, dispossession, and the literal bulldozing of history that he knew well the danger of monological principles. He continued rather to advocate the dialectical entwinement of societies and histories and the continuous rediscovery of the making of history by real people in the real world. Instead of the security of a religious-nationalist Palestinian vision, Said prefers the secular uncertainty of a state, a home that is no one's singular property: "I suppose part of my critique of Zionism is that it attaches too much importance to home. Saying, we need a home. And we'll do anything to get a home, even if it means making others homeless. . . . I want a rich fabric of some sort, which no one can fully comprehend, and no one can fully own."[28] It is no surprise then that in a much discussed interview for an Israeli journal Said is recognized by the interviewer to "sound very Jewish." Said's response, the last words of a book of collected interviews, which I can imagine being spoken with mischievous and subversive humor, should be nonetheless taken seriously: "Of course. I'm the last Jewish intellectual. You don't know anyone else. All your other Jewish intellectuals are now suburban squires. From Amos Oz to all these people here in America. So I'm the last one. The only true follower of Adorno. Let me put it this way: I'm a Jewish-Palestinian."[29]

For those claiming to represent the allegedly real world of politics, Said's critical secular vision is at best utopian, its sense of the future immaterial, literary. Yet I would argue, perhaps in a more philosophical vein, that, on the contrary, the politics of comments such as the one just quoted is drawn from the mature cognizance of humanity's finite existence, of the corporeality and mortality of subjective experience, in addition to a defiant lack of interest in transcendent solutions—all of which, together, generate a sharpened and radical focus on the actual historical future. It is possible to consider that Said makes such comments in the spirit of "lateness" or *Spätstil* (late style) as Adorno theorized it, a notion forming the basis of Said's main literary and theoretical inquiry in the last decade of his life.[30] According to Adorno, lateness exceeds what is acceptable and normal in the world, and hence submits one's presumed unity with historical time and social environment to irreconcilable dissonance. Lateness reaches beyond its present time in history, or more precisely, it makes its mode of expression achieve a suspended presentness that fissures time, disrupts the beguiling assurance of controlled temporality, and thus enables a radical historical consciousness to emerge.

Said diagnoses this kind of consciousness at work in a variety of literary and artistic contexts. In addition to Adorno himself, he has spoken specifically of Beethoven, Strauss, Proust, Beckett, Genet, Cavafy. But I find particularly insightful, in this context, his discussion of late style in Sigmund Freud's bold gesture of writing *Moses and Monotheism* as the last response of a profoundly secular mind to a world of single-minded identities and totalizing violence. Freud's own unresolved sense of identity (on many registers, not merely the cultural, but also the scientific and professional) produces a way of fissuring the imaginary core of monotheism by tying its emergence to the constitutive presence of the stranger, the foreigner, the other, within the instituted communal body. Said recognizes in what sense this remarkable gesture attests as well to how an ethnic/national exclusionary institution is also irreparably entangled with the stranger, the foreigner, the other, at the origin. The strength of Freud's thought, Said argues, "can be articulated in and speak to other besieged identities as well, not through dispensing palliatives such as tolerance and compassion, but rather by attending to it as a troubling, disabling, destabilizing secular wound, the essence of the cosmopolitan, from which there can be no recovery, no state of resolved or stoic calm, and no utopian reconciliation even within itself."[31] Only a critical secular response that attends to this wound—that realizes the limitations of history, and yet recognizes the limitless capacity of the historical imagination—would cast its eye upon the future without becoming enchanted by its conjured irrelevance, apocalyptic abolition, utopian promise, or transcendence.

It is this transgressive, transformative desire to resist the will to transcendence that animates Edward Said's conviction that "all criticism is postulated and performed on the assumption that it is to have a future."[32] The conviction as to having a future against all odds is this paradoxical affirmation of our historical being that emerges out of the acceptance of our existential finitude. Disappointingly, this is becoming rarer and rarer in our historical present. The religious imaginary revealed in and after the 9/11 events, whether intended this way or not, suggests the casualty of envisioning a future—a future in the world, of course, for the future of martyrdom is no future, strictly speaking; it is submission to a heteronomous plenitude, to the supreme authority of the Other, which knows no temporality. Sadly, but perhaps not surprisingly, the response of the American state, institutionally a secular state, exhibited a similar monological (so as not to say, outright metaphysical) attitude toward history, which might be said to cancel history's capacity to remain unpredictable, uncertain, in flux. The George W. Bush White House document titled *The National Security Strategy of the United States of America*—a document of enormous significance, if only because of its unabashed declaration of the projected terms of global domination—envisions a future so narrowly self-referential and wishfully guaranteed by sheer military power and ideological conviction in the transcendental authority of the market that it leaves one wondering if that's any future at all.

The faith that certain policies and courses of action, whether directed by the will of God or by the "rational" analysis of national security advisors, will unilaterally transcend the contradictions of the present and be fulfilled in a redemptive future means lack of thinking critically, historically. It actually abdicates humanity's self-consciousness and responsibility in the making of history, making of the future a mere game of power in order to confirm the status quo of power in the present. The grave problem laid before us is how to conduct a fight for the future that takes as supreme values, first, the untranscendable finitude of human existence and, second, the absolutely teleological danger of the destruction of the whole planet (that is, total finitude). To this extent, I argue, the tradition of transcendental thinking has never offered humanity anything better than the blissful pill of oblivion, while a transgressive, transformative thinking takes one's individual finitude as the point of departure and draws from it the energy to combat whatever forces might risk humanity's irreversible end.

Appendix: The Late Style of Edward Said

Said's interest in "late style"—a concept drawn from Adorno's account of Beethoven's late music—can be traced back to the early 1990s. It represented initially the next in a line of writings on literary and musical criticism, following *Culture and Imperialism* (1993) and *Musical Elaborations* (1991). But it would also be fair to say that "late style" was conceptualized by Said out of the disruptive experience of his illness and the consequent confrontation with mortality. Because Said had always been adverse to religious or transcendental solutions, his personal encounter with mortality was unlikely to have led to intellectual projects that exemplify some sort of spiritual quest, an exercise in philosophical redemption, or a retrospective settling of affairs.

The writing of his memoir *Out of Place* (1999)—which, by his own account, proved difficult to complete—was hardly an attempt to round out the contours of his life or provide a retrospective reference for some sort of Saidian totality. In addition to being, in a concrete and avowed sense, an attempt to recall and reconfigure in writing a social world now lost forever, the memoir strove to map a network of beginnings and hardly to account for a totality of life from some end point of thought. It might be said that *Out of Place* was Said's first exercise in late style, much as it signified, de facto, the deferral of writing the envisioned essays that would make up the book on late style. As a narrative of beginnings—and similar to the way of thinking in *Beginnings* as such—the memoir was an extensive meditation on the parameters of secular life, on a person's struggle to create meaning solely within this world, even in historical instances when the world seemed recalcitrant and adverse to any sort of meaningfulness.

The book on late style was never completed, though various essays or bits and pieces in lectures and occasional writings over the last fifteen years of Said's life suggest that the project was always alive and imminent.[33] The first posthumous publication in the *London Review of Books* of the essay "Thoughts on Late Style," a fragmentary but brilliant exposition of the problem he was pursuing, put forth a whole other framework in which to perceive Edward Said's last works.[34] (We might note, incidentally, that the graduate seminar Said occasionally taught at Columbia University during those years carried the double title "Last Works/Late Style.") By last works, I refer to his book *Humanism and Democratic Criticism* (Columbia UP, 2004) and the political journalism of the last years collected posthumously as *From Oslo to Iraq and the Road Map* (Pantheon, 2004) and published with an insightful introduction by the now late Tony Judt and an elegant and moving afterword by Wadie Said, the author's son.

Even the most elementary account of Edward Said's life and work makes evident that his literary and political worlds were intertwined in delicate but persistent fashion, though kept intact in their disciplinary parameters, conducted simultaneously as distinct but interrelated elements of a life project, which he explicitly authorized as the task of *secular criticism*. But what exactly distinguishes these last works within the protracted project of secular criticism that might enable us to speak of the late style of Edward Said?

In the aforementioned essay, Said gives the most succinct descriptions of an otherwise elusive concept. Returning to Adorno's interpretation of the late Beethoven, Said singles out the insistence on Beethoven's intransigent subjectivity in relation to his musical material, which disregards the rigorous integrative logic that was the composer's signature symphonic style in favor of "wayward and eccentric" or "episodic" approaches that reveal Beethoven's final resignation about the possibility of synthesis. Said points to Adorno's conclusion that the style of Beethoven's late works, far from achieving harmonious synthesis, produces an internal tearing, which leaves these works suspended in time and imprints them with implacable and catastrophic awe.

Said agrees that Beethoven's late works "remain unco-opted by a higher synthesis," as "they do not fit any scheme, and they cannot be reconciled and resolved, since their irresolution and fragmentariness are constitutive, neither ornamental nor symbolic of something else. The late works are about 'lost totality,' and it is in this sense that they are catastrophic." But Said underlines that Adorno's reading seeks to define lateness as a specific relation to form that goes beyond the mere biographical element of an artist late in life striving to leave his last mark. Whatever might be the relation to the biographical dimension—no one suggests it's not relevant—and hence whatever might be the relation of art to a specific reality, late style testifies to art at an extreme point that disregards conventions (including the artist's own) and breaks through the muted assurance of contemporary reality, which, until then, had provided the artist with a cogent identity.

Lateness thus becomes a condition in its own right, a disruptive response by a creative intelligence to the irreversible finitude of life, on the one hand, and to one's assimilation by the enormous memorializing forces of history, on the other. Said recognizes Adorno's own gestures of late style in his characterizations of Beethoven before proceeding to two cases suffering from the same condition but drawn from the fringes of a Mediterranean universe so dear to his own imagination: the Sicilian novelist Giuseppe di Lampedusa and the Alexandrian Greek poet Constantine Cavafy. He identifies in both an anachronistic sensibility that, paradoxically, denudes the present of its elusive and inscrutable character and thus sharpens its force as history-in-the-making. This anachronistic imaginary is conducted by taking great pleasure and having great confidence in the skewed and exilic position of a literature that disregards the authority of its present time and, therefore, does not get absorbed in the unresolved tension between what is presently trivial and what might end up being historically shattering. Such position configures instead, eccentrically and inimitably, the terms of a critical understanding of present history to be actualized in the future. Said concludes that "the prerogative of late style" is "to render disenchantment and pleasure without resolving the contradiction between them. What holds them in tension, as equal forces straining in opposite directions, is the artist's mature subjectivity, stripped of hubris and pomposity, unashamed either of its fallibility or of the modest assurance it has gained as a result of age and exile."

Late style is thus characterized by definite bravery but never naïve audacity, by remaining committed to one's singular vision but never losing touch with either the absolute limits of mortality or the defiance of limits that enables humanity to make history in the face of an indeterminate future. No careful reader, I believe, can avoid the resonance of this final paragraph in Said's definitive essay on late style. It is implicitly as self-referential as it is explicitly pertinent to a literary form and a social condition.

The essays on humanism were famous years before they found their way into print. In certain circles in the humanities, they were downright infamous, configured to bear the most concrete evidence of Said's alleged turn against theory. The argument circulated at the most simplistic level: insofar as the high days of French theory, in the spirit of '68, had made their mark through a devastating critique against the assumptions of the humanist tradition, any attempt to defend and reauthorize the discourse of humanism was tantamount to being anti-theory. This syllogism is not merely simplistic; it is entirely inaccurate in respect to both sides. Neither was Said ever simply "anti-theory," nor were the so-called post-structuralist theorists simply "anti-humanists." There is nothing a priori compatible or incompatible between the terms *theory* and *humanism*. Their interrelation is, and has always been, historically contingent, before even the terms bore any recognizable coherence, before even being thus named, from Heidegger extending backward to Nietzsche and to Marx.

Said, of course, never hid his frustration with what he perceived to be the fetishism of theory, the specific sort of academic self-fashioning by means of a rarefied language that ultimately undercut any frame of reference other than itself. He found this indeed to betray the political purposes of theory—which, from his earliest avowed allegiances to Lukács and to Gramsci, had meaning only in a dialectical relation to praxis—and he assailed such tendencies in both Europeanist and postcolonial literary studies, over whose theoretical parameters he had, at one time, presided. Hence the charge against him of a turn of face. The lectures on humanism were met, practically everywhere in American universities, with a sense of betrayal by those who had been counted among his allies in the humanities during the 1970s and 1980s and a sense of triumphalism by various adversaries, who had inaugurated themselves as the defenders of Anglo-American humanist principles against the foreign onslaught.

A careful reading of *Humanism and Democratic Criticism*, however, shows Said to confound both sides yet again. He initiates the argument with a relentless critique of latter-day American humanism (of the likes of Allan Bloom, William Bennett, and Saul Bellow), who represent "the anti-intellectualism of American life" and are characterized by "a certain dyspepsia of tone" and "the sour pursing of the lips that expresses joylessness and disapproval," all of it driven by the "unpleasant American penchant for moralizing reductiveness" and the stern conviction that "the approved culture is salubrious in an unadulterated and finally uncomplicatedly redemptive way."[35] At the same time, Said does not mince words about "lazy multiculturalism" and "specialized jargons for the humanities." He rejects "ideological anti-humanism," which he identifies as a negative practice that nullifies a priori the sovereignty of the Enlightenment subject, instead of dismantling the assumptions this subject mobilizes in the ever-changing landscape of the post-Enlightenment world, precisely in order to wrest subjectivity away from its presumably impermeable ideological trappings.

This double-sided rejection speaks of an equally double-sided purpose. Said initially proclaims his undertaking to be "critical of humanism in the name of humanism" (H, 10) and yet, later on, professes his aspiration to achieve the position of "the non-humanist humanist," which, by his own account, is a "dialectically fraught" position that takes humanism to initiate "a technique of trouble" (H, 77). Any careful reader of Said over the years knows that his language can achieve the most extraordinary intertwining of the skeptical with the utopian, but is never equivocal or sophistic. These apparently self-contradictory assertions are not driven by some perverse desire to confuse but, on the contrary, by stern commitment to elucidate the underhanded and deceitful ways in which identities—here, both the "humanist" and the "anti-humanist," but in essence *all* identities—are produced and cultivated.

For a man who had once said, simply and succinctly, "imperialism is the export of identity," the critique of identity is not merely an occasional political stance (as in the critique of "identity politics," for example) but a philosophical position that interrogates any practice of exclusion. Without ever adopting an ontological framework, Said consistently attacks any structure, discourse, or institution that renders itself unaccountable for forming identities, no matter what might be the historical necessity or political strategy. Hence, his tireless dismantling of authorities that demand strict obedience and adhesion to a priori principles: nationalism, imperialism, religion, the State, or those definitions of culture that bind societies in conceptual frameworks of "civilization"—this was, of course, the impetus of *Orientalism*. Moreover, this demands the sort of historical slowness that enables the secular imagination to unfold, unlike the ahistorical speed scale of identity-making and identity politics that the capitalist imagination in fact favors and facilitates.

The essays on humanism follow this line of thinking against identity, but focus on the core figure that drives identity production: the human as such. This focus is relentlessly sharpened by brushing aside abstract philosophizing about the "nature of the human" in order to foreground the range of human practices—the making of society, the making of history—as constitutive boundaries of the human. In this respect, Said's antinomian humanism is yet another elaboration on the task of secular criticism, which must be understood to work on both grounds of what is secular and what is critical. The text is full of descriptions of this task; I choose two: "To understand humanism at all is to understand it as democratic, open to all classes and backgrounds, and as a process of unending disclosure, discovery, self-criticism, and liberation. . . . Humanism *is* critique" (H, 21). And: "Humanism should be a force of disclosure, not of secrecy or religious illumination. . . . [It] must excavate the silences, the world of memory, of itinerant, barely surviving groups, the places of exclusion and invisibility, the kind of testimony that doesn't make it into reports" (H, 73, 81).

Taken together, these phrases target both particularist and universalist practices by demanding a disclosure—Said is fond of using just as often the word *exfoliation*—of all exclusionary strategies, whether their authority is achieved in the name of the Self (and its global expanse) or in the name of the Other (and its narrowing essence). We may thus understand Said's call "to practice a *para-doxal mode of thought*" (his emphasis) as a call to subvert any *orthodox* tendencies, no matter what their purpose or justification. It's not so difficult to see why both dogmatic traditionalists, who defend the purity of the literary canon or of human rights, and dogmatic multiculturalists, who refuse to affirm anything other than their own minoritarian niche, would find much to be sour about in this book. But they are likely to miss that Said's presumed objection is not against their position in political, historical, or even theoretical terms, but against the orthodoxy of their position, against their entrenchment, their inability to consider that their position, after all, bears as well the mark of its worldliness, of being made in a specific moment *in* the world. This inability undermines and occludes the historical accountability of such positions because it denies them the realization that they remain open to being, just as easily, unmade (and made anew, made otherwise) when worldly conditions demand it. Said certainly deserves the credit of being a global intellectual, but he achieved it by being always a worldly intellectual.

It's this worldliness that grants meaning to both humanism and criticism (which are, in any case, interwoven) as practices invariably engaged in the struggle to accept and embrace the new, the emergent, the not yet known, the unthought, the as-yet-to-be imagined. This attitude is crucial to Said's argument about humanist practice, but resides also at the core of his characterization of late style. At the point when one is "getting old"—the point of the body aging, works maturing, life-experience reaching the fullest—one is even more persistently open to the new, often to the new against the old, against the grain of what is already in place, comforting and assuring. This disquieting and restless *modernist* spirit—"rendering pleasure and disenchantment without resolving the contradiction between them" ("Thoughts on Late Style")—permeates the argument throughout and explains precisely why this book, written presumably at the summit of the author's intellectual wisdom, is so annoying to so many, so subversive.

The volume *From Oslo to Iraq and the Road Map* collects Said's political journalism of the last three years of his life. The title resonates with his call for dismantling "the technical and ultimately janitorial rearrangement of geography" (H, 143). Most of these pieces were written as regular columns in the weekly English-language edition of the Arab newspaper *Al-Ahram*, and almost all the pieces, which are short, concise, and widely accessible, were syndicated and reproduced in various newspapers around the world or broadly distributed through the Internet. In this mode of writing for large audiences, Said strives to achieve the ultimate power of the essay form to capture the demands of the transient and the ephemeral—the world of real, daily politics—as forces of history that have lasting effect, as events that exceed their temporal lifespan. Only a masterful essayist, like Said, could draw from the transient and the ephemeral a concrete sense of the unknown future: "one *invents* abductively; one hypothesizes a better situation from the known historical and social facts" (H, 140).

What distinguishes this set of writings, however, is, on the one hand, a greater sense of urgency, a fierceness of energy remarkable given the author's already awe-inspiring indefatigability, and, on the other hand, an explicit and deliberately cultivated politics of self-critique that shadows the critique of the adversary in ways hitherto unexplored. This gives these writings—which are, of course, focused on the Palestinian question but with an eye poised on its global repercussions—a distinct style, if I am permitted to address political writing with a literary term: a writing style distinguished by its sharpness and intransigence, not merely with respect to its content, but in its very form. Only the complex personality of Edward Said, a student of Adornian writing who clearly surpassed the lesson, could have produced a late style of writing in the context of political journalism. And my sense of these pieces, as a reader in retrospect and at a distance from the historical immediacy that generated them, is that Said's long-term involvement with the Palestinian struggle served to sharpen his intellectual focus in ways that even the most rigorous and self-reflexive theoretical thinking couldn't.

The main gesture in these texts is to speak to Arab audiences, to raise the stakes of discourse and reflection in and with Arab audiences. Hence, we see a great deal of energy spent on examination and critical elaboration of things Arab, not merely Palestinian. This happens in conjunction with attempts to convey the complexities of American reality and to dispel the naïve and narrow-minded (pre)judgment of American society, culture, and politics. It hardly means that Said's criticism of Israeli policy and the cowardice of Israeli intellectuals is any less relentless than it had consistently been. It's just that whatever the critique of Israel, Said strives to show, it must take place in the context of self-critique, for two reasons: (1) self-critique will sharpen the critique of the adversary and make it more useful, moving it closer to the realm of praxis; (2) self-critique and critique of the adversary must coincide because the two societies are irretrievably coimplicated and complicit, both in their history and in their present reality. This, I think, is the most radical of Said's positions on this matter in the later years of his writing, echoing his general conviction that "cultures are intertwined and can only be disentangled from each other by being mutilated" (H, 52).

For this reason, Said assails the contemporary mode of conducting politics, addressing American and Israeli policies of conquest and occupation, as well as Islamist responses, with a statement that exemplifies the secular criticism he pursued throughout his life: "demonization of the Other is not a sufficient basis for any kind of decent politics."[36] We could add, just as well, that demonization of the Other always bespeaks of a "religious politics" whose indecency is the least of its problems. In this kind of politics, the inequities of power, regardless of which position in the equation one finds oneself in, assume a metaphysical aura and are thus maintained (even if the intention is to subvert them) by fostering some sort of dogmatic exclusion or erasure of the adversary's actual existence. It is, in other words, a politics of annihilation.

Against the demonization of the Other, which is bound to leave behind real traces of atrocity and destruction (including self-destruction), Said's journalism exemplifies the politics of humanist resistance. It fosters a democratic criticism that does not make mockery of its (abused) name: a criticism that inhabits and speaks to the world, disregarding set constituencies and their approval ratings—indeed, continuously (re)shaping constituencies around the interrogative assessment of the issues, which thus lose their righteous authority and open themselves to subversive rethinking. In this world, where God is allegedly occupying the mind of political players worldwide—which hardly excuses the mindlessness and cynicism they shamelessly try to pass off as righteousness and morality—Edward Said's voice, preserved in these quick and sharp meditations on history-in-the-making, continues to provide us with arms of defiance. And though his adversaries have been all too eager to celebrate his corporeal absence, they cannot outmaneuver the altogether actual presence of his legacy. Whether writing of past history or of events unfolding in the present, Edward Said never wavered from his avowed conviction that "all criticism is postulated and performed on the assumption that it is to have a future." Late style is precisely the form that defies the infirmities of the present, as well as the palliatives of the past, in order to seek out this future, to posit it and perform it even if in words and images, gestures and representations, which now seem puzzling, untimely, or impossible.

CHAPTER 2

THE LESSON OF PIERRE CLASTRES

The essayist whose lesson we presently rehearse was by profession an anthropologist, or an ethnologist, as the French term goes. I prefer to identify him as an essayist, not only in the terms I have consistently borrowed from Adorno, but because, even within the terms of his discipline, his position and his work are paradoxical. Pierre Clastres was an anthropologist at once traditional and maverick, whose research belongs to the core of anthropology and yet decisively exceeds its boundaries. It is fair to say that, in his meteoric and hapless life (1934–77), Clastres passed through the anthropological world like a phantom. But he left behind an inimitable ethnographic and theoretical record that still has not registered its proper recognition outside France, despite the fact that the poetic and philosophical dimensions of anthropological practice have established a substantial presence outside their disciplinary boundaries. It might have something to do with the authorial personality itself. A student of Claude Lévi-Strauss, Clastres spent little time in the academic circles of his discipline and even less in the fashionable circuits of Parisian intellectuals. He seems to have been driven by a singular quest, which began with his fieldwork experience, in the early and mid-1960s, amid indigenous tribes, still remarkably in near Stone Age conditions, in the Amazon regions of Brazil, Paraguay, and Venezuela. The impetus was to chronicle and elucidate the last vestiges of what Clastres identified from the outset as "societies without power," totally cognizant of being a privileged witness to an alternative social reality that was certain to vanish in his lifetime.

His work, in this respect, is characterized by tremendous urgency and, as his friend Maurice Luciani said in his obituary, he is to be remembered "by [the] aloofness of his irony and the laconic presence of his friendship, his indifference to the spirit of the times, his contempt for derivative thinking, his solitary bearing."[1] From these words, we can understand why Clastres, whatever his training, showed no interest in either furthering the structuralist project or embarking in some sort of poststructuralist critique. And though he was, by training, an ethnologist, his work appeared in contexts one would not expect. In an essay that serves as an introduction to his translation of Clastres's first ethnography, *Chronicle of the Guayaki Indians* (1972), the great novelist Paul Auster recounts, in characteristic style, how he first came across Clastres's writing (which "seemed to combine a poet's temperament with a philosopher's depth of mind") in the last issue of the legendary literary journal *L'Éphémère*, a journal whose editors and regular contributors included Yves Bonnefoy, Michel Leiris, and, until his death in 1970, Paul Celan.[2] A few years later, Clastres became involved as a cofounder in *Libre*, another journal project, dissolved after his death, in collaboration with radical political thinkers outside the mainstream, such as Claude Lefort, Cornelius Castoriadis, Marcel Gauchet, and Miguel Abensour.[3] Clastres is celebrated for his legendary book *Society Against the State*, initially published in 1974, which elaborates on the political ramifications of his fieldwork. He was conducting a sequel work, in the pages of *Libre*, on the significance of war in primitive societies, tentatively titled *Archeology of Violence*, when his life was cut short one day at the age of forty-three, as he lost control of the wheel of his car and skidded over the edge of a mountain.

Forty years have passed since the day Pierre Clastres completed his trajectory in human history, and the lesson he bequeaths us, a lesson in historical thinking above all, remains more trenchant than ever. As is the case with all groundbreaking historians, this lesson is given in terms that go beyond the disciplinary limits of history—in this case, in terms of not only creative ethnography but political philosophy as well, with the specific aim to study the polemical origins of the archaic social imagination as a springboard for a self-reflexive relation to the contemporary. On the face of it, there is nothing unusual here. I was late in realizing how, from a certain standpoint, Clastres may be deemed perfectly canonical. His ethnographic universe is formed around the conviction that the study of the primitive encapsulates the anthropologist's task. Against the grain of post-Lévi-Straussian anthropology's deconstruction of the primitive as privileged object of research, everything for Clastres begins and ends with primitive society, defined more directly as society without a state, or, as he was eventually to call it, society *against* the state. The prepositional shift from "without" to "against" denotes a shift from the ethnographic to the political project that was his life's work, the latter being defined explicitly as the realm in which adversarial (indeed warring) relations with the other are conducted and explicit mechanisms of counterpower are developed and instituted.

Clastres goes so far as to say that societies against the state are "ethnology's privileged if not exclusive object."[4] Yet, this is hardly a traditional anthropological position insofar as the real time of this ethnography, as a political project, exists explicitly in contemporary society. Despite his ethnographic fascination with the primitive, the concept of "society against the state" is driven by Clastres's exasperation with contemporary politics, by an anarchist (for lack of a better term) aspiration that demands a radical rethinking of the terms of power. For Clastres, the modern world—which, in his heretic chronology, begins with the first agricultural societies, that is to say, in standard terms, with ancient Mesopotamia—is defined as society *with* the state, or society *coupled with* the state, in the very direct sense of the sort of society that desires the state, that desires to become one with the state. (This element of desire for oneness is indeed the epistemological crux of the problem I'm discussing.) So, according to Clastres, we study the primitive not to understand better the process of civilization, but to understand the moment prior to civilization as an instance that may teach us to overcome the perils of civilization. Overcoming civilization does not mean becoming primitive; very simply, it means relearning—*remembering* (and the matter of memory is equally crucial in this discussion)—how to free ourselves from domination.

I must underline here that in claiming a prior situation, Clastres cannot be further removed from theories of prehistorical societies, Marxist or otherwise. In fact, one of his most challenging contributions is to reframe our inherited understanding of the so-called prehistorical or prepolitical. In looking backward in history he may be said to be looking ahead. His political anthropology is not restricted to the diagnosis of a specific anthropological field. Rather, in examining societies without a state, he is also concerned with how the emergence of the state was blocked in such societies, how such societies refused to succumb to the primary division of a command-obedience structure, and what specific mechanisms, rituals, or performativities they developed in order to enact this refusal.[5] His way of reading his ethnographic material and the impetus of the theoretical project is to demonstrate the presence of politics (*la politique*) in primitive society in order to reinvest the concept of the political (*le politique*) with new and radical meaning. Indeed, he insists that the concept of the political, which we take for granted in a conceptual universe already fully formed, is a historically derived concept, and that there is a whole forgotten history of the political—forgotten because relegated to prehistory—that, if properly recalled, alters our understanding. In this sense, Clastres calls for a new anthropology, which is a matter of developing not a new methodology of ethnography, but a new way to conceive the past and future of the human, of *anthropos*. Indeed, he is not only asking us to reconceptualize primitive society per se; to use one of his own metaphors, he is asking us to engage with a Copernican revolution in the perspective of political anthropology as such.

The Polis as Primitive Society

We thus begin with a strange relation between traditional ethnography and maverick anthropology, interwoven and predicated on each other's thorough pursuit. This basic dialectical relation is exemplary of Clastres's overall methodological attitude, and though here is not the context to address this specifically, I do underline it as a signpost for the sketch I am about to draw. My interest in Clastres is not properly anthropological. It emerges as part of an inquiry of how societies institute the political, which is to say, how societies institute their own forms of freedom or domination. This is a question immediately pertinent to the understanding of the democratic imaginary, which I take to be the impetus toward a self-governing (properly *an-archic*) mode of political organization with various emergences throughout human history. In this respect, I find Clastres's account of "society against the state" especially striking in my overall interrogation of the Athenian polis, specifically in the sense that, if we engage in a rather subversive rhetorical arrangement, we may speak of the polis (after all, a society of warriors) as a primitive society. This arrangement undoes the traditional association between the polis and "civilization" and, conversely, the association between savage societies and the alleged "natural state" of humanity, a concept that, from Thomas Hobbes onward, has dominated the framework of Western political theory. In this respect, the larger framework of this sketch would be to articulate a broader and more refined understanding of the archaic moment in politics, whereby contrary terms such as *the primitive* and *the civilized* or *savage culture* and *democratic culture* are undermined by an otherwise inadmissible association.[6]

A project that seeks to understand the polis as primitive society is at once an extension of Clastres and an antithesis to Clastres. The latter is due to his refusal to see Athenian democratic politics as anything other than the source of Western culture, which is to say, the source of the politics of power and domination. Clastres's anarchist urgency is so great that his otherwise iconoclastic thinking reproduces some of the worst idealizations of ancient Greek society, entirely unaware, it seems, of the self-fashioning interest of Romantic Philhellenism and the national(ist) modernity it coveted. Hence, he altogether misses the social-imaginary investment of modernity in translating the (ancient) *polis* into (modern) *State*, thereby reproducing a whole range of misguided conclusions as to the trajectory of politics from ancient to modern times.

Be that as it may, the trenchant point of departure in this meditation is Clastres's demand that the imagination of non-power become a primary element in the theorization of power. His object of inquiry was the political imaginary of a society in which all forms of singular power are undermined as prerequisite to communal survival, and this is precisely what the Greek institution of democratic politics also signified, though the historical terms differ on numerous levels.

There are several registers in which this curious affinity between, say, Amazonians and Athenians may be traced.[7] I list just three here, with minimal commentary, as a sort of prelude to the details that follow. To speak of affinity is not to evade the unlikeness between these two social imaginaries. There is no doubt that Athenian society is profoundly differentiated, with a complex institutional structure and a psychosocial framework that enables a kind of individual initiative that would be inconceivable for the Amazonians. The easiest thing to say is that the two have nothing in common. This makes the affinities even more impressive. In light of this comparison, Clastres's own dead-ends will emerge in the end, but the ingenious impetus of his thought and the openings that he forges begin here:

1. *The unmitigated devaluation of singular power.* The arbitrary and ritualistically discredited authority of the tribal chief among the Indians is analogous to both the short-term holdings of office drawn by lot and the community's instituted power to repeal any officer at any moment in the ancient democratic polis: in both cases, the elemental substitutability of persons in office-holding or administrative duty, despite specific skills and capacities, so that no position of power is ever invested with any one person. The impetus in both social-historical situations, despite their enormous differences, is to institute modalities of governance where power can never be concentrated in the hands of one over the others because it must circulate among all, and even when one is designated to execute the authorizations of the community, one never comes to *embody* the authority of this executive, not just in perpetuity but even in the momentary occupation of this designated seat. The specific rituals—the modes of institution—are certainly different, but this difference nonetheless shares an aversion to the authority of the one, to *monarchical* power strictly speaking.

2. *The poetic performativity of political speech.* In the tribes of Clastres's ethnography, the chief is at the very most the tribe's epic poet—more precisely, the tribe's *performer*, for he is not endowed with any sort of creative *poiein*. The ritual songs he sings belong to the tribe; they chronicle its warrior glory as memorial inventory. Not only is his speech vacant of authority, but, strictly speaking, it bears no addressee. For, insofar as it is spoken by the chief, it is a speech that cannot be listened to, a speech that must be refused. The chief's speech is instituted as non-instrumental; it is performed specifically so as to fall on deaf ears. Crucial here is Clastres's claim that the tribe

does not repress or ignore the chief's speech. Rather, the tribe merely feigns the act of nonchalance toward the communal poet; its relation to the discourse of the chief is to enact a *performance* of not-listening. Although by rules of communicative action this would make both positions empty (or disingenuous), the radical importance is precisely that their mutual *emptiness* (the empty speech of the chief and the voided listening of the tribe) is in actuality mere performance.

It's inappropriate, of course, to speak of Athenian political speech as non-instrumental. The very word *demagogue* literally forecloses the possibility. However, the most original of all Athenian institutions, the theater, which is a quintessentially political space, stands witness to the profound effect of non-instrumental speech. The great tragedians who placed the entire polis before its own interrogation can hardly be understood to act (or even more to speak) instrumentally. The language of tragedy does not lie at a great distance away from the language of the oracle. Whatever might be deemed to be its truth is not apparent in the words themselves, but in the framework of action it precipitates, which would include interpretation at all levels (performers, judges, audience). Forms of speech that flourish concurrently with dramatic poetics (the public speech of the sophists or later the rhetoricians) are even more apparent as to their performative non-instrumentality. One thing, however, remains profoundly different in this comparison. Non-instrumental performativity notwithstanding, the Athenians were remarkably keen on the art of listening, a characteristic trait remarked upon even as late as the New Testament text describing the visit of the Apostle Paul to Athens.

3. *The centrality of warrior culture as groundwork for social cohesion.* This is a paradoxical but foundational condition for an autonomous politics in the archaic world, although again the specific elements of autonomy between the two cases differ substantially. Clastres's perspective, quite simply, undermines most of what is written about the social significance of war, not only in primitive societies but in the historical development of power toward the institution of modernity. In his mind, war serves as the ultimate buffer against two possible formations that would annihilate indigenous Amazon societies from within: (1) the tendency of power to become external to society and (2) the tendency toward tribal fragmentation or internal division that would produce catastrophic social inequities. In terms of the comparison, however, more important is Clastres's understanding that war in primitive societies is a permanent condition, by which he means an existentially necessary condition. On the basis of a sort of existential enmity between tribes (or societies), a kind of self-sufficiency—or, as he elaborates explicitly, using a term of great radical political currency at that time, a kind of *autogestion* (self-organization,

self-management)—is secured for each society, which prevents the development of externalized power that comes to rule in itself and for itself as One.[8]

In discussions of Athenian tragedy (or even more generally, of Athenian democracy), it has become rather common to forget that all these unprecedented developments in both theater and politics took place while the city was almost continuously at war. Thucydides remains the best source of documenting the existential necessity of war to the peculiar trajectory of Athens, including its most vulnerable aspects, but the tragedies themselves may be said to provide the most profound expression of the social imaginary that formed and was in turn transformed by this condition. Of course, from the Homeric epics onward we know very well to what extent Greek societies were quintessentially warrior societies and how the surrounding framework of war shaped their elemental character and their institutions to the minutest detail. The key argument, from my standpoint, would be to underline how, as a sort of fundamental social condition of Greek societies, war played a crucial role in the trajectory of democracy in Athens, both its creation and its (self-)destruction. Here, one could well invoke the difference in Greek between *polemos* and *stasis*—the first being the means of preventing the occurrence of the second—and also recall Herodotus's reference to how the institution of *isēgoria* in democratic Athens benefited directly the warring power of the Athenians (*Histories* 5.78). I would also add, even if without elaborating, that out of the same social-imaginary rubric Athenians introduce into the mix the notion of justice (*dikē*), another definite mark of distinction.

I understand these three elements as scale dimensions of a map. This cursory noting is but a point of departure in the course of considering the significance of Clastres's thought. The *co-incidence*, for both Amazonians and Athenians, that singular *archē* is perilous is, in the end, the most intriguing point. To get to this, we shall have to make a detour. Perhaps the very suggestion of a political theory that associates the primitive with the modern—an association that elicits all sorts of ramifications of how the archaic dwells in the core of the modern, as Walter Benjamin would say—demands that we consider instances where the modern emerges against the primitive conditions of its own historical time. What presides over Clastres's daring to shatter the chasm of "prehistory" (which is also what provokes me to make this association, within the realm of the archaic, between the Amazonian and the Athenian) is the radical gesture of a mentor-text that shadows his horizon: a notorious French Renaissance pamphlet by Étienne de la Boétie, known by the double title *Discours de la servitude volontaire* or *Le Contr'Un* (1549), which raises precisely the same demands against the monological/monarchical principle and the circuit of desire between power and submission.

La Boétie, the Rimbaud of Thought

We know little of La Boétie (1530–63), other than that he came from a wealthy and privileged family in Bordeaux, that he served as a judge, and that he was on his way toward a career in politics when he died, most likely of the plague, at the age of thirty-three. Most of what we know about his person and his life comes from Montaigne, who famously composes his essay "On Friendship" to celebrate their relation, the intimacy of which, Montaigne professes, epitomizes the essence of friendship as fraternal sharing of all that is most precious: "will, thoughts, opinions, goods, wives, children, honor, life."[9] (I shall return to this sexual marking at the end.) Of the circumstances of La Boétie's writing of the *Discours* we know nothing other than what Montaigne exclusively tells us: namely, the author was only eighteen years old when he wrote it "as a school assignment on the tyrants of Antiquity," and, as a tribute and in memory of his friend's early death, Montaigne declared his intention to publish it at the exact center point of the first volume of his essays (chapter 29). He opted against it, however, in the first edition under his supervision (1580), when he discovered a partial and anonymous publication of the *Discours* in 1574 by a Huguenot editor, an association that, given the political climate of the time, he did not wish to risk.[10] As a result, the *Discours* never gets published as part of the *Essays*, though the announcement of its imminence and its centrality is never to be erased. The complete text, still anonymous, sees the light of day in 1578, thirty years after it had allegedly been written, by a Protestant press based in Heidelberg. It remains curious why Montaigne does not include it in the publication of the collected works of La Boétie in 1571, for which he had procured official license to act as editor.

The peculiarity of this whole affair and the apparent political incompatibility between the *Discours de la servitude volontaire* and La Boétie's later essay *Mémoire sur l'Édit de Janvier 1562* (a text defending Catholic order), as well as various discrepancies between Montaigne's chronology and certain textual references in the body of the *Discours*, have led a group of historians to claim that the author of this text was not La Boétie but Montaigne himself.[11] Their argument has many persuasive elements, but it's worth noting that both Clastres and Claude Lefort, who provide the definitive political readings of La Boétie, do not seem to care one way or another.[12] And true, beyond the merit of a certain adventure in scholar-detective play, the essence of this radical document remains intact beyond the mythistorical conditions of its emergence. Nonetheless, Montaigne's essays, particularly "On Friendship" (1572–76) and "Of Cannibals" (1578–80), figure as crucial intertextual companions—as do, after all, Machiavelli's *Discorsi*—even if we don't take Montaigne to be playing the sincere forger and accept his account of the young genius named Etienne de la Boétie, about whom he concluded his essay "On Friendship" saying: "His mind [ésprit] was fashioned on a model of another age than this." In the same spirit, Clastres's idea to name La Boétie "the Rimbaud of thought" (AV, 93) still stands unchallenged, even if this genius might have been Montaigne's mythical invention. For in the performative nature of myth lies precisely the capacity to produce historical accuracy even from historically forged premises.

La Boétie's essay certainly exhibits many characteristics of the acknowledged master of the essay form, including the classic device of the meandering argument, with a trail of tangential excursions, and a Plutarchian skill of mining the most obscure details from the Greco-Roman world as exemplary instances. It also demonstrates a similar political attitude, though, unlike Montaigne's highly refined gestures of understatement, it opts for a directness that makes this text one of the most incendiary documents ever written.[13] But true to the genre, the political problem is addressed here not in contemporary terms, but by allusions to past history and a philosophical penchant to ruminate on matters of human nature. The overall trajectory is to ponder a condition that exceeds reasonable contemplation, a condition whose legitimacy cannot be retrieved from history, which thus leads the essayist to consider it an outcome of utter perversion. This is altogether a modern psychological term, and not entirely accurate; however, it speaks of the essence: La Boétie calls voluntary servitude a condition of being denatured (*dénaturé*). From the outset, the essay registers a mode of inquiry that refuses to compromise with real historical existence, which it perceives to be scandalous, and seeks instead to establish the undercurrent terms that authorize and veil this scandal. The essay deploys the gestures of grand refusal toward all authority, including the authority of historical explanation. It is thus quintessentially *anarchist*—and I use this term not in its contemporary political sense, but according to its literal meaning.

The Misfortunate Encounter

After a clever introduction that places Odysseus, the master of cunning and deception, at the center, La Boétie opens the core argument by wondering aloud: "What can that be? What shall we call this vice, this horrible vice? Isn't it shameful to see an infinite number of people not just obey, but crawl; not just be governed, but tyrannized? . . . Shall we call this cowardice? Shall we say that those who submit to this yoke are cowards and weaklings?" (SV, 176/192–93). This barrage of questions is aimed at an elusive object, elusive because its reality—which is indisputable—is nonetheless unfathomable, incomprehensible, inexplicable. What sort of object can this be then, whose existence, though real and indeed ever present, nonetheless boggles the mind and escapes all identification? La Boétie continues wondering, as if under the spell of an echo:

"What kind of monster of vice is this, then, which does not deserve even the name of cowardice, for which all expression is lacking, which nature disavows and the tongue refuses to name?" (193/177). The elusive object thus establishes its law—interrogation without end—and the essay may be said to begin when all registers of accessible meaning are proven a failure.

La Boétie establishes a discourse around a definitively paradoxical object. He is not merely interested in questioning the conditions of power and submission, or what we have come to understand philosophically since Hegel as the dialectically binding self-consciousness of master and slave. The rhetoric of mastery leaves him otherwise unmoved and unimpressed, and the reality of slavery—*servitude*, which in French carries a multiplicity of meanings, including literally service but also bondage—is merely unconvincing, insofar as he can conceive of no real power that can truly enforce it. The whole puzzle emerges precisely because the exercise of power is not commensurate to the production of submission. (In this whole quandary, there exists a peculiar arithmetic to which I will return.) La Boétie rehearses various historical instances in order to demonstrate this incommensurability. The conclusion is the evident paradox: submission is the outcome of certain willingness, quite independent of the enforced will of mastery. In fact, by the perverse logic of this paradox, no master can command and ensure a successful regime without being dependent on—being *subjected* to—the will of the servant.

"Voluntary servitude" is, from the standpoint of standard ontological grammar, a nonsensical concept because the agent is placed in the position of both master and servant simultaneously, being and acting as both subject and object of desire at one and the same time. By the same token, in terms of political grammar, the concept of voluntary servitude and the discourse it mobilizes nullify the concept (and discourse) of sovereignty in conventional terms. In both cases—in both grammars—voluntary servitude is an ill-logic that, as Abensour has argued, opens the way to the abyss of unworldliness, to a condition where subjective power loses all contact with the world that makes it be, that gives it meaning.[14]

Before we might jump, in our contemporary post-Freudian minds, into thoughts about the self-enclosing circuit of primary narcissism, we should note the centrality of the concept of desire in a mid-sixteenth-century text. La Boétie first calls upon it before he actually names it, by registering its absence—or the negativity of its presence, and I am not being sophistic. He marks this negative terrain with exceeding passion:

> Yet there is no need to combat this lone tyrant; there is no need to defend oneself against him. He is defeated by himself, as soon as the country does not consent to its servitude. One need not take anything away from him, so long as one doesn't give him anything. There is no need for a nation to put itself to

> the trouble of doing anything for its happiness; it suffices that it does not work to achieve its ruin. It is thus the peoples [*les peuples*] who let themselves be throttled [*garrotter*], or rather cause themselves to be throttled, since if only by ceasing to serve they would break their bonds. It is the people [*le peuple*] that subjugates itself. It is the people that cuts its own throat. Having the choice of being either subjugated or free, it rejects this freedom and takes the yoke. It is the people that consents to its own unhappiness [*son mal*] or rather, pursues it.
> (SV, 179/194–95)

To which he adds later on, as a sort of directive: "Be resolved no longer to serve, and you will find yourselves free. I do not want you to push or to shake him, but only no longer support him, and you will see him, like a great colossus stripped of his base, collapse of his own weight and break" (SV, 183/196–97). I will bypass yet again, but only for the moment, another instance of peculiar arithmetic, the noticeable shift in the agent of the nation from the plurality of "peoples" to the singularity of the unified subject ("the people") and then back, in order to focus not yet on the subject, but on the nature of the action.

To begin with, it behooves any contemporary reader to encounter in a mid-sixteenth-century text a clear notion that power is constructed around a vacuum of meaning, that mastery produces nothing: "One need not take anything away from [the master], so long as one doesn't give him anything." This is not a dialectical equation. The master is a mere shadow on his own; the dialectics emerges solely as fantasy, that is, literally, by the phantasmatic projection of power onto a screen, which is thus animated and reflects back the illusion of autonomous authority. Seen from a reverse angle, this occurs simultaneously with what Cornelius Castoriadis has named "the self-occultation of society": namely, the projection outward, which returns, as if bearing its own independent source of light, and succeeds—meaning, *becomes apparent*—only because the agent of projection produces simultaneously a self-enveloping darkness, a self-erasure. By an incomparable piece of magic, the agent of the action vanishes, producing a void that then becomes the basis for what is perceived as external authority. In this respect, the void of power is both real and unreal. It is real insofar as the agent of the action produces a void against himself—*actually voids himself.* It is unreal insofar as the entity predicated on the void—the master—is *actually* predicated on a thoroughly veiled transference of authority. This is precisely why we're facing an act of magic.

Except, magic works because it mobilizes the charming art of conjuring reality, which in our deepest sense we know to be none other than the psychic energy to make the world according to our desire—this ultimately unsocializable psychic capacity to do to ourselves (and others, but more to ourselves than others) what we please, even if what we please is tantamount to what causes us great displeasure: "It is the people that consents to its own unhappiness [*son mal*] or rather, pursues it." The void that occupies the kernel of power is wholly commensurate, in our post-Freudian terms, with the void that occupies the kernel of desire. And here La Boétie proceeds to an extraordinary gesture. He exempts from the realm of desire only one thing: "There is only one thing which, I know not how, men do not possess the force of desiring. It's liberty. . . . Liberty alone, men uniquely disdain for no other reason, it seems, than because if they desired it they would have it. It is as though they refused to make this precious acquisition only because it is too easy" (SV, 181/195). On second thought, I'm wrong. He does not exempt liberty from the realm of desire. He does something stranger. He makes desire for liberty altogether unique, insofar as, perversely, it exempts itself from realization because, by all accounts, it is tantamount to possession. Desire for liberty exists only insofar as one has liberty. Only those who have known liberty, who possess it (even as erstwhile experience), can fully engage in the desire for it. In this sense, precisely because liberty exists only as possession it cannot work as desire—presuming here the most standard understanding of desire as lack.

Let us consider it by following La Boétie's thought directly. Historically, he claims, the desire for liberty is manifested in instances of peoples who have come to know it. La Boétie specifically recalls the stand of ancient Greek cities during the Persian wars. But this specific example is only meant to serve as marker for the historical actuality of liberty, which, in light of what he takes to be the conditions of servitude of his contemporaries, suggests, on the scale of human history as a whole, a reversal, a repression, an abrogation. If nothing else, this historical reversal raises an enormous question that boggles the mind, for it entails self-dispossession. Claude Lefort, in his analysis of La Boétie, has put it succinctly: "In effect, the unthinkable is not only that man may cease being free, that is, cease being what he is by nature. The unthinkable is born out of the operative disjunction between desire and liberty in the very moment we articulate 'desire of liberty'—indeed, the moment we become able to affirm that liberty does not defend the desire for liberty."[15] In other words, the ruse by which La Boétie (de)links desire and liberty, as a condition of exception, runs itself ultimately into a logical dead end. Let us assume, following a psychoanalytic logic, that any possession produces a lack in turn. In this case, the possession of liberty produces another desire that runs counter to the desire in possession, a desire that is truly *other*. If we extend ourselves along these lines, we would likely reach the conclusion—perverse, no doubt, within psychoanalytic terms—that the desire for servitude is predicated on the possession of liberty, insofar as this possession produces an otherness as its lack and therefore a desire for it. And, in a peculiar way, we will have thus returned to La Boétie's original paradox: *voluntary* servitude, submission as the mastering of a desire.

Be that as it may, this psychological register engages a discourse that the essay, though it traffics in matters of desire by name, nonetheless does not share.

La Boétie writes in terms of history and politics,[16] and for him, this condition of reversal, of self-dispossession, is altogether real and altogether incomprehensible:

> What sort of unfortunate accident [*malencontre*] is it that has so denatured man—the only being truly born to live freely—as to make him lose his remembrance of his original state and the desire to regain it? . . . One can scarcely imagine *up to what extent* of vileness people, already subjected to a perfidious traitor, fall—and into such profound oblivion of all their rights, that it seems impossible to wake from their stupor in order to regain such rights, serving so well and so willingly that, upon seeing them, one would say that they have not only lost their liberty, but have won their servitude.
>
> (SV, 187, 189–90/199, 201)

At this juncture, La Boétie shows no qualms in assuming outright the existence of an original state, a nature, which humanity has explicitly and voluntarily betrayed. There is nothing provocative in the first part of this assumption, given the historical imaginary that produces this text. The discourse of human nature, after all, will not even be put into question until Marx, and even then a whole other framework regarding what he called "species-being" (*Gattungswesen*) will be substituted. That, in La Boétie's mind, the natural state happens to be a state of liberty certainly means no more than what, less than one hundred years later, Thomas Hobbes will imagine as utter mayhem.

What is striking instead is, first, the claim of being *denatured* and, second, the association of this being with the casualty of memory. La Boétie cannot come to terms with his own astonishment except by positing a process of erasure, the cause of which is but an unfortunate, accidental encounter (*malencontre*), though even this leads to an aporia, insofar as there is no evidence of an external other that makes this unfortunate encounter possible. The implication is that the mal-encountered *otherness* that produces desire for servitude is internal, self-produced. It is also, as such, not the agent but the outcome of oblivion, precisely because the entire schema is configured as voluntary and any external wielding of power is rejected as a factor. In fact, external coercion emerges as a *symptom* of voluntary servitude, which is exactly why it produces a colossus with no legs to stand on when the force of desire is recalled. Likewise, the originally self-produced oblivion yields as symptom the power of custom.[17]

So, voluntary servitude perpetuates itself via a reproduction of oblivion, which, if one looks at it from another angle, is none other than the curious reproduction of a distorted memory—moreover, a memory that is never renewed, a static memory of servitude whose original moment (as loss of liberty) is irrecoverable. Insofar as servitude enforces a condition where no new memories can be produced in relation to experience, it resembles the condition of the confused investigator in the film *Memento* (2001), which introduced a corruptive variation to the classic theme of amnesia in film noir. But unlike this hero, who is both master and slave to his condition, La Boétie's slaves have instituted no rituals, no tattoos on their bodies—I'm alluding both to the film and to the discussion of Clastres that follows—which will ensure a permanent engraving of reality in order to evade its loss. In mapping La Boétie's trajectory retrospectively, we might speak here of the passage *from voluntary servitude to the involuntary memory of servitude*, a memory that has turned fantasy into reality (even against the grain of nature) and has granted this reality an independence that, in yet another turn, occupies the entire phantasmatic terrain. In other words, we might have here an unusually precise depiction of the social-imaginary institution of heteronomy.

Singular in Their Fantasies

It is time to return to Clastres, though we have by no means concluded with La Boétie, as neither the peculiar arithmetic nor the puzzle of unfortunate encounter (with what exactly?) has been duly unraveled. Clastres writes his essay on La Boétie's text—evocatively titled "Liberty, Misfortune, the Unnamable"—after he has published both his ethnography on Indian tribes and his theoretical extrapolation on the politics of primitive society and while he is contemplating the next phase: the archeology of violence and the significance of war culture. He perceives in La Boétie a confirmation of his findings in the Amazon, particularly in the sense that La Boétie dares posit, even if as an imaginary instance, the possibility of a people that will have never known servitude.[18] What goes beyond Clastres's self-confirmation, however, is an explicit admiration of La Boétie for raising the question of whether humanity's desire for submission is innate or acquired and, moreover, for understanding the paradoxical nature of how an acquired desire can in fact become innate—a phrase that is utterly nonsensical but is, nonetheless, accurate: "Did his desire preexist the misfortune which would then have permitted its realization? Or is its emergence due instead, *ex nihilo*, to the occasion of the misfortune, like a lethal mutation that defies all explanation?" The answer merely confirms the aporia since it points to an undeconstructible paradox: "Such is [La Boétie's] new presentation of man: denatured, yet still free, since he chooses alienation. Strange synthesis, unthinkable conjunction, unnamable reality" (AV, 98).

But he confesses to being amazed at La Boétie's acknowledgment of the incomprehensible rupture in history that inaugurates the dialectic of power and submission, a dialectic whose range and effects become since that moment transhistorical: "Misfortune [*malencontre*]: tragic accident, inaugural mishap [*malchance*], whose effects do not stop expanding to the point of abolishing previous memory, to the point of substituting the love [*amour*] of servitude for the desire [*désir*] of freedom" (AV, 94). I draw our attention to how this historical accident splits the field of desire, perhaps even abrogates desire by fostering a love, which already by La Boétie's time denotes a certain *attachment* (in opposition to the *yearning* denoted by "desire"), whose commonest reference—and the cornerstone of post-sixteenth-century discussions of natural law—is the attachment to self-preservation: "self-love" (*l'amour de soi*). Clastres seems obsessed by this small difference, a shift that might itself articulate precisely the process of denaturation:

> Denaturation is expressed both in the contempt necessarily felt by he who commands for those who obey and in the love of the subjects for the prince, in the worship [*culte*] the people devote to the person of the tyrant. Now, this flow of love which unceasingly springs up from below to gush ever higher, this love of subjects for the master equally denatures the relations between subjects. Excluding all freedom, these relations dictate the new law that rules society: one must love the tyrant.
>
> (AV, 104)

I mentioned at the outset how for Clastres the institution of the state is not merely the establishment of domination over society. It is the establishment of a relation, of a coupling, whereby the explicit signs of domination are occluded by fostering a self-willed love for the state, a sense of necessity, and a drive to become one with it, which produces in turn the modern state's characteristic permeation of all registers of social existence. Bracketing for the moment the incisive observation regarding the "denaturing" of relations between subjects—that is, the very bonds of friendship within and across the ranks of society—we must hold on to the image of this law that emerges from the fragmentation of the ranks: the concentration of energies of adoration, of worship, on the Supreme Subject to which all else is subjugated. In Clastres's terms, the "Supreme Subject" is the State. In La Boétie's time, the contrarian desire that propels the author of the *Discours* or *Le Contr'Un* is specifically directed against monarchical authority. I don't mean to refer to monarchy merely as a specific mode of government, which may or may not be tyrannical, but literally, according to its Greek derived meaning: *μόνη ἀρχή*—singular authority, unique authority, but also, given the double meaning of *archē*, singular origin, unique origin.[19] The "new law that rules society" is, in this respect, a desire to love the origin, to couple with the origin—of power, of course, but that's the least of it. Insofar as it is also origin, authority becomes the *singular* source of primary meaning in a situation where social fragmentation erases the possibility of seeking (and making) meaning within the social domain.

La Boétie's text marks this effect with a notably "modern" phrasing: "The good zeal and affection of those who have preserved their devotion to freedom [*franchise*], in spite of the times, no matter how numerous they may be, remain without effect because they do not recognize one another. The liberty of action and speech, and almost of thought, is completely taken away from them under the tyrant. They become altogether singular in their fantasies [*ils deviennent tous singuliers en leur fantasies*]" (SV, 197/206).[20] This last phrase is striking. In our cognitive universe, it couldn't have been more precise. Not only does it posit explicitly the perilous conditions of singularity to which everyone regardless—including those who nominally deny themselves love for the tyrant—is subjected, but, in addition, it comprehends the profound dimensions of this peril: namely, the fostered conditions of singularity not only affect social practices of association but already occur in the realm of social fantasy, in the imaginary domain itself. This condition makes the *real* presence of the other inadmissible—or, just as well, makes *otherness as internal reality* inadmissible—so that submission to the singular authority of the (external) Other is open as a self-willing path. In other words, this sort of self-referential—strictly speaking, *autistic*—condition in relation to the social imagination might explain in part, without necessarily entering the vast depths of psychoanalytic theory, why we can say the phrase: *the desire for power is the desire for submission*. The ultimate point of this equation, the limit point of power and submission, is monological. The desire is to submit to singular power, in the sense that the love for the Master is, in the last instance, unique, unshareable, and unreproducible—locked intact within the strict bounds of singular fantasy.

Desire for Power Is Desire for Submission

This is actually Clastres's point of departure. His ethnographic reflections converge on this point in an uncompromising critique of monological thinking, which, he argues, underlies the obsession of the Western imagination with oneness. Hence, as a contrarian, he centers his attention on the painstaking rituals developed by Indian societies in order to obliterate the notion of the One. For Clastres, oneness is history's most oppressive force, fueling the social imagination with a death-drive. In the remainder of the essay, I will attend specifically to how monological thinking and the desire for or refusal of the One operates on cultural memory, with the aim of rethinking the politics of the democratic imagination from a different (and unlikely) historical standpoint.

In an essay included in his *Society Against the State* and titled "Of the One Without the Multiple"—the very same essay that caught Paul Auster's attention in *L'Ephémère* (1972)—Clastres sketches quickly and delicately the Indians' metaphysics of power (or non-power), which he posits explicitly against the political metaphysics of the Greeks (singling out Heraclitus by name, but also widely alluding to Plato). I won't elaborate here on why the very notion of political metaphysics in the world of the Greek polis is a nonsensical proposition, not just for the materialist Heraclitus but even for the idealist Plato. If there is anything remarkable about Greek politics—about the institution of the political—it is being alien to metaphysical concerns.[21] But what is of interest here is less Clastres's misapprehension of Greek philosophy and politics and more his conceptualization of so-called primitive society in terms that shatter any logical foundation of the singularity principle upon which modern civilization is based, where by "singularity" we mean not the radical principle of iterability, which cannot be multiplied (reiterated) and even in that sense mathematized, but the principle that reduces all mathematics to the One: the unitary, indeed even the universal.

Clastres quotes an old shaman saying whose origin the Guarani tribe has forgotten: "Things in their totality are one; and for us who did not desire it to be so, they are evil."[22] The fact that the origin of this saying cannot be established gives it a different authorization: it makes it mythical. Its purpose as myth is to address "the genealogy of misfortune," as Clastres calls it, the indisputably historical experience of living in an imperfect world, which is historical despite the fact that the question of meaning in such a state of imperfection appears as an existential ontological problem. This is what Marcel Gauchet, under the influence of Clastres, identified as an originary deficit, a debt of meaning, a debt in the creation of meaning.[23] "Why is the world like this and why do I live in it?" is a question that always emerges from historical experience, even though it is often answered in other terms. "The grandeur of the question is matched by the heroism of the reply: Men are not to blame if existence is unjust. We need not beat our breasts because we exist in a condition of imperfection" (SaS, 171). The myth here rises out of a guiltless relation to the universe and is constituted around a decision (*krisis*): we do not desire this state of imperfection or injustice and we consider its causes, the causes of our misfortune, evil. Conversely, our misfortune arises from what we don't desire—it is an external condition against our decision for life—and this is explicitly identified as the principle of the One. This perfect syllogism concludes with a stunning realization: the One is the principle of imperfection; Oneness is an imperfect condition.

The Indians' continuous revolt against the tyranny of the One precipitates the myth of the journey to the Land Without Evil, a mythical terrain that, in our terms, would represent the utopian desire for existence away from the constitutive power of the singular principle. Most Indian rituals, as Clastres describes them, are traceable to this aversion and the desire to obliterate oneness at all costs. That the chief holds the position of non-power par excellence is one such symptom. Clastres provides eloquent descriptions of how the chief is forced to give up all his possessions upon assuming office; how he is never listened to in any instrumental way, although he is required to speak as the poet of the tribe; how he is literally beaten to submission in order to qualify for the office of the chief. To speak precisely, the office of the chief is executed by a demonstration of limitless generosity: "Greed and power are incompatible; to be chief it is necessary to be generous" (SaS, 30). But this generosity is instituted as a requirement. It is hardly voluntary, but binding—essentially an occasion to remind the chief that his office bars any possession: "This obligation to give, to which the chief is bound, is experienced by the Indians as a kind of right to submit him to continuous looting" (SaS, 31). Of course, when he steps down from office, the chief has all his looted possessions rightfully returned to him as an explicit signal that he is now again like everyone else, one of the tribe. Similarly, the alimentary taboo—the prohibition against eating one's own hunt—is precisely calculated to eliminate singularity. Hunting for the others safeguards societal unity. One cannot hunt alone, for he will either break the taboo and die spiritually—which is an actual death in an animist society (analogous with being *apolis* in the Greek world)—or not break the taboo and die of starvation.

Clastres's analysis of the hunter's song as the only individual domain, a domain of utter self-referentiality in whose imaginary terrain the hunter is relieved of his duty to share, might be said to repeat the significance of the ritual beating and looting that enforce the chief's dispossession. Given that the only significant role of the chief—except for leading the tribe into battle—is the composition of memorial epic songs, the hunter and the chief occupy the front line of defense against the perils of the One: in their solitary song, they embody a pure non-instrumentality of language. "The chief's discourse recalls, by its solitude, the speech of a poet for whom words are values before they are signs" (SaS, 47).

But the chief's discourse, his solitary right to speak, is never autonomous: "If in societies with a State speech is power's *right*, in societies without a State speech is power's *duty*" (SaS, 153). And although "speech is an imperative obligation for the chief," although the chief *must* speak in order to be chief—must speak *as* chief—his speech is not spoken in order to be listened to. The event of the chief's obligatory speech is a non-event. It must fall on deaf ears, or, rather, on ears that pretend to be deaf. "The chief's discourse is empty because it is not a discourse of power" (SaS, 154), says Clastres, but it is more accurate to say that the chief's discourse is what enables him—at the level of poetic language—to escape being the chief. In this the circle is complete. The chief is chief precisely because he does not act like a chief. This nonsensical, non-instrumentalist position maintains the tribe's core necessity of existence: "The tribe maintains a disjunction between chiefdom and power, because it does not want the chief to become the holder of power; it refuses to allow the chief to be a chief. Primitive societies are societies that refuse obedience" (AV, 98).

One might well ask: Why then should there be a chief at all? What is the meaning of chiefdom in a society that refuses the command-obedience structure? Clastres answers directly:

> A society that would not have a *leader* [English in the original], the guy who speaks, would be incomplete, in the sense that the figure of potential power (that is, the very thing society wants to impede) must not be lost. Its place must remain defined. There must be someone about whom one can say "Here is the chief, and he is precisely the one we will prevent from being chief." If you cannot have someone to address in order to demand certain things, if there is not this figure there to occupy the space of possible power, then you cannot impede power from becoming real.[24]

Much can be said here of how Clastres's thinking reconfigures Lefort's famous notion of the empty space of power—not only in the sense that he recognizes it to exist in societies at the furthest possible remove from modernity, but also in that he understands that the space of power is always ontologically empty but never performatively empty. In fact, in order to assure that the space of power remains empty, it must always be performatively filled. And it must be filled, so that a society against the state would not lose sight of where the debilitating power of the state would come from. What matters is not that the chief is a continuous target, a kind of prisoner in his non-functional function (even though he is no doubt trapped in his space of empty eloquence), but that his function is precisely to embody the always imminent threat of emerging as a singular power figure. The real target is the state, that is, the condition of a external, autonomized, singular source of power, which the chief, *though a reminder of it,* is nonetheless deliberately and concretely prevented from achieving. The production of refusal, of disobedience, is thus not merely an anarchist gesture, but an outcome of defensive protection of the collective cohesion, a defensive affirmation of non-power against the threat of being conquered by power.

What we see throughout this analysis is an equivocal logic (A = B), which is meant precisely to subvert the production of singular meaning. It also enables the subject that claims such a language to outmaneuver the otherwise strict social order of primitive society. Consider how language works in the case of the hunter's song. Says Clastres: "the Guayaki hunters found in their song the innocent and profound ruse that enables them to reject in the domain of language the exchange they are unable to abolish in the domain of goods and women" (SaS, 122). This moment of utter and glorious solitude, this imaginary abolition of the rules of exchange, is the moment of Indian society's own necessity of art. The explicit impetus is "to escape the subjection of man to the general network of signs . . . by aggression against language in the form of a transgression of its function" (SaS, 125). Words are thus stripped of their communicative duty. They achieve pure self-referentiality, a transformation of social language into poetic language.

Poetry occupies here explicitly the domain of the metasocial, as a kind of *poiein* embodied in the social imaginary itself. I quote from Clastres again in what appears to be retrospectively a supplement to Gauchet's thesis about the originary deficit or debt in meaning: "The meta-social is not the infra-individual, the hunter's solitary song is not the discourse of a madman, and his words are not so many cries. Meaning persists, detached from any message, and it is its absolute permanence that supplies the ground on which speech can stand as value and nothing else" (SaS, 125). The hunter's song "gives voice to the universal dream of no longer being what one is" (SaS, 126). This is precisely the order of myth, as I have argued repeatedly—*not* a desire for transcendence (for no otherworldly telos exists), but a desire for transformation, where the desired form remains permanently unknown and unknowable. The order of myth breaks open the established externality of language we have come to take for granted in monotheistic societies. It produces an order of internal discourse that shields the community from the miraculous Word establishing an autonomous, self-reliant elsewhere.[25]

The same principle operates in the tribal ethos constituted around the torturous marking of the body of the young men, a ritual engraving whereby the tribe leaves its collective mark on the individual body. These ritual traces not only register the signs, the body language (literally) of the tribe, but also register forever the memory of nearly death-wielding pain that is itself the concrete signature of the engraving, the seal of language becoming *embodied*. The body becomes explicitly marked as the domain of tribal memory and thus turns into a permanent presence of the involuntary memory of tribal history. The tribe's secrets—its collective memory—do not form a narrative preserved and suspended in some realm of its own. Collective memory is an open secret, literally inscribed on everyone's flesh by the same exact means, *as the same exact text*—which is hardly to be understood as a text of words, but as a texture of signs, of scars, that tell everyone that each one is of no more and no less worth than any other. Tribal memory, preserved in the pain of the tribal secrets—essentially the pain of its historical existence—and traced indelibly on every individual body, becomes thus the explicit, always apparent and incessantly readable by all, collective text of the law. As Clastres concludes: "Archaic societies, societies of the mark, are societies against the State. The mark on the body, on all bodies alike, declares: *You will not have the desire for power; you will not have the desire for submission*" (SaS, 188).

Of course, the key here is, once again, that the desire for power *is* the desire for submission; the two are entirely consubstantial and interwoven. This is not paradoxical at all and follows a strict logic predicated on preventing the singular principle from remaining intact. The socially instituted imaginary determines that the moment any individual dares conceive himself to be more worthy than others he is automatically rendered less worthy than others. The real outcome is that he is either abandoned by the tribe or killed (AV, 100). To be more is to be less; to be dominant is to be dominated; to be the One is to be the Other (apart from everyone). This latter aspect is the most interesting and the most troubling: the point from which I can say that in this book I embark on an extension of Clastres, but also where my antithesis with Clastres begins.

The One Is the Other

Clastres makes a point of disrupting the traditional dichotomy between the One and the Multiple, by arguing that the Indians' aversion for singularity is predicated not on a desire for plurality or multiplicity but on their conception of the sacred duality of things. Once again, in contradistinction, he relegates the Greek polytheist principle to a particular outcome of the belief in a singular origin. This is in essence inaccurate. An elementary reading of the Anaximander fragment, the first philosophical articulation of Greek cosmology, is enough to show that the Greek ontological framework is dyadic: chaos and cosmos, *physis* and *nomos*, infinity and finitude, and so on. The Indians' quest for the not-One, the utopian Land Without Evil, is the last expression of their own double nature as they claim with grand audacity: their simultaneous humanity and divinity. Yet, a contradiction emerges from Clastres's insistence on the foundational indivisibility of Amazonian societies. Although he tries hard to argue that this indivisibility is due to sustaining symbolically the dual nature of the simultaneous human/divine essence, he nonetheless ascribes to it the external foundation of indigenous societies. Indivisibility is the foundational myth, society's law engraved on the body, which not only makes law constantly present but is meant to refute, tangibly, law's externality. The law is literally incorporated; it lives in the temporal domain of the body. The body is the terrain where mythic time and historical time are interwoven.

And yet, there is a silence regarding the actual moment when the body becomes open to inscription, open to receive the memory of history. There is something terrifying about this moment, which Clastres stops short of addressing. It isn't so much the cruelty of the act, as this is after all entirely underwritten by a social imaginary that institutes it as a moment of collective sublimation, and there is no way to justify a privileged external position, from another social imaginary altogether, that claims to know cruelty as cruelty. It is rather what Lefort has called very simply "the violent intrusion of the law into the body" as such.[26] The scene surely brings to mind Franz Kafka's Apparatus in

The Penal Colony, where the ultimate purpose in inscribing the body with the law is the production of Enlightenment. The Prisoner will come to know both the *meaning* of the sentence and the *meaning* of his crime by *reading* the actual *sentence*—in the case reviewed in the story this sentence is "Be Just!"—as it is being written on his actual body, in the actual temporality of writing. This reading will not take place by sight, because the sentence is written on the prisoner's back. It will take place in the mind as a result of the corporeal sensation produced by the brutal repetition of excruciating pain continuously retraced in a precise pattern that spells "Be Just!" The comprehension will come as the reading is completed, in a moment of revelation—enlightenment—that is also the moment of death: the moment when pain finally ceases after it has accomplished the goal. In this respect, knowledge and punishment coincide, or, equally, death and justice coincide, in what is one of Kafka's most ingenious indictments of the criminal—*paranomic*—metaphysics of Enlightenment law.[27]

Clastres does mention this text, but as a point of contrasting logics. Kafka's terrifying mythology is meant to show how, in societies of the State, the incorporation of the law is precisely the scar of power—the mark that memorializes the unbridgeable externality of power. Yet, Clastres's claim that, in primitive society, the writing on the body seals society's instituted indivisibility may carry us over into another register of what the meaning of sealing—I would also say "mystifying"—might actually be. The sealed structure of commandment that abolishes any order of command also erases its inaugural gap: the fact that in the actual moment of inscription, in this synchronic cut in historical time, the law as history and the law as ever-present memory reveal a certain doubleness, a certain gap. The erasure of this gap, in the name of defending indivisibility, might also erase the possibility of interrogation of the law, which would be the key in ultimately defending society against the law's external singularity, defending society against the state.[28]

Indeed, when answering the essential question "where does law come from?" Clastres does not seem to be at all alarmed by his avowal that the self-institution of Indian society was rendered external to it, drafted into the order of myth. Justifying this by saying simply that, for primitive tribes, law occurs in mythic time means nothing. It's true of all societies in human history, including those who claim to have vanquished myth by reason. What are, after all, the foundational constitutional moments of the Enlightenment, the Bill of Rights, the Declaration of the Rights of Man and the Citizen but modern society's moments of mythic time? The crucial question is, Who creates this mythic time?—creates in a *poietic* sense. I quote Clastres at length:

> Where is Law as legitimate foundation of society born? In a time prior to society, mythic time; its birthplace is at once immediate and infinitely faraway, the space of the Ancestors, of cultural heroes, of gods. It is there that society

> institutes itself as an undivided body; it is they who decree the Law as a system of norms, the Law that religion has a mission to transmit and to make sure is eternally respected. What does this mean? It means that society's foundation is exterior to itself, society is not the founder of itself: the foundation of primitive society does not stem from human decision, but from divine action. (AV, 123)

I am amazed by this statement. It is a classic instance of being entrapped in the "Western" metaphysics of power. It accepts for a fact society's voluntary disavowal of its self-institution: in other words, the self-occultation of autonomy that produces a heteronomous symbolic universe—the bane of all religions that claim an ontotheological theory of the origin of society. This misapprehension is traceable in the very language of the passage. Reading backward, we see that society's foundation is not exterior to itself, despite what the Indians believe, precisely because it is they who fashion this exteriority—the external origin—by fostering a religious ritual that chronicles a mythic time from whose inaugural moment (poetic *Ursprung*) they have severed themselves. Nothing unusual: the self-consciousness of society's self-institution has been rare in history and always short-lived. But even this rare, tentative, and ultimately self-defeated emergence of autonomy in history was achieved precisely because the notion of absolute singularity, the omnipotent external law, was put radically into question.[29]

Perhaps, we might mobilize in Clastres's defense Lefort's reading, which finds the alterity of the Indian religious myths and rituals to be ultimately unlocalizable, as if the heterotopia of alterity might prevent the institution of heteronomy. In other words, unlike in conditions of monotheistic modernity, this exterior foundation never comes to occupy the authority position of the Great Other, internalized intact in its unassailable exteriority as the guilty inner conscience. No doubt, the threat that the Indians perceive registers as an actuality, given the grave extent to which they go in order to anticipate it and block it. That they name this threat the Evil of the One also speaks of their refusal to define its place, to locate it even in mythic time. Far be it for them to even imagine what we know very well as an inherited principle: that the One achieves its totalizing power by being ubiquitous, by occupying every place and no place at once. The trajectory from society without a state to society coupled with the state might be mapped as the shift from the mythical Land Without Evil to the ideological condition of Evil Without Land. The modern experience teaches us that the One wields its most debilitating seductive powers when it is the least tangible or localizable, when it is fully signifiable as a mere Name. La Boétie himself opens his treatise by exclaiming his amazement that servitude is due not to some severe constraints but to being somehow "enchanted and charmed by the mere name of the One" (SV, 175/192).

In his reflection on La Boétie's use of the "name of the One," Claude Lefort might be said to complement his reflections on Clastres. He speaks specifically in terms of "the production of the One" in modern society by a kind of self-refutation of the active plurality out of which emerges the position of an all-presiding Other.[30] This is, in another language, the shift from the masses of people (the heterogeneous plurality of society) to the People, the self-authorizing singular entity that abrogates its instituting power in the name of the *sacred* authority of the Constitution or the Nation—to speak of the remarkably consistent scenario of the post-Enlightenment national imaginary—an authority that is rendered sacred precisely because it is assumed to bear the transcendental truth of the community, suspended in some universal netherland. I quote an illuminating passage from Lefort:

> The desire pursuing the illusion of the One and brought under the image of all is anchored in merely exhibiting itself as desire: such is servitude. We would gain if we present what is evoked by *voluntary servitude*, an otherwise self-defeating articulation, as self-love, as social narcissism. . . . With servitude, the charm of the name of the One has destroyed the articulation of a political language. The people have willfully named themselves, but the name that abolishes the enigma of social division, the difference between each and every one, the process of indefinitely motivating mutual recognition, is the name of the tyrant. His loved name becomes the one on which everyone remains suspended under penalty of otherwise being nothing. This detached name, as if it has emerged from nowhere, as if it has resumed its own beginning, becomes the name of the Other, the name of the only one who has the power to speak at a distance to all others who cannot but listen.[31]

Oneness, or singular *archē*, entails, in other words, the most precise articulation of the identity principle: in modern politics, the purpose and animus of a social collective that recognizes itself in terms of unitary exclusivity. The terms of this exclusivity, though historically multiple, belong to a unitary order of substitution: the tribal ethnos, the people, the state, the nation—and as such, specifically, national language, national religion, national identity. All these are monological/monovalent entities, regardless of what social heterogeneity, what cultural and lingual plurality, they may represent on historical grounds.

Indivisibility Is Not Unity

The production of the One in its total singularity is the production of the Other in its absolute pervasiveness. This is something that eludes Clastres, even when, for example, he speaks of the One as anathema to Amazonian society's indivisibility. The relation between oneness and nondivision in Clastres's text indeed remains an aporia. Common sense suggests that there is no discernible distance in meaning between the two. Yet, what links them is a wayward path. Ultimately, it is a path that leads nowhere because the relation between these two terms poses an intractable question. On a certain level, one may speak of a contradiction in Clastres's thinking, or an unconscious inconsistency, perhaps even a little prejudice—literally, in the sense of prejudgment. His thesis is that societies who refuse the One, who consider oneness to be absolute Evil, are societies committed to nondivision. In fact, they refuse the One precisely in order to defend and to preserve their indivisibility. Clastres does not give us any explicit signs of pondering this question: In what sense does indivisibility foster an institution of oneness, perhaps not the domination of external singular *archē*, but oneness nonetheless?

We are entering here the mysterious domain of Clastres's (and La Boétie's) peculiar arithmetic. In his last work, "Archeology of Violence: War in Primitive Society," Clastres dares a definition: "What is primitive society? A multiplicity of indivisible communities all of which obey the same centrifugal logic" (AV, 166). The institution that expresses and ensures this logic, Clastres would eventually come to argue, is war. He interpreted the tendency of indigenous Amazon societies to wage continuous war between themselves as a deep-structural means of making the fragmentation of intertribal life permanent. He did not see war as the result of the failure of the law of exchange, caused by the antagonism emerging from scarcity (which is the Lévi-Straussian position), but quite the opposite: as an element of *co-incidence* with the law of exchange that safeguards, in different planes, the autonomy of each tribe. For Clastres, war in primitive society was the key element in an immanent centrifugal logic that, in effect, blocked the converse: the centripetal logic that aspires to unite and homogenize, the drive that derives itself from and leads everything to the domination of the One.[32] Characteristically, he goes on to say: "The war machine is the motor of the social machine; the primitive social being relies entirely on war, primitive society cannot survive without war. The more war there is, the less unification there is, and the best enemy of the State is war. Primitive society is society against the State in that it is society-for-war" (AV, 166).

The memorable phrase "the best enemy of the State is war" would confound any theorist of sovereignty who takes Carl Schmitt's thinking as a reference point, even those who would combat it. It's difficult to argue, historically speaking, that war isn't anything but the quintessential register of the sovereign state, that without war the significance of sovereignty would weaken to the point of irrelevance. What Clastres is positing here is war as an endemic social condition, which, first of all, works to control the demographic problem and, in addition, secures a kind of primal autonomy—where primal, as resonant of primitive, describes an elemental materiality, a kind of societal nature (not at all in the sense that Hobbes would imagine). Earlier Clastres claims: "Refusal of unification, refusal of the separate One, society against the state. Each primitive community wants to remain under the sign of its own Law (autonomy, political independence) which excludes social change (society will remain what it is: an undivided being). The refusal of the State is the refusal of exonomy, of exterior Law; it is quite simply the refusal of submission, inscribed as such in the very structure of primitive society" (AV, 166).

As a parenthesis, which cannot really be elaborated without losing focus, it is important to register the resonance of this position with several concerns concurrent at the time, which precipitated much greater influence in contemporary thought than those of Clastres. First, the phrase "war-machine" recalls Deleuze and Guattari, and we know that Clastres's *Society Against the State* draws from *Anti-Oedipus* and informs explicitly *A Thousand Plateaus* in turn. Moreover, Foucault's famous 1975–1976 lectures make several unacknowledged gestures to Clastres's thinking in the process of developing an argument about the significance of war to modern sovereignty.[33] I note all this in addition to the direct dialogues between Clastres and the team of Castoriadis, Lefort, and Gauchet, which we have already established.

Foucault's lectures are especially important here. What Clastres bars from his concern—the problem of how societies against the state produce (or disintegrate into) societies with the state—is Foucault's explicit concern in his analysis of the vicissitudes of power where war resides at the crux. We know well Foucault's reversal of Clausewitz's famous thesis: namely, politics is the continuation of war by other means. Foucault reiterates Clastres when he separates the significance of war in what he calls characteristically "societies before the state" from the historical dimensions he is researching,[34] but he nonetheless seems to counter Clastres by suggesting that (1) the emergence of the state does not end this condition of war, even if it is presumably destined to do so, but rather pushes it back into prehistory, and (2) it is indeed this condition of war that gives birth to the state and leaves indelible marks (Foucault says "stigmata") upon its body. For Foucault, the lesson of Pierre Clastres, on this specific issue at least, is to elucidate the fact that, beneath the established fantasy that proclaims the state to be the conqueror of war and the safeguard against it, the phantom of war is never exorcised. War remains forever in the backdrop as the very foundation of societies that have enabled the emergence of the state.

From this complex—and without needing to leave Clastres's text and seek aid in Foucault—several questions arise within Clastres's own terms that he doesn't quite address: Would war foster a society of warriors above all else, above even the fundamental significance of the hunter, which would thus threaten indivisibility? Under what conditions does social division appear in an indivisible society? And in what sense is war precisely the modal threshold that traditionally preserves indivisibility and historically nonetheless fosters division? Clastres recoils before this question. Could it be that prolonged conditions of war may produce war itself as a singular fantasy? The claim is that the continuous upheaval of war as a constant repetition secures ungrowth, unchangeability: a strange proposition, not only logically but politically. I take it as a rhetorical gesture, for no society is possible as an unchangeable entity; in the case Clastres describes one can say at best that change takes place inordinately slowly, almost imperceptibly. Extending this and as a consequence of the last Clastres quotation given, we can only wonder: What sort of autonomy is there for a society that refuses to change, a society whose essential purpose, its elemental survival, is to pursue an instituted reverence for unchangeability?—where by using the word *instituted* we come very close to something that has become exonomous, something intrinsic that has become other, a mark of heteronomy. Can there ever be autonomy without alteration—indeed, as I have argued repeatedly, without self-alteration?

By way of La Boétie, Clastres settles this matter as an unfortunate accident that alters social history. For him, simply, indivisibility in indigenous Amazon society is comprehensible because it is a society of mere hunters and warriors. Indivisibility against the terrifying threat of the unitary One is, in this respect, analogous to La Boétie's privileging of friendship as the one untamable intrinsic element that antagonizes tyranny. For La Boétie, humanity is naturally endowed with the gift of friendship, just as it is with liberty; indeed, the two terms presuppose each other's condition. As usual, his phrasing is wonderfully complicated: "If [nature] has shown in all things that she did not want to make us all united so much as making us all one(s)—[*qu'elle ne vouloit pas tant nous faire tout unis, que tous uns*]—we cannot doubt that we are all naturally free, since we are all companions [in certain manuscripts we find the term *equal—égaux*]; and it cannot enter anyone's mind that nature has placed anyone in servitude, having put us all in companionship" (SV, 185/198). One marvels at the interplay between *unis* and *uns*, whereby Clastres's problem of indivisibility against oneness emerges retrospectively in La Boétie, but in reverse: oneness is superceded via fraternal association, which breaks down any unifying tendencies while keeping individual autonomy ("the indivisibility of the free mind") intact.[35] The ultimate claim is that friendship is not merely antagonistic to tyranny; it is precisely what tyranny cannot achieve: "Friendship never occurs except between honorable people, and it arises from mutual esteem. It maintains itself not so much by means of good deeds as by a good life. What renders a friend assured of the other is the knowledge of his integrity. . . . There cannot be friendship where there is cruelty, disloyalty, or injustice. In the assembly of the wicked, there is complicity, not society. They do not provide for one another but fear one another. They are not friends but accomplices" (SV, 221/220).[36]

Evoking the difficult terrain of the politics of friendship at this point, without elaborating on it specifically, might seem adventurous, if not cavalier. But it's the key to resolving the peculiar arithmetic. Nicole Loraux, by way of thinking Greek—as one of the greatest historians of the ancient Greek polis (and Athens in particular)—raises the stakes and provides a trenchant challenge to Clastres's argument precisely in these terms. To read Loraux's essay, which she wrote in homage to Clastres (and with great admiration), means embarrassingly to confront the obvious. La Boétie's and Clastres's theories of how companionship resists the tyranny of singular authority invoke entirely androcentric views of society.[37] They compose an image of society that necessarily excludes women in exactly the same way that it refuses the state, Loraux argues. Although to turn this into an Aristotelian syllogism would be absurd—women are *not* the state (whether as the entity feared by the Indians or the entity realized in modernity)—women nonetheless occupy the same syntactical position in the grammatical equation that pits society *against*. Loraux calls Clastres into question precisely for not meditating more rigorously on the political-epistemological parameters of the word *contre*.

This is not a matter of simple feminist calculation. The implication is that, from a standpoint other than that of the hunter, the warrior, the chief, or the one whose body is tattooed with the tribe's historical memory, Indian society is already divided. It is a society—like all societies in history—keeping an other(ness) in its midst. But this otherness, being structurally internal, resists the equivocation of the logic that is the Indians' greatest fear: the logic of power and submission, of A equaling B. As Loraux says, in terms of internal logic "A and B are two ways of being one."[38] They are two numbers that do not add up to one, yet also do not signify division. Division in all archaic societies (including, of course, the Greeks), Loraux argues, is signified by the social position of women—in the Greek case literally the presence that breaks up the identity between *andres* and *anthropoi* from Hesiod onward. Throughout her work and in truly radical ways, Loraux raises the issue of sexual difference as a disruptive calculus, which she in fact counts to be the underlying force that makes tragedy both the expression and the interrogation of Athenian democracy. Tragedy challenges both monological/monovalent attitudes and the very process of identity formation with an elaborate process of self-interrogation, of staging oneself as an other (in ways whereby, on numerous occasions, sexual difference is staged as the primary problem), in order to achieve (or, more precisely, to reinstitute) society's autonomy.

In Indian thought, Loraux counters, "there is somewhat of a gap between the metaphysical hostility against the One and thinking on matters of sexuality, which is riveted on the verification of the principle of identity" (169). There is, in other words, a principle of *contr'un* that works on the basis of a whole other arithmetic, which is in fact silenced by the arithmetic that Clastres proposes. "How do the Indians count?" asks Loraux, mocking Clastres's own rather famous question "How do Indians laugh?" "What sorts of operations do they accomplish," she asks further, "in order to efface the One within the two, the two within the multiple, but also the two within the One, in order to keep alive the principle of identity while dreaming of a world where identity would no longer have a place of existence?" (169). Clastres does not raise the question of whether there may be multiple meanings of the One—of whether oneness, nondivision, and unity may occupy different places, or even occasionally share a place in coexistence but even then, just as well, in contradiction, whether the place of the One is just as important, or even more important, than the nature of the One. Once this set of questions is posed, there might be multiple meanings of *contr'un*: say, on the one hand, the possibility of a contested articulation between a movement against the division of the sexes that affirms a partial oneness, the point where the indivisibility becomes an ideologeme (even in a preideological sphere), or, on the other hand, a movement against oneness that is registered by the social presence of sexual difference.

These are hastily raised questions that certainly provide no resolution. Yet, despite many of his misapprehensions, Clastres's formulation that the society of nonpower, the society against the state, owes its existence to its aversion to oneness is essential to an interrogative relation to the origin of the law, which is fundamental to the democratic imaginary. To rehearse again the succinct division, I quote Clastres's explicit distinction from his interview with *L'Anti-Mythes*, the very last text bearing his signature: "Primitive societies are on the side of the small, the limited, the restricted, of permanent division [*scission*], of the multiple, while societies of the State are the exact contrary: on the side of growth [*croissance*], of integration, of unification, of the One. Primitive societies are societies of the multiple; non-primitive societies of the State are societies of the One. The State is the triumph of the One."[39]

As the state occupies an externalized position, other to society, the power of the One resides precisely in deploying the discourse of the Other, to follow the pattern of shifting terms to their opposites that Clastres's dialectical analysis of indigenous Amazon societies so brilliantly accomplishes. According to my own concerns, which I have identified all along as the task of secular criticism, the discourse of the Other is nowadays often occluded in ways that reproduce precisely the disempowering heteronomous structures that produce otherness as a marginalized and disenfranchised condition. This was my impetus in the essay "On the Catachresis of Otherness," which concludes *Dream Nation*, written some thirty years ago in a California campus in the midst of the Culture Wars. The problem continues to persist, and is perhaps even exaggerated by the surge of outright religious notions of political power throughout the globe that stake the virtue of their Otherness in their unabashed adoration of the authority of the One.

In these terms, it does become urgent to understand that the discourse of the Other camouflages the power of the One precisely when it is configured as a principle that monopolizes authority *outside* the boundaries of the social-historical. There, the One is the element most radically external to the immanent plurality and heterogenerity of society but, paradoxically, it fosters the symbolic safety net of social cohesion, social unity, by way of a heteronomous command. This is why the attempt to challenge the institutions of the One produces a mirroring paradox. Configured as failed socialization—as abrogated sublimation—it leads to enforced solitude or even expulsion, exteriorization, and finally extinction. To use the terminology of the indigenous Amazonians, the One is evil because it entails an absolute monopoly of power, the absolute heteronomy of external Otherness, an otherness that abolishes the self because it is unreachable and thus irreversibly, *undialectically* dominant. To undo the equivocal logic of domination—"the desire for power is the desire for submission"—the sovereignty of monological, indeed monomythical, Otherness (of the One) must be dismantled. Only an internal otherness, whose source would be an immanent desire (constitutive of the human animal) to alter its world, would liberate society's radical transformative potential. A society against the state is a society against external otherness. To the degree that this position, in modern terms, entails a transformative, not transcendentalist, politics, it animates a capacity for self-alteration that is wholly internal, embodied in the sort of social imagination that privileges the othering of itself.

CHAPTER 3

ON SELF-ALTERATION

To think is not to get out of the cave; it is not to replace the uncertainty of shadows by the clear-cut outlines of things themselves, the flame's flickering glow by the light of the true sun. To think is to enter the Labyrinth; more exactly, it is to create an appearance and a being of a Labyrinth when we might have stayed "lying among the flowers, facing the sky." It is to lose oneself amidst galleries which exist only because we never tire of digging them; to turn round and round at the end of a cul-de-sac whose entrance has been shut off behind us—until, inexplicably, this spinning round opens up in the surrounding walls cracks which offer passage.

—Cornelius Castoriadis, *Crossroads in the Labyrinth* (1978)

I am militating politically for the impossible, which doesn't mean I am a utopian. Rather what I want does not yet exist, as the only possibility of a future.

—Luce Irigaray, *J'aime à toi* (1992)

The terrain suggested by a *co-incident* reading of the two quotations above configures the path of this essay's primary orientation. Examining these two writers together is dictated by this path, not by some sort of preconfigured or presently contrived affinity.

Castoriadis's rumination disengages thinking from all Platonic derivatives that map the journey to Enlightenment, which would pertain to a whole range of transcendentalist aspirations, revelations, epiphanies, but also intensions of perfectibility, including any pretensions to arrive at a clearing (*Lichtung*). He sees thinking as a peculiar mode of architecture in which the instrumental is always secondary to the creative. That this architecture is labyrinthine means that it is ultimately without end, despite its many, its ubiquitous dead ends. It is without end because, on its own terms, it is interminable and boundless, because the limits that emerge on every turn are of the thinker's own making. Castoriadis's mode is to leave behind the elegy-inducing Rilke "among the flowers" for the enigma-provoking Kafka, recognizing in the latter's vein that the labyrinthine galleries of one's burrow are one's thoughts in-the-making, with yet an important deviation: not as ideal projections of self-making (as for Kafka's paranoid architectural creature) but as wondrous openings of self-othering. In this respect, thought becomes quintessentially *poietic*, that is to say, creative/destructive: a (self-)altering force that sometimes produces cul-de-sacs and other times opens windows onto chaos. Indeed, Castoriadis's description of how a dead-end becomes a window onto chaos is one of the most dramatic encapsulations of his entire way of thinking. To think is thus to enact an alterity both toward yourself and toward the world. It is not to derive or emerge from an alterity, and surely not to desire alterity as telos—the labyrinth, a space resplendent with otherness, is always one's own.

In turn, Irigaray's personal account clarifies how the utopian and the impossible are hardly identical. This is not because the utopian may also be in fact possible, but because desiring the impossible is an entirely real and actual way to commit oneself to what is possible in the future. Her emphasis on "what does not yet exist" does not entail investment in a predetermined or providential element that will come to be in the future—some sort of future nascent in the present. Rather, "what does not yet exist" is configured as a permanent condition of alterity within present existence, a kind of unknown variable in the equation of what may come to be possible in the future, an equation that obviously carries no mathematical consistency but remains permeable to the ever-unpredictable contingencies of human action. This condition, therefore, knows no time—as X factor, it is *achronos*—but nonetheless lies in place across the entire range of history's temporalities, perhaps as an already inscribed heterotopia. It is a condition open to the indefinite possibility of something whose "nonexistence" as "the only possibility of a future" is a presently existing condition, insofar as without this X the equation (present or future) cannot be constituted.

The coveted object in both quotations, therefore, is some measure of the impossible, of what indeed appears impossible because the horizon of possibility in the perception is rendered inadequate by the reigning preconception. The impetus here is to imagine that human beings are characterized precisely by their daring to make the impossible happen, which has nothing to do with making miracles but it does have to do with encountering and acting in the world with a sense of wonder. Inquiring what animates and encapsulates this daring for the impossible will lead us to the fact that *human-being*, as a living condition, is immanently differential, which is to say that alterity is intrinsic to it.

The way of this inquiry is to contemplate an arguably impossible concept: *self-alteration*. Strictly speaking, self-alteration signifies a process by which alterity is internally produced, dissolving the very thing that enables it, the very thing whose existence derives meaning from being altered, *from othering itself.* In terms of inherited thought, this is indeed an impossible concept—at least, within the conceptual framework that identifies alterity to be external, a framework, I might add, that is essential to any semantics (and, of course, politics) of identity. Such a framework cannot but vehemently defend, by contradistinction, the bona fide existence of what can thus be called without hesitation "internality," even if, in a gesture of cognitive magnanimity, it may accept a fragmented, fissured, indeterminate, or even boundless internality. But internality thus conceived, however "open-ended" it claims to be, cannot enact self-alteration because alterity will always remain external to it, precisely so as to secure its meaning.

Having said that, let us also concede that this framework of an internally/externally conceived distinction of identity and difference gives meaning to the language I am using at this very moment. It is, inevitably, the framework that enables us to build communicative avenues by positing totalities and identities that we consider recognizable even if we might significantly disagree over their content. I understand that, in this framework, self-alteration is an impossible concept, but I have a hunch that it is nonetheless possible, that it *takes place* in the only way anything can take place in the world—*in* history, *as* history. At the limit, the conceptual inquiry I am suggesting, labyrinthine though it is in its own turn, configures its groundwork in the world of human action, not in the universe of concepts and propositions.

Creation/Destruction

Self-alteration is a central concept in Castoriadis's thought, and we could say that he understands it as essential to all living being, perhaps as even tantamount to *physis* itself. In this first order, the concept owes a lot to Aristotle's notion of movement as change—in Greek *alloiosis*. But though Aristotle may be Castoriadis's favorite philosopher, Castoriadis is by no means an Aristotelian; for him there is no *physis* without *nomos*. This comes into play particularly when we discuss the world of the human being—the most peculiar of all living beings. In this register, one other word for alteration in Greek, which we indeed find in Castoriadis's Greek texts, is more provoking: *heterōsis*. It is this meaning that I use as an anchor, in order to examine self-alteration, in the world of the human being, both as a psycho-ontological and as a social-historical dimension.

A basic kind of starting point would be to consider self-alteration in the context of Castoriadis's persistent view of the living being as self-creative and of the human being, specifically, as a social-historical being that exists via its interminable and indeed unlimited capacity for the creation/destruction of form in the world. Hence, self-alteration is articulated in direct connection with self-creation as an ontological standpoint that Castoriadis understands as *vis formandi*, a kind of morphopoietic force or life-power that reconfigures the world by creating radically new forms or indeed, more precisely, radically other forms. It is important to understand the *co-incidence* of this notion of self-creative being with a destructive, catastrophic element. Castoriadis is not consistent on this matter, but one often sees in his writings the formulation *creation/destruction*. Certainly, in his analysis of tragedy (*Antigone* especially) and in much of his discussion of pre-Socratic cosmology, where the emphasis is on an ever-present dyadic cosmological imaginary (*apeiron/peras, chaos/kosmos, physis/nomos*), no notion of creation can be configured without a simultaneously enacted destruction.[1] The crucial element here is the simultaneity of two distinct forces. We're certainly not speaking of some monstrous concept, like the neoliberal notion of "creative destruction" or some such thing. Nor are we speaking of any sort of simple dialectical relation, despite the inherent antagonism of such originary dyadic frameworks; in Castoriadis at least, the matter of dialectics as preferable epistemological mode is ambiguous.

This simultaneous or *co-incident* double figure elucidates one of the most controversial of Castoriadis's philosophical tropes, the notion of creation ex nihilo. Given the texts, we don't really need to wonder why Castoriadis insists on this figure. His entire anthropo-ontological framework is based on the idea that what distinguishes the human animal specifically is the capacity to create form (*eidos*) that is entirely unprecedented, previously inconceivable, and indeed nonexistent in any sense prior to the moment and fact of its creation. He insists time and again that creation does not entail the production of difference but the emergence of otherness. This capacity for the wholly new, wholly other is what distinguishes the radical imagination. The ex nihilo is there to accentuate the fact that we are not talking about reformulation, or infinite variation, or creative assembly or rearrangement of already existing forms. His example that the invention of the wheel is a more radical and splendorous creation in the universe than a new galaxy is well known, for every new galaxy emerging in space is ultimately but another instance of the galaxy form, whereas the wheel is entirely unprecedented.[2] The often used idiomatic injunction in English encapsulates what Castoriadis has in mind: "you're reinventing the wheel!" means you're not being creative, you're not using your imagination, you are wasting your effort in reproducing what exists (however we are to consider the merits or inevitabilities of this kind of effort).

But especially in late years and in order to defend himself from likely misunderstandings, Castoriadis insisted on the clarification that *ex nihilo* did not mean *in nihilo* or *cum nihilo*. Unprecedented radical creation *out of nothing* does not mean with(in) nothing, *in a vacuum*. On the contrary, what makes it radical is precisely that it takes place in history, *as* history—that indeed it makes history anew. There is no way such creation can register as history anew without destroying, in some form or other, what exists in place, whether we conceive this simply as what resists the new or merely what resides there unwitting of whatever will newly emerge to displace it or efface it. New social-imaginary creations do contribute to the vanishing of social-imaginary institutions already there. That's why we don't have Pharaonic priests, Spartan warriors, or Knights of the Round Table running around in the streets of New York or the suburbs of Paris.

In retrospect, it is possible to construct a description—to write a history—of how and what elements and processes characterize the creation of new social-historical being. A common example in Castoriadis, discussed at various junctures in his work and arguably culminating in the years that made up the seminars of *Ce qui fait la Grèce* (1982–85), is how the specifics of the Cleisthenes reforms that encapsulate the creation of Athenian democracy as new social-historical being are 'traceable'—if that's the proper word—in the complexities of the social-imaginary institution of the Greek polis, which duly points all the way back to the earliest Greek textual documentation: Homer, Hesiod, Anaximander, Sappho. In other words, Castoriadis's theory of creation ex nihilo is not entirely unrelated to various theories of discontinuity in history. I cannot pursue here this line of comparison, but it's a worthwhile path of reflection to consider the line, otherwise alien to Castoriadis, that extends (in the French tradition at least) from Bachelard to Foucault. If we don't adhere dogmatically to the notion of the "epistemological rupture" characteristic of this line—in the same way that we would not heed the accusations against Castoriadis that creation ex nihilo ushers some sort of theology in the back door—then we might arrive at a more nuanced understanding of the notion.[3]

But there is also another dimension to this issue that I don't think has been adequately attended to. In his classic essay "Fait et à faire" (1989), Castoriadis speaks of what grants validity to creation: its encounter with the world. I quote extensively:

> Newton certainly did not "discover," he invented and created the theory of gravitation; but it happens (and this is the why we are still talking about it) that this creation *encounters* [*rencontre*] in a fruitful way *what is*, in one of its strata.
>
> We create knowledge. In certain cases (mathematics) we also create, thereby, the *outside of time*. In other cases, (mathematical physics) we create under the constraint of encounter; it is this encounter that validates or invalidates our creations.

And later on: "To the extent that we can effectively comprehend something about a foreign society, or say something valid about it, we proceed to a re-creation of significations, which encounter the originary creation. . . . A being without the re-creative capacity of the imagination will understand nothing about it."[4] Let us focus for a moment on two elements: "the constraint of encounter" and "the re-creative capacity of the imagination." The first is precisely to emphasize that *ex nihilo* does not mean *in nihilo* or *cum nihilo*. Not only is radical creation out of nothing always enacted in the world, but it is enacted as and constrained by an encounter. The "nothing" out of which radical creation emerges exists, in the most precise sense, *in* the world; it is not, in other words, some sort of transcendental nowhere. And though we should not at all compromise the notion—we indeed mean out of nothing; we mean, in the ancient Greek sense, to note the passage "out of nonbeing into being"—we have to allow ourselves the paradoxical capacity to imagine both that this nothing, this nonbeing, is worldly and that, instantly upon coming to be something, this newly created being registers its worldliness by an unavoidable encounter with what exists, whether in the dimension of logic and calculation (what Castoriadis calls, by means of a neologism, *ensidic*—ensemblist-identitary) or beyond it, in the *poietic* dimension as such.

Second, it is not enough to stick to a kind of straight surging forth of the new, of the other. We need also to put our imagination to work on re-creating the entire domain of the surging forth, the full dimensions of emergence of the new. This too can be understood in different ways. One recognizable instance of imaginative re-creation is the hermeneutical act itself, as Suzi Adams has pointed out astutely.[5] This is at play not only in philosophical work but surely in historical work. The best historians are the ones who can re-creatively imagine the horizon of emergence of the historical shift they are investigating. But in both cases (philosophical and historical), as I've argued in *Does Literature Think?*, one engages in the work of *poiein*—of imagining form in the case of radical creation, of shaping matter into form (which is to say, of signifying form) in the case of imaginative re-creation. The *poietic* dimension in society's imaginary institution pertains indeed to society's creative/destructive capacity and is essential to the radical interrogation of (self-)instituted laws/forms that enables in turn the radical creation of new forms—in other words, both to the question of autonomy and the question of self-alteration.

Sublimation

This epistemological level of situating self-alteration—but also ontological, to the degree that it conceptualizes a *physis*—should serve as a certain groundwork, shifting though it is, which needs to be elucidated, however, by a psychic dimension, in order to lead us to the social-historical concerns that pertain to the *physis* of human-being as such. For Castoriadis, this is the crossroads between his psychoanalytic and his philosophical writings, where self-alteration becomes a key notion entwining the elaboration of a politics of sublimation, on the one hand, and the project of social autonomy, on the other.[6]

As an impossibly quick clarification, let me recount that, for Castoriadis, sublimation is not the transmutation of libidinal drive to the nonsexualized activity of the imagination, as is traditionally conceived in the wider sense of the so-called repression-hypothesis—in two ways: First, if nothing else, on account of the unquestionable human capacity for and proclivity toward non-functional sexuality that foregrounds sexuality first and foremost as a matter of the pleasure of fantasy (that is, the privilege of phantasmatic representation over simple organ pleasure). Because the pleasure of fantasy informs every aspect of human existence, it becomes difficult to determine in what sense sublimatory investment might ever involve desexualized pleasure. In other words, even in the process of sublimation the primacy of phantasmatic (or representational) pleasure still occurs on the somatic or sensuous register. Sublimation is not meant to be understood as some sort of abstract spiritualization. Even ascetics experience pleasure in their asceticism, and the *jouissance* of mysticism is all too evident in a variety of expressions through the ages. What matters is the autonomization of desire, which goes hand in hand with the defunctionalization of desire—the *co-incidence* is precisely what makes the human imagination independent of instinct or drive and, in this respect, "functional" in an altogether different sense of the term.

Second: Because sublimation is the necessary mode of socialization—or precisely, as Castoriadis says, of humanization—that is, the mode by which the indomitable psyche cathects its primal desire for omnipotence onto the pleasure of social community, at the expense, of course, of this omnipotence but at the gain of the "security" of ego-constitution through the provision of meaning (with all the traumatic elements this entails). Because, however, socialization/humanization is a social-historical process and sublimatory objects are always part of the imaginary institution of society (even when they are objects of radical interrogation of society, or indeed even when they are objects of society's destruction, suicidal or genocidal), sublimation is not some sort of natural process, with consistent and immanent elements, but always involves a politics. It is precisely the politics of sublimation that makes an inquiry of this properly psychoanalytic domain be at the same time an interrogation of the political ontology of subjugation and heteronomy against which the concept of self-alteration emerges as an emancipatory force.

The problem of heteronomy in sublimation is insurmountable within a purely Freudian register. It involves a basic contradiction in the epistemology of psychoanalysis, which Freud never quite theorized, perhaps because he never resolved for himself the conceptual struggle inherent in the psychoanalytic project between the phylogenetic and the social-historical nature of the human. I am referring to Freud's inability to reconcile the fact that, on the one hand, civilization must be condemned for repressing human drives in the service of domination and exploitation, while, on the other hand, this same repression of drives (according to the notion of the "renunciation of instinct") must be accepted as a prerequisite for humanity's actualization of its higher potential, a prerequisite of civilization's very existence. This, in Freud, necessarily links sublimation with repression and, given his admitted lack of theoretical elaboration on the work of sublimation, becomes responsible for the dismissive (or at best, narrowly conceived) treatment of sublimation at the hands of many psychoanalytic and cultural theorists. Sublimation has thus been tainted with the mark of a perverse condition, as a sort of necessary evil inevitable for mental health. The implication can only be that the human animal is irrevocably perverse or pathological by nature. We can say a lot of things about the human animal's biological incapacity, but it's terribly problematic to consider this pathological; the very assumption of "incapacity" renders impossible the very concept of the normal and thereby its critical dismantling.

There is indeed another implication, which I cannot address here, but deserves to be mentioned: the fact that a radical indecision arises at the core of psychoanalytic theory and practice, a split between the emancipatory project of liberating repressed libidinal potential and a kind of ingrained conservatism in recognizing repression as the necessary cost for the progress of civilization. Ego-psychology, as we know, bypasses the dilemma by making a conscious decision in favor of the second solution and subscribing directly to what we could call the domestication of the unconscious, whereby liberation of repressed desire is to be managed by an all-powerful healthy ego that will, for all practical purposes, replace the injunctions of the superego with its own. To what extend this entails a double repression in turn, a repression not only of unconscious potential but also of superego activity—thereby occluding the workings of authority for the subject—should be evident. I hardly mean to disavow the standard thesis that recognizes the superego as the psychic locus of heteronomy.

But at this point I am not concerned with sublimation as a protoformative process but as a practico-poietic process, and here the ego (secondarily, but for me essentially) becomes key. The ego is the locus of society's *conscious* agency, and a heteronomous ego becomes the agent of heteronomous sublimation on a grand social-cultural scale. This is precisely a matter of the *politics* of sublimation and cannot be exorcised by some sort of "pure" psychoanalysis.

An evocative way to consider this problem is the radical significance of Castoriadis's reversal of Freud's classic motto of *Wo Es war, soll Ich werden* (Where It was, I shall be) to *Wo Ich bin, soll Es auftauchen* (Where I am, It shall spring forth). What Castoriadis argues instead is that the creative/destructive capacity of the unconscious will emerge in the ego's location in such a way as to disrupt the ego's reliance on gaining signification solely from the social-imaginary institution present in the superego. This disruption hardly means the end of sublimation. Such an end is essentially impossible; were it to occur, it would signify the evolutionary regression of the human animal. But it does mean, potentially, the alteration of the standard ways of sublimation, as we know them in history. In a concrete sense, it also means an altered relation to history as such, as ceaseless flow of human thought and praxis.

Let us return to Castoriadis's insistence that sublimation is tantamount to humanization. The point is that sublimation means not merely the hand of civilization upon the human individual (the classic repression hypothesis), but the process by which one achieves the condition of human-being out of a primal psychic organism that may fulfill the terms of living being but does not constitute the sufficient terms of being human. This primal organism, the monadic core of the psyche, as Castoriadis calls it, cannot possibly survive on its own merely driven by its insatiable desire for atomic omnipotence at all costs. To live up to the terms of this drive would mean literally to die of starvation. For the sake of its existence, therefore, the psyche requires connection to the world of other living beings, which must be effected immediately upon birth as its first "subjective act"—keeping in mind that the notions of "act" and "subject" (not to mention "human") have no meaning prior to their being existentially enacted. In this respect, sublimation does not put into place the agency of civilization and it surely involves something more than the creation of civilization: it is an element intrinsic to the process of human existence that makes human existence possible, an *autopoietic* element. Of course, from the standpoint of the monadic core of the psyche, sublimation will always appear as—and *is* in fact—heteronomous rule because it opens the gates for otherness to enter. From this standpoint, sublimation does entail violent disruption of the plenitude—the closure—of protopsychic existence and its relentless refusal of reality. At this level, heteronomous sublimation is not a problem; it is a fact. But the level of the monadic core of the psyche is hardly a sustainable standpoint from which to understand (even to view) the complications of human existence. The problem arises precisely at the moment this elemental but *partial* fact is taken for the whole.

What do I mean? Castoriadis's insistence on the defunctionalized nature of the human psyche, even at the level of the monadic core—a point, by the way, entirely commensurate with Freud—enables us to understand that, although it is indeed the work of social-imaginary institution, sublimation is not enacted as external imposition (nor should we be tricked to think that it is a brute internalization of superego-type injunctions). What enables it to happen is the psyche's own ability to operate and respond at the level of representation, of imagistic flux (*Vorstellung*). The psyche's imaginary capacity exists already at the level of drives; it is not a meta-attribute, some sort of *cultured* capacity. It is already present at the moment sublimation is enacted. We might even say, it enables sublimation precisely because it provides a language that can translate society's forms into psychic terms. In this respect, though the monadic core of the psyche experiences a violation and cannot but resist, it also experiences—against itself but from within itself—an elemental pleasure, which is what ultimately allows sublimation to work. Otherwise, given the insatiable autoscopic nature of the psyche, no sublimation would have been socially effective and one can only wonder what this would mean for human history.[7]

This tempers the sublimation-as-repression theory, if it does not render it inadequate, because simultaneously with the experience of radical violation of plenitude there is an equally powerful experience of elemental pleasure, an immanent pleasure, one could say, in the object-investment that sublimation affords. One could choose to pathologize this double condition—which is actually to say, *naturalize* it—or one could choose to view it in social-historical terms, which would entail making a political decision as to the significance and distinction, indeed the value, among the multitude of sublimatory objects in the course of human history. In this respect, the heteronomy of sublimation, simply understood, does become a problem precisely because it is not a *naturally* inevitable outcome, but is rather conditioned by the historical dimensions of a specific social-imaginary institution.

Subjection

Already, given the terms of our inquiry so far, a trajectory is set up to pass through the conceptual straits of alterity with the enormous weight of heterological discourses that shadow it. Be that as it may, the impetus is to attain, in a certain dialectical sense, an *altered relation to alterity*, with an aspiration ultimately to counteract the allure of transcendence that has become elemental in the contemporary lexicon of the Other, to such an extent as to reproduce consistently a cognitive figure of transcendence that is itself untranscendable. At the same time, I am aware that this trajectory thereby plunges us into the chimerical waters of the Self, whose own conceptual lexicon has long been the target of the most radical tendencies in psychoanalytic and feminist theory, as well as today's insurrectionary politics. This is all the more complicated by the often irresistible association of discourses concerning the subject with discourses concerning the self, which makes conspicuously evident indeed how problematic—that is to say, how political—any theory of subjectification becomes insofar as it must involve a theory (or, in essence, a politics) of sublimation, whether acknowledged or not. In the last instance, we must restate the utterly obvious because it is so crucial: subject-formation is a political matter, as it signifies the inaugural negotiation with power—indeed, with the power of the other, or with power *as* other, but also, inevitably, with power as altering (*othering*) force. It is this latter aspect that problematizes the entire equation, raising, by its very constitution, the question of the political pure and simple: Where does the power of othering, of alteration, of transformation, reside? Wherefrom does it emerge? What is its referential frame? Its location? Its standpoint of interlocution? And finally, what is its mode and terms of articulation?

In *The Psychic Life of Power*, Judith Butler made a bold intervention in response to these questions, working from the Hegelian basis of the negotiation of power in the dialectics of self-recognition but clearly exceeding it—or, more precisely, altering its terms—so that the always theoretically precarious terrain of the construction of the subject can reemerge in its full complicity with the construction of subjection. Butler's overall understanding of the forces involved in this complicitous relation is profoundly dialectical. Indeed, in a basic sense, it forges an altered relation to dialectical thinking, very much in defiance of recent critiques, which demonstrates the capacity of dialectical thinking to frame questions and responses that outmaneuver the deadlock of identitarian logic. Let us traverse the terms of her argument for a moment, with an eye to their implications as groundwork for an inquiry into self-alteration.

* * *

Butler predicates her argument on the rather controversial assertion that subject-formation is always intertwined with subjection: that is, with subordination to the power of an other, or, more precisely, to power as an other entity that retains the force of its otherness even when it is (as it must be) "internalized" in the process of the subject's emergence into being. Internalization here does not mean the ideological assumption of the terms of external power, in the classic sense of all political and psychological figures of subjugation, precisely because, Butler argues, the moment of internalization is itself a formative moment—indeed, a *transformative* moment—whereby the subject's inaugural act of existence signifies both the "absorption" of power as otherness and the enactment of the forming capacity of this power.

In other words, there is a foundational simultaneity at work in the inaugural moment of subjectification that points both inwardly toward the psychic nucleus and yet outwardly in excess of the determinant domain of the other.[8] This paradoxical simultaneity, whereby the other both forms the subject and yet is formed by the subject, plunges the entire ontological equation into uncertainty and makes signification enigmatic. Butler calls it explicitly a "tropological quandary," mining from language itself the full range of the Greek meaning of *tropē* (both turn and manner, both shift and figure): "The form this power takes is relentlessly marked by a figure of turning, a turning back upon itself or even a turning *on* oneself. This figure operates as part of the explanation of how a subject is produced, and so there is no subject, strictly speaking, who makes this turn. On the contrary, the turn appears to function as a tropological inauguration of the subject, a founding moment whose ontological status remains permanently uncertain."[9] In this respect, the very language of subject-formation turns on a figure of uncertainty, whereby all structural and temporal order (of principles, elements, forces, loci, and so on) makes for an undeconstructible enigma.

Right away then, the discourse of subjection as discourse of subject-formation can hardly be mapped as a specifically directional vector force, the force of subjugation pure and simple. As order (*taxis*) is foundationally enigmatic, no paratactic or syntactic (or even tactical) arrangement of power can be assumed. Taking this rhetorical rubric to its full extent, I would argue here the same for subordination (the *hypotactic* element) in a grammatical but also philosophical sense, something that Butler does not address as such but, nonetheless, leads us to by implication. In any case, although power does exist "external" to the subject—by definition, insofar as it is recognized as a formative force—its externality is impossible to determine, precisely because, in a dialectical sense, power is itself subjected to the transformative force of the subject's inaugural act of making this power "internal." Conversely, the subject's inaugural position, as itself "external" to power (to whose formative force it is subjected), is also impossible to determine. There is no a priori subject. Rather, the subject enters the domain of determination at the very moment it "internalizes" power as its own, thereby transforming—*altering*—power both in terms of power's location and the elements of its force. It is crucial to keep in mind here that this alteration is a moment of rupture, an interruption. Otherwise, internalization would merely signify the worst aspect of heteronomous enslavement, and the significational alterity in the force of alteration would be entirely lost. This is why Butler repeatedly insists on the discontinuity between "the power that initiates the subject" and "the power that is the subject's agency" (P, 12).

* * *

The logic in the figural encounter that Butler describes resonates uncannily with Castoriadis's own psychoanalytic account of both subject-formation and social-imaginary institution. The similarity of both registers is quite remarkable, with some important differences in language—Castoriadis does not grant such authorizing force to "power" but prefers to keep in this position the term *society*—and in this respect it deserves a study on its own. For our purposes, however, let me note the following: Whenever Castoriadis speaks of imaginary institution he always assumes a groundless, abyssal simultaneity at the origin, a simultaneity that thus forms a consubstantial, co-determinant, co-incident origin—what he explicitly calls "the primitive circle of creation." In his basic terms, every society is the "subject" of its imaginary institution in the sense that every society emerges from the magma of its own significations: significations that society institutes as its own at the very time it is instituted by them, since, like the subject, no society can exist a priori to a social imaginary—there is no vacuum space in history. To say that society is the subject (and, conversely, that the subject is an institution of society) is neither to imply a notion of collective consciousness (or, for that matter, collective unconscious) nor to assume that subjects are, simply speaking, social-historical products. Society/subject is a dialectical form that has no a priori origin and no teleological meaning. Precisely because there is no historical vacuum, the subject is always instituted as a social form insofar as it assumes the imaginary significations particular to the social-historical moment that pertains to it. At the same time, however, social-imaginary significations at any historical moment are themselves meaningless (i.e., unsignifiable) without the subject that institutes them: confers upon them relevant meaning.[10]

Castoriadis conceptualizes this structure in the psychoanalytic terms that pertain to subjectification, as well in the domain he calls "the radical imagination," which enables him to speak in terms of an ontology of society, of *physis* with *nomos*. At the level of the radical imaginary, the untamable core of the psyche encounters what appears to it to be the pure alterity of societal institution in a moment that signals simultaneously the psyche's defeat and emancipation: the inaugural moment of subject-formation. I'm reiterating that, for Castoriadis, the monadic core of the psyche remains insubordinate to the power of societal institution, while thus providing the nuclear energy, so to speak, that powers the institution: it is, at a foundational level, the *instituting* imagination—limitless, indeterminable, unsignifiable, untamable, abyssal flux of image/affect/representation: pure *Vorstellung*. This psychic insubordination, even if it is the consequent source of radical imagination, preserves the constitutive internal schism on which it leans—the fact that the first real stranger that rends asunder the primal corporeal undifferentiation of the psyche is the ego itself, that is, the psyche's very own renegade ambassador to the outside world. The later psychoanalytic work of Castoriadis elucidates especially this primary production of otherness within, which animates the psyche with an elemental self-hatred that always lies in ambush even in the most extreme manifestations of primary narcissism (self-love). For Castoriadis, the radical hatred of the other, observed indicatively in racist affect, leans precisely on this outmaneuverable psychic self-hatred. What averts racist desire is, in this respect, a specific politics of sublimation that enables an encounter with otherness as difference instead of as existential threat to the self—in psychic terms, radical treason of self. Conversely, a politics of sublimation that empowers racist hatred always bears an intrinsic genocidal potential, even if it does not always reach this extent.[11]

Obviously, the psychic monad as such (as pure *Vorstellung*) is a nonsensical entity in any sort of simple terms of human-being. It is entirely meaningless and its survival hinges on its being endowed with meaning, with signification. Going back directly to Freud, in this respect, Castoriadis speaks of the psyche's translation of the images/affects/representations of societal institution at the very moment of this encounter, which may be conceived as a moment inaugurally, but is obviously conducted again and again in an individual's lifetime, insofar as subject-formation is never exhausted in a single instance but is inevitably an open-ended (re)iteration, a historical enactment. In this translation, the psyche receives the instituted significations that identify it as a subject in a given social-historical domain, in which (significations) it then invests—as it must, in order to emerge out of its autistic monadic condition—but in such a way as never to be reducible to the overall instituted framework of signification. Were it to be so, the psyche would be terminally defeated and an unconscious would be unimaginable. This translation is therefore a *poietic* performance, a transformative act that subjects instituted signification to alteration. By the same token, subject-formation is the limitless process (indeed limited only by the certainty of mortality) by which the radical imagination of the psyche retains its capacity to make and unmake (alter) the horizon of possibility of social-imaginary institution by accepting (and acceding to) social-imaginary signification, by accepting (and acceding to) the specific social-historical content it then comes to recognize as its worldly existence.

This relation renders any idea of absolute alterity unfeasible and unsignifiable, except as a condition of perspective. While from the radical standpoint of the psyche the institution of society does indeed appear as pure alterity—as does, conversely, the psychic core appear as absolute alterity to the logic of society (despite ceaseless efforts to explain it or conjure it away, whether by religion, philosophy, or psychoanalysis)—there is no way to signify a location external to these standpoints that would determine the other's existence. To put it in a rather clumsy way: there is no self to the other, or in another sort of language, the other is not a subject. The other is a force of alteration that enacts and is enacted by the subject—this is the position that power holds in Butler's conception: a force that brings the subject into existence, yet is nonexistent without the subject. Thus, the crucial element to determine is not the figure of the other but the force of alteration. Butler raises a succinct question in this regard: "how is subjection to become a site of alteration?" (P, 11). The political ramifications of this way of phrasing the question should be obvious: subjection must be (re)considered not as site of enforcement of instituted power but as site of transformative power—in Castoriadis's terms, of *instituting* power. In Butler's words, "the act of [the subject's] appropriation may involve an alteration of power such that the power assumed or appropriated works against the power that made that assumption possible" (P, 13).

In this respect, Butler's inquiry into the complicity between subject-formation and subjection demands that we reconsider the terrain of the other in a way that opens up the possibility of subjectification as self-alteration. This requires us to reorient ourselves theoretically from attending to the internalization of the other toward recognizing the internal force of othering, which, in the broadest sense, constitutes the creative/destructive (*poietic*) capacity of humans to alter the forms of their historical existence, for better or worse. The obstacle in enabling this reorientation resides in the indicative gesture of concealment that seems to occur at the subject's inaugural moment: in order for the subject to emerge as power—or in order for the subject's power to emerge—the subject seems to conceal the formative force of power, so that, as Butler says, "agency [appears to] exceed the power by which it is enabled" (P, 15). In other words, the subject appears to enact a gesture of self-referentiality at the origin that actually occludes the autonomy of self-reflexivity to be achieved. This is the ideological content of all autopoetic figures in the post-Enlightenment and post-Romantic imaginary, whether variants of the self-made entrepreneur or variants of the autonomous genius of the Artist.

This dissimulation—or, to quote Butler, "the metaleptic reversal in which the subject produced by power becomes heralded as the subject who *founds* power" (P, 16)—occurs also at the level of societal institution, except in the other direction, a point that Butler does not address: namely, as history has shown it to be prevalent, societies tend to conceal their own instituting force, potential and actual, conferring thereby authorization of their origin and survival upon social-imaginary significations that are constructed as instances of transcendent rule: God, the father, the king, the nation, the constitution, the market, and so on. Indeed, even in cases of nominally secular societies, these instances of transcendent rule are explicitly rendered sacred, and this sacralization becomes in effect the most profound expression of subjection as subjugation. In this respect, the force of subjection does not merely concern the psychic domain of subject-formation but pertains to the social imaginary as such. Most social imaginaries in human history enact a heteronomous institution, that is, most societies submit the self-altering force emerging in the internalization of power to self-occultation, as Castoriadis says all too often. They prefer to (re) institute the perspective of an "external" authority of subjection into pure alterity, into occult heteronomous order.

Sexual Difference

A reconsideration of Irigaray's work may be useful here, if we consider that, of all philosophers in recent decades—except perhaps for Levinas, but his impetus could not be further askew—she has placed "alterity" and "the other" at the core of her epistemological inquiries, thereby granting us, in especially incisive fashion, a novel armory with which to encounter the question of how a politics of the other may not disintegrate into heteronomous politics. My objection to decontextualized uses of "otherness" as an allegedly pure philosophical concept (in ethics, ontology, or even psychoanalysis) or simply as a formal rhetorical category (in aesthetics or politics) still holds.[12] My impetus has always been to draw attention to how certain heterological discourses efface tangible indications of otherness by virtue of an avalanche-like process of ever-increasing abstraction.

At the height of identity politics during the so-called Culture Wars of the late 1980s, the Other had already come to mean nothing, while at the same time signifying anything deemed marginal, minoritarian, oppositional, or disenfranchised. As a formal category, and essentially emptied of historical content even when ascribed to specific historical terms, otherness was suffering, I argued at the time, a *catachresis*. I meant the term rather literally, in the Greek sense, as *abuse*: a kind of ultimate counterutility that, in plain language, entails an essential uselessness. It might be worthwhile, however, to resurrect the rhetorical content of the term in the English language and consider additionally the "catachresis of otherness" to signify an improper transfer of the sense and attributes of the other, an inappropriateness that returns to haunt whoever claims the domain of the other as an alibi for abstracting meaning away from the real historical battlefield. In either case, my concern remains essentially the same: an abstracted, disembodied other lends itself seamlessly to authorizing a total and empty Other—an absolutist, indeed totalitarian Other. In this sense, even the most articulate heterology becomes an authorization of heteronomy, if it fails to configure otherness as a limit concept—that is, a concept permeated by an undeconstructible *différance* at the same time that it unleashes conditions of *différance* on all other concepts it encounters.

Levinas certainly enjoys heterology as heteronomy, but Irigaray does not. At least, there remains a certain *an-archic* element in her thinking, even in the later work of heterosexual affirmation, which refuses to grant to the other the markings of *archē* and *telos*.[13] The reason is the singular importance that the notion of sexual difference has held for her throughout her work, despite the obvious shifts in terminology and orientation this work has taken over the decades. Reading Irigaray without latching on to the issue of her various turns and periods—bracketing, that is, the otherwise important historical reading of an oeuvre that does indeed follow a circuitous and at times contradictory path—helps us recontextualize her insistence on sexual difference as a concept that acts like a hinge to the opening and closing of her various pathways: not simply a key concept, that is, whose content remains stable, uniquely comprehensible, and transferable across discourses, but an epistemological threshold whose crossing requires and also produces a continually altered (and altering) mode of raising and thinking about certain questions (even the same questions).

Irigaray alerts us to the fact that sexual difference can never be described in terms or signs of an equation, even a differential equation. Its mathematics, as it were, is incalculable. This is not simply because there is no equality between the different parts, between the sexes, but because the two contrasting elements of difference cannot possibly share a mutual means of measure. Even in the most complex differential equation one equals one. But the other, in this case, is not one—or, more precisely, not merely one. She is at least double, or not merely double. She is multiple, though hardly multiplied as mere reproductions of the one. This enables her to be one, to register as singular presence, without ever occupying the position of the one. The other who is always more and less than one is always else than one. And this else cannot be signified even by the mathematical capacity to designate it as X, the unknown one, the variable one, the one that can have many (or any) values, the one who can have many faces or any face. This is because the many faces of X become possible—calculable—only within the terms of the equation, an equation that X, in a peculiar self-authorizing way through its unknown presence, makes possible and calculable. In terms of sexual difference, the other defies even setting the terms of the equation, perhaps because she knows (although who knows how she knows?) that any equation to which she grants her otherness will erase sexual difference.[14]

In this respect, Irigaray's insistence on sexual difference transforms it from a concept to an epistemological condition that ultimately reaches beyond the strict referential framework of sexual relations. Incidentally, let us note that Irigaray increasingly opts to reconfigure the phrase as "sexed difference" (*la difference sexué*), which may be a bit awkward in English, but is nonetheless more precise: sexual difference has meaning insofar as it denotes the fact that difference itself is sexed, not as a matter of sexuality but as a matter of disjunction between the sexes and repression of this disjunction in favor of one sex over the other. Sexual difference therefore pertains to matters beyond sexual relations, strictly speaking, because its specific epistemology is already grounded in a *différance*, a kind of irreducible separation from the presence of a simple difference—let us say, a "natural" biological difference, or, strictly speaking, the "formal" philosophical difference between Self and Other. This irreducible separation enables the risk to conceptualize otherness as an "internal" position, as an exteriority within. The tremendous complication of this positioning—always marked by *différance*, as *différance*—is an essential departure point for any meditation on self-alteration, conceptual, epistemological, or psychoanalytic.

In this context, I would therefore suggest that Irigaray's insistence on an epistemology of sexual difference has consistently aimed—despite the different terms, concerns, or textual targets—at disrupting the classic philosophical adherence to the "universal," without which, in any case, no conceptual possibility of the Other would have arisen. Irigaray has always acted as a philosopher—in the Greek sense as much as against the Greek sense. (To be provocative, but also more precise: inasmuch as she acts against the Greek sense, she has always acted as a philosopher in the Greek sense.) One might argue that her epistemology of sexual difference enables a self-interrogation of alterity—an interrogation of alterity within alterity and by virtue of alterity—that alters in turn any possibility that the politics of the other might lend itself to simple politics of identity. In this sort of argument, one could, very productively, place Irigaray at the core of the Hegelian problematic of subjectification as subjugation that we broached at the outset as a departure point in investigating the trajectory of autonomy as self-alteration. But Irigaray might also be said to reconfigure this Hegelian frame as a mode of interrogating the universalist morality of traditional philosophy—this is at least what I understand her to be doing in the series of texts collected under the title *Sexes and Genealogies*.

She finds Hegelian *Sittlichkeit*, for example, to be haunted by an unacknowledged content of a fissured doubleness, the repression of which cannot be exorcised by a progressive dialectics of the spirit in history. According to her reading of Hegel, this doubleness arises from two instances: (1) the chasm opened between a primary social imaginary (the "law of the ancestors") and its contemporary manifestation (modernity's "emancipatory" ethical predicament after the French Revolution), a symptom of not addressing genealogy in history as a problem, as Nietzsche would shortly thereafter; (2) the fissure the social imaginary opens in its configuration of nature as it passes into history, which silences the fact that both nature and this passage are undeconstructibly sexed. The two instances are obviously interwoven as a genealogical problem—the epistemic framework is not merely the juxtaposition of sexes and genealogies, but the fact that all genealogies in all societies are sexed. But the second instance, specifically, enables Irigaray to underscore Hegel's implicit (unacknowledged) *double nature* of the spirit. As it becomes (part of) history, a sublated (and in a very real sense always sublimated) nature exceeds itself but is hardly abolished as nature: "History is the soil in which a second nature, a double nature grows: cultural, spiritual nature, which goes beyond its natural potential."[15] That this soil cultivates a condition—let us say, in Hegelian terms, a civil society—that deliberately (by necessity) occludes this double nature corresponds, metaphorically at least, to the self-occultation of the universal as unmediated exteriority, as objective singularity, which cannot but ultimately assume, even in strict historico-political matters, a theological (indeed theocratic) content.

Against it, Irigaray proposes what she calls "the ethics of the couple," a differential entity that does not repress the doubleness of nature in history. This requires that "the ethics of the couple" be understood in light of the deconstructive mathematics of "the sex which is not one." I understand the legitimacy of various objections to the explicitly heterosexual content Irigaray grants to the notion of the couple, although obviously this heterosexual double is not a matter of sexuality but strictly of gender. In any case, such critique will gain further if it diverts its attention from the content of this figure and (re)considers the form. By insisting on the "ethics of the couple," Irigaray challenges the formal identitary monism of the ethical demand that permeates traditional philosophy, in terms of not only Kantian autonomy but Hegelian *Sittlichkeit* as well:[16] "The most powerful goal of interpretation is the analysis of discourse as sexed [*sexué*] and not neuter. This can be demonstrated with linguistic and semiotic tools. To undertake this task is to complete that extra turn into self-consciousness that Hegel failed to make: reflexion upon discourse itself as a content that is the outcome of its forms, forms that are arbitrary" (SG, 138).

Going ahead to practice this sort of interpretation, Irigaray disputes the capacity of the Hegelian dialectic to account for sexual difference; in fact, she points to sexual difference as the limit point of Hegelian dialectics. She does so because she exempts the law of sex from contradiction, preferring instead to ascribe to it a sort of mimetic performativity: "Sex does not obey the law of contradiction. It bends and folds to accommodate that logic but it does not conform. Forced to follow that logic it is drawn into a mimetic game that moves faraway from life" (SG, 139). Irigaray enables herself to make this argument by taking Hegel literally, at his word, that social action is but an interminable (re)enaction of the spirit. In that respect, she is right to point out the alienation—literally, the despiritualization—that the lack of acknowledgment of sexual difference brings to human relations. Fair enough, but I cannot resist insisting that, whatever might be Hegel's absolutist aspirations regarding the various embodiments or even purity of the Spirit, the dialectical method itself is not even possible except as a performative process that is, moreover, characterized not even simply by mimesis but by bona fide impersonation: as a series of instances where one is, becomes, acts as an other—indeed, even as an other within oneself. Irigaray seems cautious here not to be understood in terms of a vulgar Hegelianism, whereby, as dialectics is contorted into confirmation of identity, ultimately "the one is reduced to the other" (139). This is not the occasion to delve into disputes over interpretations of Hegel, but this caution is unnecessary. Hegelian dialectics can be dissociated from the march of the Spirit, as an enormous and vastly varied procession of Hegelian dialectical practices that reject Hegelianism tout court (from Marx, to Adorno and Benjamin, to Žižek, Butler, and, I would argue, Irigaray herself), after all, testifies to. Dialectics is a performative method whose content is therefore always provisional and occasional, (over)determined by whatever may be the historical or epistemic demands of the dialectical instance.

Be that as it may, what interests us here is not Irigaray's outright claim that "there is no dialectic between the sexes" but that Hegel fails (as does all traditional philosophy) because "he gives no thought to the living being as a sexed being" (SG, 139–40). To think the two assertions together, one might say, as Walter Benjamin did in his own way, that only a dialectics of the living really matters. Irigaray adds the obvious but deeply repressed qualification: life matters are irreducibly sexed. This is to say, in so many words, that the inability of philosophy to come to terms with sexual difference makes it unfit for matters of life. But Irigaray's grander point, and the one most crucial to our inquiry, is that the universality traditional philosophy produces is essentially anchored in a monistic mathematics, capable (even if in relatively rare instances) of contemplating contradiction, yet even then reducing contradiction to singular units of time whereby the integrity of the opposed agents (subject-object, self-other, man-woman, history-nature, internal-external, and so on) ultimately remains total, separate, and closed. Against this, Irigaray argues that the universal is itself nothing more than a mediation: on the one hand, historically speaking, because the human animal's yearning for its spiritual nature always comes up against the necessity for its worldliness, and on the other hand, because the human animal's worldliness—whatever might be the flights of spirit or plunges into repression—is itself a constant reiteration of the problematic of sexual difference, a problematic that registers precisely in the enormous expenditure of significational energy to efface it.[17]

The gesture of depicting the universal as mediation also aims at destabilizing the equation by which the figure of the Other lends itself to certain theological imaginaries—monotheistic ones, to be sure. Despite Irigaray's own peculiar investment in a certain recuperation of religious significations (whether her romanticized evocations of early Christianity or her uninterrogated exoticism of Hinduist or Buddhist categories), she nonetheless succeeds in making alterity concrete at the same time that she makes sexual difference historical—in other words, the primary condition in the human animal's production of meaning in the real world. In the same way that the epistemology of sexual difference exposes the universal as mediation, it configures alterity as a worldly condition, limited by its interruption of history while at the same time unlimited as psychic energy of human transformation. As threshold to history, sexual difference dismantles the fetishism of absolute, monological alterity—it detheologizes alterity. It is, of course, banal to note here that monotheism is the theological symptom of a patriarchical imaginary. The self-congratulatory delusion one sees in various New Age discourses that like to refer to God as She makes for a stunning confirmation of their subjugation to this imaginary, no matter what might be their feminist predilections. God cannot be a She in the same sense that a world conducted in terms of a female imaginary cannot possibly invent monotheism. A sex which is not one cannot imagine a god who is merely (and only) One. Worshiping the Absolute Other, the One-and-Only Other, paralyzes the conduits of an open relation to the other. Monotheism channels an obsession with the power of the One—an obsession with submitting to a monopoly of power—into the worship of the absolute, transcendental Other. This devotion to the One who is the Other makes engagement with otherness literally impossible. It is an instance when subjectification by means of the power of subjection is, very simply, incapacitation, pure heteronomy.

Praxis/Poiēsis

This raises the most salient political question of all: Can a process of subject-formation that takes place distinctly through a process of subjection conjured as pure subjugation produce an autonomous subject? To put it directly, can—or how can—an autonomous subject emerge out of a heteronomous order? Obviously, in risking the use of the term *autonomous subject*, I do not mean to suggest a self-enclosed, self-supposing, narcissistic subject, suspended in the ahistorical void of its own essence. Pure autonomy is itself a theological concept, even in Kant's glorious rationalist mind. It pertains to a self-referential, tautological meaning that the monotheistic mind—in fact, any monomythical mind, as the German philosopher Odo Marquard has so incisively put it—attributes to the one and only power of signification. In a philosophical language, the name "I am that I am" is the name for the total attributes of Being, including, of course, all the possible languages of Being, the plurality of which is abolished by the monistic source that enables them. Thus, such pure ("autonomous") ontology cannot be named, cannot be represented. By extension, it cannot enter history because it cannot "know" history—it cannot know anything other than what it knows absolutely, which is (and can only be) itself. Hence, it cannot change—not merely history, but anything at all, including itself. Not only does this Being not "know" alterity; it has no altering—and most significantly, no *self-altering*—powers. At its most extreme, it may be said to exist as absolute alterity for someone else, someone who believes his or her being to be determined by it, derived from it. In other words, this absolute and tautological equation of Being-in-itself has meaning only in a heteronomous universe of meanings, in a universe whose signification is guaranteed by the presence of an unreachable, unutterable, and unapproachable Other who precludes any alternative authorization.

In the way Castoriadis understands it, very much against the grain of traditional philosophy, autonomy can exist only as project: an ever-presently restaged project whose primary condition or rule (*archē*) is explicitly drawn from the capacity for self-alteration. This means an *archē* that always begins anew, *othered*—therefore, an *archē* that reauthorizes itself as an other. That's why autonomy as explicit self-alteration is not some fancy way of considering self-constitution, or *autopoiēsis*. In fact, as an ever-restaged and ever-interrupted *archē*, self-alteration renders all received paradigms of self-constitution unfeasible, unconstitutible claims. From the standpoint of self-alteration, the autonomous subject engages in a kind of interminable self-determination, whereby both the "self" and the determinant elements are under perpetual interrogation. In literal terms, by autonomous subject I am considering here a subject who makes the law—a poet of the law—whose most prized achievement is the limitless interrogation of the law in its full range: first of all, law's emergence, and then its referential framework and justification, its authorization and canonical execution, and most of all, its metatextual presumption of authority. To be the poet of the law is first and foremost to recognize the existence of the law not as transcendental dimension but as historical privilege. This is tantamount to thinking of the subject (whether of oneself or one's society) as a historical entity, whose ground is otherwise abyssal, whose *archē* is indeterminate, and whose telos is nothing other than the very project of self-interrogated, worldly, mortal existence.

***

It is unclear what social-historical conditions are needed for subjectification to take this form. It is safe to say, however, that social autonomy is hardly a natural condition of human-being. It can only emerge as the *praxis/poiēsis* within a certain social imaginary, which surely does not mean that it is the mere expression or application of a certain social imaginary. On the contrary, in such an instance, the radical interrogation of the terms of one's existence would be itself the ground of *praxis/poiēsis*, in full cognizance of its otherwise ontological groundlessness. Autonomy is impossible without limitless self-interrogation, in the sense that autonomy cannot be attained once and for all but must be, by definition, open to reinstitution (i.e., alteration), whose limits cannot be set outside the process of alteration. Contrary, then, to traditional notions of autonomous subjectivity that, one way or another, cannot avoid equating self-determination with the self-presupposition of both origin and end, Castoriadis's notion insists on an open figure in which the limits of both "subject" and "autonomy" remain indeterminate as a matter of *physis*. The determination of limit that presumably distinguishes the domain of relation between subject and object, internal and external, individual and society, and so on is always a political determination, a matter of *nomos*.

To conclude, it would be essential to add, following this Castoriadian terminology, that autonomy signifies a particular sublimation: a politics of sublimation that confronts the definitional heteronomy "experienced" by the psyche when it encounters the social imaginary—the nature of subjection in Butler's terms; the effacement of sexual difference in Irigaray's—as the pleasure of/in the force of alteration itself. This sort of sublimation would enact a subject whose psychic reception of society's *Vorstellung*—enacted, in turn, by the psyche's translation of society's imagistic/affective/representational flux into its own terms—would consist in a *poietic* experience: a performative experience of self-othering, which moreover signifies the non-self-referential poetic pleasure of altering one's world. In this respect, it seems apt to recall John Cage's often quoted phrase "Art is self alteration"—provided, however, that we don't take it to mean a sort of artistic redemption or self-actualization (in some New Age sense), but that self-alteration names the core process by which our worldly existence can be radically transformed, which is also, after all, the deepest significance of art: the radical transfiguration of form. To this end, self-alteration cannot be conceptualized or articulated if the self remains a notion within the signifying limits of identity. The process of self-alteration is deadly to the sovereignty of identity. It presupposes—it enables and performs—an *identicide*: the self-dissolution of the self, or, in another idiom, the production of nonidentity as self-transformative force.

CHAPTER 4

ŽIŽEK'S REALISM

Slavoj Žižek is a realist thinker. I understand not many people would put it this way, yet I say this because in a basic sense Žižek is always trying to think from the standpoint of the real and, at the same time, to think through the standpoint of the real. I am not merely speaking of the Lacanian Real—what "resists symbolization" or marks the limit that is both obstacle and access to the real. I am speaking, in rather unsophisticated fashion, of those *real elements* (which may or may not resist symbolization) that constitute the nodal points of our worldly existence, the points that undermine all systematic attempts to determine this existence in advance and by means of externally derived iron laws. It is unlikely that Žižek himself would put the matter in this fashion. This is because his strategy is precisely to flirt with "iron principles" (what he has also named "lost causes") in order to expose how the political contingencies of our world are nowadays veiled by a palliative language that uses the alibi of contingency to defeat principles.

The matter is contradictory, perhaps (as Žižek would prefer to say) perverse. And the contradiction, the perversion, is evident in his very mode of operation, the rhetoric, the performance. Many of Žižek's remarkable musings and readings of things around us—sometimes the most trivial, most concrete things, other times the most abstract, most speculative things (but in Hegelian terms, the most abstract is the most concrete)—may themselves be seen as gestures of the real and therefore as gestures of resistance to symbolization. There is an attempt here—how conscious I am not entirely sure—to perform under the calling of the real as a way of thinking from and through the standpoint of the real: in other words, to think the realm of the possible, the realm of symbolization (particularly insofar as this symbolization eludes us) from the standpoint of the impossible, of the unsymbolizable.

In this specific sense—and I am continuing in rather unsophisticated fashion—Žižek's realism is a Hegelian realism. This is itself a perverse notion in any philosophical framework, except a Hegelian one. Yet, I would argue, it is this peculiar way with which Hegel weighs his thought upon the real—on the Idea as the abyssal mark of the Real (a gesture as far away from Platonic considerations as can be imagined)—that has animated Žižek's engagement from the outset. And parenthetically, I would add that it is the persistently self-reflexive wrestling with Hegel—not quite with Lacan, who most of the time remains uninterrogated—that has consistently provided Žižek with his most radical interventions. In short and as a point of departure, whatever might be Žižek's particular concern with the virtual is in effect an extension of his consistent concern with the real.

The Theology Machine

But before we get into this specific relation in detail, there is another crucial element in this staging. Žižek may not say he is a realist thinker but he explicitly ascribes to himself the task of being a dialectical materialist thinker. Let us note that this self-ascription is also consciously perverse, in the sense that, although it obviously draws its meaning from a Marxist language and does so bearing the full force of a politically subversive project, it is hardly reducible to standard understandings of what Marxism (and the Marxist language) is conventionally thought to bear.[1] The other major thinker who comes to mind, who also used this self-ascription in similar subversive fashion, is Walter Benjamin. Žižek does not often refer to Benjamin but he does, in a significant gesture, in his introductory pages of *The Puppet and the Dwarf*. In fact, the book's title is drawn from one of Benjamin's most famous allegories in his *Theses on the Concept of History*.

Let us recall that Benjamin opens his *Theses* with a description of the chess automaton model, as realized by the Hungarian inventor Wolfgang von Kempelen in 1769 and later acquired and made famous by Joahnn Nepomuk Mälzel, which consisted of a large puppet figure of a Turk with a hookah conducting himself as an indomitable chess player. This is because inside the box (underneath the chessboard), which is made to seem transparent by an intricate play of mirrors, sits a chess master hunchback dwarf, who authorizes every chess move by pulling the strings of the puppet Turk. When he acquired the machine, Mälzel refined some of its features of mechanical illusion by implanting a voice box that would declare "Échec!" every time the opponent's king was checked. Mälzel was a well-known German engineer and inventor in his own right, a maker of machines of all kinds, primarily ones related to mechanical music (including the metronome and a set of ear trumpets to help Beethoven with his hearing loss). But he was also a bit of a showman and he took his "Turk" (as he indicatively called the chess machine) on the road for a series of performances that courted the miraculous nature of a sort of primitive artificial intelligence, until its "fraudulent" nature was discovered during an American tour. Edgar Allan Poe, in a gesture exemplifying literature's resistance to the mechanization of intelligence, had already made public his certainty of the "Turk" being a fraud before it was in fact discovered. It should be noted that the whole concept, including the specific preference for Orientalia, deformed bodies, technological mastery, marionette theatricality, and, above all, the classic motif of the "ghost in the machine," bears the full imprint of German Romantic aesthetics.

After his description, Benjamin offers a philosophical counterpart to this arrangement, dubbing the puppet "historical materialism" and the dwarf "theology," which, he adds, "is small and ugly and has to keep out of sight." Benjamin then insists, without the least irony, that historical materialism is to "win every time." Most readers of this allegory, with good reason, no doubt, have interpreted it as a distillation of the author's underlying theological preferences, citing the usual suspects of influence: Scholem, Schmitt, Rosenzweig. Such readings, as a rule, don't pay enough attention to Benjamin's insistence on historical materialism's victorious certainty.[2] If and when they do, these readings assume that historical materialism triumphs because theology is secretly guiding it. Yet, to attribute the simplest causality to this relationship may indeed pay tribute to Mälzel's mechanistic performance but does little to honor Benjamin's profoundly radical dialectical thinking. There is an analogy here with the conventional reception of Marx's famous phrase from *The 18th Brumaire*: "Men make their own history, but they do not make it as they please." The phrase has been traditionally interpreted as a staple of "structural Marxism": history has its own way, its own structure, which overcomes people's desires. In the process, the most radical element is waived aside: history is made by people; it is a worldly affair; people can make and unmake their conditions, even if not quite as they please. Whatever his theological predilections, Benjamin weaves this allegory in order to speak about historical materialism, and significantly its performative victory at a time of the quintessential performance of its defeat. He reminds us, in other words, that history is of human making, whether for emancipation or annihilation.

The temporal conjuncture is crucial on both occasions. Žižek uses it to reverse in turn Benjamin's assertion regarding the allegory of the "Turk":

> Today, when the historical materialist analysis is receding, practiced as it were under cover, rarely called by its proper name, while the theological dimension

> is given a new lease on life in the guise of "postsecular" Messianic turn of deconstruction, the time has come to reverse Walter Benjamin's first thesis on the philosophy of history: "The puppet called 'theology' is to win all the time. It can easily be a match for anyone if it enlists the service of historical materialism, which today, as we know, is wizened and has to keep out of sight."[3]

This is the opening paragraph of *The Puppet and the Dwarf*, which is meant to further the work of the materialist historian, a work most assuredly trained on the real, by taking on, in my opinion, one of the most profound virtual realities of human history: Christianity. Again, Žižek would not quite name Christianity a "virtual reality," but, I argue, his method of interrogation does so—a path of thinking that elucidates the "undercover" core of perversion within a specific logic.

The Liberal Reality of the Virtual

The Puppet and the Dwarf may present the most focused work on this matter and deserves specific attention, but it must be considered as an element in a network of concerns in which religion, politics, reality, and all their alleged "postface" manifestations are relentlessly turned inside out.[4] The lecture presented in the film *Slavoj Žižek: The Reality of the Virtual* (2007) is entirely contiguous to this endeavor, even if not specifically trained on theological matters. Indeed, as attested to by the multiple references in the film to matters of religion, the theological inquiry undertaken in the texts I have mentioned can just as well be inducted in the inquiry of the virtual—a realist (and dialectical materialist) inquiry in the terms I developed at the outset.[5]

If one were to produce an outline of the network of notions and significations that Žižek contemplates in this film, it would be the following: virtuality, modernity, universality, reality, truth, freedom. This network of notions bears an evidently readable Enlightenment trajectory, though obviously traversed—as Žižek never permits us to forget—by the utmost contemporary dimension of daily life on this planet. In other words, the standpoint of this trajectory—one might also say, the elemental fantasy of this particular net-weaving of notions—is not that of an archivist of concepts or a philologist of meaning, but, as the task of the dialectical materialist historian would entail, the work of a political thinker. More than anything else, it is the idiotic presumption to have overcome the political that draws Žižek's wrath, and it is the widespread symptom, in contemporary society, of the drive to depoliticization that becomes the object of both philosophical and psychoanalytic critique.

This widespread depoliticization is directly linked to what we might call the performance of permissibility—the sense or the belief that all is permissible.

This sense or belief is, moreover, escorted by a feeling of superior civilization versus those who are allegedly subjects (thus subjugated) to a regime of belief, those whose belief system determines what is permissible and in that sense forbids the permissible as such. The most ludicrous but, unfortunately, also the most forceful and real indication of this prejudiced sense of cultural superiority is the classic American ideologeme that Islamic fundamentalists, who are entirely imprisoned in their own belief system (much as their women are "imprisoned" inside a burka), nonetheless desire our system of permissibility (so callously called "freedom"), and, insofar as it is unreachable to them, they seek to destroy it. This altogether ridiculous ideologeme, indicative of an essentially paranoid racism, becomes the convenient alibi for the preemptive destruction the US government unleashes on these "backward" Muslim societies, with the idea that they are to be forced to submit, under penalty of annihilation, to our culture of permissibility. In this extraordinary fiasco, the depoliticized society that allegedly enjoys this permissibility stands aside and permits its leaders to conduct such violence over hapless others—on the one hand, because it really swallows the ideological candy bar ("these people are really after our way of life") and yet, on the other hand, because it does indeed feel unable or unwilling to resist its own leaders, thereby attesting (even if it does not lead to any sort of understanding) to the actual limits of permissibility, to the virtuality of this permissibility.[6]

Of course, the point is that this virtual permissibility is perfectly real. It is not real as permissibility; it is real as virtuality—meaning that it is real precisely insofar as it is not really permissibility but its opposite. Žižek unwinds the knot of this contradiction in a variety of ways. His examples of how the culture of permissibility produces in fact a practice of the crudest restriction abound. So does his dialectical dismantling of the logic by which the culture of permissibility empties out the very content of what it allegedly permits (beer without alcohol, coffee without caffeine, chocolate without chocolate, and so on), thereby permitting nothing. The delusion of permission is only one dimension of Žižek's point of critique. The more important dimension is the fact that this delusion is itself forbidding. In other words, the sense of freedom one perceives in today's Western societies, largely speaking, insofar as it is freedom to enjoy nothing—the emptying out of pleasure—turns out to be a binding regime against pleasure, against the risk of pleasure to be exact (the risk that is the core of pleasure, to be perfectly exact).

But this too would have been a point of minor consequence—after all, one can seek to go against the grain of this sort of culture—if it did not pertain directly to the general demobilization or deactivation of society's political will and, concurrently, the blunting of the powers of social conscience. The reason why Žižek insists on the reality of the virtual conditions of our contemporary existence is precisely because this virtual permissibility, this virtual reality of pleasure, establishes the *real* horizon of life; it is actualized on real bodies; it stupefies real minds.

One of the many consequences is what might be called the pluralization of reality. The classic *liberal* response—speaking with historical accuracy—to the paranoid fantasy of those "fundamentalist" others who want to steal our enjoyment (bomb our buildings, take our SUVs, withhold our oil, infiltrate our neighborhoods and our schools, generally destroy our way of life, *because they can't have it*) is to suggest that they be left alone because they too belong to a modernity to which they too have a specific right. Žižek exposes the prejudicial underlogic of this liberal fantasy with exceeding menace, perhaps because he finds it more insidious than the brutish overtly racist response. The point is well taken, as it exposes another particularly dissimulating dimension of the reality of the virtual.

Žižek's argument stands here along with Fredric Jameson's notion of the singularity of modernity, not because modernity is, let us say stupidly, a "Western invention" (and therefore no other can have it), but because its core historical characteristic is the interrogation and (re)invention of its ephemeral and singular intersection with history. If anything may be said to characterize modernity as a specific social-historical formation, it is that it remains inordinately open to its own undoing. For this reason, beyond Habermas's characterization of modernity as an "unfinished project," I have argued for modernity being "unfinishable" by definition. In other words, modernity is constituted on the basis of an internal antagonism that sustains the possibility of a self-generated otherness that may (and often does) alter entirely the generating self. The singularity of modernity resides in actualizing the capacity for self-alteration on a historical scale, which is the quintessential condition for social autonomy, but it is also bound by no guarantee and, therefore, may just as well produce the destruction of autonomy.

In his critique of the liberal palliative of "alternative modernities"—often posed as counterforce to the overt imposition of Western cultural superiority—Žižek is right to point out a case of "historical nominalism." The logic of multiple modernities reduces the intrinsic antagonism of modernity (the dialectic of modernity, we might say) to just one kind of modernity among many. This isn't a matter determined by Western and non-Western antipathies. Žižek, for example, considers fascism as the first explicit attempt to build an "alternate modernity." Most important, this multiplication of modernity relativizes its historical magnitude effectively down to nothing, often equating modernity with modernization (a technical ideology of a specific historico-geographical moment), and thereby, in place of modernity, releasing modernization into pure form, as an ideology that can be duly exported since, as form, it can find shape under any condition. At the very least, this false equation and pluralization lose sight of contemporary problems as the core antagonism of modernity continuing in other guises, and therefore eliminate the force of self-critique that modernity entails. In short, the notion of alternative modernities achieves nothing; it's pure self-occultation. Not only does it not transcend the domination of Western modernity; it effectively effaces modernity's truly radical work.

Žižek extends the same type of argument against the currently fashionable critiques of universality: "the Universal as such is the site of unbearable antagonism, self-contradiction, and (the multitude of) its particular species are ultimately nothing but so many attempts to obfuscate, reconcile, master this antagonism. In other words, the Universal names a site of a problem-deadlock, of a burning question, and the particulars are the attempted but failed answers to this problem."[7] It must be added that the Universal, signified as the site of antagonism, is what modernity elucidates in a specific and new way—new insofar as whatever has preceded it will now be understood as premodernity. That we occasionally retrospectively recognize, in what we call premodern social-historical formations, a certain kind of antagonistic universality does not mean that it was signified or understood as such. The resignification of universality via modernity is what makes universality possible—a universality to which the particular does not occupy an outside. If we insist on the particulars as myriad outsides—as do the advocates of antiuniversalism—we merely confirm universality as a monolithic category, the very thing we are presumably combating. If, on the other hand, we see in these multiple particulars the esoteric elements of what is often called (with a touch of evident derision) "universal modernity," then we can decode this universal modernity as a virtual category, a condition whose appearance as such is its reality, but which is, nonetheless, plural and differential by virtue of its core antagonism.

Žižek evocatively argues that "multitude is an effect of the intrinsic discrepancy of the One with itself," a kind of pure self-difference, a *différance*, which certainly belongs to the realm of critiques against monological thinking, critiques that perceive the problem with the One to be precisely the suturing of signification. The dispersal of forces at the core of universality's antagonism is in fact traceable in the shards of particulars that are thus posited and signified. In the sense that these particulars are neither alternatives to the universal nor relativized faces of the universal, they enable access to the universal antagonism in terms of their own irredeemable partiality. Hence, Žižek repeatedly argues that truth—to the degree that it can be signified as universal and safeguarded from multiplicity and relativism—is accessible only from the specific partial standpoint whose presence is signified always in a condition of struggle, and therefore does not occupy an unshakeable ground, a timeless moment.

Different Dialectics

The sense of dialectical time forbids dwelling in any moment, including the moment of initial Being, including the moment of *Aufhebung*. Hence the performance of beginnings, as Edward Said would say in another idiom, whereby a content—of truth, of universality, of the real, and the like—is posited, "invented," or, in any case, given a material determination. Since, at least in Hegelian terms, the concept of *matter as such* is incoherent, this positing, this material determination, is the work of negation. The identity of a thing is established by first determining its *not*. Theodor Adorno is the first to really understand the esoteric nonidentitary force of Hegelian thinking, which he eventually developed into what he called negative dialectics. Žižek, who in his early Slovenian and French writings paid a lot of attention to Adorno before moving his reference frame elsewhere, might be said to read his Hegel in similar negative nonidentitary fashion (as he has emphasized, quoting Hegel, "tarrying with the negative"). In a perverse way, nonidentitary thinking, though doing the work of negation, is affirmative thinking, the kind of thinking that moves beyond the determinants of what something is not to the open (interrogative and performative) supposition of what something is in the process of its becoming—more specifically, becoming other.

Dialectical thinking has nothing to do with unification, even when it pursues objects as singular, even when it evokes totalities. Rather, it seeks the self-contradictory condition of the unity of the nonunified, perhaps even the nonunifiable. But thought, *in itself*, cannot possibly theorize the nonunifiable. This is the elementary radicalism of dialectics. If thought can be considered this way, by the strictest standards of theory, it could only be so as a symptom of a worldly *prattein* that establishes itself as ground for thought (*Zugrund*). In other words, thought does not occur as a reflection on an outcome (as an instrumental result), but as an event, a practico-poetic event of the dispersal of the real.

The Perversion of Christianity

In his alertness to this dispersal of the real, Žižek rails against the sort of thinking that dampens the sources of transgression that make the real *sensible*—literally, as an event that registers itself in the corporeal sensibility of the psyche. It is in this context that he welcomes what he calls "the new emergent fundamentalisms" that will open up a new space of freedom, the freedom that will reempower the force of transgression. What Žižek signifies, counter-intuitively, as fundamentalist power can be summed up in his invocation of

Lacan's reversal of Dostoyevsky's famous warning "if God does not exist, everything is permitted" to "if God does not exist, everything is prohibited." But he does so with yet another reversal, the reversal of the reversal, which reiterates Dostoyevsky in a new era: if you can demonstrate that God exists (by talking with him or hearing his voice or something similar), then everything is permitted. The perversion of this thought does not reside, as one would imagine, in its casual handling of people who admit to having a regular chat with God—people whose self-satisfied confession would otherwise be considered a paranoid episode and would send them straight to the loony bin if they didn't happen to be world leaders. The perversion lies in the idea that "Christianity offers a devious stratagem for indulging our desires *without having to pay the price for them*, for enjoying life without the fear for decay and debilitating pain awaiting us at the end of the day,"[8] because, presumably—and the presumption here involves an entire self-enclosed social imaginary—God himself has taken upon himself the totality of death, decay, and pain in an act of totally redemptive self-sacrifice.

My view of Christianity and Žižek's are divided by an epistemological chasm. The details of this matter are not my immediate concern on this occasion. Suffice it to say, as a first-order objection, it is precisely the enjoyment of life without fear of decay—which emerges out of the imaginary of a strictly nontheistic, tragic, guiltless sense of human mortality, of finitude without redemption, of existential emptiness—that abolishes all transcendental fear. What concerns us here, more specifically in terms of the vicissitudes of the real in the virtual—and, by all means, the necessity for a brutal critique against the indulgences of liberal relativism and identity multi-ism—is Žižek's attempt to rekindle the flames of transgression in a world self-subjugated to an erasure of political will.

It is likely that Žižek follows here Paul's exhortation that "where there is no law there is no transgression" (Romans 5:13) in order to argue in favor of the emancipatory necessity of law. In following this, however, he disregards that Paul's exhortation is meaningful only in heteronomous conditions, whereby law is the imposition of an external rule, the rule of an Other, against which I must enact a transgression if I am to get anywhere near an understanding and experience of freedom. In conditions of autonomy, however, where the primary rule is self-alteration—that is to say, otherness internally brought forth against self-mastery and the law authorized by those who recognize themselves in it—the whole dependency of transgression on the presence of the law, which Žižek configures as the core of his argument, is a nonsensical proposition. This lapse produces a mode of argument that leads to Žižek's claims in favor of authority and orthodoxy—"there never was anything so perilous and so exciting as orthodoxy," he declares—which is, moreover, conducted in the guise of a professed materialist (and, by his account, perverse) theorization of Christianity in order to repoliticize the conditions of Western societies.

I reiterate that Žižek rightly directs his wrath against the contemporary oppression of the permissible, the privatization of politics and desire that disciplines both politics and desire away from any sort of emancipatory action, the fetishism of identity politics and submission to the heteronomous idealization of the Other, and so on. But he does hesitate to go even further in theorizing a politics that places all authority—*authority itself*—under radical interrogation. Believing that such an all out interrogation would undo the dialectical interdependence between law and transgression, he cannot envision how an interrogative politics bears the kind of negative affirmation that is properly Hegelian and surely not some sort of degeneration into the "postmodernist," "postpolitical," cynical conditions of our times. So, he embraces instead—out of sheer stubborn resistance to the unacceptable reality of our contemporary life, of which there is no doubt—a politics that requires a kernel of authority, of orthodoxy, of faith, which he, of course, duly shapes with all kinds of brilliant negative dialectical gestures. No matter, the kernel of perversity (in Pauline Christianity, Leninism, Lacanian psychoanalysis, and so on) remains, to my mind, unreshapable. In a sense, this too is Žižek's point. The most perverse gesture of the master dialectician is to dialecticize a condition to the point where it "returns" *by virtue of having been thus altered* to its initially posited state.

In this light, Žižek's attraction to the great British mystery writer G. K. Chesterton, for example, is understandable. It emerges from his attraction to detective fiction and the thrilling thirst of the mystery genre. Perhaps, this might be a way to elucidate his attraction to metaphysical mystery as well. As a Catholic Christian thinker, Chesterton makes this specific connection his life's work. His motivation, like Žižek's, is worthy of being shared. But it also produces a desperate justification of dogma by correcting—one might even generously say, enriching—the inherited *doxa* of this dogma. I am happy, as a reader, to encounter this specific *doxa* enriched, but the dogma, unreshapable by definition, produces a distressing politics that annihilates all *doxa*.

One of Chesterton's arguments, which Žižek is fond of repeating, is that Christianity is the only religious imaginary in which God doubts his own existence. The reference is the occasion of Christ's evocation on the cross of having been forsaken. I cast aside, on this occasion, the crucial slippage of determining Christ on the cross as God pure and simple, so that thereby, in declaring God's forsaking, Christ would be addressing himself. The matter is hardly pure and simple, not merely theologically, about which brutal wars have been fought, but even in terms of ontological definition. Suffice it to say here, the ontological perversion in the figuration of Christ as both human and divine would falter if either of these essences were not taken in utter strictness, or if one essence would take precedence or ontological privilege over the other. But there is nonetheless a difference between the two, and it reflects the theological understanding of ontology basic to Christianity as a monotheistic religion: Christ is man, like any man (any wavering on this equivalence brings the whole paradoxical edifice crashing down), but he is God, not any god (quite obviously), but the One-and-Only God. The paradox of doubling the One-and-Only might be just as well theorized in terms of the constitutive non-coincidence of the one with itself, a basic *différance*, which is one of Žižek's favorite figures, except that curiously on this issue he does not venture in this direction. In any case, the two instances of like being are not of the same order *only* in this one sense: the being of any (man) vs. the being of the one-and-only (God). But because, as far as Christ is concerned, God and man (as essences) are always present together at once, the cry of having been forsaken cannot be entered into the logic of divine tautology, of God addressing—doubting, forsaking, declaring the absence of—himself, because at this very moment Christ is *also* (a simultaneity that alters the entire proposition) behaving like any man who doubts God in a moment of insufferable torment. This is Christ's greatest humanizing gesture. The gesture doesn't just humanize himself—therefore providing the *humanist* point of identification that will eventually, by the insidious ingenuity of Paul, spread Christianity beyond ethnoreligious divisions. It also humanizes God—because God is the father of a human, not in a symbolic sense, but in a *real-virtual* sense.

There is yet another issue in this example that Žižek doesn't quite figure out. His theorizing moment of "God being forsaken by God" is a moment of reading—a textual figure—whose language is recognizable only by an atheist Christian. A believer cannot possibly read this moment. For the believer, it is understandable—or, more precisely, it is readable—as a human moment: Jesus the man, the son, is expressing his despair at having been forsaken by his father (who also just happens to be God). The father's existence as such is never in doubt. The son is experiencing the reality of a painful delusion, as familiar as any in real life: the despair that all is for not. The impact of this story in the community of Christian believers resides precisely in this familiarity, and the whole matter is settled by the mystery of the Resurrection, which puts an irreversible end to Christ's human story and returns epistemological stability to the realm of monotheistic divinity.

Žižek misses the contours of this reading because his underlying point in evoking Chesterton is a critique against atheism, which he perceives a bit like he does liberalism: namely, it lacks the capacity for conviction and therefore succumbs to power without struggle. But, I would argue, Žižek's critique is leveled against Christian-derived atheism, no doubt the most widespread sort and the underlying imaginary for secularist dogmatism. Christian atheism is distilled in the declaration "I don't believe in God" (or "I don't believe there is a God"), which is a self-deluded statement in that it refuses to acknowledge that this negation participates in the terminological framework of belief, a discourse that, as far as matters of religion go, belongs to the epistemology of God. An atheism that will have emancipated itself from Christianity would render this matter irrelevant, or, more significantly, would recognize it as a matter of performance.

The all-out interrogation of authority I am suggesting—an interrogation that would further Žižek's polemic against conformity and depoliticization—would hinge on how one can perform one's worldly existence without God, not out of some sort of conviction, of belief in unbelief, but as a performance of a fact that eschews conviction, a performance of a fact that requires no demonstration or verification. This performance is always ephemeral, if nothing else because its object is groundless. It has to be constantly reperformed, each time anew, discontinuously even if constantly, repeated in utter singularity, untimely, ungrounded. The reality of this performance resides in its virtuality. Such real-virtual atheism would not be deconstructible; it is certainly not reducible to a convenient pretension, comfort zone, or conventional cynicism. Instead, it would stake out a position of living without presuming a content for the void of the Real, of living by assuming the void as core with no need to justify it, explain it, theorize it—without a need for a transcendental, metaperformative guarantee.

This radical performative (real-virtual) atheism would leave Christianity and all its social-imaginary mechanisms far behind. It would mean to live not as if God does not exist but *to live as if God does not matter*. It goes without saying that an argument about the irrelevance of the divine can't be conducted neutrally, as a moral, philosophical, or scientific argument; it is embedded in the performative politics of worldliness. A succinct moment of such atheist performativity is Woody Allen's quip in *Stardust Memories* (1980), where his character responds to the accusation of being an atheist with "To *you* I'm atheist. To God I'm the loyal opposition." Such performative politics renders belief or unbelief in God immaterial, much as it renders the question of God's existence or nonexistence irrelevant. Even more significantly, it thereby exposes that both discourses (belief and unbelief) consist in producing an authority materialized out of the immaterial, which occludes the encounter with worldly things that really matter. There is no way that the issue can be resolved by taking cover behind some sort of noncommittal agnosticism: "I don't really know if God exists or not, so I withdraw judgment in the matter." I side here with Ludwig Wittgenstein's sense that the strictly agnostic position is impossible. I cannot presume not to know with the certainty of knowledge. In Wittgenstein's (sense of) language, I cannot say, "I know that I don't know," Socrates notwithstanding, without compromising the radical power of nonknowledge (which obviously has nothing to do with ignorance). I cannot presume not to know because I would have to imagine (therefore, know) what it is I don't or cannot know. In this respect, a dogmatic atheism—or a "fundamentalist atheism," as Žižek invites us to consider, though he never quite develops it—would entail a self-defeating principle, entirely self-enclosed in the regime of belief in the name of unbelief. Indeed, a dogmatic atheism assumes that it can speak of God's nonexistence as a transcendental position, that is to say, as if this nonexistence exists beyond the world. In Wittgenstein's language: "the world is all that is the case."

What's left then? Following the Wittgensteinian demand, the point is to perform atheism without the least necessity, desire, or investment in its truth—to be an atheist without the least care to prove the validity of its meaning. But why should one do this at all—especially if one rejects the appeal to "reason" (or, in this case, secularism) as another instance of transcendentalist metaphysics? Apart from the strategic answer that pertains to a politics that seeks to counter the globality of religious politics, which has been efficiently disguised in Samuel Huntington's culturalist language of "the clash of civilizations," the answer involves a crucial subversive dimension. Living your life by performing the *fact* that God does not exist—solely, in the sense that God does not *matter*, not because you have a stake in the ontological status of the question of whether "God is or is not"—is to destabilize any guarantee of providence or destiny. Such lack of guarantee in meaning entails, of course, a tragic condition in altogether extreme terms. In moments of absolute happiness, of fulfillment, I have to remember—though this memory will do nothing *in itself* (as *value*) to compromise, subvert, or avert this condition—that such moments may constitute just as well moments of unraveling, of undoing, perhaps of destruction and horror.

This opens life to infinite possibility, or, even more, to the horizon of impossibility. Although Žižek rejects the tragic sensibility in the modern world as pseudopagan or simply cynical,[9] the conclusion of his lesson in the film *The Reality of the Virtual* speaks precisely of the tragic conditions under which one can practice (perform) the impossible. This he identifies as a utopian force, not in terms of some sort of futurist longing, but rather as the "presently impossible"—before adding, evocatively: "The point is not planning utopias but practicing utopias. The future will either be utopian or will be none." Yet, the politics of the *presently impossible* can only be a tragic politics, which embraces the performance and theatricality of life's decision at a social level, in the polis—in other words, a real-virtual *poiein-prattein*. This is, as well, another way of saying a radical democratic politics, a *realist* politics that exposes the heteronomy of permissibility and confronts it with the poetic praxis of othering oneself, of self-alteration.

Appendix: Recoil from the Real?—Žižek Out of Athens

Slavoj Žižek has emerged as a kind of oracular figure in contemporary radical politics.[10] No other intellectual commands instant attention when things go aflame or when things get so confused as to render all inherited political discourse unusable, which seems routine nowadays. This makes his silence on the December 2008 events in Greek cities all the more puzzling, especially when, by all accounts, these events reverberated profoundly in radical antiglobalization ranks and European state ranks alike. That the Invisible Committee, who claims authorship of *The Coming Insurrection* and the texts that followed (arguably some of the most incendiary texts in recent years), place their position in perspective with a reflection on the Greek events or that rebelling youth from Barcelona to Istanbul and from Cairo to Oakland index this specific insurrectionary manifestation in their own aspirations for action suggests that these events have acceded to worldwide significance and merit extensive rethinking.

Ten years after their occurrence, the Greek December events remain undeniably complex enough as to defy easy explanation and standard classification. The fact that the nihilist rebellion of high-school bourgeois kids was joined by immigrant youth from a variety of Balkan, Middle Eastern, and African backgrounds—many of them raised and even born in Greece, but bearing no citizenship rights—attests to a phenomenon that operates on a social, cultural, and political surplus in relation to strict nationally driven protests or marginal underclass explosions. Is Žižek's silence, regarding one of the major radical events in the first decade of the twenty-first century, evidence of his reluctance to engage with Balkan surplus when it does not fit standard "postsocialist" parameters? Or is there something about these particular events that exceeds the qualifications of most social-analytical rubrics, not just Žižek's? However we are to decide this, Žižek's inimitable trajectory against the grain of established norms demands that we engage the matter in his language. So, following the trail of Žižekian excursions in and out of the desert of the Real, we are compelled to ask this question again, in different terms, as possible recoil from the Real.

My brief comments here are predicated on two assertions. First, as I have already argued (and against typical assessments by devotees and detractors alike), Slavoj Žižek is a realist thinker. By this I mean to ascribe neither characteristics of a certain philosophical school nor some sort of commonsense pragmatist attitude. As to the first, Žižek's psychoanalytic way of thinking cannot be mathematized, although it would be worthwhile to consider how his Hegelian materialism does privilege a certain factuality of things. As to the second, the Žižekian idiom, no matter how much it flirts with the everyday, cannot be convincingly configured to trade in the realm of the commonsensical. Instead, I mean realism more in the way Brecht would have meant it: a realist thinker is the one who makes the worldly most tangible by foregrounding and elucidating its distortions—the distortions it produces and the distortions it suffers. In this respect, Žižek's long-term critique of postmodernist comfort and liberal delusion has been consistently accurate and indeed even predictive of all kinds of social and political calamities.

Second, whatever happened in Greece during December 2008 deserves to be called an insurrection, and, as all insurrections in history, it was spontaneous and uncontrolled: an eruption of extraordinary rage against all and in demand of nothing—or, just as well (to borrow a bit from the poetic language of the actors), in demand of all and against all established order, an order that, in their minds, amounts to nothing. It was an insurrection conducted initially by high-school students, who were eventually joined by a significant number of university students and undocumented immigrant workers, as well as by weathered anarchist groups and youth belonging to autonomist and freethinking circles of all kinds, politically, socially, and sexually. It is utterly misguided, however, to consider that autonomists and anarchists controlled the contours of the action in any way, and it goes without saying that the official parties on the Left were completely uninvolved—decidedly suspicious from the outset and, with few individual exceptions in the ranks, ultimately opposed to the movement in ways so typical as to be banal.[11]

In all honesty, my intellectual response to these events remains one of puzzlement. I refused, at the time, to rush into the realm of public assessment, as I felt that all the analytical tools I have inherited were indeed ineffective. In retrospect, puzzlement honors the seriousness of the event, which isn't to say that, as intellectuals, we should not try genuinely to evaluate the significance of what happens as it is happening. I cannot possibly account for why Žižek responded to the events with silence (or possibly even suggest that his silence is the outcome of his puzzlement or whatever else), but I do think there is a point in considering the significance of these events in relation to a Žižekian understanding of both radical politics and the psychic dimensions of societal unraveling. All the more so, since Žižek, unlike liberal thinkers of the Left, does not in fact recoil from the consideration of violence as a mode of societal transformation. To the contrary, he has endeavored to theorize societal violence beyond its conventionally understood political boundaries. I am referring specifically to his book *Violence* (2008), which, in expectantly Žižekian "sideways" fashion, treats the matter beyond the merely conceptual and historical.

It's worth noting here, in light of my confessed puzzlement, Žižek's following stipulation in regard to the Paris *banlieues* riots in the autumn of 2005:

> What needs to be resisted when faced with the shocking reports and images of the burning Paris suburbs is what I call the hermeneutic temptation: the search for some deeper meaning or message hidden in these outbursts. What is most difficult to accept is precisely the riots' meaninglessness: more than a form of protest, they are what Lacan called a *passage à l'acte*—an impulsive movement

> into action which can't be translated into speech or thought and carries with it an intolerable weight of frustration.[12]

I would certainly not hasten to equate the Paris events with the Athens events, but I do register our mutual resistance to the "hermeneutical temptation" regarding both cases. Most important is the reasoning behind such resistance. What one faces in such events is not an allegorical structure whose peculiar or even inscrutable language we must decipher, but a direct action whose language is untranslatable yet otherwise straight-up and overt, even if extreme and exaggerated. It is gestic, to remember Brecht again. This gestic language demands to be thought, sensed, and perhaps written, but not interpreted. Or rather, it may be interpreted but it is doubtful that whatever emerges as interpretation would not be mere recirculation of patented and projected meanings. This isn't to say that meanings are lacking. "Meaninglessness" here is used catachrestically. For, precisely because it is the gesture of an event, this untranslatable and uninterpretable gesture is otherwise profoundly signifying. It registers an abundance of signification (meaning), even while it remains meaningless in the recognizable syntax of contemporary politics.

Žižek accentuates this notion of meaninglessness because he wants to dismantle any causally minded, instrumentalist, or transcendentalist presumption in response to this sort of action, any imposition of meaning that would act as palliative for the terrible trouble the event compels:

> The riots were simply a direct effort to gain *visibility*. . . . [The protesters] found themselves on the other side of the wall which separates the visible from the invisible part of the republican social space. They were neither offering a solution nor constituting a movement for providing a solution. Their aim was to create a problem, to signal that they were a problem that could no longer be ignored. This is why violence was necessary.
>
> (V, 77)

In other words, if there is something communicated by the protesters, it is phatic: the sheer registration of their being—their *being-thus*, the sheer existence that is denied them, obscured and dissimulated by the continuous production of an identity conferred upon everyone: the consumer subject. In Athens, vicious attacks were made against shops of ubiquitous consumerism: computer stores, clothing boutiques, stores selling expensive eyeglasses, as well as, of course, banks. Government buildings—or university buildings (which, in Greece, belong to the state, as universities are public)—were secondary targets. The voluminous visual production of slogans, pamphlets, posters, stencils, graffiti, and so on also targeted not some specific ideology, but an insufferable way of life: the imposition of consumerist ways of being. The production and imposition of consumer subjectivity does indeed also produce specific conditions of what is visible and what slides under the horizon of vision. Middle class high-school students and immigrant youth came together on a specifically shared, even if uncanny, common ground: their non-participation in the travesty of citizenship, which duly renders them invisible in the present much as it sells out (thereby barring them from) their future. This particular point was made evident in the riotous action with brutal force and the sharpest sort of self-understanding, thus rendering further elaboration or interpretation useless (or, if nothing else, disingenuous). The insurgency sufficed as an unquestionable and untranslatable assertion, a frontal assault on presumed and conventionally accepted meaning.

This assertion of *being-thus* or *being-here*, if we may put it this way, produces a peculiar insurgency without demand. This is not to suggest, however, some sort of existential transcendentalism, but rather the undoing of the silent inclusion of masses of people into a position of invisibility and marginality—an inclusion that is indeed an exclusion. It's crucial to underline that this sort of assertion also bears, at a core level, the structural violence that is in fact an "objective" feature of contemporary societies. In this respect, violent insurgencies are symptomatic of the conditions they reject. This is not to compromise their radical significance, but to dispel notions of their abnormality, aberration, depravity, or what have you, which is how the language of liberal order defines them. Yet, orbiting this core level, there is, as Žižek points out, a dimension of "subjective violence" characterizing this assertion, a kind of counterviolence to the "objective" structural violence of the system that excludes it. In this sense, the conventional configuration of revolutionary violence as countermeasure to a status quo of violence exercised in the order of daily life has not been epistemologically overcome. So long as we don't get hung up on some sort of fetishization of alterity here (whether aberrant or redemptive), we can emphasize that this countering dimension indeed entails an altering (and self-altering) unfolding of the contradiction, even if the overt "ideological" demand is not present.

I certainly concur with Žižek's understanding of this kind of "subjective violence" as the emergent assertion of a placeless nonpart of society that thereby destroys social cohesion. More precisely, it thereby exposes the fact that social cohesion is a sham. No longer tied, even marginally, to the class structure of capitalist production, this placeless/invisible nonpart of the social body nonetheless restages the signification held once by the proletariat of industrial capitalism: "those who stand for a universal singularity, those who belong to a situation without having a specific 'place' in the situation, included but without any part in the social edifice. As such, this excluded non-part stands for the universal."[13] Žižek borrows Marx's notion of the proletariat's "insubstantial subjectivity" (*substanzlose Subjektivität*) in order to buttress his argument about this new placeless political subject that seemingly shows no respect for conventional politics. For Žižek, Marx is enhanced with a certain Jacobinism, stripped, of course, of its class interests down to its pure form: performing the sort of violence that alters the conditions of violence: "The standard liberal motto—that violence is never legitimate, even though it may be sometimes necessary to resort to it—is insufficient. From a radical emancipatory perspective, this formula should be reversed: for the oppressed, violence is always legitimate (since their status is the result of the violence they are exposed to) but never necessary (it will always be a matter of strategy whether or not to use violence against the enemy)."[14]

Formally speaking, I find this refreshing, especially after the many decades following François Furet's denigration of the legacy of the French Revolution to totalitarian politics, and the spinning out of this, in the hands of the old *nouveaux philosophes* (Bernard Henri-Lévy indefatigably chief among them) but also a curious cohort in France that spans from Alain Finkielkraut to Marcel Gauchet to some broad phantasm of terrorist violence that eventually comes to match the insurrection in the Paris *banlieues* with Islamic insurgency tout court. However, this daring reconfiguration of the Jacobin imaginary against the grain of insipid postmodern liberalism loses ground when it collapses into grandstanding callings for a new communism, following primarily Alain Badiou's directions. Here too, Žižek's position is more nuanced, but at the same time confuses the deserved demolition of postmodern liberalism with a nostalgic invocation of the language of "lost causes"—lost universals. The desire is right on mark; but the name of desire means a historical somersault. Let's look at an indicative passage: "The only way to grasp the true novelty of the New is to analyze the world through the lenses of what was 'eternal' in the Old. If communism really is an 'eternal' Idea, then it works as a Hegelian 'concrete universality': it is eternal not in the sense of a series of abstract-universal features that may be applied everywhere, but in the sense that it has to be re-invented in each new historical situation."[15] But, of course, communism is not an eternal idea. The very thought would make Marx's skeleton rattle. It is a social-historical formation and, as such, a finite one, except for the added twist that it is a core element of modernity, a social-historical formation that has *so far* defied its finitude. The very notion of "being re-invented in each new historical situation" is the way of modernity—and indeed (although this is another conversation) the way of secularity. With this much clear—that modernity enables communism to work itself out of the strict social-historical bounds of its institution, to be invented anew—it would be essential to guard against a recent trend to seek, on behalf of communism, some premodern analogue. This entails an unfortunate confusion of communism with various traditions of communalism, most of which—and this is hardly accidental—underline representations of the ways of early Christianity.

This gets very close to territory carved out by Charles Taylor and his acolytes into which Badiou and Žižek, in their adoration of Pauline thinking, unwittingly slide. Of course, Taylor hardly has communism in mind, but his investment in Early Christian communities as models of radical institution that repeal the excesses of both modernity and postmodernity amounts to the same delusion. The fact of the matter is that communism *and* capitalism, the two great enemies, are both bound by their social-imaginary institution within the historical range of modernity, whether we like it or not. (Here, the question of the presumed difference of postmodernity would not take us very far.) And while the victory of one over the other may remain a genuine fantasy in the various ideological positions that claim it on either side, the imaginary dialectical *co-incidence* of the two formations cannot be exorcised by gestures of a desire to return to some sort of premodernity, no matter what may be the seriousness of the impetus or the sophistication of the argument. Moreover, in the end, Christian-based communalism is nothing more than the stripping away of worldly hierarchy in the name of collective slavery to God—a reprehensible proposition on any political ground, short of the politics of *doulocracy* or a contemporary affirmation of what Etienne de la Boétie once called "voluntary servitude."[16]

So a question arises relative specifically to Žižek's quotation: Why wouldn't one formulate this exact phrasing—the Hegelian concrete universal "to be reinvented in each new historical situation"—using radical democracy in place of communism? Surely, to enact provocation by the mere use of a name that can be reinvented precisely in the moment when it is most discredited is not sufficient grounds for radical thinking. Besides, one may additionally protest: Why is the name of communism more (or less?) discredited than the name of democracy? What matters is obviously not the performative undoing of the ideology that discredits, but the very terms of the proposition. In this sense, the reinvention of significational terms in relation to new historical situations is paradigmatic of radical democracy, whose epitome is relentless attention to contingency as epistemological source. This brings into the form of radical democracy all kinds of radical anticapitalist and antiliberal content, including, of course, anarchism and anarcho-syndicalism, as well as communism—at least, workers' councils communism, which was communism's most radical and emancipatory content. (To think that one would opt to invoke Christian communalism over workers' councils communism in order to renew the content of the name simply boggles the mind.) In the end, communism without democracy is nothing. Or rather, it is Communism, that is, the very authoritarian bureaucratic formation that precipitated some of the most reprehensible moments of twentieth-century history.

Žižek's total repudiation of democracy parallels his repudiation of liberalism, marred perhaps by an unthoughtful collapse of the two in his uncritical reproduction of the conventional meaning of the name *democracy*. This name is surely overburdened and may be beyond rehabilitation—that too is another discussion—but the same can be said about the name *communism*. Curiously, in one of his many attacks against postmodern liberal depoliticization and production of social stupidity, Žižek, with the full relish of perversion, gives the name of *liberal communists* to the likes of Bill Gates and George Soros and the general capitalist defanging of human self-empowerment that their world precipitates (V, 15–39). Again, Žižek's demolition of the pernicious edifice of privilege in postmodern capitalist societies is correct and insightful—indeed, welcome. Yet, behind it stands an equally pernicious predilection for what, from my standpoint, figures as faux asceticism, which ultimately subverts the radical impetus.

Žižek assails the machinery of pleasure that gets in the way of the larger things in life, the life-altering things, the real encounters with the other—which is to say, the real encounters with the Real. Hence, he identifies pleasures as narcissistic, petty, or stupid. There is, however, something puritanical in this sensibility, something Christian and Communist alike (to my mind, not so different when it comes to matters of morality or desire). I understand and share his frustration with the incapacity of contemporary "Western" societies to embrace large causes that exceed (and undo) the restricted dimensions of everyday petty demands. But it is everywhere present in Žižek's sensibility that, in spite of the evident *jouissance* of his writing, his gesture marks an option for the abstract way of looking at the largeness of things social—and here I don't mean "abstract" in the Hegelian sense, which would mean the most concrete, but literally as the unworldly, the disembodied, the formalistic.

Pleasure need not be confined in the prison house of private desire, no matter what postmodern capitalism enacts as entertainment industry. Nor is pleasure that is, strictly speaking, individual or personal (which isn't at all to say, private) restricted to some figure of the imaginary of modernity. Rather, pleasure is partial to the most concrete ways of the human animal, and this defies temporal/cultural characteristics, although obviously it does not transcend the historical determinations of the human-animal psyche. Who is to say that carving the insides of a cave in Lascaux was not a moment of personal pleasure—even if the sense of "personal" may have been perhaps unattainable, and even if the meaning (the imaginary signification) of pleasure may have been profoundly other to what we now understand? In the end, whichever way, we're merely theorizing. But theorizations that seek to diminish (or even eradicate) the concrete knowledge of how even the smallest, most ephemeral pleasures of life emerge from the most profound encounter with the other, the most real encounter with the Real, are just empty theorizations, gestures of grandstanding, indeed transcendentalizing pseudoaspirations.

The sheer, unadulterated, maddeningly unavoidable knowledge of our mortality demands that we show care toward even the most ephemeral pleasure in full cognizance of its unavoidable vanishing. For the real encounter with other, the real encounter with the Real, occurs in the full light of this cognizance. And although, yes, revolutions are not made as symphonies of ephemeral pleasures, who could possibly dispute that revolutions are not as such, as events, ephemeral moments of unlimited psychic excess, of *jouissance*, as well? In the end, Žižek's limit point is the foreignness—the dissonance in his ears—procured by any encounter with the tragic sense of Eros. This is why he bristles at any suggestion of tragic life and ridicules any suggestion of the pagan as New Age hedonism. Generally, Žižek's facile determination of pagan sensibility in New Age terms betrays a stressful incapacity to deal with tragic being. He ridicules the New Age obsession with balance (ying-yang principle or the symmetry of "male" and "female" principles), ignoring the fact that this naïve notion of balance is totally foreign to, say, the pre-Socratic imaginary of balance achieved by the multiplicity of forces in interminable and terrifying antagonism framing the groundless and infinite chaos of existence, in relation to which there is neither calculation nor redemption.

For similar reasons, Žižek's understanding of myth remains conventional, which at the very least compromises the radical elements of his critique.[17] Moreover, he fails at the theorization of the cryptomythical elements of all theological imaginaries, whereby mythification turns to mystification. This ubiquitous conflation of the mythical with the mystical is achieved precisely because the tragic element of myth is effaced. Without the tragic, myth becomes simply a social identification mechanism or, as it is taken for granted, it gets harnessed to the regime of truth as its opposite. Even Žižek's intelligent argument in favor of atheism in *Violence*, which could be said to roll back some of his previous (self-admittedly perverse) adorations of Pauline Christianity, resonates doubtfully because it is an atheism that doesn't understand the unmasterable indeterminacy of the tragic—an indeterminacy that is archaic and has nothing to do with the imaginary that reveres indeterminacy in contemporary theory. In the end, Žižek's invoked atheism is an atheism that denies the tragic by not annihilating the unconscious Christianity that authorizes it. And to deny the tragic is to recoil from the Real.

Which brings me to the historical context that animated these reflections at the outset. Žižek's nonresponse to the Greek events of December 2008 continues to register its deafening silence. The question it poses is double: First, what is it about this event that rescinds Žižek's inimitable discursive affluence? And second, how does this silence (re)signify the otherwise uninterrupted discursive flow? I'm not sure I can answer the first question without merely speculating. This does not diminish whatsoever the question's bona fide accession to the Real. But the second question is more tangible. At least, it points directly to the core problem of the Žižek phenomenon. Nothing is more powerful and more problematic than Žižek's discursive onslaught. It's not merely the incomparable speed of textual production and, consequently, the immeasurable volume of positions and counterpositions amassed over the years. It is the inimitable panache of addressing everything, of speaking about everything, and of evaluating everything all together and all at once. It would be false to characterize this as a symptom of a certain immanent tendency in both psychoanalytic and Marxist thinking (Žižek's incontestable discursive pillars) toward totalizing exegesis. I say this because, although this tendency is indeed immanent, both psychoanalysis and Marxism are not *necessarily* (that is, in a deterministic way) totalizing, but rather, because of an equally immanent tendency toward dialectical self-interrogation, they can just as well be (or become) fragmentational toward both the totalization of knowledge and themselves. So, there may be something in Žižek-speak itself that precipitates this problem.

If that's the case, we can perhaps consider the question from another angle: What sort of readership practices does Žižek's writing produce? Or even more crudely: What sort of reader does Žižek produce? Let's be clear: I'm speaking of serious engaged readers, not dismissive enemies or adoring fans. When one speaks of everything all together and all at once, one is caught inevitably in a web of repetition and contradiction. In and of itself, this is not a problem, unless there are demands for systematic thinking. Contrary to what may be the impression, there is nothing systematic in Žižek's thinking. This is another confirmation of his being a realist. But Žižek does not present himself as some sort of belles lettres essayist who dazzles the small community of a cultured salon. This very image would bring out of him the most vehement of sarcasms. His work is attractive, in large part, because of its passionate calling for action, for its irreverent, insurrectionary fervor. And yet, this is precisely where his machine-like mode of production fails him. The boundless proliferation of discursive spinning out of everything all together and all at once produces a debilitated reader (again, dismissive enemies and adoring fans exempted), a reader caught in the sea of repetition and contradiction, a reader disheveled by switching back and forth between marginal scribbling of "Brilliant!" and "Nonsense!": a reader debilitated by ambivalence and thus dissociated from the *real* stakes of the work's relation to reality—in this sense, yes, a "psychotic" reader whose capacity for action in the real world is likely to be deployed in the realm of fantasy.

It is precisely for these reasons, for the fact that reading Žižek is a serious, arduous, and in the best sense provocative task and for the fact that action in fantasy must somehow discover again its pathway to the world, that we must be poised to read not what Žižek says but what he doesn't say. We must be attuned not just to his repetitions and contradictions but to his silences, to those nodal points in his voluminous writerly excess where he does indeed, unwittingly or not, recoil from the Real. Only then, perhaps, we may begin to really engage with his politics.

Postscript

And there is yet another turn. Two years after this last section was written, and in the midst of the Greek economic crisis and the Greek people's struggle to resist the punitive domination of global capital, Žižek took an explicit and vocal position on the side of those resisting in precisely the way that the best of his radical thinking demands.[18] *All this was further theorized in his book* The Year of Dreaming Dangerously *(2012), where his analysis of the Greek situation figures prominently in his overall political ruminations. His insights here are commendable. There is much for us to learn in thinking critically and in thinking ahead into the future about the Greek situation, just as there is much here to show that Žižek too has learned a great deal from being closely engaged with Greek politics. His subsequent intervention on behalf of the SYRIZA government against the grain of idiotic self-satisfied leftism that criticized it in the moment of its first (self-)defeat is indeed memorable and, for me personally, refreshing as we both struggled to articulate the importance of governmental power of the Left in the midst of neoliberal order, no matter what may be, always in easy retrospect, the Left's incapacities.*[19]

CHAPTER 5

PAUL'S GREEK

The Pope's Word

The lecture by Pope Benedict XVI at the University of Regensburg (where he had been a student and later professor of theology) became an instant cause celèbre. The clamor was such that, in the American headlines, it displaced the aftermath of the fifth anniversary of 9/11—the lecture took place just one day later, on September 12, 2006—which had been orchestrated by a media blitz as an outpouring of Christian faith and patriotic resolve. The controversy centered on what was to become for weeks afterward a notorious quotation: "Show me just what Mohammed brought that was new, and there you will find things that are only wicked and inhumane, such as his command to spread by the sword the faith he preached." The fact that these were not the pope's own words, that he was quoting the fourteenth-century Byzantine emperor Manuel II Paleologus, was dismissed as inconsequential, with remarks attributing to him the shrewdness of a rhetorician—using a front to speak his mind—and going so far as to claim that, whatever the rhetorical technique, slighting Islam was indeed the pope's intention.[1]

Setting aside discourses of intentionality, no doubt the quotation carries an anti-Islamic gesture. But this disparaging gesture should hardly raise our eyebrows, when considered next to such profoundly anti-Islamic practices of American government officials—or, for that matter, the overall history of Christianity. That it became such an issue is the outcome of mass media, both Christian and Islamic, feeding precisely on such rhetoric of polarization. That scholars and academics got hung up on this phrase, however, is a disappointing reminder that, in fact, they do not read. Surely the pope's lecture could be deemed controversial from a certain standpoint, yet this standpoint—as the impetus and theses of the lecture demonstrate—has only symptomatically to do with Islam. The lecture addresses the contemporary conditions of Christianity, both internal and external, and serves as a call to reconsider current theological and religious practices.[2]

The lecture is aptly titled "Faith, Reason, and the University," and it delivers what it promises with stark symmetry. The three notions are used as coextensive tools of an inquiry into how Christianity can reclaim the ground of *universitas* from the domain of secular life: "the reality that, despite our specializations which at times make it difficult to communicate with each other, we make up a whole, working in everything on the basis of a *single rationality* with its various aspects and *sharing responsibility for the right use of reason*" (my emphasis). Whatever its multiplicity, this ground is marked by a single language—it may be conjured up as the passage by which *communitas* becomes *universitas*—and this language is at once something more than a language, or perhaps something more than language as such. It is "more than" because, however we measure it, this ground is accessible specifically by a sort of compulsion to exceed—a compulsion to be more than ourselves, more than our one self, by a commitment to sharing what might be called our indebtedness to reason. For, from the outset, the stipulation is that *universitas*, this univocal space, is achieved not merely by the community that exists in it and by virtue of it, but in many ways against it, beyond it, and, it might be fair to add, in spite of it. Unlike the notion that a university is a space where a multitude (a *community*) of discourses—indeed, antagonistic, contentious discourses—exists in abundance, the pope's notion is animated by an injunction: "sharing responsibility for the right use of reason."

I don't need to belabor the point that this sharing (this *communitas*) is, in effect, a misnomer, since the plurality to which it alludes is automatically undone by its object: the univocal, the unique, the *one and only*, which is how the pope understands *universitas*. Reason is right by virtue of this monological framing—not the other way around. Again, the pope's invocation is not a call but an injunction. It is not a call to enter the community of rational exchange, whereby presumably there exists de facto the understanding of contention and antagonism (in other words, the dream space of liberalism), but it is an injunction to participate—sharing, yes, but in *one voice* (a "single rationality")—in the *right use* of reason. Nor do I need, in addition, to belabor the point that this move from exchange to sharing spells out a move from the secular university to the univocal congregation of the faithful.

This passage is exactly what the lecture conceives as its object, what it calls forth (from the darkness of history, we might say) as the singular space that claims to know, claims to own, *what is right*. That this, in essence, dogmatic claim showcases the work of reason cannot be simply reduced to yet another play of the dialectic of Enlightenment. But, no doubt, it mobilizes the most authoritative Enlightenment rationalism in order to raise the stakes beyond a simple devotional exhortation or theological intervention. In speaking of "reasonableness of faith" or "coherence within the universe of reason" the pope is speaking like a Kantian. Given Kant's own piety, this is hardly a joke. In a lecture in which she briefly glossed over this passage, Judith Butler quipped aside bemusedly, in reference to the pope: "Whom has he been reading?"—the playful answer presumably being "theory." But there is a real and obvious answer, as far as I'm concerned. He has, of course, been reading Manuel Paleologus, but there is no doubt he has already (long ago and at length) read his Kant, his Hegel, his Nietzsche, his Heidegger. And although he embodies the supreme authority of Catholic theology, he knows his Martin Luther by heart. There is a simple, worldly, secular fact here that everyone deems too trivial to notice: the pope is a German intellectual and as such he is the product of German *Bildung*. If we ignore this historical element, if we read the pope as another dogmatist speaking to the servile constituency of the faithful, then his extraordinary demand to repeal "the dehellenization of Christianity" would appear either capricious or inscrutable.[3]

Whatever we might want to say about this lecture, whether we concentrate on its anti-Islamism, its anti-mysticism, its anti-Protestantism, or its anti-secularism—and it pertains to all at once—or however we might want to criticize it, attack it, or discredit it, we will have achieved nothing if we don't encounter this demand as its core thesis, its raison d'être. What the pope names straight out as the "dehellenization of Christianity" is what he brings to the table for consideration, discussion, critique—what, by the conclusion of his lecture, he will define in expressly Kantian terms as a "critique of modern reason from within." His decision to bring Manuel Paleologus out of the library dust—by way, it must be said, of Adel Théodore Khoury, an Arab Catholic theologian and one of the most eminent Church scholars of Islamic theology and history—cannot be understood outside this gesture.

In the continuation of the controversial passage about Islam, the pope focuses on Manuel's secondary elaboration: "not acting reasonably is contrary to God's nature." The translation (drafted directly from Khoury's French) pales before the Greek phrasing, burdened as it is with modernity's weight on signification. The original—*τὸ μὴ σὺν λόγῳ ποιεῖν ἀλλότριον Θεοῦ*—could be rendered, somewhat clumsily, as follows: "not creating [*poiein*] by partaking of reason [*syn logō*] is alien [*allotrion*] to God." It is important to notice here the detail of the phrasing *syn logō* (with or alongside reason, partaking of reason) and not *en logō* (within reason, in the purview of reason). Nowhere do we see a sense of the total inclusiveness or total significational dominance of *logos*. Given the multiple meanings of *poiein* and *logos*, of course, the phrase could easily mean, in simple language: "not acting with words is alien to God." In any case, for Manuel Paleologus, God is merely—but so profoundly and essentially—a matter of *logos*, which is almost banal considering the famous opening of John's Gospel. Whatever is deemed to be *alogon* (as Paleologus goes on to elaborate) is confined to an essential otherness, a domain radically excluded from the provenance of God, an alien space. Given that, the erudite Byzantine emperor frames this otherness around the use of violence in the profession of faith and the proliferation of conviction (i.e., religious conversion) is inordinately ironic, not in reference to Islam (to which it is addressed), but in light of the entire history of Christianity, not to mention the fact that it was produced at an encampment site during a respite from battling the infidels.

Dehellenization?

Pope Benedict's key question is brutally clear: "Is the conviction that acting unreasonably contradicts God's nature merely a Greek idea, or is it always and intrinsically true?" For those who don't dismiss him out of hand as just the pope, the question is classic: Is knowledge and praxis a matter of external historical dynamics or immanent to itself, intrinsic to the very terms that make it knowable? This classic, perhaps typical, question is treated with a rather typical equivocation: history—in this case, very specifically, the historical import of Greek philosophy—is commensurate (his word is "harmonious") with the internal plenitude of the Christian faith. In other words, an old problem is shoved right in our face: What is the relation of Christianity to ancient Hellenism? That the pope opts to situate the beginnings of an answer in the famous opening of John's Gospel—"In the beginning was the Word"—is a gesture far beneath the magnitude of the question and hardly flattering to his evident intellect. But dogma is dogma, after all, and to demand more from him—much as to demand from him respect for Islam—is a useless expectation.

The question he articulates, however, is extremely important, particularly since it pertains to one of the most significant institutions of secular modernity: the university. Given, moreover, the historical specifics of the situation, the object in question is the German university, the institution that bears the quintessential tradition of German *Bildung* from Wilhelm von Humboldt onward. (This historical signpost is not a pedantic matter but the cipher to the whole problem.) The point is that, whatever the resort to the immanence and prescience of dogma, the examination of this tumultuous conjuncture in the Hellenistic world that eventually produced the global domination of the Christian Church cannot be conducted strictly in terms of ancient history proper. It passes through the history of modernity, indeed the history of secularization itself, through which it achieves a paradoxical condition: On the one hand, it expands the domination of Christianity even further, to extents unfathomable even by the Pauline ambition of universal expansion. On the other hand, it produces the social imaginary (in the last instance, unavoidably Nietzschean) that will dare proclaim a horizon beyond Christianity, even if such a horizon could only be a void.

The pope essays a clever path that presumably would outmaneuver this quandary by proclaiming modernity itself, in its paradoxical condition, to embody the annihilation of the ancient conjuncture that made it possible. That he does this with the weapons of modernity—as I said, he speaks like a Kantian—is one of the most glaring lapses in his argument. But let us consider what he says more carefully. The pope predictably refers to the Apostle Paul as the exemplar of the fact that "the encounter between the Biblical message and Greek thought did not happen by chance." That he attributes a providential character to a historical accident, by invoking Paul's dream-visions of the call to convert the Gentiles as a divine "distillation of the intrinsic necessity of a rapprochement between Biblical faith and Greek inquiry," hardly bears comment. What should be underlined instead is his insistence on the *necessary* entwinement of a decidedly pagan sensibility of interrogating the divine with the spiritual affirmation of an imagination that is existentially dependent on the certainty of revelation and redemption. What is the nature of this necessity? What produces it? In what terms, internal or external, is it justified? What sort of cognitive armory does it mobilize in order to abolish the historical contingency that produces it? These questions are not addressed, but we cannot allow them to remain unaddressable.

The pope's historical consciousness paints a picture in which the "profound encounter between faith and reason, . . . between enlightenment and religion" in the antiquity of early Christianity is betrayed first by medieval theology (in the hands on Duns Scotus, he tells us) and then—no surprise here—by the Reformation. The result is the emergence of an idea of God that propels divinity to the position of absolute alterity and an idea of religious practice that propels the faithful to a boundless voluntaristic devotion to communicating with this alterity by means of the Word: the Lutheran call for *sola scriptura*. We might say that, in both gestures, we discern an enchantment. The Word becomes magic, as much as the encounter with God, now an unnamable mystery, precipitates the workings of a radically personal miracle.

The pope sees the "dehellenization of Christianity" conducted in three historical instances: sixteenth-century Reformation; nineteenth- and twentieth-century liberal theology; the contemporary conjunction between theological fundamentalism and cultural relativism. It isn't immediately clear what thread might have brought these instances together in a process that takes up the last four centuries of "Western" history. The first instance inaugurates a radical disengagement of faith from knowledge, but also, as a consequence, from history, understood here in terms of Antonio Gramsci's notion of "inventories of the present." According to this logic, the Reformation granted to faith a disembodied otherworldliness that solidified its heteronomous hold over the human sphere, even beyond its strict adherence to the discourse of religion. This leads Pope Benedict, interestingly, to argue that Kant's radical opening to practical reason was forged out of borrowing the otherworldly space of faith, even when his explicit object was a worldly morality. In effect, the pope argues that both Luther and Kant eradicate philosophy in favor of morality and make knowledge the object of faith—in God and reason, respectively.

In the second instance, whose identified patrimony is the liberal theology of Adolf von Harnack, theology and morality were reduced to a sort of humanistic scientism, ultimately pushing not only philosophy but also faith as such out of the axiomatic boundaries of knowledge. As a result, theology becomes religion (by now split between the customary practices of the faithful and an academic discipline of comparative historical inquiry), much as the project of practical reason turns into the project of natural science. For Pope Benedict, classic nineteenth-century secularization signifies the second defeat of philosophy.

He says the least about the third instance, which he identifies as "dehellenization in progress." The implicit gesture alludes to the danger of a cultural relativism that has no tolerance for even the historical construction of the so-called Greco-Western imaginary institution, producing crude, uneducated anti-Westernisms. There seems to be an attempt here to criticize whatever efforts seek to return to a primary Christianity that can be absolved from the excesses of modernity and, having thus been cleansed, can be made available to whatever new "inculturation" may seem fit. His target is both the secular dismissal of the cognitive propensities of religion and, yet also, the (equally secular) politics of identity that claim Christianity to be an ahistorical entity that can be bent and shaped according to whatever—here we must say (though the pope does not) *political*—purposes a given constituency (Christian or non-Christian, Western or non-Western) sees fit. Secularist reason "which is deaf to the divine and which relegates religion to the realm of subcultures is incapable of entering into the dialogue of cultures," Pope Benedict concludes, though he is either unaware or dismissive of the implications that his concern—"the dialogue of cultures"—finds its essential significance in a secular cognitive realm, regardless of the specific residual theological content. What he does imply, as far as I can tell, but does not engage in any direct sense is that the degradation of Protestant sectarianism, which has produced American fundamentalist evangelical cults, is but one more instance in the long process of the "dehellenization of Christianity." This process, much like Christianity itself, he implies, is a historical matter. This historicity doesn't take anything away from the internal theological integrity of the faith. On the contrary, "dehellenization" is a code term for the charge of disregarding and violating the historical parameters of the faith, which de facto signifies the distortion and violation of the theological plenitude of the faith.

Taking seriously this assertion of "the dehellenization of Christianity" hardly means adopting Pope Benedict's concerns, or his conceptions of what this assertion might mean. Nevertheless, the assertion does demand that, by inference, we best consider the question of Christianity's Hellenization. What might this mean? Did it ever happen? If not, what the hell is the pope talking about? If yes, it did happen, then is the field of inquiry opened up by the event of Hellenization a matter of historical or philosophical inquiry? And what does "Hellenized" mean in relation to "Hellenic"? Surely, they are not equivalent. The past participle denotes a transformation: Christianity was at some point Helleniz*ed*, therefore it was not Hellenic, which in turn leads to the question of what it was before this moment of alleged Hellenization. Was it Christianity, or was it something else? If it was not Christianity, the notion of its Hellenization becomes incomprehensible—what was indeed the entity that was Hellenized?—unless we go so far as to assert that it is precisely this event named "Hellenization" that makes Christianity comprehensible, that *makes it Christianity.* But then, the charge of its having been dehellenized would have to mean that Christianity has long ago been annihilated, and the brutal reality of history disputes such hypotheses.

These questions regarding Hellenization haven't concerned theologians since antiquity, in effect since the time that Hellenes who still hadn't become Christians existed in the outer contours of the early Christian communities. When the question is broached by historians, it can either yield some important insights into what Peter Brown has famously named "the making of late antiquity" or it can easily be reduced to those neoclassical Orientalist theses that laid the foundations for the institution of world religions in the nineteenth century.[4] Whatever the case, the theological (or, some would say, philosophical) dimensions of the matter remain at the level of cliché indicatively invoked by the pope with a matter-of-factness that, from a historical standpoint, is mind-boggling: "The New Testament was written in Greek and bears the imprint of the Greek spirit, which had already come to maturity as the Old Testament developed."

Serious commentary fails against this baffling statement. Let me just say that even simply the notion of "the Greek spirit" is quintessentially un-Greek. I mean this in historical terms, if measured according to the self-conceptualization of society and its modes of knowledge that prevailed in antiquity, even late antiquity. We can perhaps speak, as Cornelius Castoriadis does, of a Greek imaginary (and even then he specifies it precisely as a "political imaginary"). We can speak of Greek conceptions of the polis or the psyche, even (with an enormous degree of generalization) of divinity or the cosmos. But to speak of "the Greek spirit" is already to speak in a Christian sense that remains tacit behind the assertion that modernity, as a "Greco-Western" institution, can lend its terms to all of history, past and present.[5] No doubt, to further say that this spirit had matured along with the prophetic development of the Old Testament into the New is dogmatically (i.e., theologically) Christian and absurd in any other sense. What remains is the equally absurd—or, let us say kindly, intellectually stretched-out—notion that the language in which a text is written—well, *the* text—is inspired, instilled, imbued, imprinted with a spirit that bears the name of this language. The very phrasing attributes an a priori sacredness to the Greek by virtue of a spirit inhabiting and passing on through language, which is—this, if nothing else—positively un-Greek. It establishes, in other words, a Christianization of the Greek at the primary level of signification, thereby provoking us to consider, contrary to the pope's logic, that it is the advent of Christianity instead, particularly insofar as it is textually woven with the Greek language, which signifies de facto—in a specific historical sense—the dehellenization of a great number of societies in the ancient Mediterranean.

Paul's Greek

Yet, this query is a matter of language, all the more because it isn't a matter of spirit. It is noteworthy (though hardly curious) that the pope mentions the New Testament in general as the Greek text in question, at least in terms of the language that provides its textuality, instead of, even if only parenthetically (noting the point of its inclusion), naming Christianity's actual first encounter with the Greek language: the texts of the Apostle Paul.

The significance of Paul's writings, before one ventures to examine their philosophical and political value, is that they are the initial Christian texts, predating the first Gospel by two decades. They are the only texts that can literally be called a testament, because, as epistles, they are declamatory and testimonial, with a specific addressee and always with a specific and deliberate purpose. These texts encounter their addressees and their purpose with the same clarity they encounter the specific conditions of their production. Paul may articulate, with grand and poetic gestures, the power of the void, but he makes sure we all know that he does not address the void—that he addresses real Christians in real circumstances, with real bodies and real minds, with the mark of the world all over them, in them, and around them. It would be more precise to say that he addresses the real—the *worldly*, for that is what he is most anxious to encounter—conditions of becoming and being a Christian, *the reality of being a Christian.*[6]

This reality, this outmaneuverable specificity, demands that Paul addresses his audience in Greek. The Greek language merely bears the *worldly* reality of his project. It is not incidental or instrumental in his project; it is immanent to his project insofar as this project has an explicit political and institutional aim. Thus, Greek is the language of Christianity not as a philosophical language but as the language of reality. It is the most tangible element of Christianity's worldliness, no matter what may be the content or the signification established in this language that promises to abolish worldliness altogether. By the hand of Paul, Christianity learns to speak Greek in order to enter the world, in order to actualize itself as a worldly project, and only as a consequence of this actualization does Christianity then get to claim Greek as its idiom. Christianity desires the philosophical currency of Greek only to the extent that it seeks to make its newfangled theology current. To make theology current means not only to make it contemporary with its time frame (which in another language will come to mean to *secularize* theology) but, at the same time, to endow theology with a powerful force that flows across boundaries—in effect, universalizing it. The resulting theologization of a philosophical idiom with the aim of universalism subsequently becomes the very mark of Christianity's occultation, for there is nothing generically universalist in Greek philosophy, despite the enormous hegemonic legacy of Platonism.

The contemporary reinvocations of Paul as a political theologian of actual philosophical power (even when this is coded in an anti-philosophical gesture, as in Alain Badiou's reading) propose a different account of this encounter, to the degree that they bother at all. The most drastic and impressive remark about Paul's Greek occurs in Jacob Taubes's anecdotal introduction to his remarkable lectures on Paul at Heidelberg in 1987. These lectures mark a rare occasion when a text honestly merits the claim of being a life's work. They are the *actual* culmination of an idiosyncratic intellectual life, as they chronicle the battle of a restless mind to persevere against the finality of a body already (and irredeemably) claimed by death, as Taubes's cancer is by then in an advanced state. Consequently, he strikes from the outset a testimonial tone, for his evident object of inquiry (Paul) is in effect himself. I am not saying stupidly that Taubes sees himself in Paul. I am saying that contemplating the significance of Paul is tantamount to the most elemental philosophical gesture: contemplating the question of life as this is signified by the encounter between oneself and the world. To risk a blunt conclusion from my impression of reading this text, I could say that Taubes's desire for Paul's vision is so overwhelming as to provoke us to imagine that he could in effect desire to be a Christian solely and exclusively on this basis, while at the same time relishing, as a Jew, a celebration of the most radical Jewishness of Paul, a Jewishness that the overwhelming majority of Jews, Taubes implies, just don't understand.[7]

Therefore, the testimonial drama of this text rightly demands an anecdotal, self-referential introduction to the problem of Paul's Greek, which also happens to be the veritable introduction to the text proper—as it very well should be.

The question of Paul's Greek, as I have said, is not merely a matter of using language. It is a matter of *the world signifying and being signified by this language*, and in this sense being the core figure in the assessment of Paul's historical significance. So, Taubes relates two instances: one in which his teacher in Zurich, Emil Steiger (a Germanist and classicist), quips ("with great bitterness," Taubes tells us) that Paul's language "isn't Greek, it's Yiddish!"; and second, some years later in New York, when Taubes pursues the issue by posing the same problem to Kurt Latte, a historian of religion and "a great philologist" with an allegedly "special ear for Greek and Latin," in order to receive the answer: "You know, Mr. Taubes, I cannot grasp [Paul's Letters] with my Greek ear."[8]

This stunning statement, if not Taubes's entire enterprise, deserves a pause. We fail profoundly if we don't ask, very simply: A Greek ear? What is a Greek ear? Surely not the ear of a philologist. No more than the ear of an Orientalist is a Persian ear, an Arab ear, or a Jewish ear. Or perhaps I'm acting quickly. The ear of a German philologist may be the quintessential Greek ear. Insofar as the stigma of one's language cannot—does not—register its meaning without the action of what Jacques Derrida, so long ago already, called "the ear of the other"; insofar as from the entire history of modernity read backward we glean the stigma of "the Greek" as always having been registered by ears other than Greek; insofar as the so-called Greco-Western institution attributes to "what is Greek" all the projections of myriad histories of myriad others as to "what is Greek" (others within it and others against it)—well, then, yes, the Greek ear *is* the ear that discerns in the Greek its own otherness. Or, we might equally say, by the most elemental demand of dialectics: it is the ear that discerns the otherness in the Greek.

But in evoking this resonance, I'm moving too fast. The *otography* that Taubes finds necessary to procure from his "Hellenized" teachers and colleagues is a double for the explicit *autography* his contemplation of Paul signifies: "This is the point at which little Jacob Taubes comes along and enters into the business of gathering the heretic back into the fold, because I regard him [Paul]—*this is my own personal business*—as more Jewish than any Reform rabbi, or any Liberal rabbi, I ever heard in Germany, England, America, Switzerland, or anywhere" (T, 11, my emphasis). The blunt idiosyncrasy of this phrasing is positively Nietzschean. "I live on my own credit," says Nietzsche in *Ecce Homo*, the quintessential gesture of declaring the matter of one's life to be radically one's "own personal business" unencumbered by an external *archē*. The literary gesture by which the fictionalized figure of autography sheds the rhetorical play of the diminutive third person for the gravity of first-person witness to the story of oneself—a story of multiple spaces within the presumed single history of a diasporic people, the presumption of which Taubes exposes while simultaneously, by virtue of reconfiguring the heretic Paul, he reaffirms—showcases the daring of the gesture in *Ecce Homo* that Derrida explicitly draws upon to articulate the question of historical destination in writing an *otobiography*.[9] In this case, the ear of the other is just as much the ear of the Jewish political theologian trained in the sounds of Judaism as of the classicist philologist trained to the sounds of Hellenism. To say that Paul is a heretic to Judaism is as elementary as saying that Christianity itself, theologically speaking, is a Jewish heresy. Both are disregarded here. Taubes's excavation purports to establish the Messianism of Paul as a diasporic Messianism—not only in a historical sense but in the metaphorical one as well: a Messianism of dispersal at the core of the Law, a rebellious Messianism that elicits out of the Law not a conformist tradition but an intransigent "unlawful" tradition.

Taubes's treatment of Paul is utterly idiosyncratic, but this does not mean it does not leave behind demands for a path to be retraced. Certainly, Giorgio Agamben picks up the strands in full acknowledgment of his predecessor (including the claim to Paul's idiosyncratic Messianism),[10] adopting in fact Taubes's anecdotal beginning as his own historiographical beginning. Yes, Paul's Greek sounds like Yiddish, Agamben says, because "Paul belongs to a Jewish Diaspora community that thinks and speaks in Greek (Judeo-Greek) in precisely the same manner that the Sephardim would speak Ladino (or Judeo-Spanish) and the Ashkenazi Yiddish."[11] And he goes on further in a manner somewhat reminiscent of Derrida's argument in *Monolingualism of the Other*: "There's nothing more genuinely Jewish than to inhabit a language of exile and to labor it from within, up to the point of confounding its very identity and turning it into more than just a grammatical language, making it a minor language, a jargon (as Kafka called Yiddish)" (A, 4–5).[12] To be fair, Derrida would never allow the phrasing "more genuinely" or determine the confounding of identity to be the outcome of a willful, independent act. His point, rather, would be that, yes, one inhabits language as an other, yet language is the space where identity is in fact made unintelligible at the same moment that, as an ideological phantasm we might say, it is (thought to be) consolidated. In this respect, the identity of exile too, or diaspora for that matter, can be constructed, like any identity, as a self-same condition, its minoritarian phantasm being yet another instance of the self-occultation of a heteronomous command.

Although historically accurate, Agamben's reasoning is ultimately facile when viewed in this light. There's nothing jargonish about Paul's Greek; on the contrary, the idiom is perfectly canonical. And I mean, canonical as a language, as enunciation, not by virtue of its theological content. If I may be allowed the conceit, to my ear—certainly not the ear of a philologist—Paul's Greek is not disruptive in the least. In fact, Paul's phrasing has established one of the richest inventories of style in contemporary Greek poetry. This is, I repeat, in spite of its content. The crucial point that needs to be interrogated here—that none of the recent excavations of Paul dares posit—is precisely the discrepancy between the content and the language. The "foreignness" of Paul is due not to his use of Greek, but to the fact that he uses a perfectly recognizable Greek to expound on an engagement with the world that is, if not quite inconceivable, certainly otherworldly to the Greek frame of mind. What needs to be interrogated—and this is a massive task, of which a bare skeleton is produced here—is the occluded underside of this disjunction: not the alleged "un-Greekness" but precisely the problematic "Greekness" of this language, problematic insofar as it threads together a set of worldly injunctions and prohibitions with an uncannily (by the historical terms of Greek societies) unworldly set of eschatological exhortations. The disjunction is also, simultaneously, a conjunction. The alienation of Hellenism by virtue of the stark deployment of a Hellenic idiom against the grain is marked by a double and duplicitous gesture: Christianity's de facto dehellenization of society (in historical terms) is at the same time fashioned as an extension of a Hellenic intellectual architecture that, in this case, will exponentially surpass even the Roman assimilation.

Athens Unknown

A notorious incident from Pauline history, as reported in the Acts, exemplifies this duplicitous condition. Although the presumed author of the Acts (Luke the Evangelist) is not considered altogether reliable—since his purpose was to produce an hagiographical construction of apostolic history that would consolidate into a narrative corpus the early principles of Christian practice and the institution of the new Church—the story itself nonetheless seems likely enough. In any case, the actuality of its truth as event is irrelevant. Indeed, the real event is the rhetorical actuality of Paul's gesture, as it is reported in self-evident convention, whether it occurred or not. After all, this gesture is what remains, what becomes canonical, indeed sacred. I speak of the famous scene of Paul's visit to Athens, about which so much has been written as to deserve an exclusive book-length annotated bibliography. Here, I touch on just a couple of things, pertaining specifically to language.

The narrative situates Paul's appearance amid the Athenians in conventionally Athenian terms, foregrounding the social conditions that are conducive to expounding and discussing new ideas: *Ἀθηναῖοι δε πάντες καὶ οἱ ἐπιδημοῦντες ξένοι εἰς οὐδέν ἕτερον εὐκαίρουν ἤ λέγειν τι καὶ ἀκούειν καινότερον*—which I would translate, in the barest terms, as follows: "All Athenians and foreign inhabitants found it best to spend their time in nothing other than talking about or listening to the newest thing" (Acts 17:21). The forward simplicity of this sentence, borne out by the trope of stating the obvious,[13] is nonetheless framed by a pair of terms that are crucial: *foreign* (*xenos*) and *new* (*kainon*). Evident terms of alterity in all other contexts, here these words register as quintessential figures of what the polis does and by what it is bound. The suggestion is that alterity is *internal* to the polis; it's difficult to imagine another phrase that could spell this out more succinctly. To Athenians, alterity *in-habits* the polis; it is the register of inclusion, and even more, the foremost bar none (*ouden heteron*) conduit of desire for all (*pantes*) inhabitants, even those who do not cease to remain foreign. This hardly signifies the desire to assimilate—thus to annihilate the foreign and the new—but rather the urge to encounter it (indeed to seek it out) in its full foreignness and unknowability. Assimilation is not the purpose because alterity already belongs to the imaginary of the city and does not need to be eliminated.

Let us note that the text has already articulated two instances of the foreign, one for each side—Paul and the Athenians. The very first sentence of the passage pronounces Paul's distress—"the aggravation of his spirit" (*παρωξύνετο τὸ πνεῦμα αὐτοῦ*)—at encountering the sight of the city resplendent with idols (*κατείδωλον*).[14] Altogether contrary, the Athenians' response is to invite Paul to the Areopagus, the venerated space of free and public discourse, precisely because what he has been disseminating in the streets—and he is indeed identified as a disseminator (*spermologos*)—sounds foreign: *ξενίζοντα γαρ τινα εἰσφέρεις εἰς τὰς ἀκοάς ἡμῶν* literally means "because you bring alien matters to our ears" (17:20). Curiously, this ancient text stages the very rhetoric of the "ear of the other" we've encountered in the question of the authenticity of Paul's Greek. But what decidedly resonates as other to the ears of the Athenians is not, let us say, the syntactical parameters of the language but the tactical ones: the foreign or "alienating" elements (*ξενίζοντα*) pertain explicitly to Paul's "proclaimed teaching" (*λαλούμενη διδαχή*). The contrast between Paul's initial impression upon entering Athens and the city's response is striking. For him, the sight (of idols) distresses and repulses the spirit; for them, the sound (of words) prickles the senses (the ears) with impulsive curiosity for elaboration. There is indeed an epistemological chasm—which is, after all, articulated precisely in Romans. On the one side, the spirit cannot tolerate the senses because it is terrified of the worldliness of the body; on the other side, the senses cannot grasp the disembodiment of the spirit because there is no world without the body, except the netherworld, the (un)world of shades. This is why the Athenians draw the line on one thing only in Paul's discourse: the resurrection from the dead as a worldly event (17:32).

But Paul's politics also finds the end of the line on this same issue. It is not a matter of language; it is a matter of what a language can or cannot say. The hunch that Paul's Greek was impeccable is confirmed by the mode of addressing the Athenians. The discursive convention is unmistakable and revealing. Not only is the rhetorical form deliberately Socratic, but the gesture of extending an invitation to listen is predicated on the acknowledgment of Athenian hospitality, of the *political* conditions that enable Paul to extend such an invitation in the first place—conditions that distinguish the polis essentially as a space of listening. Paul's trick is to declare, in as flattering a mode as possible and with an explicit gesture of veneration—"as even certain of your own poets have said" (17:28)—that the Athenians, precisely because they are "in all ways most adept at matters of the divine" (17:22), already know what he proclaims. Except, despite their knowledge, they are not listening carefully, properly. Evangelism has been relentlessly attached to reception and receptivity from the outset, always seeking to determine and control the conditions of listening, indeed, to eradicate all other modes of listening.

Counting on their listening, Paul engages them with a peculiar philosophical gesture. He frames the matter in terms of how one configures the known. They may know what he proclaims, yet, he suggests, they do not know *it*—this essence, this substance—as they should, as it must be known, as it can only *be* known: essentially, substantially (17:23). Configuring the known is conditioned precisely by some mode of knowing the unknown. Paul recognizes that he faces a great predicament that, at the same time, offers a fabulous opportunity. The Athenians, in their inimitable sophistic care to hedge their bets with the divine realm, had set aside a temple dedicated to divinities they did not know. This, in itself, is an extraordinary gesture that nonetheless feeds on an elemental plane of the Greek sense of the world, certainly inconceivable outside a polytheistic cognitive universe and evidently linked to the primacy of the imaginary of hospitality (*philoxenia*), of hosting precisely what is alien. But this gesture is also—or had become by that time—a figure in a perfunctory cult, an almost pedant attitude toward the devotional terrain that rounds out the multiplicity of gods by closing off the set with a determined and thus exhaustible X factor. Paul latches on to this very sense of conventional and lax relation to the divine, exploiting hospitality in the most actual sense.

The temple's dedication literally lacks definition. The unknown element of whatever divinity is to be worshiped there is all pervasive; the unknown is addressed to the entire range of names and representations. In fact, it is only insofar as a divinity is worshiped at this site that he or she is—*becomes thus*—unknown. But by this same structure, the unknown is, as such, provisional. The presumption is that, as new divinities become known and cults develop around them, proper temples, named and dedicated, will be built, with the added satisfaction that the path of this now-professed worship had already been laid. The meaning of *provisional* is, in this respect, exceedingly accurate and profoundly embedded in the whole structure of time in the polis: it encompasses both the temporary (the transient and timeless present) and the providential (the future, projected and anterior).

One of the most remarkable aspects of the Greek understanding of divinity is that the gods, although they are immortal, are nonetheless not eternal. Their immortality refers to divine nature—the only register of meaning that absolutely differentiates the divine from the human. Eternity concerns merely power.

The Greek imaginary understands the divine realm to be like everything else in the universe: a struggle between rival powers. Gods reign by assuming power, and whenever power is open to struggle, eternity is meaningless. But, of course, to lose power does not mean to lose your divine nature (*physis*); it merely means to lose your position in the grid of divine power (*nomos*). For this reason, gods from different historical moments—how we understand the significance of the divine being open to history is one of the most crucial registers in understanding the Greek political imaginary—can come to coexist without the least contradiction according to how power relations shift. This suggests that the practice of worship, even when certain gods or certain rituals are favored (and each city, or even groups within each city, had a particularly instituted and ritualized mode of favoritism), can, nonetheless, never be exclusive. The call for a singular or exclusive devotion to one god, one ritual, one idea, and the like was a major transgression (the hubris of *monos phronein*, as is criticized in *Antigone*). Instead, the tendency is to go to the opposite extreme: to extend inclusion even to the unknown, not, of course, as *the* bona fide Unknown but, rather simply, as the not-yet-known.[15]

To say that the Athenian temple's dedication lacks definition is to say that the devotional inscription literally lacks the definite article. It's simply Ἀγνώστῳ Θεῷ—the distinctive capitalization of both God and Unknown is obviously biblical. The clear translation is "to god unknown." The temple thus refers to the primordial universe from which gods emerge indefinitely but not eternally, whereby they belong to an otherness that precedes the institution of the Other as absolute singular limit. Paul's brazen and ingenious notion of reading the inscription otherwise, of transfiguring it from the provisionally unknown to knowing the quintessentially unknown—from "god unknown" to *the* God, the One-and-Only God, who is by definition *the* Unknown (the Unnamable)—may be seen as the practical application of a shift in the understanding of alterity that grants the other absolute singularity.

I have in mind here Hans Blumenberg's argument concerning the shift from the power of the other as absolute neutrality (*das Andere*) to absolute singularity (*der Andere*), which, of course, personifies alterity and shifts its internal affinity with the cosmic chaos to the configuration of an object that mobilizes a singular psychic investment. Monotheism may be exemplary of the shift from *das Andere* to *der Andere*, from the Other to the One (and only other); Paul's reconfiguration of the inscription on the temple is certainly the practical application of this shift. Interestingly, Blumenberg considers Paul's reconfiguration unintentional, an instance of misreading, an interpretive error. In terms of apostolic textuality error does not exist and, in any case, since the historical verity of the matter is undecidable, his point is not a helpful path. But he is right to call it a demythifying gesture that signals Christianity's initial transfiguration of *mythos* to *logos*, which will appropriate and at the same time demolish the primacy of Hellenic thought in the Mediterranean world.[16]

Paul's God is the other par excellence, the One-and-Only-Other, who now commands exclusively the terms of social definition. Ironically, this God cannot belong to this Athenian temple of devotion, for in the polytheistic horizon he would be just another god, a god whose name is not unknowable but, for the time being, just unknown. In the universe of the Athenian psyche, the unknown is provisional because the possibility of knowledge is a worldly matter. But Paul presents the unknowable as terminal, prohibitively singular and singular because prohibitive. Once God is known as *the Unknowable*, he occupies the entire range of the prohibition of knowledge, prohibiting all other gods at the same time that he prohibits access to his own name.

No doubt, there is more to say here about the *co-incidence* of prohibition and devotion. One of the core elements of Paul's political theology, which is foundational to Christian morality, is precisely the establishment of a devotional mode based on prohibition. (The matter is primarily political and only symptomatically theological.) Perhaps this is why Paul's gesture, for all its rhetorical ingenuity, fails. Of all the instances of proclaiming the Gospel in Greek cities, as recounted in the Acts, Athens is the only place where Paul fails to establish a congregation, taking the few converts along to the next stop in his journey. Yet, his invocation of this Unknown God is a gesture of erasure that the imaginary of a temple to "god unknown" cannot fathom. In effect, Paul's invocation has abolished the symbolic field and, as a radioactive proposition, has set in motion an unbeknown annihilating power. The Athenians, whom Paul leaves behind unconvinced and unconverted, thus remain, in their inconvertibility, a dying breed.

The Itinerant Trauma

As disseminator, Paul exists in constant vagrancy; the most meaningful mode for him is to be on the road. Even his texts are mobile. The epistolary form confirms his errant condition at the same time that it seals the permanence of the addressee. These missives are also missiles of foundation. They mean to eradicate the runaway tendencies of doubt and strengthen the rooting of the newly established congregations, or, more precisely, to immobilize the instituted community of the faithful while mobilizing the instituting force of the faith. Without its conscious instrumentality, its avowed purpose to establish an institution, Paul's language is pure delirium. Being on the road becomes thus an essential precondition of foundation, the errant distance needed to make the power of the word more proximate. Such is, literally, the nature of apostolic labor. In Paul's case, however, it is all a matter of repetition, the compulsive reenactment of an inaugural traumatic event. Paul is perpetually on the road to Damascus.

His restless peregrinations may be driven by the singular obsession of a man utterly convinced that his access to the truth demands that it be available to all. This is the basic psychic framework of all evangelism, which will be instituted as a collective repetition compulsion of Christian missionary work for centuries on end. Yet, underneath this self-evident demand, Paul's peregrinations are driven by something darker and singular. Paul goes on the road in a desperate attempt to re-create the shuddering disruption of his own interpellation. This is not merely narcissistic or self-referential. It carries the added exigency of putting into action the disruptive mechanics of a reproducible *coup de foudre*, so as to engineer what must be henceforth self-generating and self-proliferating. He labors under the compulsion both to reenact his own traumatic experience and, at the same time, to reproduce this experience in others. The point is therefore to *produce* a myriad others who are thus ordained into an infectious state, no less traumatic, which can be managed only by further externalization and wider dissemination of the trauma. This extraordinary passing on of the contaminant-traumatic kernel from self to other constitutes an order whose condition can only be characterized—and I understand the risk of this metaphor—as viral.

The traumatic event of Paul's interpellation on the road to Damascus cannot be labeled simply a conversion. It becomes the arch-event for all subsequent evangelical Christianity and the born-again syndrome. The common enunciation "I have found God!"—to which a genuine believer can only, incredulously, respond, "I didn't know He had been lost!"—reveals a truth that is immediately repressed, whereby the (self-)authorizing subject occludes the autonomy of the act. The undercurrent meaning is to confirm that God has called me, has found me, lost among the sinners, etc. It must be a real experience of interpellation if it is to have the power of transforming the subject, who will from now on, evidently, begin a new life. But, like all interpellation, it is, in the last instance, a self-interpellation: after all, *I* am the one who got the call; *I* am the one who has been born again in Christ; *I* am the one who is to bear henceforth God's word, etc. Equally evocative is the, henceforth, conventional utterance "God has spoken to me!" which transfers to an anonymous and disembodied voice the fact of my enunciation. What is implied and, one assumes, registers its full force in the unconscious at its moment of oblivion is a self-confirmation: indeed, a bona fide moment of *subjection*. The occlusion of self-authorization is essential to the whole process. There is no image more magically evocative of this than the description of a transformed Paul, who is blinded by having his eyes finally opened!

In the symbolic power of the narrative of the event on the road to Damascus (where he was, after all, on a zealot mission to persecute Christians), Paul exemplifies the heteronomous gesture. He embodies an act of extraordinary desublimation by which the victimizer joins the ranks of the victims in order to endow the victims with a victimizing zeal whose dogmatism will henceforth wreak havoc throughout the centuries. This repetition compulsion is crucial to Christianity's proliferation. Alain Badiou goes further by taking even the incident at Damascus to signal a repetition, to "mimic the founding event," Christ's Resurrection: "The event—'it happened,' purely and simply, in the anonymity of the road—is the subjective sign of the event proper that is the Resurrection of Christ. Within Paul himself, it is the (re)surgence [*(ré)surrection*] of the subject."[17] In a more subtle rendering, we could consider, alongside Badiou's observation, Taubes's insistence that Paul reproduces the Jewish trope of the "elect" by involving himself, symbolically, in a process of "outbidding" Moses (the word is Taubes's) and outdoing Mosaic law (T, 28–54). We thus have a composite figure, whereby Paul simultaneously incorporates a fundamental element of the Jewish imaginary within a new fundamental (foundational) element that abolishes it. This composite figure is crucial to understanding what Paul will eventually come to signify as "grace."

The phrase from Romans is often quoted: *οὐ γαρ ἔστε ὑπό νόμον ἀλλά ὑπό χάριν* ("for you are not under law but under grace," Romans 6:14). It's difficult to understand exactly how Paul himself understands the meaning of the two enormously complicated Greek notions (*nomos, charis*) he uses with such abandon. But let us assume, along with Badiou (but also Taubes, Agamben, and Žižek, although they all angle things differently), that, whatever the historical usage, Paul does institute a new set of significations. The deviation from established meaning matters only in our assessment of the meaning of Paul's project, which can only be a contemporary assessment. In this sense, the polemics are conducted against the inheritors of Paul and their own response to the new institution. Badiou's execution of this inheritance is crucial because of the kind of politics he pursues, whose emancipatory claims are indeed undermined by the signifying framework he imposes on this particular nexus of Pauline notions.

One of Badiou's central claims regarding Paul is that, as an antiphilosophical enterprise, the Pauline theology of resurrection shatters the rules of the dialectical relation between life and death: "I shall maintain that Paul's position is antidialectical, and that for it death is in no way the obligatory exercise of the negative's immanent power. Grace, consequently, is not a 'moment' of the Absolute. It is affirmation without preliminary negation; it is what comes upon us in the caesura of the law. It is pure and simple *encounter*" (B, 66). And also: "Resurrection is neither a sublation nor an overcoming of death. They are two distinct functions, whose articulation contains no necessity. For the event's sudden emergence never follows from the existence of an evental site. Although it requires conditions of immanence, that sudden emergence nevertheless remains of the order of grace" (B, 71).

Clearly, without the triumphant history of Christianity, Badiou would have no ground to grant to the Resurrection the status of such rupture. But the ground emerges out of the groundlessness this figure fosters for itself and its legacy, via a theology and a politics that are, in fact, hardly rupturing, but, on the contrary, assimilative to an unprecedented extent. The Resurrection itself, as a figure, is a particular performance of the *nomos empsychos* principle, which was the most prevalent juridical and political notion in the Hellenistic kingdoms of the era. The animation of law in the body of the king—or, simultaneously, the spiritual animation of the king's body by the incorporation of the law—can easily be perceived in the figure of Christ that Paul sought relentlessly to sculpt. Paul resignifies the notion of the permanent presence of the divine within the human by a shift in direction: from assimilating the unworldly into the worldly to elevating the worldly into the unworldly. This shift exemplifies the very force that eventually will animate Christianity's peculiar relation with secularization.

From Badiou's two statements, which express his theorization of the event, let us now consider together the two notations of grace as interruption (caesura) and as encounter. The co-articulation is caught in an elementary contradiction. Even if an encounter precipitates an interruption, it brings forth a connection, an emergent relation. Although this encounter becomes the archreferent of a new radical imagining—let us note, by the way, that as archreferent it becomes itself absolute—it does so by repressing the contours of its very emergence, both the unavoidably aleatory nature of its occurrence (true of any encounter) and the actual traces of the discontinuity it celebrates. Badiou disputes the notion that the event is equivalent to creation *ex nihilo*, precisely because, he argues, the event is always worldly and this worldliness is what enables its rupturing power, whose elements are significantly traceable (even if retrospectively) in the new historical parameters that the event radically institutes.

Of course, the very distinction would come into play only if creation *ex nihilo* is conceptualized theologically. Otherwise, there is no distinction. Castoriadis has given us the most thoroughly materialist theorization of creation *ex nihilo*, and in his formulation the figure signifies merely the capacity of the human animal to imagine things that don't exist in the world and act on that basis. The nothingness out of which a human creation emerges makes sense only if we cannot, retrospectively, place the creation in an altogether signifiable and identifiable field of causes already in place, already present in their potentiality. This hardly means that human creation conjures things out of thin air. One of the more radical ways we can understand the overused notion of the "cunning of history" is to understand that history can produce conditions of radical alteration that are not traceable to an a priori intact (or merely just recognizable) formation—in other words, events that, in comparison to existing formations, do seem to emerge from nothing and do signify nothing by reference to what exists. Creation *ex nihilo* marks Castoriadis's own way of exploring the problem of discontinuity in history—an enormous and vital domain of historical study that has, nonetheless, nothing theological about it.[18]

The event matters historically because it emerges out of the historical matter of which it is composed, even if in an altogether altered (and therefore rupturing) configuration. The relation between what once was and now is—as something altered, as an emergent radical otherness—is the most important element in theorizing the event, although I doubt Badiou would place emphasis there. It is certainly more important than the rupture itself, if we are not to become mere pawns to the forces the event unleashes. In any case, by virtue of its worldly character, no evental site can efface entirely the parameters of the rupture the event produces; otherwise, the rupture would be unreadable and the event would never register at all. An elementary understanding of Foucault's attention to historical discontinuity (including what he called "history's unrealized instances") would be a good thing to employ here. In these terms, the encounter at Damascus may produce the birth of Paul, but, as Paul himself never ceases to recount, this birth is a rebirth. It is linked to a network of significations that it does, of course, set out to destroy, but in this very destruction it continues to be linked to them, no matter what the rhetoric. No born-again discourse can do without the again, despite the aspiration to have erased or severed all past traces. The sheer zealotry of the Christian Paul is but an elementary particle of the force of anti-Christian zealotry that brought about the event of his apostolic election. There is no way out of this equation, and neither the most apocalyptic evangelism nor the most revolutionary theory of rupture can conjure a way out, even as mere language.

God's Gift

Language here is hardly straight. Paul's opposition between law and grace is but one fold in a multifold opposition that sometimes is articulated as flesh (*sarx*) vs. spirit (*pneuma*) or, at the core, as death vs. life: *τὸ γαρ φρόνημα τῆς σαρκός θάνατος, τὸ δε φρόνημα τοῦ πνεύματος ζωή*—"because the thought of the flesh is death, while the thought of the spirit is life" (Romans 8:6). Badiou goes to great lengths to disengage all these notions from their philosophical parameters, as Paul would have inherited them in a Hellenistic world. This world, however, already provides unprecedented conditions of syncretism, which makes whatever Paul is said to be inheriting already nebulous and multivalent. Even the philosophical/antiphilosophical juxtaposition, as Badiou theorizes it, becomes problematic. Because, even if we accept the radical resignification that Paul is said to enact, we cannot summarily qualify, at least with any demonstrable clarity, the already signified material against which he signifies a rupture. This makes the rupture itself unclear. Be that as it may, Paul's enormous success at altering the signification of a widely used Greek vocabulary (whether popular or philosophical, strictly speaking, makes no difference) by enacting an extraordinary manipulation and downright occlusion of his own signifying process is much graver and worthier of interrogation than any theorization of rupture.

It is impossible to understand "grace" outside the social-imaginary parameters of the gift. I understand both Badiou's logic and his strategy of declaring this notion an antidialectical gesture that undoes the dialectical engagement of the subject with the law. But I sense that this logic involves instead a gesture of cryptodialectics that not only dissimulates the dialectical encounter it mobilizes but disallows any possibility of the dialectical undoing of this encounter, any possibility of real self-alteration. Surely, no bona fide Christian discourse would dispute that God's grace is God's gift. Yet, while the association that comes immediately to mind is one of gratuity and graciousness, this is but an instance of veiling what is really at work: an order of economy and exchange.[19] Indeed, grace and faith (its necessary twin) are the two foundational notions of the economy of Christianity, and this is to be understood both in the classic etymology of the term (*oikonomia*: the laws that keep one's house in order) and in the conventionally modern meaning: the signifying framework of producing, regulating, and circulating wealth. It is essential to emphasize here that what sustains the economic integrity of the gift is not acquisition and accumulation but expenditure and dissipation, as Marcel Mauss and Georges Bataille have theorized in exemplary fashion. And expenditure requires an effective mechanism of exchange that is based on the commitment—or, more accurately, the conviction—that the stakes are all consuming.

In Mauss's apt formulation, "the gift necessarily entails the notion of credit."[20] His impetus is to assail evolutionary economic theories that suppose the trajectory from barter to cash sales to credit as the map of civilization's progress, arguing not only that the gift is the primary stratum of all social exchange but also that the institution of credit is present in all archaic economic and juridical systems, from Babylonian societies onward. The phrase, however, is apt for our purposes. If we apply to it a Pauline idiom, as we might mix two substances in a catalytic encounter, we see that the pair gift/credit is no different from the pair grace/faith. The relation is the same and even the signification is the same, because each pair intrinsically deciphers the other. Although the Latin derivative etymology is different, faith is a condition that partakes of all the signifying variants of *credo*. Drawing on Emile Benveniste's pioneering linguistic studies, Agamben argues for an intimate relation between *credo* and *fides* in the Roman world, whereby the more archaic root of the first eventually yields to the hegemonic position of the second, especially in juridical discourses (A, 115).

What is more interesting is the explicit association of the root signification of *credo—kred*—with the notion of giving and of giving in: in effect, trusting. The whole signifying complex (in all its variants) between gift, credit, faith, and trust is evoked in the Greek word *pistis*, which becomes Christianity's key imaginary signification, registering the first instance whereby *pistis* achieves an autonomously religious signification, if not the signification of religion as such.

Agamben quotes David Flusser, the most recent editor of Martin Buber's works, on the fact that this complex of meanings inhabiting the Greek word *pistis* is the same as in the Hebrew word *emunah*, thereby disputing one of Buber's crucial arguments about the differences between the Christian and Jewish notions of faith. In the context of the entwinement between the economic, the religious, and the juridical that characterized archaic societies in the Mediterranean, this makes sense. The difference lies not where Buber sees it but in the fact that Christianity institutes as its foundation the notion of *pistis* as an exclusively religious term, thereby occluding the word's other worldly parameters. In economic terms, Christianity (re)signifies faith as a religious monopoly. Flusser, nonetheless, attempts to rescue from Buber an unacknowledged (perhaps unwitting) understanding about a difference that, he claims, exists in the juxtaposition between *pistis* and *emunah*: namely, that in Christianity there is an inherent split within the notion of faith between the faith *of* Jesus (according to the historical narrative of a man and his actions in Judea) and faith *in* Jesus (according to a theological institution of the notion that the Son of God died for our sins and was resurrected). Although one might argue that these two instances reflect the tension—arguably traceable in the entire history of Christianity up to our time—between a secular narrative of religious foundation and a messianic performative of a transcendental desire, nonetheless both Flusser and Agamben, who builds on his argument, are rather careless in disavowing the paradoxical signification that has reigned at the heart of Christian theology since the defeat of the Monophysites and is designated by a Greek word that does not correspond to any sort of Greek concept: *theanthropos* (god-man).[21] This utterly illogical neologism bypasses even the father-son complex (insofar as it enables the two notions to become consubstantial) and forms the significational basis of the Trinitarian substance. In effect, Christianity is incomprehensible without assuming the impossible identification of the divine and the human in a single figure that is at once both individual and total and, as a sort of protean substance, can assume the form of either or both together, as the occasion demands.

We will delve further into this particular terrain in the next essay. What concerns us here is that, despite an incisive discussion of the notion of grace, Agamben does not acknowledge that, in institutionalizing Paul's obsessions, Christianity enacts a religious monopoly over the signification of *pistis*, whereby gift, trust, credit, and faith are all robbed of their juridical-economic meanings.

No doubt, the whole edifice is built on Paul's own (re)signification of the notion of grace (*charis*), the first term of the pair. The word may be one of the most multivalent in the Greek language, a language where multivalence is the norm. The primary substratum of meaning, already present in the Homeric texts, seems to be aesthetic: *charis*, in the most objective sense, pertains to an idiomatic quality of beauty, what we have come to translate as "gracefulness." The subjective extrapolation from this objective substratum divides meaning between the one performing the action (distributing goodness, bestowing favor, showing preference) and the one receiving it (which includes all the notions of thankfulness and appreciation—gratitude). In all these meanings, already in place in the Aeschylean era, one finds connotations of pleasure, in both giving and receiving, which is often (but not necessarily) sexualized—in both hetero- and homoeroticism—and coupled with adoration, with all the accoutrements of appreciating what is adored and adoring, the elements of worship. Eventually, the term comes to bear the signification of cause, rarely seen in English (perhaps, but not quite, in the phrase "by the grace of"). Nowhere do we see the meaning of gratuity in the sense signified colloquially by the phrase "as a favor"—*gratis*. The exchange inherent in the notion of *charis* remains intact throughout, if nothing else, because articulating appreciation is a necessary component. This dimension has never been absent in Christian discourse and is most precisely signified in the speech act (and ritual) of "saying grace"—not to mention in the literal meaning of the Eucharist, which is the liturgical application of total exchange and total expenditure between God's gift and the appreciation/incorporation of grace by the entrusted faithful (*pistoi*).

Yet, Paul's injunction that "we are not under the law but under grace" epitomizes the mode of thought that occludes the principle of exchange by putting forth an exclusive resignification of *charis* as gratuity, charity. Of this, Agamben remains uncritical, indeed gratuitous. His interest is to uphold Paul's direct opposition between *charis* and *nomos*, which he takes to be a symptom of (and, yet, a cure for) an already instituted split between the juridical and the religious that, in effect, inaugurates the two realms of law and religion as such. If there were a split at all (which would, as a result, establish the boundaries of a prelegal or prereligious society, a highly precarious enterprise), it would consist of whatever enacts a differentiation in the discourses and rituals of obedience. This is an enormous matter for discussion, but in this context we can safely say that Paul did aspire to reconfigure the terms of both the practice and the understanding of obedience. His obsession with discounting the exchange mechanism in God's grace has to do, more than anything else, with his drive to establish a new imaginary of obedience. In this, he is driven both by his renunciation of Mosaic law and by his enmity toward the remnants of the juridical imaginary of the polis in the Hellenistic world. His frustration at not succeeding in Athens must have reinforced his resolve. After all, his object was to conquer (convert)

Rome, which is why Romans is the gravest and most canonical of the Pauline texts.[22]

In any case, Agamben sees Paul's notion of grace as an excessive term that reverses its symptomatic nature and acts as a cure for the fracture between law and faith: "The promise [of grace] exceeds any claim that could supposedly ground itself in it, just as faith surpasses any obligation whatsoever. Grace is that excess, which, while it always divides the two elements of prelaw and prevents them from coinciding, does not allow them to completely break apart" (A, 120). I have no investment in disputing Agamben's insistence that Paul sought to articulate a complex relation between law and faith that rescinded their centrifugal tendencies.[23] I merely question his attachment to the signification of grace as total excess, which is no doubt motivated by his general attraction to the exceptional. In this case, the exceptional, configured as the messianic, signifies a mere reproduction of the Pauline denial of the gift's exchange economy, of what Mauss, in Agamben's words, understood as "the paradoxical bond between gratuitousness and obligation" (A, 123). Agamben correctly criticizes Mauss's political incentives as "social-democratic and progressivist" but misses the radicalism of this particular formulation of the gift economy, which ultimately challenges this politics, much as he misses Bataille's correction of Mauss, which he also invokes.

God's grace has meaning only insofar as it is God's gift. The essential Pauline phrase is *δωρεά ἐν χάριτι* (Romans 5:15). When read with utmost precision, the phrase actually (grammatically) shows that *charis* does not as a rule imply gratuity, but only in this case. Only by the hand of God does grace bear a gift: "gift in the form of grace"; "gift by means of grace"; "gift within grace." What most readers of Paul miss is that the hermeneutical emphasis should be placed on "gift," not "grace"—or at least, on the fact that this phrase separates the gesture in two words, of which "gift" has the defining force. It's useful to look at Bataille's formulation more carefully: "The gift would be senseless (and so we would never decide to give) if it did not take on the meaning of an acquisition. Hence *giving* must become *acquiring a power.* Gift-giving has the virtue of a surpassing of the subject who gives, but in exchange for the object given, the subject appropriates the surpassing: he regards his virtue, that which he had the capacity for, as an asset, as a *power* that he now possesses."[24] What Bataille sees here so sharply is that excess produces power for the one who wields it. God's grace as God's gift empowers God, not the faithful—even when it appears to be an act of gratuitous giving, of gracious magnanimity. Or, more precisely, it empowers God because it actually stages an act of gratuitous giving, which, much like a mimetic performance, produces the sense in the recipient—the spectator—of having been endowed, blessed, with great power by being witness (*martyr*) to something extraordinarily altering and singular. As witnesses to God's grace, the faithful perceive God's performance to pertain to themselves directly. The discourse of "God gave me this gift" is ubiquitous in Christian America, but what enables it is this attention to "me," this discursive self-empowerment that occludes the interpellation. The often-used phrase has less to do with God than it has to do with me, the recipient of the gift, the one who believes he enacts the power of the gift and is thus confirmed as a believer. The power resides and is (grammatically) attributed to God, but always pertains to, signifies, and is performed by "me"—the position that is simultaneously subject and object of the act. It is *this* position that seals in fact the exchange economy, precisely what theorizing the gift as gratuity misses. Let us see exactly how Bataille specifies this acquisition of power, what sort of relation it entails:

> But [the gift giver] would not be able by himself to acquire a power constituted by a relinquishment of power: if he destroyed the object in solitude, in silence, no sort of *power* would result from the act; there would not be anything for the subject but a separation from power without any compensation. . . . The wealth actualized in the potlatch, *in consumption for others*, has no real existence except insofar as the other is changed by the consumption. In a sense, authentic consumption ought to be solitary, but then it would not have the completion that the action it has on the other confers on it.[25]

Bataille not only confirms the Maussian exchange economy of total expenditure, but adds an element that Mauss's essentially structuralist system does not allow: the exchange hinges on a transformation, on an alteration of the power relation, which is why the expenditure is total only provisionally. The gift actually empowers the giver, who may indeed have expended his all, but regains it in the form of power over the other, who is thus transformed by believing that he has been endowed with power. (It is elementary to note that the other *becomes* other in the very process of this exchange, of becoming a believer.) I cannot think of a more precise and evocative depiction of the relation between grace and faith, in which the silent and essential third term—the hinge—is obedience. Under God's infinite grace, I thus become the subject of faith, which means both that I become faithful and that I enter the faith; I achieve *pistis* and I become *pistos*. Both as an internal(ized) capacity and as an external(ized) identity, faith then becomes the means by which I convey my appreciation by uttering it back ("saying grace"), as if in an infinite echo, in order to be reborn and replete with God's grace, in an interminable (that is to say, *quintessentially repetitious*) dance of gestures that ensure God's interminably (repeatedly) reauthorized power. Grace and faith, power and submission, are thus interlocked in a repetitive ritual replay ad absurdum.[26]

Doulocracy

This repetitious interplay is occluded in Paul's formulation because his impetus is to challenge obedience to the law in favor of another framework of obedience. His concept of *nomos* is predicated on an essentially Mosaic juridical understanding (even if he desires to overcome it by saving it—in classic Hegelian *Aufhebung* fashion) and therefore bars him from any sort of understanding of what *autonomia* may have once meant in the context of the democratic polis. On the contrary, he attributes to God's grace a totalizing plenitude—*en panti pantote pasan autarkeian* (2 Corinthians 9:7–8)—literally, "in everything always total self-sufficiency"—which Agamben mysteriously understands as the definition of "real 'sovereignty' (*autarkeia*) of the messianic in relation to works of law" (A, 120). I have to presume that the insertion of sovereignty here has a metaphorical impetus, because there is nothing etymologically (or even philosophically) in *autarkeia* that would link it to any permutations of *archē*. Nor would there be in it any connotation of autonomy, since any dynamic sense of autonomy would suggest an *unsettled* condition, enacting and enacted by a horizon of self-interrogation and self-alteration. *Autarkeia* presupposes an imaginary of completion in oneself, and at best, in the Hellenistic era of despotism, it might have connoted a certain self-distancing from power. This notion of self-sufficiency has nothing to do with either pre-Socratic or Socratic frameworks of meaning; it emerges with the Cynics and changes the previous boundaries of signification, as Foucault observes specifically in regard to the hereby-altered framework of *parrhēsia*, which moves from the public frankness of collective utterance to the presumption of unencumbered private self-expression.[27] Whichever the meaning, in the Athenian political imagination—which, against all odds, still persists in Paul's time, as we saw in Acts—this notion would be absurd. The complications of the Pauline juridical idiom, generally speaking, derive from the fact that he grafts onto the heteronomy of Hellenistic despotism a *nomos* that is still a matter of Mosaic law, despite the obvious condition of radically questioning and subverting established Mosaic institutions. The discrepancy between language and signification is no doubt the most exhilarating aspect of the Pauline text. Where one stands in relation to it, however, is altogether a matter of politics, nothing else. It inheres, it requires, a politics.

Perhaps better than *nomos*, the word that encapsulates this discrepancy is *ekklēsia*. Paul theorizes *ekklēsia* in such a way as to abolish the classic Greek dialectic between *polis* and *oikos*, taking over what is otherwise a technical term that, at least in Athenian democracy, pertains to government as an arch social signifier. The classic Pauline argument that encapsulates the content of *ekklēsia* is often quoted: "There is neither Jew nor Greek, there is neither slave or free, there is neither male nor female" (Galatians 3:28). A common interpretation (Badiou also abides by it) is to take this to be a revolutionary signification that undoes the exclusionary framework of the polis. This argument is either naïve or cunningly deceitful. Although, no doubt, the members of the *ekklēsia* in early Christianity are not differentiated by class, gender, or culture, this equitability is authorized and sustained by an overarching submission to a singular external authority. They are all God's slaves—the word is actually *douloi*—or, as Blumenfeld so charmingly quips: they constitute a "'doulocracy,' a republic of cheerful slaves, ruled by a saving, absolutely just God."[28]

That they are all *equally* God's slaves, that they are *all* slaves without exception, cannot possibly qualify for a figure of autonomy or freedom, except by the Orwellian logic of being free in total submission, free because of total submission. On the other hand, while no doubt the *ekklēsia* in Athens, as the assembly of free citizens, excluded women, slaves, foreigners (*xenoi*), and resident aliens (*metoikoi*), those who belonged to the *ekklēsia*, who had political rights in the city, were themselves the source of their authority. Their freedom was consubstantial with their forming and having access to an *ekklēsia*, and the *polis*, which the *ekklēsia* was meant to serve, did not exist in any greater or external sense. In the strictest terms, the alleged liberation from Greek exclusivity that Christianity effects is actually the reverse: an all-inclusive subjugation. Suffice it to say, I am not suggesting anything more than what Nietzsche theorized in *The Genealogy of Morals*, which remains inimitable in capturing the inner logic of Christian doulocracy. That this extraordinary book is systematically ignored in currently fashionable critiques against secularism—no matter what specific agenda they are serving—should be treated as scandalous scholarship (but it's not).

Incidentally, Badiou does engage with Nietzsche but only insofar as he seeks to bolster his claim of Paul's antiphilosophy. He too ignores the Nietzschean basics. In fact, his attempt to configure Paul as the retroactive dismantler of "the empty universalism of global capital" (B, 128) is spurious, if nothing else. Of course, it is true that this "empty universalism" fosters a communitarian particularity that is limited and neutralized by a petty logic of identity. Yet, the "empty universalism of global capital" enforces precisely the condition of the abolition of difference that Badiou evokes from Paul's Galatians—the emptying out of all value and the flattening of distinctions. The relativist particularism that global capital cultivates as alleged resistance to "globalization" is the virtual reality of this emptiness. As virtual reality, it is altogether painfully *real* in its virtuality, so as to shield us from the capacity to interrupt it and thus make it real. After all, there is nothing more consistent in the history of Christianity—always in the name of the same—than the pursuit of the radical delineation that nurtures racial, political, and sexual inequities, on the basis of which—this is utterly obvious—the history of Christianity is tantamount (after a certain point but yet to be reversed) to the history of global domination by capital.

In any case, something also needs to be said about the difference between the two uses of *klētos*, the root term in *ekklēsia*, which is explicitly invoked by Paul in the salutation of Romans. In Athens, *klētos* is the one *called upon* to perform his citizen duties, no more, no less. If he performs them irresponsibly, he is subject to *anaklēsis*—literally, to being recalled. In other words, he is not tied to his duties by any sort of entitlement, expertise, or authoritarian appointment. By contrast, the notion of *klētos* in Christianity, as instituted by Paul, is tantamount to being chosen or called upon *once and for all*, permanently bound to the heteronomous calling. *Klētos* and *doulos* are identical notions; they pertain to the permanent privilege of submission that produces the new (*kainē*) identity. It is likely that what influences Paul's resignification of *klētos* is the privilege that resides in the Hebraic notion of being chosen by God. Whether or not that's the case, *ekklēsia* for Paul means *the assembly of submission*, the assembly of those who *elect* heteronomy, thus effacing the autonomy of their act by attributing their *election* to the unquestioned alterity of divine authority. Even if we deemed it appropriate to hold on to the notion of the *elect* in the case of the *ekklēsia* in Athenian democracy, we would have there the crucial dimension that the *elect* (those elected) are also, simultaneously, the ones who elect. Between election by God and election by the *dēmos* exists an epistemological chasm.[29] In this respect, Christianity, which was profoundly political from the outset, effaces the *polis* from its vocabulary, and deconstitutes both its imaginary and its social hold by expanding the meaning of *oikos* to include a public dimension (which, in another way, means domesticating the public dimension) and by making *ekklēsia* the primary social and political imaginary institution, sanctioned as the House of God (*Oikos tou Theou*).

Thanatopolitical Theology

If Paul can be considered as a rule the instigator of Christianity's remarkable capacity to resignify notions of freedom into notions of submission and the reverse—in what is, in the domain of signification, a carnivalesque performance of unprecedented magnitude—nothing encapsulates his perverse ingenuity better than the way the sign of Resurrection trumps the signifying relation between life and death. Badiou is the most articulate spokesman of this Pauline daring, making it indeed the spearhead of his politics of the universalizable singularity of truth and the event, so our analysis must inevitably traverse his reading. Badiou is keenly aware that his main opponent in this domain is Nietzsche, whose understanding of Paul's thanatopolitics still remains the most incisive. Encountering Nietzsche in this regard raises the stakes on a whole lot of fronts, most significantly on the question of whether Paul's (political) theology is at all a philosophy, thereby seeking to outmaneuver Nietzsche's explicitly philosophical concerns.[30] From my standpoint, the whole encounter is staged erroneously as the moment Badiou claims that philosophy is existentially dependent on mastery (B, 58), instead of fostering, by the most conventional Socratic standards, an enterprise of interminable (self-)interrogation. In the latter terms, Paul is indeed the quintessential antiphilosopher, as Badiou desires. He is the greatest enemy of (self-)interrogation in favor of a politics of mastery at all levels, from the domain of the individual body and mind to the domain of the imperial body politic.

Philosophy as (self-)interrogation is, at an undeconstructible level, a politics of life, an interrogation of life based on the understanding of something irredeemable: the finitude of life. Therein lies the tragic dimension that shatters the allure of abounding heteronomy, the fact that its ubiquitous presence passes for reality. Christianity gave heteronomy a rejuvenated politics. Let us not lose sight of a crucial principle: When Paul speaks of "life in Christ" he is not speaking in tropes. He is indeed articulating an extraordinary condition by which life exceeds the bounds of the living body and gives itself over to the mastery of another—in this case, the One-and-Only-Other. Strictly speaking, the phrase "life in Christ" is tantamount to possession, and it is hardly surprising that the history of Christianity is replete with instances of depriving the life of all sorts of "enemies" under the charge of "spirit possession." Very simply, Paul's theology is based on the demand that people surrender their life—to God, to Christ, to faith.[31] It is a *thanatopolitical theology* ingeniously woven around a singular figure that claims to defeat all death once and for all: the Resurrection.

Badiou is following his own obsession when he dubs the Resurrection "*anastasis nekrōn*, the raising up of the dead, their uprising, which is the uprising of life" (B, 68). And later on: "Resurrection suddenly comes forth *out from* the power of death, not through its negation" (B, 73). Bracketing for a moment Badiou's explicit intention to strip from the figure of the Resurrection any sort of dialectical play in order to endow it with the rupturing power of the Event, we see that in any other sense his signification of life and death follows Paul's. Pauline scholarship abounds with discussions of how the meaning of the two notions is inverted: Biological life—dependent on the permutations of the flesh (*sarx*), which come down to one and only condition, sin—is death. Death—which in the world marked by the event of the Resurrection is in a sense no longer one's own, as Christ himself has already performed it for us all, for those who have lived and died and those who are to live and to die until the end of time—is life, insofar as it defeats the world of sin and opens the door to the rule of the spirit (*pneuma*): "But if we have died with Christ, we believe [*pisteuomen*] that we shall also live with him. For we have seen that Christ, rising from the dead, will never die again, will never be conquered by death. For the one who died in sin died once and for all, while the other lives, lives in God" (Romans 6:8–10).

One can understand the inspirational resonance of this promise to ears bereft of any sense of autonomy. It is a more refined, more alluring heteronomy than what presides over life burdened either with the ceaseless demand of the covenant with God or with the arbitrary rule of earthly despotism. Nonetheless, this splendorous promise is nothing but the promise of eternal life in an other world and by an other's law. The affirmation of life that Paul extols with such rapture is very simply the zealous adoration of the afterlife, nothing more, nothing less—an adoration, moreover, that inheres in death, as the curious tenses in Paul's quotation suggest: belief emerges out of having died with Christ (who has died for/with all). And it is this desire, this adoration for the afterlife—the life that exceeds death—that subordinates life, real life, to death. Badiou is right to see in the event of Christ's Resurrection a call for repetition. Having died for everyone, Christ calls on everyone to partake of his death as a form of eternal (after)life, in an eternal repetition ritualized in the Easter liturgy but played out in the psyche of every devout Christian every day. One thus dies continuously (in one's mind) before one actually dies, with the belief that death, as the key to eternal life, is the worthiest element of living in/with Christ. In this particular sense, Christianity is a religion essentially propelled by a death-drive.[32] It is especially interesting to note that the finality in this promise of redemption is exempted from the discourse of death, even though it is *pure death*—no other death-imaginary can even come close to the purity of Christian afterlife as a condition that annihilates all previous signification.

The death of God is a Christian proposition; the absence of God, the void, is not. Christianity is the first (and so far the only) religion to be founded on an altogether perverse notion of killing God. Of course, access to knowledge of the perversion is barred from the founding moment, because in Christianity the killing of God is neither gratuitous nor an act of rebellion. God is put to death precisely so as to claim conquest over death. The death of God in Christianity is thus marked by uncompromising instrumentality. God dies so that he may be resurrected, as simple as that. The instrumental outcome is all that matters (the abolition of sin happens with the Resurrection, not the Crucifixion), and the reality of God's death—*God's suicide*, to be exact—vanishes behind the interminable ritual repetition of a mythical spectacle rendered sacred. The ontological status of the Christian God, therefore, is somewhat like the Undead, if not quite the "living-dead." After all, these astounding monsters in horror films are inevitably associated with something Satanic—the singularity of the Evil being the Christian invention of God's other side.

In retrospect, after two millennia, it seems that the death of God in Christianity was meant to abolish once and for all the possibility that God may be rendered truly irrelevant to our existence, that God may be *voided*. It is a mark of humanity's ultimately untamable psychic core that such an imaginary possibility has still not been extinguished. Nietzsche's "death of God" may be considered, on the one hand, as the final act of Christian thinking, but, on the other hand, it may be the first act of un-Christian thinking from within, because it also signaled the death of the Resurrection and a return to life as actualization of mortality. Living with a sense of utter mortality, of plain finitude, diminishes the hold of death over life. If death is zero, then all life before it curiously becomes infinity and plenitude, in every infinitesimal, ephemeral, and unreproducible moment. If the zero of death is undone by the promise of an eternal afterlife, a promise that turns infinity itself into a promise, then death's zero expands backward all over life and, like a radioactive cloud, envelops it and removes from it all temporality. It annihilates its (life) force and hollows it out into a perfunctory shell yearning to be filled with promise.

It is one thing to identify death as the life of the flesh, even if this is the bare limit of the frail dignity of being human. In any case, the gesture belongs to a long history of renunciations of the real. Paul, after all, had an avowed aversion to all matters of the flesh—*to all matter*—to the point of having to devise the extraordinary division between flesh (*sarx*) and body (*sōma*), which he finally stripped of all things somatic. But to call life what, even by the standards of the renunciation of the real, is a kind of permanent unliving, the deprivation of all that is human, is to proliferate the present of a delusion—present, here, being understood in its double meaning: both as indication of a certain vertical temporality and as the actuality (presence) of the gift. At the very least, this thanatopolitical reconfiguration of life raises a great many questions as to the political acumen of those who seek in Pauline theology signs of human emancipation, whether they call it universalist or messianic.

CHAPTER 6

EVERY RELIGION IS IDOLATRY

The assertion I have chosen for a title is a quotation from a very important essay by Cornelius Castoriadis on the imaginary institution of religion, which is unique in his overall oeuvre and has not really gotten the attention it deserves. It is especially pertinent to the discussion of political theology and the question of what politics theology mobilizes. I will address Castoriadis's essay and the quotation specifically in due time, but only after working through a long and circuitous trajectory that begins by fielding the question of political theology, not in the abstract but specifically in regard to its endemic monarchical politics, which will then lead us to explore some of the earliest aspects of Helleno-Christianity and the political-philosophical permutations of Trinitarian thinking. This will bring forth the question of monotheism as a symptomatic mode of political theology specific to the denial of its own idolatry, an inquiry that inevitably passes through Freud's historical fictions in *Moses and Monotheism*. The problem posed by Castoriadis will then come to elucidate the contested terrain of iconoclasm's own political theology, not just in the domain of religion but in the secularist framework itself, where the politics of unrepresentability continue to hold sway unchallenged. In other words, as two instances of monarchical thinking, political theology and iconoclasm are entwined in a double sense, by virtue of serving monotheism and by occluding their own idolatry. In this sense, monotheism is not the opposite of idolatry but one of its instances. In the end, against this intricate nexus, I will propose the language of theatricality as a political antidote to theology tout court.

Political Theology as Monarchical Thought

Since the term *political theology* established itself fully in the academic theoretical scene—although originating with the advent of the Carl Schmitt obsession in the American academy, it becomes substantial with the secularism obsession, which emerged about fifteen years ago—the term that it overtook and silenced was not so much *political theory*, as Paul Kahn argues in his *Political Theology: Four New Chapters on the Concept of Sovereignty* (2011), but rather *political economy*. The eclipse of political economy as a primary interpretive concept in politics is all the more stunning given the dire circumstances of our time, when the economic sphere has come to occupy the political in undisguised fashion. While we have come to understand, after Marx, that economic interests ultimately determine the political trajectory of societies, we now see economic agents explicitly exercising governmental power, not only according to the well-documented control of American government officials by Wall Street lobbyists, but even the appointment of unelected bankers or financial managers to positions of heads-of-state (note Greece and Italy in 2011–12). Such is the condition signified by what we may call the *deregulation of the political*.[1]

So, in a context where the economic is exercising explicit regulation over the sphere of the political, while simultaneously effacing "political economy" from the language of social and historical analysis, it seems even more problematic to me that the political is ever more thought to be determined by the theological. Of course, one might say, this is endemic to the very problematic of sovereignty whose political-theological phantasm is but an overdetermination of the political-economic terrain. In the process, we have come to a situation at present where sovereignty (specifically understood as state power) occludes its dependency on society's economy, although all along the economy implicitly determines which phantasms (political, cultural, national) will become prominent until, via persistently and extensively cultivated deterritorialization, it reemerges explicitly as the authorizing force of sovereignty.

In his recent work, Giorgio Agamben complicates this picture by arguing for a split within the theological, with economy emerging as a theological category separated from the political along with the advent of Christianity.[2] This complex and virtuoso argument, whose details will occupy us as we go along, falters on one assumption: the ease with which it takes for granted as totalizing factor the theological domestication (*oikonomia*) of politics that Christianity established as an intrinsic theologization of society that is said to permeate history all the way to the institution of sovereignty in modernity. Whatever might be the (post-)Christian elements of sovereignty in Western modernity, which are in essence historically indisputable, Agamben too—like scores of contemporary thinkers—assumes that the nontheological elements of the political flourishing in the pre-Christian Greek world have been annihilated. This assumption makes for an easy narrative, whereby modernity is nothing but the child of secularization, which in turn is nothing but a disguised continuation of Christian political theology. The idea that modernity is just a lavish party of historical imposters has been one of the most lucrative paths of recent scholarship on these issues.

The first problem that concerns us here is not only that the famous Carl Schmitt assertion in *Political Theology* ("all significant concepts of the modern theory of the state are secularized theological concepts") seems to be circulated ad absurdum as fact,[3] but that, even in its own terms, Schmitt's dictum has been irresponsibly considered. To say that something has been secularized, grammatically speaking, is to mean that an action has been taken upon this something and that this something (the "theological") has thereby been altered. Secularization is an alteration of the forms and conditions of the theological, which is neither to say the annihilation of the theological, nor to say the mere repetition of the theological in another guise. While we are fond of saying that history repeats itself, it brutally doesn't. And it is precisely history as finite action that makes even the apparent repetition of form out to be actually a shift—from tragedy to farce, or what have you. As elementary as this point is, it is indicative of a profound lapse in the proliferation of Schmitt's dictum in the present secularism debates. From this standpoint, although theological elements continue to abound in contemporary societies worldwide, neither are they primary (in some sort of a priori hierarchy of determination), nor have they always existed in strict historical terms—all the more so in relation to the political.[4]

As a concept, historically speaking, political theology may be considered a Christian notion. Although accurate as to its Christian derivation, this history is rather elusive. Jacques Lezra is right to question whether political theology is indeed a concept at all. At the very least, he argues, it is a border concept, or, more precisely, an encounter, whose situational character can only produce riveted, hybrid, or cross-bordered conceptuality.[5] Carl Schmitt claims to have invented the term,[6] and though it is certain that discussions about political theology today may be unable to escape this crucial reference point, the contours of the name are archaic and circuitous. The name in its original Greek is first encountered in Stoic philosophy, where it is given the significance of one category of politics among many; *theologia politikē* is meant to be distinguished from *theologia mythikē* and *theologia physikē*. By this token, the theological is merely an account of specific elements of service to statecraft, in contradistinction from service to philosophy (via myth) and to science (via nature). The Roman glosses on the Stoics interestingly translate the notion to *theologia civilis* (Varro), which becomes status quo thinking throughout the realm of Hellenistic monarchies before inevitably turning into the pagan anathema that fueled the theological politics of Latin Christendom starting with Augustine.

But the notion gets onto the trajectory we are now debating when the Roman Empire refashions itself as a theologically endowed regime under Emperor Constantine. The first historian of Christianity, Eusebius of Caesarea (ca. 263–340), is also the first to fashion the idea that the transportation (and transformation) of Roman Imperium to Byzantium is the historico-political actualization of what is theologically announced in the biblical texts. There is an intricate nexus here, especially the relation of Eusebius's position with the theological arguments about God's Trinitarian consubstantiality, which brought about the decisions of the Council of Nicaea (325) that form the theological and juridical foundations of Christianity until the Schism in the eleventh century. Especially significant is the famous dictum of Gregory of Nazianzus (329–90) in his *Third Theological Oration* (379) that the Trinitarian *archē* consists in the notion of "the One being in *stasis* with itself" ["*τὸ Ἓν στασιάζον πρὸς ἑαυτῷ*"]—an extraordinary notion, not only as the epitome of the Christian theological imaginary and, altogether explicitly, of how political theology is necessarily monarchical, but also, more broadly, in its equally explicit contradistinction from the ancient Greek philosophical and political vocabulary that enables it to begin with. However, it is at the hands of Augustine, as is well known, that the horizon of political theology is enhanced with a transcendental teleology, the substance of which has yet to be conceptually outmaneuvered. The City of God is still the last instance (*telos*, but also *eschaton*) of political theology, whatever name might be invented for it in the course of time and the various social-historical languages deployed.[7]

As last instance, philosophically speaking, the transcendental *Civitas Dei* is the limit point of the concept of political theology, making in this sense the political ultimately subordinate to the theological, an instrument of the theological, as is after all grammatically evident: political is just an adjective to the substantive theology it qualifies. From a historical standpoint, however, political theology is to be understood from the outset, long before Carl Schmitt came to exist upon this earth, as theology grounded and constituted against an enemy; Augustine's entire position confirms this. This enemy would have to have both theological and political dimensions, although this is not to say that the two are necessarily dialectically entwined. The political history of Christianity is exemplary as a political history of the concept of enmity and has come to infect its historical enemies with the same logic.[8] While the transcendentalist element in political theology is thus outmaneuverable and primary, the usage (or actualization) of political theology in different epochs, including our present time, testifies simultaneously to its insurmountably worldly character. The discursive space of political theology, in this respect, is always the realm of the political, even when the discussion that ensues is resolutely theological.

Thinking from the nodal perspective of this naming, two crucial sets of questions emerge in need to be asked. These two sets of questions are of a different order, but are indeed linked by a demand to focus our interpretation on the political:

1. *Is theology necessarily political?* That is, can we speak of an apolitical theology? And what would this mean? How could "apolitical" possibly stand on its own, that is, undetermined by the political? And moreover, can we really speak of theology as such? Unqualified? Substantial? If the answer is "no" to any one of the last two questions, then the emphasis on the original question inevitably falls on the issue of necessity. Is theology *necessarily* political? This, I believe, is the bottom line in the discussion of what might be signified by the name "political theology" and its uses. If indeed this is the case, we need to ask further: What are the terms of this necessity? What authorizes it? My tendency would be to say that such terms cannot be merely theological, strictly speaking—that is, we cannot speak of an internal history of political theology as if it is a formal philosophical concept. In the last instance, political theology is an instrumental logic.
2. *What is the politics enacted by political theology?* Can we speak of a politics in this paradoxical singular-plural way, that is to say, of a certain *kind* of politics, an *eidos* of politics, which can nonetheless be manifested differently according to the historical specifics? All the more so, given that political theology remains articulated unquestionably in the singular—indeed, this begs the question. The question of whether political theology is monological or not is, for me, an outmaneuverable dimension of the problem. We cannot assume an agreement on this issue but cannot go ahead without seriously encountering it as a question. If in fact political theology enacts a specific politics, regardless of the theological or historical content, then a whole other can of worms is opened.

I venture on an answer, by conviction but also for the sake of argument. Schmitt is, again, a crucial reference point. I have always argued that Schmitt's notion of sovereignty as decision on the exception entails a monarchical theory—literally speaking, not in reference to royalty. This I hold in spite of his arguments in *Verfassungslehre* (1928).[9] Certainly, in *Political Theology* (1922)—"a purely juridical book" in his own words[10]—Schmitt conceives sovereignty explicitly as singular *archē*, and it's elementary to say that the radical democratic imaginary that honors Aristotle's dictum that no ruler can rule without the knowledge of being ruled and vice versa—a veritable an-archic position—could not possibly be entertained in the Schmittian universe. Even in his postwar masterpiece, *The Nomos of the Earth* (1953), Schmitt is unequivocal: "all human *nomoi* are 'nourished' by a single divine *nomos*."[11] But I would go further and argue that this literally monarchical element permeates all those (post-Hobbesian) theories of sovereignty, including those advocating popular sovereignty like Paul Kahn's, that see the sovereign position as extradimensional (exceptional) to the polity.[12] Even if we agree with many of Schmitt's interpreters that the term *political theology* in Schmitt's mind implies no more than a structural correlation beyond and against whatever are the historical contours of the two components, this analogical relation between the political and the theological is possible only insofar as both are configured to be monarchical. The sovereign who decides on the exception and thus performs something miraculous (by Schmitt's own metaphorical expression) is, by analogy, the Creator sovereign who makes light out of nothing—or as Schmitt himself says in reverse: "the omnipotent God became the omnipotent lawgiver." Omnipotence from the standpoint of singular *archē* is, of course, quintessentially monarchical.

By this token, one could paraphrase Schmitt's famous dictum in *Political Theology* to say instead that *all significant concepts of the modern theory of the state are residual monarchical concepts.* This would make political theology a language that expresses and actualizes a monarchical—and, I would add, monological, monomythical, and indeed monotheistic—imaginary.[13] Alternately stated, but by the same analogy: to the extent that it acts politically, theology obeys a monarchical logic following a long historical trajectory of theologizing the monarchical principle of archaic societies, so much that monarchy has become in turn a quintessential theological term with an imaginary all of its own, historically animating and sustaining the world's most powerful religions. In this specific sense, Schmitt's dictum signifies precisely the opposite of what it denotes: namely, it is not theological concepts that have been secularized but secular concepts—*political* concepts—that were theologized to begin with.

Jan Assmann has made a similar argument, although our few differences may be due to the fact that for him the reference frame is set by the social-imaginary of Pharaonic Egypt in relation to which monotheism—what he has famously called the Mosaic distinction—is both a theologization of the political and yet, at the same time, an antistatist gesture. We'll get to this in due time when we take up the problem of monotheism, but to begin with, Assmann essentially reverses not only Schmitt's dictum but Schmitt's entire theory of secularization:

> All significant concepts—perhaps we can rather say more modestly: several central concepts—of theology are theologized political concepts. . . . The process of secularization has an opposite direction. I call this process *theologization* and would like to prove it by showing how the theological comes to be out of central political concepts, just like Carl Schmitt wanted to prove the process of secularization by showing how the political comes to be out of central theological concepts. One could rewrite the Schmittian project of

> political theology as the birth of the political—or better, of the law of the State [or public law—*des Staatsrechts*]—out of the spirit of theology. I will turn the tables and deal with the birth of religion out of the spirit of the political.[14]

In effect, if we take seriously Assmann's notion of theologization, it's difficult to see how any concept of political theology can legitimately come to exist, at least in the way that such claimed concepts have come to be understood and have gone largely unexamined. But even more significant is that Assmann shows how theologization is actually an element in the vast process of secularization over time, which, as I have argued repeatedly, is not only unfinished but unfinishable. In this sense, theologization may be said to belong to the history of the political from the earliest instances of human society on this planet. This isn't to say that all elemental and necessary political formations in human society *had to be theologized*. Theologization is neither predetermined nor necessary. What Assmann calls "theologization" is a historical event presumed to be of generally archaic provenance, just as what is usually called "secularization" is understood to be a historical event exclusively attached to the institution of modernity: "The 'theologization' of the political had revolutionized the world of its time as fundamentally as the secularization of the theological had in the modern age" (*Herrschaft und Heil*, 30.) The historicity of both is not to be doubted, but their assumed periodization most definitely is.[15] To be sure, making theologization part of the overall secularization process means two things: on the one hand, a nonmodern understanding of secularization and, on the other hand, an understanding of the political as an elemental and outmaneuverable anthropological category that exceeds whatever is deemed to be the sacred, even if on certain historical occasions the sacred may be included in the political.

From this standpoint, Schmitt's thinking is indeed theological at its core, which isn't simply to say religious. Assmann does not replicate the argument made by Heinrich Meier that Schmitt thinks first and foremost as a Catholic, about which there is, of course, no doubt—Schmitt had no problem admitting it, and such self-descriptions abound in his postwar notebook *Glossarium*.[16] But this not an issue of religious creed. Schmitt's thinking of the political along religious lines eventually becomes paradoxical but, insofar as his investment in the totalizing capacity of the political is animated by a *monarchical* desire that is non-negotiable, it is perfectly consistent. In his preface to the second edition of *Political Theology*, arguing against Protestant notions of theological alterity (or "unpolitical" theology), we find a sort of phrasing that reflects a line of thought Schmitt had in the meanwhile developed in *The Concept of the Political* (1927), while also revealing the unquestionable air of the times (1934): "We have come to recognize that the political is the total, and as a result, we know that any decision about whether something is *unpolitical* is always a *political* decision, irrespective of who decides and what reasons are advanced. This also holds for the question whether a particular theology is a political or an unpolitical theology" (PT, 2). But while this seems to propose a framework, contra theologians, where the political occupies the last instance, it does not alleviate the fact that the *nomos* of the political is "nourished" by a single divine *nomos*, as I quoted earlier: in other words, what decides and guarantees the totality—*the existential sovereignty*—of the political is a matter of singular unitary *archē*. Contra theologians, this is Schmitt's theological testament.

As *The Nomos of the Earth* argues explicitly, Schmitt's non-negotiable assumption is that the primary building block of human societies is the sacred, and the ultimate desire that propels him is for an eschatological guarantee against primordial chaos. Of course, both chaos and the guarantee against it are historically created notions, or surely notions that become meaningful in concrete historical situations: hence the sovereign exception as guarantor of political order in real terms. Whether the sacred is indeed the building block of society is surely debatable in an anthropological framework per se, but be that as it may, the core issue for us here is that Schmitt's understanding of the sacred is *monarchical*. Whether this understanding either derives from a political orientation that privileges sovereignty as singular *archē*, which is then projected backward onto the presumably primordial sacred (which, in this sense, becomes "monotheistic" regardless of what religion it delineates historically), or indeed is based on configuring the sacred itself as singular *archē* (that is, monarchically), which then haunts the worldly terrain as ever-present shadow, may ultimately be a matter of Schmitt's psychobiography. In either case, political theology and singular *archē* are consubstantial, and the typical disregard of what is an elementary association in Schmitt's thinking has precipitated all sorts of ponderous fancies.

Let us remember that Schmitt writes his second *Political Theology* treatise practically fifty years later (1970), not at all as a sequel, despite the name, but as a response to his critics, primarily to the long essay (which he calls a "legendary document") by the Catholic theologian Erik Peterson "Monotheism as a Political Problem," written in 1935—both the date and the specific focus point to a response to the monarchical dogma of the *Führer* principle, which Schmitt acknowledges, though not exactly in these words (PT II, 43)—and secondarily to Hans Blumenberg's contemporary critique of Schmitt's understanding of secularization in *The Legitimacy of the Modern Age* (1976). But it is actually the second text (Blumenberg), addressed in Schmitt's book as an appendix, that gives reason to Schmitt's impetus to take on the first (Peterson), thereby expressly staging an argument with a theologian as a political rather than a theological matter.[17] This argument was long overdue in Schmitt's mind and psyche—there is an explicit, if passing, reference to Peterson in his reading of *Leviathan* (1938)—especially as the significance of his *Political Theology* as a theory of sovereignty must have undergone multiple reassessments in the tectonic trajectory of the epochs he experienced, from Weimar to Nazism to Cold War–divided Germany. Schmitt suggests that, if monotheism is a political problem according to Peterson, then political theology is not about monotheism—a shrewd shift of the argument's framework, very typical of Schmitt's tactics. Hence, he predicates his argument on the assertion that "Political theology is a polymorphous phenomenon [with] two different sides to it. . . . each directed to its specific concepts. This is already given in the *compositum* of the phrase. There are many political theologies because there are, on the one hand, many different religions and, on the other, many different kinds and methods of doing politics" (PT II, 66).

One does not suddenly discover a relativist Schmitt, so this passage requires an equally shrewd reading. I would draw our attention to the centrality of the *compositum*. I have always found insightful the assessment of the great German playwright Heiner Müller that Schmitt's thinking is exemplarily theatrical. He is a political thinker—for some, *the* thinker of the political—and, simultaneously, though in a furtive and circuitous manner for many reasons, driven by a theological desire. The two are in constant agonistic relation. The *compositum* is precisely the staging of this agonism disguising a *compromise formation*. Although a concept delineated in the singular (as part of a demonstrable *Begriffsgeschichte*), political theology for Schmitt becomes, by the argument of the 1970s, a performative domain, which is thereby articulated, by virtue of its very performativity, as the work of myth. Schmitt explicitly applauds Peterson's suggestion that political theology *is* a myth, albeit by turning against Peterson's negative signification of the notion of myth. Having already somewhat furtively stated in *Roman Catholicism and Political Form* (1923) that "political theology is polytheistic as every myth is polytheistic," Schmitt adopts here a Sorelian notion of political theology as the myth necessary for the specific socio-historico-political—in his language, essentially *juridical*—action he demands in most of his post–World War II texts.[18] The problem that needs in-depth investigation is in what sense this mythical performative, even in Schmitt's staging in *Political Theology II*, can outmaneuver the eschatological imperative of a politics that desires to be theological above and beyond all, a politics that, by virtue of this untamable monarchical desire, can never be democratic. Because it partakes of a monarchical imaginary, monotheism *is* a political problem first and foremost, although in terms that neither Peterson nor Schmitt can adequately handle.

The Monarchy of the Trinity

On the politics of monotheism—a long and arduous issue—I would begin by reminding us of Freud's bottom-line assessment: "Along with the belief in a single god religious intolerance was born, which had previously been alien to the ancient world and remained so long afterwards."[19] And more specifically: "This [Egyptian] imperialism was reflected in religion as universalism and monotheism" (MM, 259), which is reiterated in the book's third and longest section as "In Egypt, monotheism grew up as a by-product of imperialism: God was the reflection of the Pharaoh who was the absolute ruler of a great world-empire" (MM, 306). While Freud's impetus may have been to absolve the Hebrews from the invention of monotheism, since they were after all nomadic peoples and hardly imperial, the point remains as an *archē* for the monotheistic impulse as such, regardless of when and how this impulse arose, who claims it as authentic, whether Moses was indeed an Egyptian (and it was renegade "Egyptians" and not "Hebrews" who conquered the land of Canaan in the name of the true God), or whatever may be any sort of archeological argument. The history of monotheisms—or, equally, the histories of monotheism—proves this singular *archē* (this *monarchy*) to be indisputable, no matter what the vicissitudes of this trajectory.

We shall return to Freud, but after another sort of archeological staging. There is admirable merit to Etienne Balibar's succinct account of monotheism as a concept of European modernity.[20] Balibar conducts his argument starting from the most difficult, almost unfeasible path: before accounting for the genealogy of monotheism's presence as a self-ascribed concept, he examines the itinerary of its absence, especially in relation to what has been codified as the opposition—polytheism. He takes as point of departure the articulation of *polytheïa* or *polytheotēs* by Philo of Alexandria (20 BCE–50 CE), the most significant of Judeo-Hellenistic thinkers and contemporary of Jesus of Nazareth, who uses it to illuminate the otherwise alien conceptualization of divinity as transcendent singularity by juxtaposing it with neo-Platonic variants that interpret the condition of many gods as the refraction of the One in the midst of the Multiple. Both these tendencies (pagan neo-Platonism and Alexandrian Judeo-Hellenism) associate divinity with the One and thus, despite their differences, share a monotheistic desire, even if the name does not yet exist.

It is curious that, although bearing a Greek composite name, the term *monotheism* is absent from the Greek vocabulary, where otherwise composites of *monos* abound, *monarchia* being most indicative. Balibar correctly argues that "the question of 'polytheism' cannot be dissociated from the question of 'polyarchy' in the double sense of the term *archē*: that is, plurality of cosmic principles and plurality of services to them, commands or obediences" (27). But given that the Hellenistic era, in which Christianity emerges and eventually merges with the Roman imperial apparatus, is characterized politically by monarchy, it is all the more curious that, by the same token, a theology that privileges the One does not come to bear its name.

Balibar stipulates that the early Church debates about Trinitarian consubstantiality, which arose expressly as responses to Monophysite or Arianist tendencies, though bolstering the power of the One philosophically with extraordinarily skillful argument, nonetheless barred the possibility of any official theological enunciation of the name *monotheism*. Instead, Balibar goes on to argue, the first recorded instance of the word by the Cambridge Platonist Henry More in 1660 is accusatory and polemical against the newly formed Unitarian tendencies within Anglicanism, which was seen as restaging the Monophysite imaginary in Protestant garb. Thus, for Christianity at least, the term *monotheism* is fraught by contradictory significations: it is the mark of both dogma and heresy. This where Erik Peterson's interwar essay becomes crucial.

It is essential to keep in mind that Peterson wrote against Schmitt as a friend. Only the brilliant Jacob Taubes understood the significance of a friend's wounding message across enemy lines in the year 1935: "True are the wounds that a friend's arrow inflicts."[21] More than anyone, Schmitt would have known how his friendship with Peterson when they were colleagues at the University of Bonn in the 1920s marked the theologian's eventual conversion to Catholicism, which came at a steep price. Resignation from the Bonn professorship, professional marginalization, jobless abject poverty, and expatriation in the midst of Nazi ascendancy are the conditions of production of Peterson's 1935 essay. But even while still in his Lutheran mind (in his *Habilitation* thesis), Peterson was keenly aware of the co-implication between monarchical thought and Christian theology since its earliest days, and he genuinely struggled to work against it. It is fair to say overall that the very notion of political theology was heretical in Peterson's Catholic mind, arguably because his primary intellectual and spiritual horizon was eschatological, a standpoint from which any politicization of theology worthy of its name would mean resigning oneself to secularization, therefore to the defeat of Christian theology.

In this respect, even if the impetus was a critique of Schmitt's appropriation of "political theology" for expressly political (state juridical) purposes, the terrain of Peterson's essay is theological through and through, with specific emphasis on the early patristic debates that emerge from the remainders of Greek ways of thinking in the Eastern Mediterranean of late antiquity, where the very words *theologia politikē* would have had profound resonance. And the historical notion that most dramatically exemplified this problematic nexus was *monarchia*, insofar as it interfered with the laborious and extremely contentious process of establishing the operations of Christian monotheism, even if the term was not yet articulated. So, monotheism is configured as a political problem—as a political-theological problem—long before it exists as a name because the new emergent theology must engage with the monarchical imaginary that permeates it historically. Peterson explicitly disputes any speculation about the realization of "divine monarchy" because he refuses the charge that Christian monotheism is monarchical. For this he turns to conditions of the earliest political moments of the newly formed Eastern Roman (Byzantine) Empire, hence to Eusebius of Caesarea and the classic texts of Cappadocian theology, which is the terrain of an extraordinary flurry of debates that form the philosophical core of Early Christianity.

Of Peterson's specific concerns, most important is Gregory Nazianzus's *Third Theological Oration* (379), where the substantive configuration of the Trinity, via a discourse on the significance of the Son, finds its most sophisticated expression against the surge of hardcore monotheistic Arianism. It is fair to say that as a new Christian empire is forming, the grave task of theology becomes literally political, even if not identified as such explicitly. So, for the new Church's most able minds, the key intellectual project is how to rein in and consolidate the centrifugal tendencies of religious thought and practice over an enormous imperial territory endemically used to its multiple and multivalent—indeed *polyarchic*—ways over several centuries. The only common vein that runs through this vast heterogeneity of imperial lands and peoples is the Greek language, which carries with it a disproportionally heavy freight of sophisticated and articulated meanings, bearing almost a thousand years of philosophical tradition (sixth century BCE to fourth century CE). Indeed, understanding the problematic terrain of intersection between Christianity's initial pool of significations and the conditions of Hellenization of disparate populations over long stretches of time is key to any further discussion, not just about dogma (theology per se), but also power (politics per se). Hence, a close look at the language of the *Oration* is warranted.

Gregory Nazianzus (329–90) was a master rhetorician (by all accounts the best of his era) and profoundly learned in the tradition of Greek thought, including the art of poetry, in which he excelled and was prolific. His acrobatic use of language to render complex meanings that are entirely untraditional, even inconceivable, in that language is remarkable and often overlooked in light of his gigantic significance in the dogma as a Church Father.[22] Reading his language, one realizes that he speaks not only to Christian theologians, but to the full gamut of Hellenized intellectuals, Gentiles and Jews alike, and also to what in modern terms we would identify as the secular realities of Christianity's relation to worldly power. So, his discourse is explicitly political even while his impetus is unequivocally theological. To what extent this means that he engages in political theology per se is not so simple a matter. Peterson argues he does not; and by Schmitt's standards, the answer is also "not" in the sense that what is political in Gregory's discourse is not structurally analogical to the theology he elaborates. I would say, in simple terms, that the discourse is deliberately and thoroughly political in the basic Greek sense, while the theological configuration, though borrowing from a Hebraic spirit, is idiomatically inventive, indeed quite unprecedented. The relation between these two realms is unique. I translate here the entire second paragraph of the *Third Theological Oration*:

> The three kinds of inherited opinions (*doxai*) about God are anarchy, polyarchy, and monarchy. The first two are for the play of the children of Greeks, and may they continue to be so. For anarchy is a thing without order (*to te gar anarchon atakton*); and the rule of many is discordant/factious (*to te polyarchon stasiōdes*), and thus anarchic, and thus disorderly (*atakton*). For both these tend to the same thing, namely, disorder (*ataxia*); and this then to dissolution (*lysis*), for disorder is an exercise in dissolution (*ataxia gar meletē lyseōs*). But monarchy is what we hold in honor. However, not monarchy where the One is circumscribed in one person, for the One can be in discordance/faction with itself and establish plurality (*esti gar kai to en stasiazōn pros eautō polla kathistasthai*), but one that is composed of equivalence (*homotimia*) with nature and a spiritual union (*sympnoia*) with knowledge, as well as identity of movement and convergence (*synneusis*) of these elements toward the One—something ineffable in terms of generated nature (*oper amēchanon epi tēs gennētēs physeōs*)—so that, though numerically distinct, there is no severance of essence (*ousia*). Therefore, oneness (*monas*), from the beginning and by rule (*ap' archēs*) moving toward duality, came to be in trinity. This is what we mean by Father and Son and Holy Ghost. The Father is the Generator (*gennētōr*) and the Emitter (or Projector, *proboleus*); but, of course, without passion (*apathōs*), without reference to time (*achronōs*), and without corporeality (*asōmatōs*). The Son is the Generated (*gennēma*), and the Holy Ghost the Emission (or Project—*problēma*); for I know not how this could be expressed in terms that altogether exclude visible things. But we shall not venture to speak of "an overflow of goodness," as one of the Greek philosophers [Plato] dared say explicitly in his discourse on the first and second causes, as if it were an overflowing bowl. Let us not ever assert that this generation is involuntary, like some natural overflow difficult to retain, thus by no means befitting our conjecture of what is divine (*peri theotētos hyponoias prepon*). Rather, remaining steadfast within our terms, let us assert the Ungenerated (*agennēton*) and the Generated (*gennēton*) and that which proceeds from the Father (*to ek tou patros ekporeuomenon*), as uttered by God Himself and his Word (*ōs pou phēsin autos o theos kai logos*).[23]

We see explicitly how well versed the theologian is in the discourse of politics and secular thinking in general, and how self-aware he is of positing a set of notions that cannot be fathomed in the very language he uses. The continuous reminder of being compelled to put into concrete sensible language the ineffable and the nonsensical is in fact embedded in the rhetorical gesture. Indeed, beyond religious practice per se (such as, say, the performance of prayer), there is no way to engage this bizarre mode of thinking other than by oratory.

On the political end of things, it is quite clear, from the outset, that only monarchy is appropriate to the discourse (*doxa*) about God—that is, to theology as such. Leaving aside the issue of anarchy, about which he says nothing other than its being a plaything of Greek children, polyarchy (the rule of the many), therefore democracy, is the most adversarial of notions for, even if it too is a plaything of Greek children, it is the mode of rule—by name, at least—most resonant of the surrounding polytheism (*polytheotēs*), which has not yet been conquered.[24] After all in 361, some fifteen years before the orations are composed, Gregory Nazianzus's erstwhile friend and fellow student of rhetoric in Athens Flavius Claudius Julianus was crowned Emperor of Byzantium as a professed pagan, henceforth to be known shamefully as Julian the Apostate. Gregory's invectives against Julian were notoriously rabid. Theology is a battlefield and the oration thus belongs to the most polemical of genres. Subsequently, Gregory Nazianzus will be appointed Bishop of Constantinople by Emperor Theodosius, the most extreme opposite of Julian, since by his decree Christianity will become the empire's sole religion, with all sorts of punitive actions against summarily outlawed polytheistic practices—the temple of Apollo in Delphi and the Alexandrian Serapeum demolished, the Olympic Games and the Roman feast of Vestal Virgins abolished, and so on.

The very notion of the Trinity—an extraordinary conceptualization by any philosophical standard—may be said to have been configured specifically in order to battle the inveterate polyarchy of divinities in the Hellenistic world in its very own language. Although the impetus is theological, the reality that the notion of the Trinity confronts and within which it stands is altogether political. The theological debates about the Trinity in Early Christianity are characterized by a double discursive terrain: the configuration of *archē* (origin, rule, power) and the configuration of number or measure (order, calculation)—simply speaking, politics and economy. But this not a matter of a split between political theology and economic theology, as Agamben argues in *The Kingdom and the Glory*, although his historical account is accurate. The discourse is double-pronged throughout but the terrain is consistently configured and focused on the crucial intersection: political economy. The Trinitarian debates conceal the stakes of political economy in a veil of theology, not the other way around. That is why when the intersection between politics and economy reappears in modernity, however we are to date this precisely, it is not a matter of the secularization of theological concepts. On the contrary, the original terrain on which Christianity imagined itself, fought for its principles, and instituted its signature was a matter of theologization of political-economic concepts. Therefore, what is called secularization in modernity is but a reiteration of the stakes of order and power where the theological veil no longer quite holds. This extraordinary misconception has marred a whole slew of analyses, whose volume in recent decades has become exasperating.

The tricks of this language are precisely what the master rhetorician Gregory Nazianzus juggles with rare inventiveness inasmuch as, all the while, they remain insurmountable. We are told from the outset that polyarchy is quintessentially driven by (and driving to) *stasis*: discordance, faction, rebellion, self-dissolution. And yet, what characterizes the substance of the Christian God—the One-and-Only-God—is that the oneness God alone encapsulates is in *stasis* with itself: the One is in a quintessential condition of self-discordance, of rebellion against itself within itself, which, Gregory adds, establishes a plurality (*polla kathistasthai*). Does this mean that the Trinity is polyarchic? Any serious Christian—and not necessarily with the intellectual prowess of a theologian—would obviously answer "of course not." And yet, in Gregory's mind, in the language that he bears (inherits, carries, puts forth), this is not a contradiction.

The paradoxical concept of *stasis*, as Nicole Loraux (the premier classicist thinker on the subject) has argued, is quintessentially Greek and has never found equivalence or even analogy in the Roman (and subsequently Latin) tradition.[25] Therefore, as an operative term in the most eloquent and significant of Early Christian theorizations of the Trinity, it cannot be easily translated and may in fact prove to be a conceptual obstacle to the process by which political theology is linked to sovereignty in Latin Christendom and then, by the typical analogy, to sovereignty in modernity. The literal notation of *stasis* precipitates a constellation of adversarial meanings. *Stasis* is a concept literally in *stasis* with itself. As substantive of the verb *istamai* (to stand), it obviously means arrest of movement, stillness, and therefore stability: in political terms, establishment, status—*status quo*. But it also means what is evidently the opposite: rebellion, strife, discord, faction. The latter set of terms, in their original Greek significations, is always conceived within an internal terrain, as aspects of the self. As a set of polemical meanings, these terms do not reside in the realm of enmity but of kinship—hence, the most consistent political meaning of *stasis* being "civil war."[26]

Surely, this is what Plato has in mind in the *Republic* (book 8, 556e 5) when he speaks of democracy's sick body (*sōma nosōdes*) as the condition of a polity in *stasis* with itself (*stasiazei auto autō*). The phrasing is uncannily close to Gregory's (*stasiazōn pros eautō*). But the contradictory meaning of the word does not allow for strict equivalence. For Plato, *stasis* is democracy's illness, its tendency toward internal strife. For Gregory, *stasis* within the One is the mark of internal plurality. Gregory would agree with Plato that democracy (polyarchy in his terms) tends to self-dissolution; he uses after all the same language (*to te polyarchon stasiōdes*). Monarchy is the politics he explicitly espouses, and the plurality introduced by the condition of *stasis* within the One may be essential to its substantive order, but it does not break up (dissolve) the essence of its singular *archē*. The Trinitarian hypo*stasis* does not alleviate the monarchical imaginary of Christianity, despite its peculiar numerical logic.

This is where Schmitt is overtaken by his own monarchical desire and misses the bizarre gesture: "At the heart of the doctrine of the Trinity we encounter a genuine politico-theological *stasiology*. Thus, the problem of enmity and of the enemy cannot be ignored" (PT II, 123). It's absurd to consider that Gregory Nazianzus conceived some sort of immanent enmity within the Trinity. There is no war within the Godhead. Nor can we simply read *stasis* in the Trinity symptomatically, as if the concept of the enemy enters through the back door. The split within the One that Gregory aspires to theorize—with a very specific external enemy in mind, Arian monotheism—is the pluralization of the one and unreproducible substance: a nonsensical notion, strictly speaking, that plunges logic into turbulence, unrest, *stasis*. The nonsensical proposition is, moreover, predicated on the radical misconfiguration of the current meaning of the word *stasis*—in effect, its depoliticization. That Schmitt continues to read it as a political notion in the original sense is an exercise of his own normative impulse—both political (monarchical) and theological (Christian). Thus, the absurdity of the Trinitarian figure just eludes him.

Indeed, the Trinity employs a paralogic. Although a configuration of order, of administration or economy (*oikonomia*), nonetheless it does not belong to the order of calculation or logic, strictly speaking. It cannot be mathematized. As all great imaginary significations, it is poetic. A very strange *co-incidence* is enacted between the Generator and the Generated (God and His Son) or the Emitter and the Emitted (God and His Spirit), which exceeds all measure and all nature. We have to understand that, although the grammatical distinction is kept intact—there is an action between a subject and an object, noun and participle, grammatically speaking—nonetheless, there is no dimensional distance (spatial or temporal) between the two positions. As I have been arguing since *Dream Nation*, where I first coined this figure, the notion of *co-incidence* is inconceivable within a framework that follows the demands of the logic of identity. *Co-incidence* occurs in a magmatic sense of both time and space, never in succession of time or distinction in space. This is not a theological figure per se; it is entirely pertinent to a real historical framework. Because even in actual history no event (or form or logic or pronouncement or anything similar) can occupy a designated place (spatial or temporal) that is exclusively its own, a place in which it can *identify itself* entirely unimpeded by an Other.

In the figure of the Trinity, of course, otherness is not visible as subject/object. The figure itself is other—to language, to logic, to reality. Entirely aware, Gregory is quick to say that the very words he uses signal the necessary compromise of using language that inevitably represents reality—"for I know not how this could be expressed in terms that altogether exclude visible things" (*ouk oid' opōs an tis tauta kalesein aphelōn pantē tōn horōmenōn*)—but what he configures cannot be *actually* represented. Whatever the language, the figure defies both likeness and distinction. Trinitarian paralogic is quintessentially figural, or, more precisely, iconic, but in the terms we have learned from Freud: namely, the fundamentally misrepresentational nature of dream-thoughts, where even words are figural (and figurative) but with referents that are inexorably distorted and ultimately lost in an abyss of uninterpretability. The symbolic logic of the Trinity, if we choose to call it that, lies at the extreme point of both symbol and logic, defying the integrity of both, in a way that only the enigmatic nature of iconic thinking can manage. It's become commonplace to point to the Trinity as evidence for Christianity's idolatrous tendencies. But what might be idolatrous about the Trinity is not what is usually argued—the allegedly polytheistic arithmetic—because, as I go on to show, even the strictest monotheism is idolatrous. Rather, what is evidently idolatrous about the Trinity is the quintessential iconicity of a logic that defies and distorts both logic and representability, an enigmatic configuration that defies both likeness and distinction.[27]

Against Arian Monophysites, for whom God's nature is monistic so that it cannot contain the divine Son except as born in likeness (*homoiousios*)—like all of God's children, after all (*kat' eikonan, kath' homoiosin* is the Greek translation of the phrasing of Genesis regarding the creation of Adam)—the imperial dogma, established by the Council of Nicaea (325) and sealed with the Second Council of Constantinople (381), in which Gregory Nazianzus also delivered an oration, decrees that the Son is of one essence with the Father (*homoousios*). This difference of one iota, as it has famously come to be known, marks the passage from the logic of measure to the imaginary of form. In Greek terms, we could say it passes from the mathematics of *physis* to the poetics of *nomos*, except that we are already far from Greek terms when *physis* and *nomos* are distended in this fashion. However, what is preserved from Greek thinking (specifically from the Stoics) is the possibility of multiple attributes of substance, so much that even the word *substance*—in the way we understand it in modern English—is not quite applicable, since, as Gregory argues, consubstantiality in the triune hypostasis of the Trinity implies that substance is not a singular entity but a relation between the elements it contains.[28]

Expressing succinctly the Nicene Creed, shortly before it becomes the sole state religion in perfectly monarchical fashion, Gregory's configuration of Trinitarian consubstantiality enacts a certain kind of exceptional juridical decision, without this necessarily meaning that we invoke Schmitt. God, as Father, retains the total creative power of generation, of Genesis, as One-and-Only, while at the same time remaining the source (the Emitter) of All. As source

(*Ursprung*), God the Father enacts the procession of the Spirit (*ek tou Patros ekporeuomenon*), much as He *enacts* the Son, for generation does not follow the law of nature, but the (performative) act of the Word. This is what the evangelical "Word becomes Flesh" means, and in this particular sense the iconic unreality of the Trinity comes around full circle to meet the iconic unreality of the Virgin Birth—they belong to the same economy. Of course, such enactment defies the order of time. It happens at the same "time" as God happens, except that God does not happen—there is no moment of action for His happening; God just is. "There was never a time when He was not," Gregory goes on in the Oration's third paragraph: *ouk ēn hote ouk ēn*—literally, "there never was when he never was." And, he adds, it is the same with the Son and the Spirit, though they are generated and emitted. They are so *ap' archēs*, which means both "from the outset" and "by rule": from the outset of no-time and by rule of fiat. In this sense, both the Son and the Spirit, the Generated and the Emitted, are *anarcha* and *aidia*, unoriginated and eternal, except only insofar as they are the objects (grammatically speaking) of an eternal *archē* or cause (*aitia*), which is "not necessarily prior to its effects, as the sun is not prior to its light"—Gregory's phrase resonating here with modern physics—as "the sources of time are not subject to time" (*ou gar hypo chronon ta ex ōn ho chronos*).

This paralogic that defies all logic, the numerical plurality that defies all measure, nonetheless does not defy the double play of *archē*—neither as the Source of All (*Ursprung*) nor, most significantly in terms of our argument, as the very Being of Rule. This is why the Trinitarian consubstantiality is quintessentially a political figure, and why, despite his deft and imaginative reading, Agamben's claim that the Trinity is ultimately an administrative figure, an economic order of theology (the *nomos* of the divine *oikos*), points to a secondary attribute. From a certain standpoint, Agamben's framework is political as well; *oikonomia* is a sort of governmental figure, the management of order, or, as he says repeatedly, a technical apparatus, especially given its translation in Latin Christology as *dispositio* and *dispensatio*. But when the political is reduced to the administrative or the procedural, its crucial connection to contestation and conflict lapses, and a formalized machine-like figure emerges that tends toward harmonization and unification: "With a further development of—even its rhetorical—meaning of 'ordered arrangement' economy now is the activity—as such truly mysterious—that articulates the divine being into a trinity and, at the same time, preserves and 'harmonizes' it into a unity" (*The Kingdom and the Glory*, 39). And as we know well from modern political realities, when politics is reduced to formalized administration the polity is depoliticized.[29] There is nonetheless merit in Agamben's argument that (following Aristotle's distinction) the politics of *oikonomia* are monarchical, so when the Trinity is perceived as an economic apparatus, it becomes an instrument to implement a certain kind of politics and forbid another: "In Gregory, the *logos* of 'economy' is specifically designed to prevent the Trinity from introducing a stasiological, *or political*, fracture in God. Insofar as even a monarchy can give rise to a civil war, an internal *stasis*, it is only a displacement from a *political* to an 'economic' rationality that can protect us from this danger" (*The Kingdom and the Glory*, 13–14). I emphasize the *political* here, which Agamben uses in perfect awareness and without qualification, while the *economic* is notated (in inverted commas) as something more than just its name. Of course, this 'more' that shadows the name of the economic is the political, so this begs the question "what kind of political?"—a veritable political question as such.

But let us return to the political language (*archē*, *stasis*) in Gregory Nazianzus's Trinitarian configuration and to the Peterson-Schmitt debate, in which it prominently figures. From a Greek philosophical standpoint—at least, the one inaugurated by Anaximander and elaborated all the way to Aristotle—Gregory's play with the notion of *archē* in describing the workings of the Trinity is, of course, nonsensical but more importantly compromised and manipulated by an a priori thesis. Unlike Anaximander's understanding of *archē* existing in the midst (*meson* = middle) of the infinite, which disarticulates the notion of ultimate beginning as source (*Ursprung*), and surely contrary to Aristotle's notion in the *Politics*, where *archon/archomenos* (ruler and ruled) are entirely coincidental and therefore *archē* is split at the origin by a kind of endemic *différance*, Gregory tries to conceptualize a multilateral *archē* in which the anarchical is a mere attribute ultimately subordinate to an overarching unity. In 381, at an advanced age, Gregory delivers what is known as Oration 42 *Synaktērios*, that is, literally, the Inaugural Address at the Second Synod in Constantinople, which as we know seals the political hegemony of the Nicene Creed under Emperor Theodosius. The occasion is political-theological par excellence, and Gregory reiterates his argument from the famous *Third Oration*, written two years earlier (379), as a theological fait accompli. I quote again this remarkable language:

> The *anarchon* [anarchical, but really "unfounded"], the *archē*, and that which is with the *archē* [are] one God [*ἄναρχον, καὶ ἀρχὴ, καὶ τὸ μετὰ τῆς ἀρχῆς, εἷς Θεός*]. For the nature of what is anarchical does not consist in being anarchical, but in being ungenerated [or unbegotten, *agennēton*]. For the nature of anything lies, not in what it is not, but in what it is. It is the positing [*thesis*] of what is, not the withdrawal [or cancellation, *anairesis*] of what is not [*Ἡ τοῦ ὄντος θέσις, οὐχὶ τοῦ μὴ ὄντος ἀναίρεσις*]. And the *archē* is not what it is because it is separated from the anarchical: *archē* is its own nature, just as what is anarchical is whatever is not of its own nature. For these things pertain to nature, but are not nature itself. Again, that which is with the anarchical, and with the *archē*, is not anything different from what they are. Now, the name of the anarchical is the Father, the name of *archē* is the Son, and the name of what is with

> the *archē* is the Holy Spirit. And the nature of the three is one: God. And the union is the Father, from whom and to whom all is traced (*anagetai*) as follows: not so as to be confounded, but as to be possessed, without distinction of time, of will, or of power. For us these things create plurality (*polla pepoiēken*), since each belongs to itself and remains different from the other (*pros to heteron stasiazontos*). But for those of simple nature whose being is none other than just itself, the One remains sovereign (*to en kyrion*).

Let me briefly decipher this paralogical argument that is bolstered by some of the semantic marvels of the Greek language. First of all, Gregory proceeds on the principle of strict identity, or what, closer to our discourse here, both Peter Sloterdijk and Jean-Luc Nancy have called "monovalence": something is because it is, and whatever stands as negative to what is, as a kind of abolition or cancelation (say, an-archy), simply is not; its being is negative, meaning there can never be a thesis (affirmation) of negativity, but negativity nonetheless registers its presence by annulling itself. Accordingly, insofar as the *anarchon* has no *archē*, it does not have a definite existence. Its nature is precisely not to have a definite existence, which is hardly to say no existence but rather existence that is All Beyond All, including all beyond time: "there never was when He never was." This enables Gregory to place the Father in the position of the void that exists beyond the world, dismantling thus the heretical notion that would attribute to the Father a definite (singular) substance. The definite substance may be said to come with the Son, who is thus an *archē*—he enters the space of time—because he is generated, albeit not in a corporeal, materialist manner, or, we must add, as mere continuity (extension) from the Ungenerated, Unbegotten, Anarchon Father. The fact that Jesus of Nazareth may have had a human body does not alleviate the fact that, as the Son of God, he obeys no law of human generation; he is generated consubstantially from the Ungenerated—that is the whole point of the Immaculate Conception. For this reason, we also cannot say that the Son stands alone, in likeness (*homoiousios*) to the Father's substance because he is generated. The Father may be *anarchos*, the Son may be *archē*, but they are not other to each other: they are of one nature and one undivided essence (*homoousios*). Here, a very strange notion of *archē* is articulated, for it is an *archē* insofar as it is definite—it has its own being—but not an *archē*, strictly speaking, insofar as it is generated by an other.

Moreover, the third element (the Holy Spirit) is literally a metaelement and cannot be thought to have an *archē* as such, for it comes to be "with the *archē*": *meta tēs archēs*. I will not get into the permutations of Heideggerian *Mitsein* (being with) here, but somewhere in the back of our mind we can imagine the strange way in which Heidegger folds otherness into Being as one of the dimensions of Gregory's paralogical argument. For the third element is an element of otherness, with neither ontological *archē* nor infinite indeterminate *an-archē*.

Moreover, the Spirit is not generated by the Father, but rather projected/emitted (*ekporeuomenon*): in other words, literally set into motion and side by side with the generated Son ("with the *archē*"). Yet, because of the marvelous multiplicity of meaning in the Greek word *meta*, the Spirit also illuminates both the anarchic primacy of the Father and the precedence of the generated *archē* of the Son relative to both of which it figures as a metaelement, not, of course, in the order of time—there is no sequence here—but in the order of being. Gregory allows all these ambiguities—and even logical contradictions—to stand because he wants to hold on to both the plurality of the Trinity and the Oneness of God.

For Agamben this is a matter of economy. It necessitates an economy, for how can this paralogic be made to work, if not by an administered order? "The function of the Trinitarian economy is to hypostasize, to give real existence to the logos and to the praxis of God and, at the same time, to affirm that this hypostatization does not divide the unity but 'economizes' it" (*The Kingdom and the Glory*, 59–60).[30] To economize here means to give unifying order to what is in discord with itself, to account for the internal dis-order brought about by *stasis*. Strictly speaking, Agamben is correct, except for his single-minded obsession with seeing this administered order as a theological figure per se. What might be said instead is that this economizing—this governing force that keeps the house in order, that unifies its multiplicity—is a force in the service of the One. Like the political theology that it cements and unleashes forth into history as empire, the political economy of Christianity, as seen in the imaginary of the Holy Trinity, works in the service of a one and only politics: the politics of monarchy.[31]

For Peterson, who thinks as a theologian within the dogma—to his mind theology exists only in the absolute dogma of incarnated logos—Gregory's brilliant exposition of the triune hypostasis is totally convincing as a repulse of Arianist aspirations to identify imperial power with divine providence. Looking back, Peterson sees the problem that Gregory solves as having begun with Eusebius in his propagating an imperial sanctification of Christian dogma: "his voice is not [that] of a scholar but a propagandist."[32] Peterson sees Eusebius as a symptom of residual Roman trouble: "In principle, monotheism had begun with the monarchy of Augustus. Monotheism is the metaphysical corollary of the Roman Empire, which dissolves nationalities. But what began in principle with Augustus has become a reality in the present under Constantine" (94). Moreover: "National sovereignty is allied ultimately with polytheism, with the effect that the Roman Empire is then pressed into service in the struggle against polytheism" (96). In order to conclude: "Monotheism is a political imperative, a piece of *Reichspolitik*" (102). The language is deliberately resonant with the conditions of writing at that time (1935) and alerts us to the deeper purpose of Peterson's intervention. Surely, no one could convincingly argue that this intervention is not political and only a matter of theological explication—that it is not political-theological. Yet, Peterson registers his explicit disdain of the notion as pertinent to Christianity. For him, political theology is a residual archaic notion that has no place in Christianity's eschatological universe. Nor does monotheism because, according to this argument, monotheism is constitutively driven to its manifestation via secular—that is to say, historical, not eschatological—monarchical institutions.

For Peterson, Gregory Nazianzus is the superlative figure that dismantles this entire mode of thinking: "With [his] arguments, monotheism is laid to rest as a political problem" (103). And he concludes his essay with the most explicit revelation of what propels the trajectory of his thinking: "Monotheism as a political problem had originated in the Hellenistic transformation of the Jewish faith in God. Insofar as the God of the Jews was amalgamated with the monarchical principle of the Greek philosophers, the concept of the divine Monarchy at first acquired the function of a political-theological propaganda formula for Jews. . . . Only on the basis of Judaism and paganism can such a thing as 'political theology' exist" (104–5).

Obviously, charges of Catholic anti-Semitism have been raised against Peterson on the basis of this conclusion. But this accurate assessment is also the easiest response, and in its dismissiveness, not only does it fail to address the problem of monotheism, even from a Judaic perspective, but it also silences Peterson's crucial association, his double nuisance: in his mind, Christianity is threatened by Judeo-Greek ideas, the exemplification of "political theology" as a *compositum* of two otherwise alien imaginaries. Here, not surprisingly, the polar configuration of "Athens and Jerusalem" emerges in sharp relief. As opposite motifs, Athens and Jerusalem have come to exist by sharing a monism that safeguards their binary opposition. But their very existence as singular polar opposites, as well as therefore the need for translation between them, is a specific historical construction that marks and is marked by Christianity, whose own constitutive linguistic confusion (Hebrew/Greek), unique and necessary to it alone, bears them out. The monovalence of the polar opposites Athens and Jerusalem is constitutively Christian, and so is their mutual translation problem. Otherwise, disengaged from each other in their archaic Babelian plenitude, both formations are riveted by their own histories, their long-assumed monism broken by their own historical self-organization, which includes shared attributes of each other that Christianity separated out and rejoined as mutual opposition for its own purposes.

Judging the double enemy to be the Jew and the Greek is perfectly consistent with Peterson's logic. What alleviates his worry is a double projection: by virtue of being Christianized, the Judaic is absolved of its Jewishness (Paul) and the Greek is absolved of its Greekness (Gregory). Surely, given the historical convergence between pagan neo-Platonism and Judeo-Hellenism, it's rather preposterous to argue that this convergence is alien to Christianity's emergence and development. Peterson expressly downplays the philosophical affiliations, not to mention the intersection of mentalities, since, in the expansive coexistence of populations in the Alexandrian terrain of the Roman Empire, such matters were not privy to just a handful of intellectuals. Gregory's impetus is precisely to wrestle with those heterogeneous mentalities and gather them into the fold, not as an imperial bureaucrat like Eusebius (even though Bishop of Constantinople at the time), but as a hegemonic intellectual. Peterson sees Gregory Nazianzus as antimonarchical, but he is correct only in the sense that Gregory was recognizably never an imperial stooge. But he is mistaken to think that, contra Arianism and its influence, Gregory was some sort of antimonotheist. On the contrary, Gregory's intellectual sophistication and the rhetorical brilliance of articulating the Trinitarian consubstantiality lend an ever more powerful credibility to the permutations of the One-and-Only, and thus to the constitutive monarchical essence of Christian monotheism.[33]

Gregory Nazianzus exemplifies the intersecting terrain between philosophy and theology as it existed in those early years in Hellenic Christianity. It is as if the Greek language in which his extravagant syllogisms are conducted is born (again) as the language of Christianity, and that whatever existed six to eight centuries prior has been folded into this moment and vanished. His exemplary theological status is evident in the singularity of his sanctified name: Saint Gregory, *the* Theologian. But precisely because Gregory epitomized the terrain that bore the last vestiges of a Greek philosophical world, Peterson was mistaken in considering Gregory not to be a political thinker. Peterson explicitly depoliticizes Gregory, because he wants to depoliticize Christianity. Yet, unwittingly it seems, Peterson's theology is remarkably Pauline and harkens back to that Alexandrian mode of thought (mixed with various Egyptian and Hebraic elements) that exalts the (ideal) kingdom in place of the (always imperfect, because worldly) polis.[34] In this sense, Peterson's depoliticizing desire has a great deal in common with the antiphilosophical discourse of Pauline Christianity.[35] Both draw their fundamental impetus from an eschatological compulsion that hides its politics in the force of collective depoliticization.

In his deft reading of Spinoza, Etienne Balibar points out that one of the things that may make Christianity a rupturing event on the horizon of societal imagination is precisely how its configuration of divinity is removed from any specific social-historical anchoring and becomes instead an internalized depoliticized natural law.[36] The fiction of God becoming a sort of abstract natural substance that can be shared by all humans regardless of who, what, and where—that is, by the sole virtue of being humans alike—disengages the religious sensibility of individuals from the political dimensions of their worldly lives (their constitutive differential associations) and channels it toward an imaginary of community as if in a "state of nature." No wonder, a core element in the earliest Christian communities was the desire to dissolve this society—and all societies thereafter to the end of time. The eschatological desire in Christianity emerges from the fiction of this abstraction—and, yes, illusion—that the world of human beings exceeds politics. The actual political consequences of this self-cultivated illusion make perfect sense in retrospect: the history of Christian societies exemplifies sophisticated and indeed terrifying systems of worldly power as well as, at the same time, ubiquitous modes of mass disempowerment within society and across societies. And, while at it, it retains the allure of the eschatological desire intact. Ironically, the total separation between Church and State—were it to exist in some realm of pure theology, bearing pure eschatology—is a perfectly Christian project. This was certainly Peterson's aspiration. But the history of Christianity has proven this desire to be impossible because in turn Christianity's own political desire—a monarchical theocratic desire expressed from the outset (from the very first Pauline letter)—has proven to be untamable, no matter what metaphysical maneuvers its own theology has conjured up.

The Politics of Monotheism

It's useful to remember at this juncture Jean-Luc Nancy's statement that "Christianity is present even where—and perhaps especially where—it is no longer possible to recognize it."[37] This may bring to mind what has become by now the typical assertion that "secularism is Christianity"—a very simplistic idea that I have addressed at length in *Lessons in Secular Criticism* and will refrain from taking up here again. More provocatively, however, Nancy's statement can just as easily be taken to refer to those religious frameworks of meaning that dismiss Christianity as fraudulent, see it as an enemy, and wish themselves to be cleansed of it. For this reason, a return to monotheism as a problem in itself, and no longer simply as a Christian problem (Schmitt/Peterson), is warranted.

Two reference points are crucial here: Jan Assmann's *The Price of Monotheism* (2003) and Peter Sloterdijk's *God's Zeal: The Battle of the Three Monotheisms* (2007). Both German thinkers approach the issue with a disregard of political expediency and no compromises of the sort of political correctness that reigns in the Anglophone academy across the ranks. Both books remind us that the terrain is one of battle indeed, a *Kampfplatz* that demands the daring to see it not as a territory of enmity arising out of difference, but rather as a domain of internecine struggle, of internal war over a shared nucleus of significations, where differences arise (and are fought over with extraordinary violence) only in order to mask the contested terrain of the shared sacred object, whose constitutive exclusionary core does not indeed allow the sharing of its patrimony.

Monotheism's contested terrain belongs very much to the history of "the West." If we care to insist on using such a designation, we cannot afford to put it otherwise. Contrary to theories—deriving from and protecting the category of "the West"—that perceive the terrain of monotheism as belonging to some "clash of civilizations," it is more accurate to suggest that monotheism (however we are to determine what it is) resides at the heart of the social-historical process that bears the name "Civilization" and all the more so as it tends toward the presumption of its globalization. The politics of monotheism in this respect is politics of "Western culture" and indeed cannot but manifest itself in war—internal, internecine war and, insofar as the imaginary of globalization has triumphed, not war between states, cultures, religions, or "civilizations" but permanent internecine war, war within.[38]

As another reminder to this effect, I invite us to consider Jacques Derrida's unusually declarative comment: "The war over the 'appropriation of Jerusalem' is today's world war. It is taking place everywhere, it is the world, it is today's singular figure of the world being '*out of joint*.'"[39] To any serious reader of Derrida the blanket statement is surprising. Surely, the "messianic eschatologies" he names as the primary forces of "world war everywhere"—a kind of globality that is positively *worlding*, that is to say, creating new notions of world, new worldwide images and significations—would be a dangerous path of culturalist generality in hands less capacious than Derrida's. Yet, the sharp edge of the comment remains resistant to politically correct polishing. Jerusalem is a name—a Hebrew name, yet spoken in a number of languages that safeguard their existence by continuous mutual contestation over it. These multiple languages of the sacred are nonetheless the voice of the One-and-Only source, if we take the books that claim them as divine voice to be both the epitome and, at the same time, the reversal of Babelian confusion. For the three religions of the Book, as they are called, in their multiversal multilingual expression, are speaking of the same: the One-and-Only—not just God, but truth and world, and even language, both the language of the here and now, ephemeral and cosmic, and the language of the hereafter, the *eschaton*, the language-to-come, the monolanguage of redemption. This language is spectral, to think of Derrida again, and not because it is archaic, for it is very much the language of today, today's worlding and today's (world) war, which is—Derrida leaves no ambiguity here—the singular figure of why today's world is out of joint. This shared core cannot be shared. And in the violent contest over this (not-)sharing, the world is torn asunder.[40]

This out-of-joint world is made and unmade by this one unshareable shared core—of significations, affects, names, images, languages, mentalities. It's not about theologies or even "religions" and even if God might be the singular word that signifies it, we would need to imagine "God" as a word-system. The problematic of this system is a long-term formation with multiple social histories, yet forming around a consistent *monarchical* core of meaning, itself complex and elusive. For this core I will retain the name "monotheism" with all historical complications in mind.[41] The name is surely not reducible to the believers of the three religions that nominally claim it. The object is not *the* Jews, *the* Christians, *the* Muslims—already a set of enormous categorical simplifications—but whatever constellation in "what is Judaic" or "what is Christian" or "what is Muslim" draws its power from submission to the order of a monological otherworldly law. In this sense, this is part of the broader critique of heteronomy I have been conducting as the primary task of secular criticism.

The effects of a social imagination that conjures and submits to the figure of the One-and-Only-Other-to-the-world are hardly otherworldly. Heteronomy is always a social-historical condition, with profound psychocultural (and, surely, psychosexual) complications that animate all kinds of fiercely contentious materialities. We can return for a minute to Freud, whose thought was focused on precisely these psychocultural and psychosexual parameters of human life. Freud attributed to the human invention of monotheism the advent of a very specific sort of violence that has both as subject and as object the religion of the other and, as a consequence, the entire (both imaginary and tangibly real) territory of the other. Whatever we think of Freudian methodology, what is now called, in cavalier fashion, "religious violence" is not some natural proclivity of human beings. It is violence conducted over the existence of someone's god—in love (and for survival) of one's own, in hatred (and for extinction) of what belongs to the other. Again, I am speaking of a certain mentality, a certain social imaginary. I am not speaking of constituencies of the faithful, or even of "religions" per se, as systems of anthropological ritual and practices of social-historical cohesion. Polytheistic Hindus demolished the Babri Masjid mosque in 1992 with the same virulence that Christian zealots obliterated the Alexandrian Serapeum in 391, the Taliban dynamited the Bamiyan Buddhas in 2001, or Daesh (ISIS) in Syria demolished the ancient arches of Palmyra just yesterday. We cannot discount the specific historical and political dimensions in the conduct of such mass actions. But also we can hardly ignore the similarity in impetus, objective, and affect, which exceeds the historical particulars. This very difficult epistemological intersection is my concern here.[42]

Centuries before "religion" became a category of social analysis, "religious violence" came to be an increasingly primary cause of war and aggression and, by all historical accounts, this shift occurred when human societies began to conceive divinity as uniquely proprietary and exclusionist. Jan Assmann is right to call monotheism a regulative idea. In whatever way we are to delineate monotheism as an event, and with all the difficulties of pinpointing its advent beyond the variety of discursive formations that claim to be in the know (the Axial Age, the Abrahamic, the Book, and so on), monotheism registers as a symptomatic condition that regulates the categorical field, both backward (historically) and forward (epistemologically). As a result, new categorizations are created and new meanings are conjured: polytheism becomes a categorical description that envelopes an enormous range of heterogeneous practices only because it now comes to be targeted as the unifocal abominable enemy; idolatry is invented as a name to describe what before monotheism was a ubiquitous, nameless, and inconsequential ritual routine for millennia across societal and cultural patterns; theology is rendered an autonomous discursive field beyond the ritual parameters of a faith; faith itself becomes a categorical mode of human-being that has a singularly undemonstrable connection to the truth; the universal emerges as the most dominant epistemic field the world has ever known; and so on—the list is long.

In this sense, the literal meaning of the name "monotheism" cannot adequately cover this epistemic range. From his earliest work, Assmann sought to describe a historical phenomenon—the rise of the cult of Akhenaten in Egypt—that does break the established theological field but cannot in itself carry the full range of what the monotheistic imaginary will come to be after several instantiations in the history of societies all the way into modern times. The revolutionary potential of the Mosaic distinction, as he famously called it, may have unleashed a world-changing force, but not because it signified the invention of worshiping a single divinity, strictly speaking. Assmann's starting thesis is that conjuring a single divinity to worship is not what encapsulates the essence of monotheism. Rather, this initial monistic distinction promulgates the idea that all other divinities are false and must be forbidden and ultimately obliterated. *Exclusion is the decisive point, not oneness*, he concludes.[43]

Incidentally, the Pauline line of argument, expressed acutely by Alain Badiou, that the sign of the One is the sign "for all" and therefore the site of the universal does not extricate us from the problem of exclusion.[44] Without belaboring the obvious point that the One-as-All or the One-for-All bears the quintessential totalitarian meaning of the One, the challenge that Badiou raises resides in his insistence on the rhetorical constitution of the One, its linguistic modality. The One precipitates a specific mode of address that unifies the discursive field of addressees—this is Badiou's chief presumption. It is more of a projection, of course, or, one might say, a retroactive actualization of an already constituted Universal—historically speaking. To say that "the One inscribes no difference in the subjects in which it addresses itself" makes sense only within a Christian perspective and the trajectory this takes into secular modernity, where indeed the idea of "the whole of humanity" flourishes. One cannot really say, for example, that it is applicable in the case of the "chosen people of Israel": all Israelites are God's chosen, which surely unifies them, but precisely insofar as they are chosen they are exclusive—the nonelect, the so-called idolaters, are excluded. And, although it surely makes sense to say, as Badiou does, that the One cannot be relegated to the particular, for this is parsed (made part of, partitioned, particularized) through the differential and plural action of worldly law, the injunction of the Universal produces a totalizing monolatry under duress. Under the sign of the Universal, the One interpellates everyone, and whoever does not respond is parsed out. The violence against the infidel is fueled by this interpellating force. The All is a hardcore singularity that disguises its exclusiveness in a gesture of all-consuming centralizing power. Not surprisingly, Badiou quickly moves on to argue that Pauline monolatrous universalism is statist at the core—in my language here, simply monarchical. Whatever plurality may have been signified by the All—before it is constituted as such by Paul, indeed before it is thus capitalized—is annihilated by the universalist exclusionism of the One.

So, it is the exclusionary effect of monotheism that ultimately changes the game. This is why any sort of discourse in the anthropology or sociology of religion that argues for an evolutionary model, whereby the monotheistic imagination is but a refinement of what human societies have achieved so far—arguments about the abstraction of divinity, even intellectuality, and the like—are ultimately trapped in the dead end of their own assurance and cannot account for the extraordinary violence that trails the history of this allegedly refined achievement. Because what has given catalytic power to monotheism (however we characterize, I repeat, its various languages and historical instantiations) lies not in its evolutionary trajectory in the history of religion, but in its revolutionary rupture in the history of the social imagination. Monotheism signifies a rupture in the field of truth, or, more accurately, it signifies a rupture because it introduces knowledge of singular truth into a field of meaning otherwise unconcerned with verifiability simply because its bind to worldly ritual was enough to sustain its credibility over time. What matters in the so-called Mosaic distinction is "the distinction between true and false religion behind which, in the final instance, stands the distinction between god and the world" (PoM, 37). This radical distinction that produces the exclusive truth of the unworldly is the essence of the monotheism-effect beyond whatever religious constituencies claim it as a name or are interpellated in its name.

From the outset, the immediate effect of establishing this distinction was the exceeding violence with which obedience to the primary command—the First Commandment—was implemented. The actual historical details may be nebulous, but I concur with Assmann that no archeological story can turn the imagination that conceptualized divinity as a matter of singular exclusive truth into mere fiction. The desire to eradicate practices that are deemed to be false is and continues to be real. When, how, and by whom it was initially manifested is of secondary consequence. What matters instead is the revolutionary association of religious faith with otherworldly law, for the crux of the monotheism-effect is that it establishes not a new religious practice but a new political order. The truth of the One-and-Only God is a command, a sacred order that resides in the nether spheres of immaterial existence—unreachable, unquestionable, and unrecognizable in any prior ways of assessing power (physical attributes, geographical limitations, social institutions, even human whims)—and yet continues to operate in the worldly domain. We have a rupture in the social imagination not only because divinity and truth collapse into one unique and exclusive signification, but because divinity is for the first time made identical to the law of society. The legislator God seals his power and his singular truth because he revokes the capacity of humans to interrogate the authoritative source of the law and therefore alter it if they so wish. The outcome is the creation of what Assmann, with an inspired phrase, names "the theonomous individual" (PoM, 42).

The monotheistic imagination is thus a sublime instance of heteronomy-in-action in the most concrete terms. For it is not only an extreme instance of self-abrogation at a psychic level: the bizarre act of denying yourself the freedom to create your own law by establishing your incapacity via your own creation of a self-binding divine injunction. It is also an extreme instance of political self-subjugation to a contractual obligation with your own creation of a superior power beyond the order of power:

> *Mono*theism has a primary political meaning. One cannot serve two masters. I may enter a covenant with either God or Pharaoh, but not with both at once. . . . This either-or was unprecedented in prior religious history. One could be particularly attached to deity without for that reason attracting the wrath and jealousy of the other gods, just as one could sacrifice to another god without falling out of favor with one's own favorite deity. The jealousy of the biblical god is a political affect, roused by the wrongdoing of a contractual partner rather than the infidelity of a beloved. . . . The contract is not metaphorical. It is the matter itself, the new form to which religion—the interrelationship between god, humankind, society, and the world—is recast. This new relationship can only be with a single god, hence monotheistic.
>
> (PoM, 38–39)

Assmann is elaborating here on what he takes to be the ground rule of monotheism, which he reiterates in a variety of ways: "God's oneness is not the salient criterion but the negation of the 'other' gods" (PoM, 31). He is arguing, of course, against the extreme point—the exclusionary distinction rather than simply the monological configuration—and, no doubt, that's where the epistemological and political violence of monotheism lies. But the real challenge is to engage with oneness as such: as the necessary determination of exclusivity and exclusion, even if not quite the absolute predetermination. The dominance of the principle of the One may not necessarily lead to the exclusion of the Other, but neither the invention of the One-and-Only nor the exclusion of the Other is possible without it. In this respect, Assmann's metaphorical invocation of the two masters is useful in distinguishing polytheistic favoritism from monotheistic exclusivity but clouds the crux of monotheism as a political order. Serving two masters is always untenable; it is a nonsensical proposition—that is why it is used metaphorically to denote the impossible. If there is more than one master, there is no master. There's only one master. So, the very notion of serving a master is monotheism's built-in necessity, except that here it becomes serving *the* master, the One-and-Only master, the Master of the Universe.

In this respect, the political here is the cosmological as well, for the transcendental power of the Creator thus conceived cannot be doubted by anyone. Those who question it are infidels in the most literal sense. Not only because they do not belong to the faith—this is a much later development—but because they have no faith in the truth of the world and thus they are an affront to the universe. Therefore, "Biblical monotheism is political at the core" (PoM, 38) not only because it establishes an otherworldly religion in terms of worldly power, but because "it polemically distances itself from other religions" (PoM, 35), or, more accurately, other modes of religion. Monotheism's epistemology is quintessentially polemical, as the principle of the One, which it serves and promulgates so powerfully, is manifested through a fundamental prohibition of the Other.

The first and obvious order of prohibition—the First Commandment—is against polytheistic practices, which are soon categorized under the invented name "idolatry" since the concretely prohibited object is not only the plurality of gods but the material reproduction of divine signification, which then opens the way to plurality (Second Commandment). To idolatry we will turn shortly in detail, but what is crucial in this language of prohibition is not plurality per se, but "the indistinction between the divine and the mundane from which plurality necessarily follows" (PoM, 41). It is this prohibition against notions of divinity that are immanent in the world—what Assmann calls "cosmotheism"—that, by virtue of the geocultural triumph of Christianity, ultimately marks the fundamental divide between the archaic world and the modern and still haunts the imaginary of modernity, despite various cosmotheistic counterinstances in modernity's history. Curiously, this view is missing from most narratives of modernity, including those most critical and facile in their "anti-Westernism," which thereby blinds them both to their own monological transcendentalisms and to the fact that "anti-Westernism" is and has always been a crucial element of modernity.

But the more important factor in the polemical opposition between cosmotheism and monotheism is monotheism's conflation of the political with the theological. The monotheistic imaginary was from the outset cultivated in specific theologico-political fashion and there is no more sublime a text to celebrate this than the Book of Exodus.[45] So, political theology may be said to be inherent in monotheism, whatever again may be the multiple permutations of both names. But there is a curious logic here that deserves our attention. As the monotheistic imaginary is dependent on the necessity of separating the divine from the worldly, it creates consequently a division within the political as well between the instrumental and the transcendental, or between power and sovereignty, if we want to use that sort of language. In this sense, by a sort of dialectical backdoor play, the theological is no longer contained within the mere purview of religion as a set of rituals and practices of worship, but returns to the political to mend, as it were, the split that monotheism created in the first place. The theological comes to inhabit the transcendental part of the political split and thus enables theology in turn to merge with instrumental power.

For only in the sort of monolatry of sovereignty that monotheism ushers into the political imagination do we find theological thought achieving such power of persuasion and control in the very worldly realm that it allegedly meant to overcome. We see this animated in all sorts of "polytheistic" or "secular" practices in modernity, especially in ethnonationalist politics, as I have argued, but also in the global onslaught of "Civilization," which is surely the epitome of a *monohumanist* imaginary and can be said to carry the imprimatur of the modern divinity of World. But there is an additional consequence that Assmann correctly points out, which is nonetheless rarely, if ever, considered: As the divine realm now comes to hold and execute the ultimate law-making power, the realm of human judgment, even about elemental things concerning the physical universe, is also split (similar to the realm of the political) between the instrumental and the transcendental, and is also similarly "reunified" subsequently by the theologization of the concept of justice, which until then had been worldly and profane in all archaic societies. The imaginary of monotheism, in this respect, has crept and ensconced itself beneath virtually all notions of justice in modernity, "East" and "West" alike, stripping justice of its innate profanity, of the fact that it is no more than a framework of decision by men and women in real time, open and immanent to the action it generates and ultimately unbounded in its effect, except by time alone.

In other words, the play of monovalence that characterizes monotheism's framework of producing meaning can afford to express itself not only as strict monolingualism, but with all sorts of binary or even multilingual structures. What must remain prominent in the variety of idioms that arise, according to specific history or dogma, is a monologue of truth beyond any presumptions of verifiability: a monologue of "things as they are" that can encompass the range from the most evident and pragmatic to the most intangible and fantastic. What authorizes this great range and complexity that enables us still to use the name "monotheism" is also what, despite the "internecine" war among the dogmas, unifies it as a framework of meaning: what Sloterdijk identifies as an "ontological monarchism: the principle that a single being can and should rule over everyone and everything" (*God's Zeal*, 83). We need not quibble here about whether "single being" is tantamount to the One-and-Only God, who may be zero, absolutely infinite, three-in-one, or what have you. "God" is just a name (even when unnameable) and, as we shall see shortly, precisely as name no more than a mere idol. Ontological monarchism is not an issue of religion, even if sometimes it reigns by force of faith. It bears first and foremost a political significance no matter what may be its overt claims to belong to a discourse of nature, the ontological status of things. How it manifests itself in religion, or *as* religion, is mere symptom. Monotheism is indeed a *political* problem.

Freud's Predicament

Freud understood that monotheism is a political problem better than most thinkers of his generation (and many generations thereafter), even if politics was never really his favorite language. This is evident in the very first paragraph of the first published portion of *Moses and Monotheism*, where, in preparing his audience for the shock of unveiling the thesis that Moses was an Egyptian, Freud admits the difficulty but necessity of going against what he calls the "national interest" (MM, 243).[46] In 1937, when the world's Jews do not yet have a nation of their own, the choice of voicing the "national interest" is noteworthy. It is a political term—a designation of Freud's explicit understanding that his text is politically laden at a primary level. But it is also an indication that Freud's psycho-anthropological inquiry emerges from (and aims at) a constituency that is in the end political, no matter whether it sees itself as ethnic, cultural, or religious.

Perhaps, we might go so far as to say that this constituency is *politicized* by the very horizon drawn in Freud's text. Traces of not only addressing a constituency but even desiring to (re)gather a constituency and give it new elements for identification and cohesion abound in this text, and they certainly account for Freud's dogged persistence, so near the end of his life and against so many counterfactors, in bringing the text to completion and publication, despite an inordinate repetition of caveats. In the end, "with the audacity [*Verwegenheit*] of one who has little or nothing to lose" (MM, 295), Freud may be said to have made a deliberate decision to distance the Jewish question from an ethnological/theological matrix by substituting for the myth of God's chosen people the myth of Moses's chosen children (the paternal gesture being essential), so that, if we risk the audacity of summation before unfolding the inquiry, we may say that Freud, as father of psychoanalysis, compiles in *Moses and Monotheism* the text of a neo-Mosaic law (that is, as such, also anti-Mosaic, in that it recasts the Mosaic distinction in secular terms), which will gather the new diaspora away from and against the ethnoracialized homogenization expressed and enacted by the Nazi enemy. Freud's gesture is political in this sense as well.

And yet, the politics in *Moses and Monotheism* remains multifold. Earlier I pointed out Freud's intrinsically driven association of monotheism with imperialist expansion—a point rarely acknowledged, but which I underline again, as it is set very much in tension with the other side of the exclusionary elements of the Mosaic distinction: the inward or esoteric tendency of the exclusively unique, the divinely elect. Moreover, there is the historical context, which has been extensively discussed: the fact that Freud is writing in bifurcated fashion, on the one hand, against the emergent politics of Nazism and, on the other, in favor of the politics of psychoanalysis in light of its doubtful future after his imminent demise. In the context of the explicit charge that psychoanalysis was a (godless) Jewish science, these two dimensions come tightly together. As the Jews of German culture are being racially targeted and the "Jewishness" of psychoanalysis is being intellectually challenged (by Jung's alternatives and more), a psychoanalytic explanation of the violent hostility against the Jews that, moreover, privileges the "cultural" dimension (whereby religion would displace the paradigm of race as framework of hostility) becomes, in Freud's mind, imperative.

From the outset, of course, the problems in the assumption that a philosophical (or anthropological or scientific) argument about religion might overcome the horrific reality of violence unleashed on the basis of race are legion, and no one exposes them better than Gil Anidjar in his recent work on Christianity. Formidably mining a vast scholarly archive, Anidjar destabilizes much of *Moses and Monotheism*'s conventional reception by pointing out that the backdrop behind Freud's restaging of the Jewish question is—for the umpteenth time, he would say—the cryptic staging of the Christian question.[47] It's difficult to dispute Anidjar's argument on its own grounds, except perhaps for the fact that, much against his own skeptical tendency to invest in the enigmatic, Anidjar finds in Christianity a total (and totalizing) signifier. Be that as it may, his thesis emerges from the depths of Freud's writing, however complex (in a psychoanalytic sense) this writing is, and would have to be encountered as an outmaneuverable stake in Freud's late-style performativity.[48] Whatever the assumptions about "religion"—Freud's own, but also the assumptions of all readers who subsequently encounter his enigma (including Anidjar)—the *political* terrain of the text, the terrain it covers (again, in a psychoanalytic double sense), organizes, occupies/invests in (*besetzen*) projects and opens up in the overall sphere of the organization of society, marks, to my mind, the bottom line of this text. This would include—and this is not at all extravagant to say—the space in between the lines and in the margins of this text, or what is latent and even prohibited in this text, *l'inter-dit* of this text.

In this respect then, *Moses and Monotheism* is a text of multiple polemics, which would include, as a final undercurrent, Freud's long-term investment in a variety of tasks essential to psychoanalytic thinking: the critique of religion as illusion or obsessional neurosis, the query as to the psychic elements of social cohesion, the constitution of authority, the genesis of society, the psychophysiology of memory across time, the trauma of civilization, the conflictual processes of sublimation, and a great deal more. From this standpoint, rather than being an aberrant text or the text of a senile old man, as many critics argued from the outset, *Moses and Monotheism* is, to the contrary, the culmination of Freud's entire psychoanthropological edifice and a profound contribution to the theory of psychoanalysis, including the evidence of its many aporias and blind spots.

The already overladen context of this essay will not permit me to query *Moses and Monotheism* extensively on its own ground (not to mention the gigantic bibliography that haunts it), but only insofar as it pertains to our discussion. Nevertheless, a few words on the form of this peculiar work are essential. For one, the translated title in English may make for a fine pair of conjugal single names, but it effaces two crucial qualifiers. *Der Mann Moses und die monotheistische Religion* reveals itself to be standing at the crossroads of the study of religion with the study of a man—a broadly anthropological inquiry through the study of indeed a single man who created a religion of a single god that established his divinity through his association (election) of/by a single people: "It was the single man, Moses, who made [*geschaffen*] the Jewish people" (MM, 353),[49] Freud says, but he also says just as much that this single man also created the god of single belief, even if borrowing the fantasies of another man, the pharaoh Akhenaten. In fact, if Moses, this one man, is granted the legacy of this grand institution, as opposed to the other man (the pharaoh) who first conceived the idea, it is because he is presumed to be the founder of a society that gave this new single god a real and lasting meaning, which can be said to have changed the course of human history.

In other words, a single man Moses not only came to make a people—a single people, who came to see itself as entirely singular in the course of its existence in the world—but he also made a single god for this people alone, or, if you will, he made a people who was the only one to be elected by this god in a covenant of mutual sacred singularity. So, while monotheism, as a particular mode of religion—which, I repeat, is given over to repetition in various languages and social-historical contexts—is certainly a key objective in Freud's inquiry, the monological principle that runs throughout the problem he encounters is encapsulated in the figure of this one man, an extraordinary man no doubt (*der grosse Mann*), but nonetheless the epitome of *anthropos*, or, more precisely, the epitome of the human capacity for the violent imagination that underlies the psycho-socio-anthropological process of the historical institution of societies. After all, humans make history, even if not quite as they please.[50]

Attention to this capacity for social-imaginary institution—to use, via Castoriadis, its proper name—is indicated in another titular gesture that never quite made it into the final published project. In a much discussed letter to Arnold Zweig,[51] Freud announces his new work (and the reason he presently withholds it from publication) by pinpointing its genre (*The Man Moses: A Historical Novel*) and thus acknowledging the central power of fiction in the making of history, and all the more in the telling of history, even if this telling takes place under a scientific presumption. Of course, as the history of psychoanalysis testifies, all of Freud's work entwines scientific and empirical aspects with speculation and indeed fiction, even in the elementary sense of the poetic making of a subject: first himself, the self-analyzed subject in *The Interpretation of Dreams* through which psychoanalysis is founded, then the very theory of subjectivity that comes with the discovery of the unconscious and all its permutations, and finally the radical poetic subjectivity of the man Moses and the social-imaginary institution of a people.

A historical novel is a very specific genre, and we cannot discount here the resonance of Georg Lukács, who was its most articulate theorist, and Thomas Mann, who was one of its greatest practitioners in the German language. We know well Freud's admiration for the latter, and their correspondence at this dire historical moment testifies to their mutual concern with German culture's demise. Mann is also writing at this time his own four-part "historical novel" encounter with the biblical myth of the Jews in Egypt, *Joseph and His Brothers*, which had a similarly episodic trajectory from manuscript to publication (1926 to 1943). Mann's visit to Vienna in the spring of 1936 to celebrate publicly Freud's eightieth birthday galvanizes their discussions on the vicissitudes of biblical myth; a mutual effect on both their works is certain. Mann will subsequently publish his own novella on Moses while in American exile (*Das Gesetz*, 1943), which Ilse Grubrich-Simitis calls "a virtuosic variation on Freud's *Moses* book."[52]

With such resonance, we can then speak of *Moses and Monotheism* as a work of late modernism in perfectly literary terms: episodic, fragmented, asymmetrical, and repetitious structure; mythographic engagement with history; hybrid entwinement of prose fiction, fable, and essay with multiple and contradictory prefaces; distorted and deceptive (anti)hero protagonist; patent inconclusiveness; narrative interruptions and lacunae; ambivalent relation to the demands of realism; and so on.[53] As the advent of psychoanalysis is conventionally accepted to be a key element in the development of modernist aesthetics, this "jagged quarry" of a work, in Grubrich-Simitis's inspired phrase, which exposes some of the most difficult terrains of psychoanalytic thinking at an anthropological scale, might as well be seen, from a literary standpoint, as modernism's return to psychoanalysis of what is due.

Michel de Certeau is right to flag the notion that conjoins psychoanalysis and modernism as a key formal element. *Moses and Monotheism* is a fantasy, he argues.[54] Freud himself admits so in one of the many letters to Arnold Zweig (February 21, 1936). The text belongs just as much to fantastic literature as it is itself a dream text that, in the manner most appropriate to dream-thinking, inscribes in its very form (*textualizes*) the entire history of its motivation and production. De Certeau focuses on how this specific mode of writing fantasy implicates the history of its conditions of production. The matter is both literary and psychoanalytic in equal part. Grubrich-Simitis makes the same argument when she likens the text to the formal structure of a daydream. The irritation some readers might have with the book's elliptical structure and its uncanny protagonist, she argues, may be alleviated "if the work is read as a kind of *day-dream* generated under traumatic conditions of extreme distress."[55] Her archeological examination of Freud's *Moses* manuscripts, which is psychoanalytically motivated but conducted in the best sense of literary criticism, corroborates de Certeau's own groundbreaking archeology of how the textuality of phantasy bears the traces of real history in fictionalized form.

There are several levels of phantasy going on here. The figure of Moses alone is an object of multiple phantasies. All at the same time, he is the sacred founder of the Jewish people, the great rebel and lawgiver, the heroic progenitor of Jesus and Mohammed within the Abrahamic legacy, the archetypal liberator for many cultural strains that emerge far into Christian modernity, the very essence of untamable messianic desire. And for Freud specifically, he is a figure of kinship (both father and older sibling), the stranger-in-the-self that epitomizes the underlying splitting of the ego, a source of fascination as an art object (his essay on Michelangelo's Moses, much like *Moses and Monotheism*, is an essential text for any psychoanalytic discussion of sublimation), and an agent of a new myth—a myth of birth from death—subverting the patrimonial myth of ancestral begetting. But there is also the phantasy space that "the man Moses" encapsulates, as does any great mythical or literary figure, which is equally multiple and open to all sorts of collective investments from all sorts of standpoints: simultaneous phantasies of rebellion and yet of law and order, of foundation and yet of renegade alterity, of equally creative and yet destructive imagination, indeed of both humanity and divinity, for we must not forget that Moses does not simply create a people but he creates a god for this people. Moses is a poet of divinity like few mythical figures in the histories of humanity.[56]

Finally, the text bears the phantasies of a whole range of historical fictions—by fictions, I mean not falsehoods or falsities but, to the contrary, realities made by the grand capacity of human *poiēsis*, whether enacted by individuals or whole societies. In this, the text engages with the central—both primordial and contemporary—phantasies of the Jews, providing in fact a rubric that counters both racial and religious demarcations of culture. At the same time it engages the phantasies of Christianity, with its own presumptions of the redemptive consequences of murder, as well as the more contemporary (with Freud) phantasies of what constitutes progress in modernity: the sophisticated level of abstraction in monotheism; the "advance of intellectuality" as he terms it; the transmission of tradition that shapes the social space and the complexities involved in the making of collective identities; the coherence of the psychoanalytic method across a range of epistemological fields, from individual therapy to psycho-socio-anthropological formations; and so on.

But of all these intertwined phantasmatic networks what concerns us here the most is the network of monotheistic phantasies. The man Moses is but one of this network's figures—for Freud, a founding figure but, in essence, this doesn't matter. What is originary or foundational in a phantasy is itself nothing but a phantasm, indeed a phantasm very much produced by the phantasy network, and the figure of the man Moses encapsulates this phantasm in stark terms. Two things are of more immediate relevance to the inquiry here, whose complexities I will now try to unravel: (1) how monarchical authority comes to achieve the autonomous status of ultimate alterity; (2) how social-imaginary cohesion is reproduced in defiance of the discontinuous processes of history. In simple words, these two terrains are monotheism and religion—and, of course, they are linked, as Freud's German title certifies. At the risk of giving the game away, we may even say that what turns the One-and-Only into the quintessential figure of the transcendent Other is precisely what enables social materiality to reproduce itself, via the ties that bind peoples together (*religio*) against the grain of history's chasms.

One of the key psychoanalytic contours of Freud's account is that the peculiar imaginary of monotheism develops out of and *as* a traumatic condition. The connection to his overall theory of repression (guilt, latency, return) and to the Oedipal complex (patriarchical jealousy, parricide, guilt, repression) has been relentlessly examined. Whatever the specific merits of the theory of repression, however, the framework of the trauma is multifold and multisited. Trauma can never be reduced to a single event and its repetition formation. In this sense, as sign for trauma, Moses, the Egyptian, is not just an alien at the crux of identity, an other residing at the heart of the self who always makes (*schaffen*) and remakes the self, an other(ed) self who, in Edward Said's inimitable phrase, bears "a troubling, disabling, destabilizing secular wound" that requires continuous attention and prevents reconciliation, assimilation, self-absorption.[57] Moses is also the cause, the source, of the trauma: the strict and wrathful father who makes inordinate demands for obedience to the law, who restricts and enforces, who formalizes living practices and legislates constraints. And who, therefore, must be killed, nullified in an act of desperate liberation, of enraged disobedience, in order to register yet another wound, on top of the wound of his foreignness and his otherness, another troubling, disabling, destabilizing, and, yes, *secular* (because existentially worldly) wound—the wound of guilt for his murder and the wound of repression, of "doing away with the traces." And yet this is not all. Moses, the cause of the trauma, is also simultaneously the effect of the trauma, a traumatic object embedded deep in the flesh of the subject—because the psyche is irredeemably corporeal—producing yet another wound, one's own troubling, disabling, destabilizing, secular wound, the wound that was made and shaped (*schaffen*) by the people who bear it, the wound they inflicted on an other—a father? a foreigner? a founder? a lawmaker? a godmaker?—but, in so doing, also inflicted on themselves, on their own psychic constitution, on their constitution as a people, a wound that was made and shaped by them in order to make and shape them anew, as God's elect, as divine people.[58]

This wound is constitutive in an absolute sense. What disables actually enables; what destabilizes actually establishes. One becomes the Other. And it does not merely pertain to the story of Moses the Egyptian, to the content of the historical fiction. It is also actualized in the author/reader of this fiction himself: in the gesture of Freud, whose text enters history in a disruptive way, as an affront to the *archē* of a whole people (their religion and social identity), in order to reestablish it, to reauthorize it. Samuel Weber has given us a succinct account of this double movement: "Dispossessing a people of its founder and, in a certain sense of its origin, [makes the origin] external and extrinsic: in a certain sense, *heterogeneous*. The origin of the 'nation' would thus consist not in its 'nativity,' not in a continuity of life expressed in blood and birth, but in what follows, both individually and collectively. The identity of a people, of a nation, at least in the specific case of the Jews, comes to it from afar. It is acquired, not innate" ("Doing Away With the *Man Moses*," 72–73). Weber helps us here to enhance the meaning of *schaffen*, for the creative social imagination that founds both religions and nations (as well as their essential intertwinement), the imagination that makes and shapes whole peoples and their history across the discontinuous vastness of time, is predicated on what turns out to be an immanent and constitutive destructive element, a gesture of unmaking. In this sense, death precedes birth and the origin is barred from an *archē* (beginning). It is *originally othered*, which is what *heterogeneous* literally means, and it comes to produce an *archē* (rule) by repressing this otherness at the origin, by expelling it, indeed effacing it, in the institutionalized reenactment of its rituals of identity. The repetition of this repression/enactment that conceals the heterogeneity at the origin ensures social cohesion as well as identity transmission through time and space.

This is where Freud's configuration of *Geistigkeit*, which is the impetus and telos of the entire *Moses and Monotheism* adventure, really matters. I understand why almost all commentators insist, even if in variable ways, on engaging this notion through the psychoanalytic (and, at the limit, anthropological) lens that Freud himself establishes. Yet, the notion carries an expressly political significance. It pertains to the constitution of society: how a specific social imaginary is instituted, how it comes to be and sustain itself, how it recognizes itself and what is different from it, what sorts of practices it valorizes, what values it authorizes, what myths it promulgates, and so on. *Geistigkeit*, in this sense, is not some sort of state of being, despite Freud's anthropological (phylogenetic) argument. It is a social-historical condition, whose psychic parameters are formed by a specifically constructed (in the strict *mythistorical* sense) mentality of society whose "ethnicity" (or "nationality" or "raciality" or "religiousness") is pure fiction, in the powerful sense that fictions become hardcore realities.

From an elementary standpoint, the phrase *Fortschritt in der Geistigkeit* is ensconced in German Enlightenment language and implicated in the notions of progress, development, and advancement that cover the ground in any discourse of modernization. The coupling of this industrial qualifier (*Fortschritt*) with what, in the German language, is certainly a word of Christian provenance (*Geistigkeit*) raises all kinds of issues, especially when it is accentuated as the sign of a specific psychic condition. The ambiguities of *Geist*, with such a trail of philosophical shrapnel behind them, prevent us from examining the notion purely as Freud's invention. He is himself subjected to this regime of ambiguity.[59] English translators of *Geistigkeit* have insisted on "intellectuality" over "spirituality," no doubt led by Freud's repeated signals. Whatever the regime of the linguistic tradition, in Freud's text the word *Geistigkeit* signals precisely the *shift* from spirituality to intellectuality—from the "religious" to the "secular," from the "archaic" to the "modern," or what have you. Although the semantic ambiguity remains, the word comes to embody a shift because it is subjected to the signifying work of *Fortschritt*—the advancement, the movement of progress, the development. In this sense, Freud's *Geistigkeit* means to point to a condition, and as a condition it moves beyond its ambiguity as a word; it resolves this ambiguity by presuming a shift in a specific direction that carries with it a distinguished and unequivocal value.[60]

But, despite his strong conviction, the complexity remains. For one, the resolution of ambiguity entails a certain repression. Whatever remains of the notion of spirit in *Geist* is repressed by Freud's painstaking investment in the spirit's advancement toward intellect. One might counter by insisting that the two words (spirit and intellect) cannot be distinguished, since Freud, after all, is engaged in a certain secularization of spirit that would wrest spirit from religion and preserve it as societal character. But this would mean to ignore that what makes spirit and intellect indistinguishable in *Geist* is in the end a Christian predisposition. On this point Freud is clear. *Geistigkeit* is foremost the condition of the Mosaic experience—if not "ethnically" the mark of the Jews, then the societal character that distinguishes the followers of Moses, who in this sense become "Jews." This character, he argues, is sculpted by arduous devotion to the hardest possible regime of sublimation: not merely the renunciation of instincts, which after all signals (for Freud) the basic psycho-physiological necessity of becoming a human being, but the deliberate choice to devalorize the work of the senses in favor of the work of the mind. While the first remains in the sphere of the natural (phylogenetic), the second is positively cultural (ontogenetic) in the strictest anthropological sense. Freud describes a whole series of requisite attitudes and practices in this regard: the expulsion of anything having to do with myth, magic, and fable; the compulsion to worship a god one cannot see or name; the subsequent prohibition of pictorial representations of anything sacred (hence, the generic rejection of image in favor of language); and the overall restraint of the corporeal, the sensuous, the ritualistic, and the aesthetic in favor of the abstract, the intellectual, the faith-based, and the ethical.

In light of these requisites, Freud argues, Christianity signifies a retreat of *Geistigkeit*: "The new religion meant a cultural regression as compared with the older, Jewish one. . . . The Christian religion did not maintain the high level in things of the mind [*Vergeistigung*] to which Judaism had soared. It was no longer strictly monotheist, it took over numerous symbolic rituals from surrounding peoples, it re-established the great mother-goddess and found room to introduce many of the divine figures of polytheism only lightly veiled, though in subordinate positions" (MM 332). I consider that, in our preceding discussion of the Trinity, we have put to rest in what sense Christianity draws from and fuels further the monarchical/monotheistic imaginary in all kinds of innovative ways. To debate strictness of monotheism here is to obscure the complexities and mutabilities of monotheism in various historical times and places in favor of a simplistic explanation that does not hold well under duress. In any case, comparing monotheisms is not my concern. What's interesting is how, in comparing Judaism to Christianity—Islam is relegated to a secondary imitation of Judaism and thus carries no trauma and no internal development (MM, 337)—Freud lands in a predicament. His conviction that Christianity signifies regression underlies his investment in *Fortshritt*, in the idea that what he later calls "the dematerialization of God" (MM, 362) means advancement in the human condition. But he immediately contradicts it by a proposing a counteradvancement: "And yet in the history of religion—that is, regarding the return of the repressed—Christianity was an advance [*Fortshritt*] and from that time onward the Jewish religion was to some extent a fossil" (MM, 333).

From the standpoint of the Freudian theory of repression, of course, both moments of advancement are possible and explainable, strangely enough even as a sequence: The Jews constituted the initial advance by choosing intellect over the senses, but achieving it required the repression of the original impetus—the murderous act against the founder (thus father and in that sense God himself). The Christians recoiled from strict devotion to intellectual abstraction, but in the process of regression they allowed the repressed guilt to return in order to be acknowledged and expiated, thus (one may say) gaining back the "unmediated" relation to God that the Jews, by virtue of their guilt, had lost.

But much is commonly concealed in the tightly controlled narrative of both these moments of advancement. For one, however we judge the theory of repression—for me there is no issue there—Freud in essence behaves like a Kantian. His passionate investment in the advance of intellectuality—"the heights of sublime abstraction" (MM, 256)—which characterizes all his anthropological writings and in *Moses and Monotheism* specifically becomes an argument for collective sublimation, can easily be seen as an extension of Kant's argument on the sublime.[61] There is something ineffable, in essence beyond reason, which only the intellect can grasp, configure, and devote itself to, and it does so through continuous (and, in fact, strenuous) sublimation of the senses to the most abstract sort of internal categorical contemplation. Freud goes further in daring to imagine how such sublimation can take place collectively, so that a whole society is socialized, so to speak, which on this basis creates both customary and written law, as well as an entire intellectual tradition, that is devotedly transmitted through the ages, one manifestation of which is surely psychoanalysis. The presumption is that the affective elements of religion and all the violence they unleash are tamed by being (re)invested in the passion for abstract thought, which does not pertain merely to philosophical contemplation but in essence to all activities of language, to the regime of the letter and its constitutive openness to interpretation, to the interminable construction and deconstruction of semantic effect, the essence of which cannot ultimately be represented. Freud's historical assertion as to the abandonment of hieroglyphics (pictorial communication) for the art of alphabetic writing and a literary sensibility as an indication of progress is, in this sense, quite revealing (MM, 283, 362).

The tendency to revere "the link between imagelessness and ethics" (PoM, 98) and accept unquestionably the presumption that the repudiation of the imagistic sphere, as symptomatically parallel to the renunciation of instinct, entails a progressive intellectual development, and even more that overcoming the world of the image enables the unfolding of literary sensibility (as if image-centered societies lacked in literariness!—say, Homer?), is so widespread that it is almost taken as scientific fact. Even Assmann, for all his exceptional reading of monotheism, falls into the same trap. Insisting that for Freud "monotheism is a feat of sublimation [that] implies the same 'no to the world' as the ban on graven images" (PoM, 99), Assmann misses on both counts. First, he misunderstands sublimation as existential renunciation or estrangement from the world, while sublimation is precisely the worlding of the psychic self, without which, indeed, the human psyche would be rendered permanently unworldly, lost in its inner psychotic abyss, effectively self-destructive, and incapable of constituting even the most elementary existential operation of human-being. When he declares, in a gesture of giving account of himself, "I want to sublimate the Mosaic distinction, not revoke it" (PoM, 120), Assmann is forgetting that the Mosaic distinction is already an act of sublimation and a grand one at that. As a consequence, he also misunderstands that the prohibition on divine representation is indeed perfectly worldly, as power of social imagination and politics, not to mention the force behind a worlding and world-making machine with extraordinary capacity for forming and shaping vast realities in human history for millennia right down to the very moment I am writing this sentence.

Indeed, for all its rejection of the plastic arts and their visual sphere, whose sensuous materiality is encountered with fear, *Geistigkeit* is no less an art, a *technē*. As means to collective sublimation, *Geistigkeit* is tantamount to a technique of socialization, a perfectly worldly agent of social formation and cohesion. As technique, it is not a matter of natural inclination; it needs to be learned and this learning does not come easy. Freud goes to great lengths to describe how this arduous process becomes such a profound source of disaffection that it precipitates its own sort of murderous violence. Yet, the contradiction in the fact that the very process presumed to alleviate and overcome the violence of religious sentiment, the process venerated as a higher plane of human achievement, precipitates murderous violence in turn seems to escape Freud, and his theory of repression, as cogent an explanation as it may be for psychic phenomena, proves inadequate to the full account of what is in fact a social-political phenomenon.

In speaking of *Geistigkeit* as *technē*, I am looking beyond the obvious account of biblical technologies, which pertains to all traditions of the sacred Book, Quranic hermeneutics included. I am thinking instead that, in its full devotion to imaginative abstraction, *Geistigkeit* as collective sublimation signifies a poetics, both a poetics of socialization and a poetics of language in the broadest sense—a discursive poetics that encompasses not only the establishment of a religion, its sacred texts, and its practices of faith, but also the full complex of juridical, cultural, and philosophical practices of a polity. These practices are critical according to the essential terms of *krisis*: they are practices of judgment and distinction, and therefore unavoidably implicated in a politics of prohibition and exclusion. In this respect, they are also a politics of producing otherness. We have already seen how "the dematerialization of God" produces an exclusive transcendental alterity to which this society confers absolute power with fully materialized effects, the most trenchant of which is a theologized lawmaking capacity. What I have been naming the One-and-Only-Other-to-the-world is the nuclear signification in every monotheistic manifestation, regardless of historical, linguistic, and cultural specificity. The monotheistic imaginary does not merely establish monarchical power in a variety of worldly modalities, but it also transcendentalizes power by the creation of unworldly alterity. Such is the Kingdom of the Heavens, which may be a Christian phrasing, but as an idea it is shared by the entire Abrahamic tradition.

The creation of transcendental alterity has a parallel othering in the social-historical world, for it comes with a hardcore existential prohibition: exclusionary devotion and prohibition of representation. Both prohibitive commands concern the same object, which by virtue of this double forbidding becomes an existential enemy. The target object is obviously polytheism, which is the operative mode for rituals of divinity in every society prior—hence, a formidable adversary. The more precise name of this adversary, at least descriptively, is, in Assmann's phrasing, cosmotheism, for the plurality of gods is but a secondary manifestation of the fact that in this imaginary the divine realm belongs to the world. Within this realm, it is possible for certain communities to invest their worship in one god among many—henotheism—which Freud also acknowledges. The turn from henotheism (which still belongs to a cosmotheistic imagination) to monotheism (which is exclusively otherworldly) could not have happened without the second prohibition after the initial exclusionary worship: the barring of sacred images. From this point on, polytheists will be identified by another name—idolaters—a name denoting their patent falsehood, for monotheism brought into being for the first time the requisite association of religion with singular and absolute truth.

In her assessment of the direct connection of monotheism's anti-visuality and absolute truth claims to *Geistigkeit*, Grubrich-Simitis is right to say that "monotheism is harsh in its attitude to man's need for illusion" (69), a point that Freud does not address, though he had gone to great lengths to establish the psychic parameters of religion's investment in illusion.[62] She then goes on to add that "monotheism is harsh on the human craving of visual expression" (70), a graver assertion, which nonetheless she justifies by pointing to how *Geistigkeit*, in directing the gaze inward and away from sensory perception, "opened up the invisible field that is the province of psychoanalysis" (70). No doubt, for a psychoanalyst this justification may be elementary and perhaps indisputable. But it conceals how the condition of *Geistigkeit* that enables monotheism to occur is itself implicated in the very processes and domains it seeks to overcome or destroy.

Monotheism claims to have laid to rest the practices of magic and sorcery. But is there more formidable magic than the conjuring of a god who cannot be seen, cannot be named, and cannot be represented, but is nonetheless inordinately real and omnipresent, impossible to evade and to refute, a god who is here and elsewhere all at once? An unseeable god who can be seen by inner vision, an unnameable god whose name is God, *the* name that bars all names and monopolizes divinity? The same goes for the property that makes this magic possible (*Geistigkeit*). What is more spiritual than the condition that claims to have overcome spirituality while assuming its name? And at the same time, what intervenes more materially—that is, substantially in the world—than a condition that claims to have refused the world and refuted the worldly? What condition is more vehement about constantly reminding its adherents, in their existential estrangement from the world, of this world's dangerous seductions that they are supposed to forget?[63] And more specifically in terms of Freud's own identity drama: What is it about this condition that is announced as an affront to a people's "national interest" but is then claimed to be "preserving their very essence"? Is it the overcoming of (their) religion, or the renewed preservation of (their) religion? Is it yet another figure of renunciation of instincts, a repudiation of idols, or is it, in its purported iconoclasm, the fashioning of a furtive new idolatry, with *Geist* as the most coveted, inveterate idol?

Concealing the Abyss of Existence

And so, we return at long last to our title. For years I have been fascinated by a couple of sentences in Cornelius Castoriadis's essay "Institution of Society and Religion" (1980): "Every religion is idolatry—or is not socially effective religion. In religion, words themselves—sacred words—function, and can only function, as idols."[64] The unequivocal phrase "every religion is idolatry" comes with an explicit qualification: "or is not socially effective religion"—thereby underscoring religion as a societal (one can easily say political) issue, rather than a theological problem. In this sense, the mysticism that might produce an abyssal language in which no idols remain standing can never be, by definition, socially effective, a social binding force. Mystical practice configures instead a social unbinding, a rejection of society, and aims, at its most extreme (the lone world of hermits and prophets), at the incapacity of worldly assembly. This isn't to say that the unintelligibility of mystical language is not socially readable—as, after all, Michel de Certeau has inimitably shown. It is to say that, however society might be able to read this unintelligibility, it nonetheless cannot but turn it into an idol, thereby turn against it, read it as another language, by another language: "The 'mystical' relation to the Abyss, whether it be 'authentic' or hallucinatory phenomenon, does not matter here: there never was and there never will be mystical religion or a religion of mystics. . . . The 'lives of mystics' themselves function as . . . instituted simulacra of the Abyss" (ISR, 325).[65]

How often "socially effective religion" has turned mysticism into dangerous idolatry (even while bestowing sanctification on specific practitioners) is one of the key indications of how far it goes to deny its own idolatrous investment. This has far-reaching dimensions beyond what, in Castoriadis, remains an unacknowledged Christian reference frame for mysticism. It is difficult to dispute, for example, that the tradition of Sufi mysticism did not provide the binding communal capacity of "socially effective religion" but, at the same time, it is equally difficult to dispute the *political* complications that Sufi mysticism has produced in the history of Islamic theology.

Castoriadis's unambiguous signification of religion as idolatry is the result of his thinking about the problem of alterity and its representations. In his mind, "the need for religion corresponds to the refusal on the part of human beings to recognize absolute alterity" (ISR, 324). This is primarily an ontological problem (much as it is for Hans Blumenberg in fact), but the question of capacity or incapacity of encounter with alterity is entirely a matter of social-imaginary institution. I should clarify, even if absurdly briefly, that, in Castoriadis's language, absolute alterity is an immanent, not transcendent, condition. This is expressed in twofold fashion. On the one hand, alterity is literally internal: a radical otherness within a "self" who is forever torn between the compulsion for self-reproduction (identity) and the necessity for assimilating and counteracting the resolute otherness of the world (self-alteration). On the other hand, alterity is precisely the second: a radical otherness pertinent to the world as a natural substratum, which is immanent because upon it rests every imaginary institution of society even if this imaginary institution is not determined by it. There is no causal relation between nature and society, even if without a specific biochemical molecular structure human beings would not exist. While the first (psyche) is ontological at the level of the living being, the second (world) is always configured according to the specific social imaginary at work. If this immanent radical otherness exists at the level of *physis*, both at the psychical and at the cosmological level, it becomes the reason why, at least in the world of human animality, *physis* must be divided by *nomos*. When this *nomos* is occluded and presented as *physis*, this radical otherness of self is externalized and fashioned in all kinds of societal institutions as transcendental otherness. This is how, on behalf of society, the existential cosmological abyss is overrun by the work of the sacred: "The Sacred is the reified and instituted simulacrum of the Abyss: it endows itself [*il se donne*] with the 'immanent,' separate, localized presence of the 'transcendent'" (ISR, 325).

Responding to this existential predicament, society produces a "*compromise formation*" that emerges out of the refusal to recognize immanent alterity, which then covers over this refusal, which fills its void and therefore unwittingly fulfills it. Before the so-called secularization process takes place (which Castoriadis interestingly identifies as "the moment when the decomposition of capitalist society begins," a fascinating claim that would require an essay all on its own), this fulfillment of the refusal of abyssal alterity, which produces a precisely circumscribed and "socially meaningful" alterity in turn, accounts for what he calls religion. Religion then is instituted in order to counter the abyssal terrain of being, the fact that there is nothing in human existence that presupposes it, hypostatizes it, or exceeds it, that human existence is at the limit groundless and all established signification fails it. This abyssal condition is, of course, unrepresentable, unlocalizable, and meaningless. It may be perhaps intelligible in the desacralized language of psychoanalysis that speculates—because it can never really know, and Freud said this explicitly—on the abyssal constitution of the psyche, but even there the object is at the core unrepresentable, unlocalizable, and meaningless. Castoriadis concludes: "Religion covers the Abyss, the Chaos, the Groundlessness that society is for itself; it occults society as self-creation, as source and unmotivated origin of its own institution. Religion negates the radical imaginary and puts in its place a particular imaginary creation. It veils the enigma of the exigency for signification—which makes society as much as it is made by society—insofar as it imputes to society a signification that would come to it from elsewhere" (ISR, 326).

In this respect, to put it bluntly, "society *creates itself*—and to begin with, *creates itself as* heteronomous society" (ISR, 328). This utterly paradoxical condition is not open to simple explanation, which is why those sociological or psychological theories about some sort of structural or hardwired propensity in human beings toward heteronomy are examples of lazy thinking. Such theories never seem to wonder about the epistemological position from which their "investigations" and "explanations" are promulgated. They don't seek to explain why they conduct and achieve a self-understanding that comes from elsewhere and, doing so, as *conscious self-realization*, simultaneously obliterate this very knowledge. Theologians in monotheistic traditions have been performing these sorts of contortions for centuries. The inordinate genius for self-occultation that characterizes some of the most glorious and brilliant manifestations of the theological mind over time testifies to the fact that "*the enigma of heteronomous society and the enigma of religion are, in large part, one and the same enigma*" (ISR, 329).[66]

One may raise the counterargument that this essentially ontological signification of religion (because it pertains to a general anthropology) remains silent about the social-historical emergence of the very concept or name of religion. This name, the counterargument goes, might be said to be inscribed with the secularization claim and all its politics: namely, the geopolitical establishment of Christianity as the world's dominant religion, which claims to go beyond religion so as to emancipate itself from that constraint while relegating every other such mode to it. For those who make this argument—in a broad range of ways, from Marcel Gauchet to Talal Asad, from Tomoko Masuzawa to Gil Anidjar—the question of secularization is in a sense false or deceptive: a ruse by which Christianity effaces itself as religion in order to establish the realm of religion for all others. While I think this argument has merit—and in fact a great deal of historical accuracy—it is ultimately shortsighted and indeed compromised by its unwillingness to consider the essential animating force of what has been called "secularization": namely, the desire of (some) human beings to relieve themselves of their self-imposed constraints and confront the consequences of encountering the cosmological abyss without safeguards.

Whether or how far this desire has been realized is not the issue. Secularization—I have been arguing for some years—is unfinishable by definition; the cosmological abyss cannot be encountered once and for all. So, although one could again raise the counterargument that all kinds of other transcendental safeguards were indeed put into place—constitutions, nations, ideologies, scientific truths, or utopian dreams—the fact remains that all those new "delusions" ushered by secularization are acknowledged to be human creations, for better or worse, thereby shifting the knowledge framework so that "religion" too could be understood as a human creation. Even if secularization can be disputed as having occurred at all—whether according to Schmitt's argument in *Political Theology* or the work of the thinkers I just mentioned—this shifting in the framework of knowledge cannot be disputed. Regardless of the persistence of the faithful throughout the world, a good number (indeed impossible to measure exactly) among the world's population understands that religion is one glorious (if sometimes perilous) human creation among many. Because such numbers do not actually form an obvious constituency (not to mention a community), they are forced into categorization by being folded, often by academic fiat, into the identificatory schemas of self-acknowledged communities of faith, whether under the equation of secularism with Christianity, or via such notions as "the faith of the faithless" in Simon Critchley's phrase, or in some other way. It's interesting to note that those who dispute the existence of secularization—however we judge it or evaluate its efficacy—do so simply by ignoring it, by refusing to encounter its difference, by forcing it into theological schemas.

In the end, what one thinks of secularization is secondary. Religious practices (under different names) seem to have existed in all societies in known history, even if their exact domain of significance is both enormously varied and inordinately contested. But, I would argue, the same is true of secularization. The human animal has created gods since the beginning of its social existence on this earth and at the same time has sought to tear them down. Such is domain of culture, broadly understood. Those who advocate monotheism as an advancement, not only in religion but in human development in general, have no qualms in proclaiming that so-called pagan societies lacked the need to distinguish between religion and culture. I am not going to engage here with the terms of this assessment, except to point out that it confirms the idea that religion as culture is not the outcome of secularization in some post-Protestant phase. All religion has always been culture, despite the inadequacy of these modern words and concepts relative to the language and imaginary of archaic societies. The language of secularization articulates and makes explicit nothing more than what has always been the case in human societies, which, by creating the separation between the theological and the religious, monotheistic imaginaries have sought to encrypt. In this specific sense, one might speak of monotheism as one instance in the many variations of the world's disenchantment over time in human history.

Presently, as one category of social formation among many, religion has come to form an epistemological domain in itself. This is to say, it is religion as a categorical—or cognitive—framework that enables the recognition and naming of a certain typology of practices we call religious, and if this distinction is itself a symptom of the secularization process, it doesn't matter. Or rather, it is a matter of historical understanding—of an emergent horizon of perception that enables the recognition of religion as a human creation. Marx's thought continues to be indispensable here. I quote extensively a well-known passage:

> The basis of irreligious criticism is: *Human beings make* religion; religion does not make human beings. Religion is the self-consciousness and self-esteem (*Selbstgefühl*) of humanity which has either not yet found itself or has already lost itself again. But the *human* is no abstract being encamped outside the world. The human is *the world of humans*, state, society. This state, this society, produce religion, an *inverted world consciousness*, because they are an *inverted world*. Religion is the general theory of that world, its encyclopaedic compendium, its logic in a popular form, its spiritualistic *point d'honneur*, its enthusiasm, its moral sanction, its solemn complement, its general ground of consolation and justification. It is the *fantastic realization* of human essence because human essence has no true reality.[67]

No need to elaborate on this exquisite passage, except to point out that what Marx calls "irreligious criticism" is precisely what recognizes humanity's reality to be a concrete manifestation, a *poiētic* creation, of confronting its groundlessness, its abyssal essence. "Human essence has no true reality," he says—no ground other than itself, which is why, whatever "it" is, it derives its capacity to be from its phantasmatic propensity to imagine, create, and actualize what we call historical realities. That these realities shape or form—and thereby *make* (*poiein*)—specific modes of *human-being* does not mean that they *create* humanity in some ontological fashion, no matter the voluminous myths of such creation in all kinds of "cultural" traditions over time. Rather, the myths themselves, in their sublime multiplicity, are perfect instantiations of the insurmountable groundlessness of human essence.

As a human creation, religion is basically a social practice of encountering and concealing the abyss of existence. It does not annul the abyss; it takes place within the abyss. What Castoriadis calls "socially effective religion"—for him the only meaning of religion—is the outcome of creating a name, a representation, a locus for this abyss of interminable self-created otherness.[68] Although such creations are oftentimes concrete material objects (icons, statues, totems, sacred texts), they are equally likely and often more powerfully abstract and immaterial (the Word become Flesh, the Trinitarian substance, the unpronounceable Name of God, the 99 names of God, the Unrepresentable, the transcendental Absolute, Goddess Reason, and so on). Christ himself is called, by Paul, "the image of the invisible God"—*eikōn tou theou tou aoratou* (Colossians 1:15)—and it's worth noting that, with this very phrase (*eikōn theou*), Philo of Alexandria argues for the merits of unified Logos against polytheism. In any case, whatever their *names*, such social-imaginary creations that constitute the space of the sacred are idols, reified simulacra of the abyss they represent and at the same time conceal. This is the essence of the statement "every religion is idolatry"; the signifying weight is not on "religion" but on "idolatry."[69]

To the extent that religion is not merely the representation of society's desire to ritualize its existence and not restricted to an individual's mystical claim to merge with the abyss, but is instead the institution that occludes the groundlessness of existence as such and thus builds an imaginary institutional scaffolding on which society may find rest, the workings of religion are essentially psychical (by which I do not mean psychological) and indeed not unlike those of sublimation, whereby all invested representations are categorically objectified, be they images, words, or cognitive abstractions. This is why idolatry is at work even in those cases when a religion is formed on the basis of the foundational monotheistic injunction: the prohibition of images (*Bilderverbot*).

Prohibition and Idolatrous Iconoclasm

Idolatry, of course, is a name not of self-identity but of imputed otherness. It is refreshing to quote Voltaire in this regard, from his entry "Idolatry" in the *Encyclopédie* (1765):

> It appears that there never existed any people on earth who took the name of *idolaters*. This word is an insulting term which the gentiles, the polytheists, may have seemed to deserve, but it is quite certain that if we had asked the Roman Senate, the Areopagus of Athens, or the royal court of Persia: *Are you idolaters?* they would have hardly understood the question. None would have

> answered: We adore images and *idols*. The word *idolater* and *idolatry* is found in neither Homer, nor Hesiod, nor Herodotus, nor any other author of the gentile religion. There never was any edict, any law which commanded that *idols* should be adored, that they should be treated as gods and regarded as gods.[70]

Idolatry does not exist and has never existed as a principle of self-determination. Much like the word *pagan*, which came into use after the reign of Theodosius II, idolatry was a name invented in order to constitute the identity of enemy otherness. Not ever being a matter of self-recognizable custom or self-assumed cultural command, idolatry was indeed generated by the very same command that proclaimed its annihilation. In simple historical terms, idolatry could not even be conceptually constituted as a name without the prohibitive monotheistic injunction: "Idolatry is a word that mainly appears in the discourse of iconoclasm, a militant monotheism obsessed with its own claims to universality. . . . There is no idolatry without an iconoclasm to label it as such, since idolaters almost never call themselves by that name."[71] W. J. T. Mitchell adds yet another obvious but crucial historical dimension that is unacknowledged in theological or philosophical discussions (although Freud makes it explicit in *Moses and Monotheism*): namely, since the initial biblical injunction, the iconoclastic prohibition is directly linked to territorial claims, in terms of either exclusionary defensiveness or expansionist conquest, almost always expressing itself with annihilating violence: "the practical enforcement of the ban on images involves destroying the sacred sites of the native inhabitants" (59).

In the same collection, *Idol Anxiety*, Assmann theorized this destruction as a symptom of a twofold development in the monotheistic prohibition: in the first instance because images represent false gods—this he deems to be a matter of loyalty to the one and only true God, who is thereby provoked to extraordinary jealousy—and in the second instance because this one and only true God is unrepresentable, thereby rendering images catastrophic obstacles to accessing the divine realm. Interestingly, he also calls the first prohibition "political" insofar as it draws a contentious difference between true divinity and false divinity, or true and false mode of devotion, and therefore provokes issues of loyalty and jealousy, and the second prohibition "theological" because it concerns the very nature of God, his insurmountable unrepresentability. But he is quick to add that "on both readings the prohibition of images is given a political commentary [in the Bible] that explains it by reference to God's jealousy and his distinction between friend and enemy. . . . The prohibition of images divides the world into two parties: the idolaters and the iconoclasts, the first being the enemies and the second the friends of God. So, what's wrong with images? They prove that you are an enemy of God."[72] Thus, without elaborating, Assmann confirms one of the key points of this inquiry: political theology is always already political before it has anything to do with the theological and, insofar as it is political, it is instituted on the basis of constructing an enemy.

Assmann goes on to theorize this endemic condition of enmity also in two-fold fashion. What's wrong with images in the monotheistic injunction breaks down into (1) images that are objects of worship and in this sense gods as such, other gods, who for this reason must be banned, and (2) images that are false because (the-One-and-Only) God is invisible and unrepresentable, and for this reason they are an affront to the sacred, sources of blasphemy. While the first still accepts the existence of an enchanted (cosmotheistic) world where the battle among divinities must be won along the lines of truth and falsehood, the second denies the existence of any divinity other than the one that in effect produces "a disenchanted or disanimated world, where images are nothing else but powerless dead matter" ("What's Wrong with Images?" 25). While the first injunction in the name of the One provokes jealousy of the Other, the second demands outright denial of the Other. The first means battle over sovereignty on the basis of truth; the second means annihilation on the basis of sovereignty. In both cases, however, the enemy is the same. The shift in name from self-ascribed polytheism to the imposed appellation of idolatry is but the symptom of the newly invented existential enemy who enables monotheism's power to name new meaning. This meaning is in essence negative. God comes to be via his absence from anything tangible and verifiable and, via this absence, this voiding of divinity, comes to create a new meaning for what is considered to be divine. Insofar as it denotes an object that might be visible, tangible, or just simply conceivable, even the word *god* is rendered nonsignifiable by the name God, a name that monopolizes all naming of divinity.

So, names take over from images, even when concerning the unnameable, but do not extricate themselves from the theistic imaginary they purport to efface: "The Bible luxuriates in verbal images of God and these are obviously fully admissible" ("What's Wrong with Images?" 22). A kind of covert and denied idolatry inhabits the core of the destructive fury against idolatry. Words are taken to be the overcoming of images, but this hardly means the overcoming of idols. As a verse in Exodus has it: "The tablets were the work of God, and the writing was the writing of God, engraved on the tablets" (32:15–16). And this very notion of divine language entering the world from the void is repeated in the "Word become Flesh" of the New Testament and the operative command "Write!" in the Quran. What was newly named "idolatry" as identification of the existential enemy had always already existed as the operative framework of the sacred text in the entire monotheistic tradition, whatever its variations and vicissitudes. Carrying the most formidable injunction against idolatry, the cryptic idolatry of the word launched a structural transformation of the sacred that went a long way toward the transformation of the profane. Indeed, what finally became the sharp difference between the two is its outcome.

Perhaps because idolatry exists as the hate-filled repressed core of its own prohibition as name and notion, it is animated, in Mitchell's words, by a surplus, "a moral panic that seems completely in excess of legitimate concerns about something called 'graven images'" (58), which inspires all-out gestures of erasure, a desire to annihilate all traces of peoples and cultures, backward and forward in time—implicitly genocidal (60).[73] Thinking in psychoanalytic terms, the French feminist philosopher Luce Irigaray understands the endemic violence of iconoclasm to be inherent in idolatry's own constitutive objectification, which ultimately paralyzes or immobilizes the energies of self by barring any open encounter with the other. I quote extensively from a rather neglected essay:

> Whether it concerns a fetish statue, a political or religious authority, an ideology, or a partner in love, idolatry seems to consist always in the fact of projecting all possible energy, indeed all becoming, into something external. Some thing and not some one, because in order to satisfy our need for an idol or a fetish, we must reduce the other to an object, made thus ideal. From this standpoint, it is possible to say that the veneration of an object as such is less injurious than the reduction of the other to an object, provided that the object, the image, the representation, or the idea remains a simple marker or means of aiding our spiritual path. In any case, it signifies a paralysis of energy. And the more this ceasing of energy takes place at a spiritual level, the more difficult it will be to liberate it. This no doubt explains the murderous conflicts that various monotheisms instigate. Immobilized in a very subtle form of the one—of the One—no energy can remain really free to enable an open encounter with the other in the quest of a future more spiritual than anyone can imagine.[74]

Understanding in what ways idolatry works at the heart of iconoclasm is the key to unraveling the profound influence of *Bilderverbot* as the most prevalent all-around social command (*archē*) in today's world.

In order to succeed, the exercise of *Bilderverbot*—which conventionally may have Hebraic origins, but remains the core principle in all monotheistic imaginaries, even if performed on extreme occasions (early Christian monophysites, Byzantine iconoclasm, Franciscan or Calvinist asceticism, strict Islamism, or Protestant fundamentalism)—must involve a rather narrow construct of "image" in its most literal sense. *Bild* essentially comes to define the object of representation as such, as an object that must be identified, known, and forbidden, by virtue of representation, *as representation*. Nominally, the prohibition is against images that dare to represent God, if only because they will then be endowed with divine properties in themselves and worshiped as such, as divine objects—idols. But underneath this nominal logic what is really prohibited is the very act, the very conception, of representation, the daring to give God a form, since in the monotheistic imaginary only God forms, or, better yet, God *is* form and *the only agency of form*, of which humans are thereby the exemplary byproduct.

This is expressly noted in the extraordinary notion of humans being formed in God's image and God's likeness—the Greek words translating the Hebrew of Genesis are *eikōn* (image, icon) and *homoiōsis* (sameness, likeness)—which, insofar as it has been always invoked polemically against paganism, may be thought of as the explicit roll back of anthropomorphic divinities by, nonetheless, absorbing the principle of icon and likeness and thereby, in a Hegelian sense, preserving it by altering the core principle: namely, if God is form, then the project of human formation is theomorphic. Yet, the human animal cannot ultimately tolerate itself as God (or godlike), thereby projecting backward an anthropomorphic notion onto the category of God, who may not necessarily look like the statue of Zeus, as it would have been sculpted by Praxiteles or Pheidias, but is nonetheless imagined (since the monotheistic imaginary can only be patriarchical) as the Almighty Father, in however abstract or concrete manifestation a specific society can handle.[75]

There is much to say here, in light of this sketch, about the validity of Castoriadis's provocative assertion that the institution of religion is "the supreme hubris of human existence, an ontological hubris" (ISR 318). It's provocative because the commonsensical assumption is that hubris is committed when humans believe they are or act like gods, not when they invent or create gods. But indeed, to imagine gods presiding over the universe is one of the most extraordinary acts of human creation, an ordering of the universe by an agency that hereby makes itself conspicuously and conveniently absent. It is hubris precisely in the denial of accountability for this act of radical creation (which is also, as *radical* creation, always an act of destruction). Now, to imagine a single and exclusive God—moreover, a single and exclusive God who creates humans in image and in likeness—is an even more formidable ontological hubris, if it is at all semantically possible to produce a quantitative figure of the ontological. Not only does it confer the creation (and, of course, meaning) of being onto an entity of the imagination, but it also authorizes the very category of Being, which thus leads to the perverse inversion of subject-object authorization whereby the creative subject deliberately objectifies itself in the most outrageous denial of its own accountability for creation. Worse yet, the object (the created God) is now named Eternal Creator—the ultimate Other, the Object who has become *the* Subject, the subject without subjectivity who, moreover, proceeds with the monopoly of the means of production of the human as the unavowed creator now configured as created (in image and in likeness). This perversely contorted process facilitates outrageous delusions of grandeur: not just the concept of the chosen people (absorbed into all nationalist imaginaries, secularized or not), but the notion that the human, made of/as the face of God, is, in the last instance, of divine essence, a notion whose consequent psychic energies underlie the worst excesses of both humanist ideology (in its most conventional meaning) and religious fanaticism. This is a stunning performance in the history of the human animal as a living being that renders even the human imagination itself paralyzed before the awe of its achievement.[76]

In this respect, the prohibition of images has built into it a powerful injunction against both form and representation as such, an injunction that seems to resurface with extraordinary urgency whenever the desire of humans to *aestheticize* their universe seems to gain the upper hand.[77] In the process, another big question emerges: What is the relation between *Bildung* and *Bilderverbot*? This is in many ways a German question—crucial to the development of German philosophy, indeed both theological and antitheological strains in it—but it is also a question crucial to the imaginary of modernity.[78] It is well known that in the *Critique of Judgment* Kant equates the Hebraic and Islamic *Bilderverbot* with the sublime. On the other side of this stands the equally well-known promise by Nietzsche in *The Twilight of the Idols* to touch idols with a hammer as if it were a tuning fork. Both thoughts resonate within the same discursive economy. I take *Bilderverbot* to be the core element underlying the Protestant imaginary, which may be distilled into a notion of *Geist* without *Bild*, not merely Spirit without Image, but spirit that cannot be formed into an image because of an assertion (passed on through theology to modern philosophy) that image ultimately despiritualizes matters. The project of *Bildung*—at least in the way it was configured in Wilhelm von Humboldt's mind—is a worldly project. Self-formation is a process that creates both the human being and the human world. It is not a spiritual quest, except insofar as spirit (*Geist*) means also mind, intellect. Freud's *Geistigkeit*—which may be the only possible redeeming value of *Bilderverbot* within its tradition and this explicitly against the perils of monotheism—is, of course, a *Bildung*, a *poietic* process of forming, of creating form against the prohibition of form.

This process is linked to what Castoriadis has named the radical imagination, that is, the primary social-historical process of enabling the creation of form in advance of those institutions of society charged with reproducing form: "The term *radical* I use, first, to oppose what I am talking about to the 'secondary' imagination which is either reproductive or simply combinatory (and usually both), and, second, to emphasize the idea that this imagination lies *before* the distinction between 'real' and 'fictitious.' To put it bluntly: it is because radical imagination exists that 'reality' exists *for us*—exists *tout court*—and exists *as* it exists."[79] Hence, an understanding of the imagination as "the power to represent what *is not*" opens up a way of reconsidering the relation between image and representation so that the first is not in the service of the second. *It is not the image as representation but the image as signification that animates idolatry.*

Indeed, it is the intangible power of signification, and not the phenomenon of representation, that also animates idolatry as a hated object—what Peter Sloterdijk calls "the deep structure of the iconoclastic syndrome." I quote at length:

> The unacceptable nature of images stems from the observation that they never serve purely to reproduce that which is represented, but always assert their own significance in addition. The autonomous value of the second aspect as such becomes visible in them—and the iconoclasts will go to great lengths to destroy this. . . . In reality, however, iconoclasm seeks to attack the autonomy of the world. . . . In iconoclasm, which is actually a cosmoclasm, one finds the articulation of a resentment of any human freedom that is not prepared to accept immediate self-denial and obedience.
>
> (God's Zeal, 96)

Because it takes place in the battlefield of signification—and over the terrain of signification—this militant ordering of both self and other in iconoclasm moves further and further away from the language of representation. The modern legacy of *Bilderverbot* would come to rest on a reconfiguration—perhaps we could say, resignification—of *Bild*, whereby image would be disengaged from the discourse of representation precisely because the order of modernity is structured around an explicit desire to create images that configure the until that moment unseen and unknown: images that conceptualize and signify the until that moment inconceivable "image" that represents nothing that exists prior, the very nothingness of which is thereby *created* into existence as a conceivable thing. In the imaginary of modernity, the image is to be not only disengaged from the discourse of representation but, more so, engaged from the standpoint of formation and transformation. Hence, the invention of *Bildung* as nominal repeal of *Bilderverbot* (even if remaining steadfast in its orbit), which foregrounded the power of *poietic* (trans)formation in the language of aesthetic education. In this process, words themselves are primary imagistic units of signification. The Protestant injunction of *sola scriptura*, which belongs by definition to the economy of *Bilderverbot*, remains throughout this process one of the most powerful idolatrous gestures in the history of the modern world, reaching beyond the realm of Christianity proper, as it underlies the increasing sacralization of the letter of the law and turns legal texts into the constitutive idols of societies around the world, whether self-identified as religious or secular.[80]

I should clarify here that my account of *Bildung* exceeds its traditional meaning. In this configuration, *Bildung* ceases to be a self-identical process, whereby the Self comes to fulfill itself—this was Humboldt's idealist vision. Once the concept of the Self is no longer the agent of closure, *Bildung* becomes the very instance of the force of interminable self-alteration, re-created through critical self-interrogation as *performative pedagogy*. Therein resides its democratic element, its participation in the project of autonomy. Democratic *paideia* conducts itself on the premise and purpose that self-interrogation shatters strict self-referentiality.

Idols of Unrepresentability

The prohibition of images is a radical notion only when it operates in a desacralized universe. This was, of course, Freud's aspiration. In a monotheistic imaginary, iconoclasm merely reorients idol worship from the utterable and representable to the unutterable and unrepresentable. The prohibition on pronouncing the sacred name of God is in essence an idolatrous act. Making the name sacred circumscribes, in this gesture of erasure, of voiding, the very abyss thus announced. The sacred prohibition of the name *is a name*, an act of naming, of localizing in an immanent sense, the Abyss that must—and does by virtue of this naming that is the unnaming of the Name—remain shielded.[81] Likewise, the ritual of the Eucharist is not idolatrous in the sense often considered, that is, as a remnant of paganism, in the evocation of animistic eating of the divine body. Rather, the metaphoric configuration of flesh as bread and of blood as wine is *secondary idolatry*, in my mind literally a superfluous idolatry, a redundant repetition. The most brilliant and insidious gesture this ritual generates is to conceal the real idolatry at work: the conjured phantasm that God, who otherwise cannot be known, who has no name, who exists in ways unfathomable and unrepresentable, can indeed be part of you. In other words, the ritual of ingesting God into one's Being, even if altogether metaphorically, reveals precisely God's idol status, which is his real (that is, actual) status, in this case the status of an idol that claims to destroy all idols—"all *other* idols" would be, of course, the precise way to phrase it.

From this standpoint, Byzantine iconomachy, like all debates about the Trinitarian hypostasis in early patristic literature, which after all fed into the eighth-century theological crisis with a sort of residual or delayed anxiety, is a debate internal to the specific idolatry of Christianity. If we take seriously the notion that signification, not representation, resides at the core of idolatrous psychic investment, then the battle between iconolaters and iconoclasts in Byzantium is a bit like Freud's narcissism of petty differences, where the differences are hardly petty because they pertain to the deepest shared inner core, hence the extraordinary violence between what are in essence constituencies of competing idols. This inner core is the ineffable *Imago Dei*, in its Latin naming, whose representation is in any case impossible by definition, even for the Byzantine iconolaters who had no trouble subscribing, theologically, to the necessary anti-realism of the divine image in sacred icons, creating the distortion that has become the distinctive feature of Byzantine art.[82]

These sublime tricks exemplify the work of the sacred in social life, a work that, in the last instance, must remain secretive, literally a mystery. In contrast, a desacralized universe of meaning reconfigures the meaning of both iconoclasm and the sacred. In a capitalist world, for example, where the image is inevitably linked to the rule of commodities and the tyranny of exchange, iconoclasm may become in effect a detheologizing gesture. Such is the meaning of Adorno's notion of utopia as negative representation.[83] When iconoclasm detheologizes, it calls into question the *idola tribus* as such: the stipulation that in every society there is a last instance that cannot be questioned and, of course, cannot be represented. Whatever content this last instance may have—whatever language, symbol, sign, convention, whatever may be identified as the "idols of the tribe" even when not acknowledged as such—it is society's last instance of the sacred.

There is a whole strain in modern art that vehemently sought this capacity to expose society's last instance of the sacred through an iconoclastic strategy which paradoxically foregrounds or hyperprivileges the image. The Dadaist tradition and the irreverent performativity of Marcel Duchamp come easily to mind. Far from being deconstructive, Duchamp's ready-mades are iconic renamings. They don't bar the image in order to preserve the ideal sacred of an allegedly noncommodified space. Rather, they desacralize the contextual space of the image, for if commodities are extensions of religious idolatry, as Marx argued long ago, they are not so in themselves but insofar as they render sacred their means of existence, the space of capitalist exchange. This was also the impetus behind Situationist performativity and Guy Debord's critique of the society of the spectacle. However, Debord's conviction that the spectacle had reached beyond mere visual excess and become objective reality led him into the whirlwind of yet another round of *Bilderverbot* politics, which inevitably propels us to seek yet another space of the sacred, ad infinitum.

Much can be learned, in this respect, from the art of Maurizio Cattelan, who, unlike many of his contemporaries, seems especially aware of the deadlock of avant-gardist responses to the commodified image that breed an idolatrous aesthetic sacralization in the name of iconoclasm. It's easy, of course, to characterize Cattelan's notorious irreverence toward the entirety of the art world and its media (agents, galleries, exhibitions, patrons, fellow artists, publications, market publicity, and so on) as iconoclastic. That this can be said without much thinking is itself indicative of the profoundly ingrained and thoughtless use of the term *iconoclasm*. But Cattelan's work—in its shameless irreverence and outrageous provocation (including explicit artistic deception or downright art theft, so that many have questioned whether he should be considered an artist at all)—shows quite the opposite: namely, it is impossible to exist in a nonimagistic universe and to presume so is not only a naïve illusion, but indicative of the triumph of consumer capitalism's metaphysics of the image, a metaphysics that ultimately denies people's imaginary capacity to think otherwise. Hence Cattelan's commitment to overt proliferation of undisguised simulacra, resin wax or taxidermic reproductions of iconic living being.

The artist's retrospective at the Guggenheim Museum in New York in 2011, with which he announced his retirement from the art world, brought forth this problematic in acute, even dramatic form. Cattelan chose to exhibit almost every one of his art pieces from over the years (the exhibit is titled *All*) by decontextualizing them to an extreme—in full cognizance of the fact that all retrospectives are dependent on decontextualization—that is, by hanging them all from the museum's ceiling with steel cables, in no apparent order, as an assemblage of cadavers on display after a hangman's mass execution, a literal signification of the corps of one's artwork as corpse.[84] This much could be expected, in retrospect, from an artist whose artwork has consistently strived to showcase its death in order to animate some other (often outrageous, irreverent, or even nonexistent) image of the living environment that enables art to exist at all. But the experience of winding up and down the museum's notorious rotunda, in order to get a circular view of this enormous hanging corpse in multiple parts, surely aggravates the perilous presumption of artistic iconoclasm for its own sake. Iconoclasm on the gallows may be an apt distillation of what this exhibit was about. Yet, what makes this exhibit so radical is that, in strangulating artistic iconoclasm, it also exposes and thus incapacitates—in a sort of simultaneous double death—the latent idolatrous desire of the presumed secular spectator.

The fact that arguably the most iconic of all of Cattelan's reproductions, exercised against what is, in the Christian world, conventionally considered the quintessential icon against idolatry (the pope), was received as the most scandalous of all his works should hardly surprise us. Cattelan's depiction in 1999 of Pope John Paul II in full regalia stricken and incapacitated by a meteorite, titled indicatively *La Nona Ora* (The Ninth Hour) in a derisory invocation of Christ's moment of death on the cross, was vandalized when exhibited in the pope's native Poland in 2001. It's easy to say that such vandalism signifies the enraged response of the faithful who are responding to the injury of blasphemy. This was as well the consensus around the controversy of cartooning the Prophet Mohammed in the Danish newspaper *Jyllands-Posten* in 2005. But we learn little by anchoring ourselves to the platitude of blasphemy as an explanation, especially since such occasions are riveted by all kinds of external social-historical factors—in the case of *Jyllands-Posten* no doubt, racist depictions that would be better categorized under the domain of hate speech rather than religious blasphemy. Hence the weakness of arguments, notably by Talal Asad and Saba Mahmood, who remain caught within the moral-legal framework they seek to overcome because they cannot confront the domain of *words* themselves, whether in the legal texts of secularism or the sacred texts of religion, as a domain of idols.[85]

Exactly ten years after the *Jyllands-Posten* events, the repetition of the scene with much greater violence against the satirical French journal *Charlie Hebdo* and the vast number of accounts of the affair along the free speech vs. blasphemy axis from both sides of advocacy—sometimes achieving a remarkable mirroring in their mutual righteousness—marked the perfect illustration of the general incapacity to comprehend the complexities of the issue. In a kind of iconoclastic convergence, both sides ignored or forgot that there is nothing irreverent, strictly speaking, in the sheer depiction of the Prophet's human existence, which is nowhere barred explicitly in the Quran and bears in fact a great tradition of representation in Islamic iconography, from Ottoman illuminated manuscripts to contemporary media in Iran. What is barred, without a doubt, is an iconography of the sacred that supplants its *signification qua sacred*—that is to say, an idolatrous representation. This was obviously not the case. What justifiably provoked the rage of Muslims was that the sacred signification was violated by a deliberately mocking distortion, a humiliating depiction of the Prophet that is driven—about this there can be no doubt—by racist impulses against specific peoples still caught in the living history of colonial domination. Wretched for its brutal persistence and repetition, this involves nothing more than what Edward Said tirelessly pointed out during his entire intellectual life. From this standpoint, protests in the name of blasphemy in fact weaken the political case of those who are thus affronted.[86]

But even if we were to remain simply at the level of the question of representability of the sacred, the more difficult thing to engage with is that such rage is directed against what is perceived as an idolatrous gesture, therefore propelling nominally iconoclastic action, while at the same time, even if unwittingly, expressing an idolatrous investment in the unrepresentability of the object of worship, which thereby bars it from the realm of art. Such investment is idolatrous in the sense that it is precisely this exclusive mode of worship (*latreia*) that turns the object of worship into an *object that can be seen* (*eidolon*, idol), even when it is not represented. We witness here a perverse logic: self-acknowledged iconoclasts rage against an iconoclasm that they perceive as idolatry, not recognizing that their iconoclasm is fed by their own idolatrous desire.[87] We can speak of antagonistic idolatries perhaps, although this is admittedly cavalier, because neither the "faithful" nor the "faithless" recognize idolatry at all. Hence, there is no possibility that either side can practice what Mitchell has named "critical idolatry"—a kind of respectful or non-violent iconoclasm, as he calls it, where the idols of the other would be understood to be no less important than one's own.[88]

Incidentally, this would be a good way to elucidate the phrase "every religion is idolatry" as a rhetorical gesture that deconstructs the presumed distinction between true and false modes of worship, or, better yet, the language that proclaims one's truth to be the other's falsehood. It is also to deconstruct the presumption that idols are restricted only to visible and tangible objects that provoke sentiments of worship (*latreia*), for the range of those "objects" created by the desire to worship is infinite in number and kind, beyond any capacity to determine what is visible and tangible. This range obviously extends to the ineffable, the invisible, and the intangible, in the sense that whichever way go the mode of worship and the desire that animates it so goes the range of "idol." In this sense too, the phrase "every religion is idolatry" is accurate, even if only a rhetorical gesture, because no religion can exist without some mode of worship and the desire that animates it, thereby creating idols ad infinitum even though "idolatry" itself as a specific historical mode of religion has never existed except as an accusatory, vilifying name.

Along these lines, Assmann makes an appeal similar to Mitchell: "The solution seems to lie not in the prohibition of images but rather in the acquisition of iconic literacy" ("What's Wrong with Images?" 31). Perhaps we can even speak of iconic intelligence, as a specific mode of thinking and knowing that is not exhausted in the visual realm. Even in the strictest sense, an idol exceeds the demand placed upon it to represent the divine. It has *presentational* power—it signifies, as I have been arguing—which is why ultimately, in the space of exclusionary monotheism, it had to be forbidden. There is a sort of intrinsic bearing to the image, perhaps even a certain vulnerability because of its contingency that cannot be abolished or transcended even by means of mechanical reproduction. Andy Warhol's *Mao* or *Marilyn* paintings may be considered meditations on precisely this issue. If anything, images are nodal points of signification, very much according to the figural logic that Freud understands to permeate all dream-work, as the psyche's capacity to think—to give meaning to itself and the world—by virtue of phantasms. Images are not representations of the world; they are makings of the world, and this has been the case at least since whatever went on inside the caves of Alta Mira and Lascaux.[89]

It is here that the political workings of the concept of unrepresentability become crucial. Much can be appreciated in Jacques Rancière's argument in *The Future of the Image* that the image plays in a field between the visible and the sayable—this confirms my argument here, in reading Castoriadis: it is *image as signification* (not representation) that animates idolatry. Rancière artfully navigates this terrain in order eventually to raise the stakes on the phantom that haunts the entire discussion: the presumption of the unrepresentable. Even when invoked in the discourse of material history—or perhaps especially there (the unrepresentable event)—the iconoclastic claim to unrepresentability is the apotheosis of idolatrous metaphysics. It is, moreover, a self-annihilating gesture, whose internal debilitating contradiction is occluded by an unacknowledged denial of its moralistic negation of the sensible, of the desire to configure one's sense of the world—even its abyssal manifestation—in some form (*poiein*). I quote extensively from Rancière's passionate conclusion:

> The assertion of unrepresentabiltity claims that some things can only be represented in a certain type of form, by a type of language appropriate to their exceptionality. *Stricto sensu*, this idea is vacuous. It simply expresses a wish: the paradoxical desire that, in the very regime which abolishes the representative suitability of forms to objects, appropriate forms respecting the singularity of the exception still exist. Since this desire is contradictory in principle, it can only be realized in an exaggeration which, in order to ensure the fallacious equation between anti-representative art and an art of the unrepresentable, places a whole regime of art under the sign of holy terror. . . . In order to assert an unrepresentability in art that is commensurate with the unthinkability of the event, the latter must itself have been rendered entirely thinkable, entirely necessary according to thought. The logic of the unrepresentable can only be sustained by a hyperbole that ends up destroying it.[90]

The obvious—and I think indisputable—point is that nothing is unrepresentable because whatever signifies it as unrepresentable must configure its unrepresentability in some form, even if entirely in the realm of the sayable. But it's more important to understand that nothing is representable or unrepresentable *as such*. In fact, the very premise of a difference between the two terms is fraudulent. It already presumes that the unrepresentable exists in itself. And to say this is to re-present it. Unrepresentability is yet another idol in the interminable gallery of idols in human existence, even if a sublime idol, an idol that animates extraordinary feelings of passion at the very moment that it effaces itself as an idol.

Moreover, in simple language, nothing can ever be unrepresentable as long as humanity exists. The very encounter of humans with the abyss of the world seems to make representation (that is, the imagistic making of the world) a necessity.[91] It is the outmaneuverable requirement of the sensible life, as Emanuele Coccia has brilliantly argued.[92] But what is curious about the human animal is that the same capacity that seems to make representation a necessity—the psyche's unlimited propensity for phantasmatic projection in the encounter with an abyssal world—also propels the demand for the unrepresentable. The phantasmatic commitment to the unrepresentable is animated by the same force that necessitates representation, the vital propensity that posits no limits as to what can be represented.

Once we conceptualize this *co-incidence* and thus deconstruct its alleged paradox, we can understand very well that nothing has ever been beyond humanity's capacity for representation because the *nothing itself* has been persistently an object of representation, perhaps the most coveted object of all, the ever-nagging kernel of both philosophical and theological thought whose most forceful renditions have been the inordinate claims to its unrepresentability and the altogether real (and often violent) action to defend the materiality of such claims.

Perhaps what gets in the way of accepting our untamable desire to *give form* to anything and everything—to give form to nothing itself—and to *perform* our encounter with it as the most basic function of being in society is a kind of double investment in the sacred as both irredeemably other—and therefore secure and untouchable in its distant plenitude—and yet so very much our own that it becomes no more than a tautology, the pulse of our identity, not just proximate but one-and-the-same. We have thus removed the sacred from the world and have rendered even our most mundane aspects otherworldly, all the while clinging to phantasms of identity as if they exist in themselves and as themselves, forgetting that they are mere shades of theatrical being. Political theologies that venerate the sacred Elsewhere in such fashion unleash their annihilating force against this existential theatricality, which archaic societies with devotional rituals to divinities whose cosmos they shared never lost sight of. Jan Assmann once again: "The demonization of images and the visual domain is accompanied by a linguistic reform that seeks to desensualize religion and dismantle the theatricality of ritual. . . . Cult draws on ritual enactment, performance, and vision. Scripture leads to a deritualization and detheatricalization of religion" (PoM, 106–9).

This theater of mutable being to which "we" belong much before "we" come to "be"—the ritual space of theater as "a manageable contraction of the cosmic envelope" in Wole Soyinka's inimitable phrase[93]—is to my mind, at this point in "post-"modernity, the coveted object of any desacralization, if the term can be used unfettered by the chains of the war between religion and secularism. In simple terms, a desacralized universe would be a universe that is theatrical to the core. In such a universe, iconoclasm would be entirely and only performative; the icon would serve to remind, not shield, the elements of what is deemed to be the metaperformative domain, transcendental in yet another turn. In this peculiar sense, if theatricality were to expose the foolishness of presuming the stability of the human by refusing to deny the performativity of existence, of living being, it would just as well derail the capacity of the sacred for interminable self-referentiality and self-authorization, in favor, one might add paradoxically, of restoring the hopeless fragility of the human, its outmaneuverable mortality.

Theatricality, as the cohesive condition of the art of *hypokrisis*, the art of performing the being of an other, is often conceived, within inherited philosophical modes, as the epitome of heterological space. And yet, I would argue, as actualization of the horizon of a tragic sense of life—or even, in more modern terms, as the space of deliberately alienating the postulated identity of the other (in a kind of Brechtian *Verfremdungseffekt* applied to the essence of autopoiesis)—theatricality may be an exemplary mode in which to confront the heteronomous language of political theology.

NOTES

Preface

1. Peter Sloterdijk, *God's Zeal: The Battle of the Three Monotheisms* (London: Polity, 2009), 78. Henceforth cited parenthetically in the text.
2. Samuel Weber, *Inquiétantes singularités* (Paris: Hermann, 2014). Henceforth cited parenthetically in the text.
3. Since I wrote these words, the outcome of the 2016 US presidential election produced a triumphalism against the politics of identity, which was thoughtlessly reduced to the politics of so-called political correctness. Of course, mainstream media have largely ignored the fact that the Trump camp won the election on the basis of an identity politics of its own (white supremacy), but discussing this will take us far afield. I have been a critic of the politics of identity for a couple of decades, and even though one might say that such critiques were vindicated by the thrashing cultural liberalism took in this election, this is exactly not the time for self-satisfaction. Even though I still think that identity politics is one of the greatest ruses of liberalism and a bona fide obstacle to building the broad constituencies needed to enact radical social transformation, I recognize—I have always recognized—its importance as politics of resistance. But a key concern of secular criticism is also how to think of what it means to move from the position of resistance to the position of emancipation and in this respect thinking beyond the politics of identity remains imperative.

1. Transformation, Not Transcendence

1. This essay is indebted to Bruce Robbins, who first articulated that Said's secularism should not be opposed strictly to religion but rather to nationalism, and to Aamir

Mufti, who extends this further by perceiving Said's secular mind to be implicated in an episteme of homelessness and a political adherence to disenfranchised positions. See, indicatively, Bruce Robbins, "Secularism, Elitism, Progress, and Other Transgressions: On Edward Said's 'Voyage In'" (1994), in *Feeling Global: Internationalism in Distress* (New York: New York University Press, 1999), 115–26; Aamir Mufti, "Auerbach in Istanbul: Edward Said, Secular Criticism, and the Question of Minority Culture," *Critical Inquiry* 25 (Autumn 1998): 95–125. On the contrary, William D. Hart, *Edward Said and the Religious Effects of Culture* (Cambridge: Cambridge University Press, 2000), fails profoundly to understand these nuances of Said's grasp of the secular imagination, expending instead enormous energy to prove that Said's discourse is full of unwitting religious metaphors.

2. I have retained here the present tense in order to protect and sustain the dramatization of the historical moment. The essay was first drafted in 2002, very much in the aftermath of 9/11, and the evident uncertainty relative to the long-term significance of the event is fully commensurate with the purpose of this argument. Indeed, what has unfolded in the years that have passed since then confirms the impetus even more sharply.
3. The entire and rather baroque sequence of events, including a whole lot of explications, clarifications, justifications, retractions, and so on, from all parties involved (including Stockhausen and his entourage, the German senator Christina Weiss, and the original reporter from North German Radio who is credited with the mendacious reportage) can be found in detail in Karlheinz Stockhausen's official web site: www.stockhausen.org.
4. See Gourgouris, *Dream Nation: Enlightenment, Colonization, and the Institution of Modern Greece* (Stanford: Stanford University Press, 1996), 123–54; Gourgouris, "The Gesture of the Sirens," in *Does Literature Think? Literature as Theory for an Antimythical Era* (Stanford: Stanford University Press, 2003), 161–97.
5. This excerpt is from a statement with the title "Message from Professor Stockhausen" with date of issue September 19, 2001, www.stockhausen.org/message_from_karlheinz.html.
6. I owe this phrase to Martin Harries.
7. One of the most brilliant meditations of the intrinsic aesthetic dimensions of 9/11 as an event and the huge problems this creates is Samuel Weber's essay "Nuages" in his *Inquiétantes singularités* (Paris: Hermann, 2014), 75–119. Most significant is his analysis of Thomas Hoepker's notorious photograph of that day depicting a group of young New Yorkers hanging out on the Williamsburg side of the East River chatting in the sun while lower Manhattan is going up in clouds of smoke. The aleatory composition reminds one of Manet's impressionist country picnics. But the photograph encapsulates a real moment in time that not only manifests this intrinsic aesthetics of catastrophe but announces the event's almost immediate anesthetization as the event became history. For an equally significant account of 9/11 as aesthetic spectacle, see also Martin Harries, *Forgetting Lot's Wife* (New York: Fordham University Press, 2007).
8. Edward W. Said, "Opponents, Audiences, Constituencies, Community," in *Reflections on Exile, and Other Essays* (Cambridge, MA: Harvard University Press, 2000), 118–47, quotation from 131.
9. Edward W. Said, *Musical Elaborations* (New York: Columbia University Press, 1991), 55.
10. Edward W. Said, *The World, the Text, and the Critic* (Cambridge, MA: Harvard University Press, 1983), 26.

11. Aamir Mufti, "Critical Secularism: A Reintroduction for Perilous Times," *boundary 2* 31, no. 2 (2004): 1–9.
12. Theodor W. Adorno, "The Essay as Form," trans. Bob Hullot-Kentor and Frederick Will, *New German Critique* 32 (Spring/Summer 1984): 151–71, quotation from 155.
13. Adorno, 161.
14. Said, *Musical Elaborations*, 70.
15. Daniel Barenboim and Edward W. Said, *Parallels and Paradoxes: Explorations in Music and Society*, ed. Ara Guzelimian (New York: Pantheon, 2002), 12.
16. I discuss the poetics and politics of impersonation at length in "A Lucid Drunkenness (Genet's Poetics of Revolution)" in *Does Literature Think?*, 249–91. Said's affinity for Genet (particularly for his ability to enter the world of the other without appropriating it) is well known. See Edward W. Said, "On Jean Genet," in *On Late Style: Music and Literature Against the Grain* (New York: Vintage, 2007), 73–90.
17. Edward W. Said, *Out of Place: A Memoir* (New York: Knopf, 1999), 3–4.
18. Marcel Proust, *The Past Recaptured*, trans. Andreas Mayor (New York: Vintage, 1971), 186.
19. Edward W. Said, "People's Rights and Literature," interview with Jonathan Rée (Cairo, 1993), in *Power, Politics, and Culture: Interviews with Edward Said*, ed. Gauri Viswanathan (New York: Pantheon, 2001), 248–61, quotation from 257.
20. Edward W. Said, "Returning to Ourselves," interview with Jacqueline Rose (London, 1997–98), in Viswanathan, *Power, Politics, and Culture*, 419–31, quotation from 421–22.
21. Edward W. Said, "*Orientalism* and After," interview with Eleanor Wachtel (Toronto, 1996), in Viswanathan, *Power, Politics, and Culture*, 208–47, quotation from 226.
22. Said, "Returning to Ourselves," 429.
23. Stathis Gourgouris, "A Conversation with Edward Said" (New York, 1990), *Planodion* 16 (June 1992): 392–401.
24. Edward W. Said, "The One-State Solution," *New York Times Magazine*, January 10, 1999, 36–39.
25. I am keeping this sentence in the present tense because it is still pertinent. Silencing the memory of Said's voice is still the task of those who will do everything in the world to prevent equal coexistence between the two peoples in Palestine. The present of fifteen years ago is, alas, still the brutal present.
26. Said relates the episode at length in "Literary Theory at the Crossroads of Public Life," interview with Imre Saluzinsky (London, 1987), in Viswanathan, *Power, Politics, and Culture*, 69–93.
27. Edward W. Said, "Criticism and the Art of Politics," interview with Jennifer Wicke and Michael Sprinker, in *Edward Said: A Critical Reader*, ed. Michael Sprinker (Oxford: Blackwell, 1992), 221–64, quotation from 232.
28. Edward W. Said, "My Right of Return," interview with Ari Shavit (Tel Aviv, 2000), in Viswanathan, *Power, Politics, and Culture*, 443–58, quotation from 457.
29. Said, 458.
30. See, indicatively, "Adorno as Lateness Itself," in *Adorno: A Critical Reader*, ed. Nigel Gibson and Andrew Rubin (Oxford: Blackwell, 2002), 193–208, as well as the posthumous *On Late Style*.
31. Edward W. Said, *Freud and the Non-European* (London: Verso, 2003), 54.
32. Edward W. Said, "The Future of Criticism," in *Reflections on Exile, and Other Essays*, 165–172, quotation from 171.
33. This text that I have noted as an appendix was written before the posthumous publication that collected Said's various fragments on late style. However, my argument

here—in somewhat unorthodox fashion—seeks to determine Said's late style in writings other than the ones trained on this concept as explicit object of inquiry; hence, my decision is not to update the text, lest I derail the focus on Said's own late style as such.

34. See Edward Said, "Thoughts on Late Style," *London Review of Books* 26, no. 15 (August 5, 2004). Henceforth cited in the text.
35. See Edward Said, *Humanism and Democratic Criticism* (New York: Columbia University Press, 2004), 18–21. Henceforth cited in the text as H, followed by page number.
36. See Edward Said, *From Oslo to Iraq and the Road Map* (New York: Pantheon, 2004), 111.

2. The Lesson of Pierre Clastres

1. Quoted in Claude Lefort, "Dialogue with Pierre Clastres," in *Writing: the Political Test*, trans. David Ames Curtis (Durham: Duke University Press, 2000), 207.
2. For an in-depth study of the significance of this journal in the French literary world, see James Petterson, *Postwar Figures of* L'Éphémère (Plainsboro, NJ: Associated University Presses, 2000).
3. There are three extremely valuable analyses of this conjuncture. For a meticulous account of Clastres's relation to the full-fledged parameters of this particular French intellectual strain, see Samuel Moyn, "Of Savagery and Civil Society: Pierre Clastres and the Transformation of French Political Thought," *Modern Intellectual History* 1, no. 1 (2004): 55–80; and Moyn, "Savage and Modern Liberty: Marcel Gauchet and the Origins of New French Thought," *European Journal of Political Theory* 4, no. 2 (2005): 164–87. Moyn's argument that Clastres's anthropological thought is exclusively motivated by an aversion to his earlier investment in Marxism, through accurate in terms of the Zeitgeist, may be a bit overstated. Curiously, he also leaves out of this configuration Clastres's decisive relation with the thought of Cornelius Castoriadis. This dimension is picked up in another, equally significant essay that rounds out these studies of an important but rather neglected intersection of French political thought in the 1970s: Warren Breckman, "Democracy Between Disenchantment and Political Theology: French Post-Marxism and the Return of Religion," *New German Critique* 94 (Winter 2005): 72–105. But Breckman too overstates in turn the political-theological dimensions of this configuration. If there is one thing we can say with certainty about Clastres, it would be that he is resolutely antitheological; if anything, his thinking tends toward the mythical.
4. Pierre Clastres, *Archeology of Violence*, trans. Jeanine Herman (New York: Autonomedia, 1994), 96. Henceforth cited in the text as AV, followed by page number.
5. Pierre Clastres, *Entretien avec L'Anti-Mythes*, ed. Miguel Abensour (1974; Paris: Sens et Tonka, 2011), 13–16. In positing the command-obedience structure as the primary anthropological division between state and society, Clastres may be said to be following Castoriadis's earliest post-Marxist understandings from the late phases of *Socialisme ou Barbarie* in the mid-1960s.
6. Crucial (and perhaps unique) in this respect is Miguel Abensour, "'Savage Democracy' and 'Principle of Anarchy,'" *Philosophy and Social Criticism* 28, no. 6:703–26.
7. On rare occasions, one has the pleasure to see one's thought confirmed by discovering it to have already existed in the work of a great thinker. This trajectory of thinking together Amazon Indians with ancient Greeks through Clastres was also

conducted by Nicole Loraux—the only other such instance I know, which still remains neglected and unpursued. Loraux puts forth an ingenious critique of Clastres, to which we will attend at the end, but let us note that she opens her argument, speaking as a classicist, by remembering her first reading of Clastres as an experience of an altogether familiar land. See Loraux, "Notes sur l'un, le deux, et le multiple," in *L'Esprit des lois sauvages: Pierre Clastres ou une nouvelle anthropologie politique*, ed. Miguel Abensour (Paris: Seuil, 1987), 155–71.

8. Clastres, *Entretien avec L'Anti-Mythes*, 34.
9. Montaigne, *The Complete Essays of Montaigne*, ed. and trans. Donald M. Frame (Stanford: Stanford University Press, 1998), 141. The great French novelist Michel Butor argues that Montaigne's friendship with La Boétie is born out of Montaigne's encounter with this text. Montaigne, the reader, finds, by means of the text, a kindred soul in its author and seeks to make his acquaintance in real life. Moreover, Butor argues, La Boétie's death becomes the source of Montaigne's commitment to writing his own text in turn: "The book that Montaigne desires to write, which will become the first volume of the *Essays*, must be, among other things, a monument to La Boètie, his tomb." See Michel Butor, *Essais sur les Essais* (Paris: Gallimard, 1968), 33.
10. The edited text is published first in Basel in Latin, and then in Edinburgh in French under the name Eusèbe Philadelphe Cosmopolite. See Marie Gaille-Nikodimov, "Les Ambuiguïtès de La Boétie," *Magazine Littéraire* 436 (November 2004): 39.
11. See David Lewis Schaefer, ed., *Freedom Over Servitude: Montaigne, La Boétie, and* On Voluntary Servitude (Westport, CT: Greenwood, 1998). See especially the articles by David Lewis Schaefer, "Montaigne and La Boétie" (1–30), and Daniel Martin, "Montaigne, Author of *On Voluntary Servitude*" (127–88). The volume includes a translation of the *Discours de la servitude volontaire* by David Lewis Schaefer.
12. The same can be said of Marcel Gauchet and Miguel Abensour, who supervise an edition of *Le Discours de la Servitude Volontaire* that includes the dossier *La Boétie et la Question du Politique*, which is edited by Claude Lefort and Pierre Clastres (Paris: Payot, 1976). In this volume, see, especially, Gauchet and Abensour, "Les Leçons de *La Servitude* et leur destin" (vii–xxix); Clastres, "Liberté, Malencontre, Innommable" (229–46), translated and included in *The Archeology of Violence* (henceforth cited in the text as AV, followed by page number); Lefort, "Le nom d'Un" (247–307). Henceforth all references to La Boétie's *Discours* will marked in the text as SV followed by page number, first, of this French edition and, second, of the Schaefer English translation mentioned cited in note 11. I modified the translation where necessary.
13. As such, its legacy is complex and problematic, drawing attention from a variety of quarters that would otherwise be in fierce antagonism. Gauchet and Abensour provide an intriguing trajectory of interest in La Boétie over the years, ranging from Calvinism to anarcho-syndicalism, Richelieu to Spinoza, Jean Marat to Sainte-Beuve, Simone Weil to Pierre Clastres. See Gauchet and Abensour, "Les Leçons de *La Servitude* et leur destin," x–xviii.
14. Miguel Abensour, "Du bon usage de l'hypothèse de la servitude volontaire," *Réfractions* 17 (Winter 2006): 65–84.
15. Lefort, "Le nom d'Un," 262.
16. Clastres identifies La Boétie in similar terms: "[He] does his research not as a psychologist but as a mechanic: he is interested in the functioning of social machines" (AV, 95).
17. The whole schema, including the argument of being denatured and forming a self-willing habitus of servitude, carries over to Rousseau's famous *Discourse on the*

Origin of Inequality (1755), except that here is an additional warning about the perils of insurrectionary energies, which, when lacking the impetus of self-rule, merely perpetuate the habitus of servitude: "Once people are accustomed to masters, they can no longer do without them. If they attempt to shake off the yoke, they move all the farther away from freedom because, as they mistake unbridled license for freedom, which is its very opposite, their revolutions almost always deliver them up to seducers who only increase their chains." Rousseau, *The First and Second Discourses*, ed. and trans. Victor Gourevitch (New York: Harper and Row, 1986), 126.

18. Clastres also claims—and history is on his side—the likelihood that La Boétie's treatise was influenced by descriptions of indigenous societies in the New World, whose discovery is chronicled with abandon and circulated with extraordinary speed throughout sixteenth-century Europe. Montaigne's brilliant essay "Of Cannibals" raises similar questions to La Boétie's (as does Thomas More's *Utopia* before them), though Montaigne angles the matter in terms of cultural, not political, difference, and, while his sharpest irony abounds, he stages the scene via a careful (politically speaking) metaphoric distancing. It's one of those fine moments that one often sees in Clastres when he situates this mid-sixteenth-century antiauthoritarian text to lie between, on the one hand, the Renaissance reinvocation of Greek and Roman ideals and, on the other hand, their refraction through the indigenous Other of the New World (see AV, 101–2).
19. La Boétie's thinking may be said to echo discourses prevalent among certain Huguenot jurists in mid-sixteenth-century France who came to be known as the Monarchomachs, which also explains why the first publication of the *Discours* under a pseudonym was by a Huguenot press. The key difference, however, is that the Monarchomachs advocated tyrannicide as a divine right, since they saw the Catholic king's actions as the violation of man's union with God. Such metaphysics is totally absent in La Boétie, as is tyrannicide as such. His antimonarchist politics consists in the simple withdrawal of consent; in that respect, it belongs essentially to democratic theory.
20. For an interesting view on the ramifications of this passage, see André Tournon, "Singuliers en leur fantasies," in *Cité des Hommes, Cité de Dieu* (Geneva: Droz, 2003), 111–22.
21. Nicole Loraux, in reference to this exact passage, responds bemusedly: "Here the historian of Greece will not understand herself at all, perhaps because Clastres has constructed a Greece to his measure." See Loraux, "Notes sur l'un, le deux et le multiple," 160.
22. Pierre Clastres, *La Société contre l'État* (Paris: Minuit, 1974), translated by Robert Hurley as *Society Against the State* (New York: Zone, 1989), 170. Henceforth cited in the text as SaS, followed by page numbers of the English edition; translation modified when necessary.
23. First published in the pages of *Libre* (1977), in the same issue as Clastres's last text on war in primitive societies. See Marcel Gauchet, "La dette du sens et les racines de l'État," in *La condition politique* (Paris: Gallimard, 2005), 45–90.
24. Clastres, *Entretien avec L'Anti-Mythes*, 40.
25. Understanding the structural operation of knowledge in all these rituals in terms of mythical thinking is explained by Clastres, in terms he borrows avowedly from Deleuze and Guattari's *Anti-Oedipus*, as a circulating code. Primitive societies exist in continuous encoded flux. Indeed, he argues, they are defined by a kind of impersonal control of the multiple flow of codes, as the body controls its circulation:

"Primitive society encodes—that is to say, controls, takes hold—its entire flow, all its organs. I mean to say that it takes hold of what we can call the flow of power. It takes good hold of it and does not let it get out beyond its limits. . . . Primitive society controls the organ called chiefdom." Clastres, *Entretien avec L'Anti-Mythes*, 35.

26. Lefort, "Dialogue with Pierre Clastres," 224.
27. I discuss this at length in Gourgouris, "Enlightenment and Paranomia," in *Does Literature Think?* (Stanford: Stanford University Press, 2003), 49–89.
28. This gap is brilliantly conceptualized by Jacques Derrida, in one of his most skillful essays, as the double instance of *l'interdit*, both the forbidden and the forbidding, hence also the interstitial and the in between—the space of the law in Kafka. See Derrida, "Devant la loi," in *Kafka and the Contemporary Critical Performance*, ed. Alan Udoff (Bloomington: Indiana University Press, 1987), 128–49.
29. This is a far cry from presuming, as Gauchet does, borrowing from Clastres, that there is an unavoidable scission at the heart of society as a form where meaning (as well as power) is intrinsically exterior to it—what Gauchet has named "the debt of meaning" or the deficit in the creation of meaning, which for him also marks the point of the emergence of religion. See Gauchet, "La dette du sens et les racines de l'État." Gauchet's argument thus boils down to the fact that heteronomy is the necessary presupposition of autonomy, what enables the project of autonomy to come to consciousness. But put in those terms—that is, without looking into the specific historical complexities of this consciousness when and where it arises—this is no more than the naturalization of heteronomy.
30. Lefort, "Le nom d'Un," 267–68.
31. Lefort, 274.
32. He reiterates this notion in his treatment of the concept of ethnocide, originally written for the *Encyclopaedia Universalis* (1974): "Ethnocide results in the dissolution of the multiple into the One. What happens with the State? Essentially, a centripetal force enters the game, which, when circumstances demand it, tends to crush the opposite centrifugal forces. The State conceives and proclaims itself to be the center of society, the totality of the social body, the absolute master of its diverse organs. We discover here at the heart of the essence of the State the acting power of the One, the work of refusal of the multiple, the fear and horror of difference." See Clastres, "De l'ethnocide," *L'Homme* 14, nos. 3–4 (July-December 1974): 101–10.
33. In a relatively unknown text, Judith Revel articulates the complexities of this triple conjuncture in exemplary fashion. See Revel, "L'altra faccia della guerra: Clastres—Deleuze—Foucault," *Antasofia* 1 (2003): 127–42. On the other hand, Miguel Abensour, in his "La voix de Pierre Clastres," which serves as editorial introduction to *Entretien avec L'Anti-Mythes*, disputes any significant convergence between Clastres and Deleuze and Guattari, despite the explicit mutual references.
34. "The primitive war, the war of every man against every man, is born of equality and takes place in the element of that equality. War is the immediate effect of nondifferences, or at least the insufficient differences." The obvious reference is, of course, unacknowledged. See Michel Foucault, *Society Must Be Defended* (New York: Picador, 2003), 90.
35. Lefort seizes on this passage and problematizes it further: "When we say '*tous uns*,' despite the plural form, we hear '*tous un*.' No doubt, language presupposes the division between the one and the other [form] as the passage from one to the other, as a shift in speech mode, as the indefinitely accountable dissociation between speaking and hearing, the difference between two voices. But this menacing enchantment is

inscribed within the phrase, as if the produced *Name* had the power to be self-sufficient, to be a pure utterance purely heard, whereby everything resonates as one voice." Lefort, "Le nom d'Un," 272.

36. Keeping in mind Montaigne's tribute to friendship in similar terms and in explicit dedication to La Boétie, we can muse in retrospect that the alleged indeterminacy of the authorship of the *Discours* figures as a double deconstruction of the One: not only as a perfectly apt realization of the antityrannical celebration of friendship but also as a dismantling of the monarchical residue in the notion of the author.
37. Jacques Derrida would say it could not be otherwise. See Derrida, *Politics of Friendship*, trans. George Collins (London: Verso, 1997).
38. Loraux, "Notes sur l'un, le deux et le multiple," 169. Henceforth cited in the text. In responding to the interviewer in *Entretien avec L'Anti-Mythes* who poses the same challenge as Loraux, Clastres claims that social divisions along the lines of sexual difference (as well as other aspects pertinent to the domestic space, to the *oikos*, such as the education of children and so on) are not relations of power that lead to or affect the development of power that separates society from an entity that is called "state." He sees the two domains—the domestic space vs. the warrior/hunter space—as separated by a radical epistemological difference. Clastres, *Entretien avec L'Anti-Mythes*, 24–26. Loraux would not dispute the epistemological difference—to the contrary. Indeed, it is precisely this difference that she brings into play: a society-against-the-state cannot be conceptualized outside the epistemology of sexual difference.
39. Clastres, *Entretien avec L'Anti-Mythes*, 20.

3. On Self-Alteration

1. See Castoriadis, "Aeschylian Anthropogony and Sophoclean Self-Creation of *Anthropos*," in *Figures of the Thinkable*, trans. Helen Arnold (Stanford: Stanford University Press, 2007), 1–20; and Castoriadis, *Ce qui fait la Grèce* (Paris: Seuil, 2004).
2. "The wheel revolving around an axis is an absolute ontological creation. It is a greater creation, it weighs, ontologically, more than a new galaxy that would arise tomorrow evening out of nothing between the Milky Way and the Andromeda. For *there are already* millions of galaxies—but the person who invented the wheel, or a written sign, was imitating and repeating *nothing* at all." Cornelius Castoriadis, *The Imaginary Institution of Society*, trans. Kathleen Blamey (Cambridge, MA: MIT Press, 1987), 197.
3. For an interesting such example, see Laurent Van Eynde, "Castoriadis et Bachelard: Un imaginaire en partage," *Cahiers critiques de philosophie* 6 (Summer 2008): 179–78.
4. Cornelius Castoriadis, "Done and To Be Done," in *The Castoriadis Reader*, ed. David Ames Curtis (Oxford: Blackwell, 1997), 396–97.
5. See Suzi Adams, *Castoriadis' Ontology: Being and Creation* (New York: Fordham University Press, 2011).
6. Castoriadis elaborates on his own theory of sublimation at great length in his signature work *The Imaginary Institution of Society* (Cambridge, MA: MIT Press, 1987), but for a concise depiction of his psychoanalytic theory in general (in which sublimation and, of course, self-alteration play a central role), see also the psychoanalytic section in the collection of essays *World in Fragments*, ed. David Ames Curtis (Stanford: Stanford University Press, 1997), 125–212, and *Figures of the Thinkable*, 153–222. For an elaboration on this intricate crossroads in Castoriadis's work (and a predicate to this

section here), see Gourgouris, "Philosophy and Sublimation," *Thesis Eleven* 49 (Spring 1997): 31–43.

7. A learned and thought-provoking discussion of how the psychic monad may enact/ be enacted by the autonomous subject is conducted by Sophie Klimis, "Décrire l'irreprésentable, ou comment dire l'indicible originaire," *Cahiers Castoriadis* 3 (Brussels: Facultés Universitaires Saint-Louis, 2007), 25–54.
8. Reiterating what I mentioned at the outset, the inner-outer distinction is just a figure of rhetorical usefulness. This isn't to say that the distinction is meaningless; rather, its meaning is a constructed condition of difference, as will become evident in the discussion that follows.
9. Judith Butler, *The Psychic Life of Power* (Stanford: Stanford University Press, 1997), 3–4. Henceforth cited in the text as P, followed by page number.
10. Of the numerous texts Castoriadis has written on these matters, the most essential is "The State of the Subject Today," in *World in Fragments*, 137–71.
11. Castoriadis's distinctive mark for the racist relation to the other is the commitment to the other's inconvertibility, that is, absolutely barring the other from possibly entering the domain of the self, an important notion to consider in the historical inquiry into the politics of religious conversion. This particular discussion is useful in corroborating the dimension of internal otherness, but it speaks to a much broader domain that cannot be, in this context, adequately dealt with. See Castoriadis, "Reflections on Racism," in *World in Fragments*, 19–31; and Castoriadis, "The Psychical and Social Roots of Hate," in *Figures of the Thinkable*, 153–59.
12. See Gourgouris, "On the Catachresis of Otherness," in *Dream Nation* (Stanford: Stanford University Press, 1996), 267–82. The mentoring in this discussion was conducted at the time by Gayatri Spivak's work.
13. This doesn't altogether mean she avoids lapsing into a certain heterological transcendentalism on occasion. See, for example, Irigaray, "Approaching the Other as Other," in *Between East and West* (New York: Columbia University Press, 2002), 121–30; and Irigaray, "La transcendance de l'autre," in *Autour de l'idolâtrie*, ed. Bernard Van Meenen (Brussels: Publications des Facultés Universitaires Saint-Louis, 2003), 43–54. But at least Irigaray is careful to refrain from those positions that declare otherness epistemologically off limits, those that bristle at the suggestion that one can speak from the position of an other. While I understand suspicion against imperializing discourses that preside over monopolies of representation by proxy, the fight is to be conducted strictly on political grounds. It can never be an ontological argument. In presuming to put oneself in the position of an other, one does not strive to *be* the other—the very law of performativity does not allow it. In fact, it makes it impossible. One of the most articulate, radical, and moving examples of how one can indeed speak from the position of the other in full cognizance of the impossibility of *being the other* is, to my mind, Jean Genet's last work, *Un captif amoureux* (1986).
14. I am drawing here on Irigaray's famous essay "This Sex Which Is Not One" (1977), which remains one of the most groundbreaking and influential texts in feminist thought.
15. Luce Irigaray, "The Universal as Mediation" (1986), in *Sexes and Genealogies*, trans. Gillian C. Gill (New York: Columbia University Press, 1993), 133. Henceforth cited in the text as SG, followed by page number. I cannot resist pointing out that this is precisely what Benjamin and Adorno also perceived as a problem in Hegel and attempted to resolve first by "the idea of natural history" and later by "dialectics at a standstill" and "negative dialectics," respectively. The notion of history as second nature (nature's

second nature) is a concept that Adorno never abandoned. Neither of them, of course, addressed this differential relation as a matter of sexual difference, despite various insinuations.

16. Consider that one of the key figures in Hegel's theorization of *Sittlichkeit* is Antigone, whom Hegel never even entertains as being herself possibly an embodiment of *hubris* insofar as she too stages, from her own standpoint (legitimate though it is), a politics of *monos phronein*—the dogmatic singularity of excepting oneself from the polis. I have reviewed this issue at length in Gourgouris, "Philosophy's Need for Antigone," in *Does Literature Think?* (Stanford: Stanford University Press 2003), 116–57.
17. It is essential to note that, while many have criticized Irigaray's later work as a kind of softening of position, the point is not to restrict ourselves to a mode of evaluation that presumes the polemical to be superior to the evocative. No doubt, Irigaray, in her later work, wrestles with the articulation of an emancipatory humanism, a humanism that proceeds through its own sublation and the sublation of the terms of so-called French theory of the 1960s and 1970s, in which Irigaray was an unquestionable protagonist. One of the elemental meanings of sublation, let us not forget, is the preservation (*albeit in an altered relation*) of the sublated terms—in this case, the critique of traditional humanism. (Hegelian *Aufhebung*—as method, not as means to an end—is an exemplary figure of self-alteration.) I would argue that Irigaray's wrestling with the project of an emancipatory humanism lends a much greater and sharper gravity to her feminism, and specifically to her pursuit of sexual difference as an epistemological condition that explodes at the core of the history of thought. And I would add that the discomfort with her late humanism is analogous to what is expressed against the late writings of Edward Said—both cases marred by similar misapprehensions, though obviously their domains of discussion are different.

4. Žižek's Realism

1. With the possible exception of Brecht perhaps, whom Žižek quotes fondly on numerous occasions and for whom realism had an evident connection to dialectical materialism—in both cases, divergent from and eccentric for Marxist convention.
2. One of the most insightful close readings along these lines is Michael Löwy, *Fire Alarm: Walter Benjamin's "On the Concept of History"* (London: Verso, 2005).
3. Slavoj Žižek, *The Puppet and the Dwarf: The Perverse Core of Christianity* (Cambridge, MA: MIT Press, 2003), 3.
4. See, for example, Žižek *The Ticklish Subject: the Absent Center of Ontology* (London: Verso, 1999); Žižek, *The Fragile Absolute—or Why Is the Christian Legacy Worth Fighting For* (London: Verso, 2000); Žižek, *On Belief* (New York: Routledge, 2001).
5. The first part of this essay was originally commissioned and written to accompany the DVD release of the film *Slavoj Žižek: The Reality of the Virtual*, produced by Ben Wright and Olive Films (2007). For historical reasons, I have decided to keep this contextual tenet intact, although obviously the overall scope goes beyond the occasion and the purview of the film, addressing directly the concerns of this book.
6. This paragraph and the ones that follow were written in the midst of the George W. Bush years. Nothing about them, however, has historically lapsed in essence. If anything, this callous attitude on the part of US policy has strengthened the equally callous and abhorrent attitude of the opposition, which under a perversion of Islam has precipitated a violent regime of absolutism that is the perfect mirror of permissibility, indeed a regime of permissibility of horror.

7. Slavoj Žižek, "A Plea for a Return to *Différance* (with a Minor *Pro Domo Sua*)," *Critical Inquiry* 32 (Winter 2006): 241–42.
8. Žižek, *The Puppet and the Dwarf*, 49.
9. Žižek's misapprehension of the tragic (and, of course, pagan) sensibility may be linked to his extensive occlusion of the intersection between early Christian theology and ancient Hellenism, particularly concerning his avowedly perverse reading of Paul, who is positively unreadable without a theoretical assessment of this intersection. This conjuncture of elements—which would require a theoretical assessment of the epistemology of *hubris* as counter to the epistemology of God—is obviously too broad for me to engage here, but it is the key for any position that will extend Žižek's radicalism beyond his strategic (materialist) attachment to the Christian imaginary.
10. These two texts are separated by five years. For the sake of retaining the historical dimensions that permeate them, I have decided neither to merge them nor to update them, but to juxtapose them intact, except for minor adjustments for clarification of meaning. The discussion of things Greek in the early pages of this second text addresses conditions before the breakout of the so-called Greek crisis. What seems to have been forgotten in the volumes of ink spilled over analyses of the Greek economic crisis is how the insurrectionary events of December 2008 carried intact in their emergence the full signification of what followed. The youth of Greece *knew* what was at stake long before the cynical elites of the world announced it and pronounced it.
11. One gets a distinct sense of what went on during those days by testimonies and analyses by the actors involved in the collection A. G. Schwarz, Tasos Sagris, and Void Network, eds., *We Are an Image of the Future: The Greek Revolt of December 2008* (Oakland, CA: AK Press, 2010).
12. Slavoj Žižek, *Violence: Six Sideways Reflections* (New York: Picador, 2008), 76. Henceforth cited in the text as V, followed by page number.
13. See "Divine Violence and Liberated Territories—SOFT TARGETS talks with Slavoj Žižek," www.softtargetsjournal.com/web/zizek.php.
14. Slavoj Žižek, "The Jacobin Spirit," *Jacobin Magazine* (Summer 2011): 2.
15. Slavoj Žižek, *First Time as Tragedy, Then as Farce* (London: Verso, 2009), 6.
16. This looks backward and forward in this book, to the preceding essay on Clastres and the essay on Saint Paul that directly follows.
17. See Žižek, "From Myth to Agape," *European Journal of Psychoanalysis* 8–9 (Winter-Fall 1999), www.psychomedia.it/jep/number8–9/zizek.htm.
18. See Slavoj Žižek, "Save Us from Our Saviors," *London Review of Books* 34, no. 11 (June 7, 2012), 13, as well as in a public event in Athens on June 3, 2012: www.youtube.com/watch?v=SWtn7iECkyY.
19. See Slavoj Žižek, "The Courage of Hopelessness," *New Statesman*, July 20, 2015, www.newstatesman.com/world-affairs/2015/07/slavoj-i-ek-greece-courage-hopelessness; Stathis Gourgouris, "The SYRIZA Problem: Radical Democracy and Left Governmentality in Greece," *Open Democracy*, August 6, 2015, www.opendemocracy.net/can-europe-make-it/stathis-gourgouris/syriza-problem-radical-democracy-and-left-governmentality-in-g.

5. Paul's Greek

1. I am quoting from the English translation distributed by the Catholic Church, after they corrected the initial phrasing "things only evil and inhuman" to "things wretched and inhumane"—the German text being "Schlechtes und Inhumanes." The original

Greek text (χεῖρον καὶ ἀπανθρωπότατον) is clearly closer to the German and the revised English phrasing. The notion of evil, whether in the typical Christian sense or any other, is altogether absent. The original text (a letter sent by the Byzantine emperor to his brother from the battlefield in 1391), along with its French translation and meticulous introduction by the theologian and historian Adel Théodore Khoury, was published as Manuel, II Paléologue, *Entretiens avec un Musulman (7e Controverse)* (Paris: Cerf, 1966). The pope's text can be retrieved easily from the *Libreria Editrice Vaticana* online on the Vatican's website.

2. An extraordinary number of responses were issued to the pope's Regensburg address, worthy of an altogether separate study. Most famous among them, from the Muslim world, was the *Open Letter to His Holiness Pope Benedict XVI*, issued exactly a month after the address by thirty-eight Muslim authorities and scholars worldwide (www.ammanmessage.com/media/openLetter/english.pdf), and a year later *A Common Word Between Us and You*, which was a statement by a broader group of clerics and intellectuals declaring the common ground between Christianity and Islam (www.acommonword.com). Of the multitude of critical texts circulated on the web, I select two that deviate from the horde (albeit in different directions) and engage the pope on issues that matter: "The Final Word on the Pope: History, New Worlds, and Islam" by Radwan al Sayyid, professor of Islamic Studies at the Lebanese University, which was published in the *Asharq Alawsat* newspaper website in English (www.asharq-e.com/news.asp?section=3&id=6607); and "Greek Reason at Regensburg" by Dimitri Krallis, professor of Byzantine History at Simon Fraser University, posted on the website of Modern Greek Studies at the University of Michigan (www.lsa.umich.edu/modgreek/detail/0,2250,6740%255Farticle%255F49228,00.html).
3. All these dimensions were already evident and at play in Cardinal Joseph Ratzinger's *tête à tête* encounter with Jürgen Habermas, a year before he was elected pope. The conversation was published as Habermas and Ratzinger, *The Dialectics of Secularization: On Reason and Religion* (San Francisco: Ignatius, 2005).
4. See, indicatively, the thesis of Tomoko Masuzawa in *The Invention of World Religions* (Chicago: University of Chicago Press, 2005). See also Peter Brown, *The Making of Late Antiquity* (Cambridge, MA: Harvard University Press, 1978).
5. The often rendered notion "Greco-Western institution" is comprehensible only as a Christian notion. It has little to do with the pre-Christian world in the Eastern Mediterranean, which has also been just as erroneously summarized as "Greco-Roman." In this respect, much can be learned from Jacques Derrida's insistence on his neologism *globalatinization*, especially as a qualifier for discourses of and about religion. If the discourse on religion is derived from Latin, we can no longer speak thoughtlessly of the Greco-Roman. If indeed the Greco-Roman has some meaning, this would be starkly different from the Global-Latin that now comes to stand for the Greco-Western. Understanding the provenance of this naming is precisely what the interrogation of the relation between Hellenism and Christianity is about. The Latinized Greek of the Greco-Roman is obliterated in the Latin of globalatinization, whereas the Greek in the Greco-Roman is obviously pre-Christian. And although Christianity Hellenized itself in order to succeed, this Hellenization in language was quickly surpassed by the latinization of Christianity as an institution—at least, the Christianity that became a global religion, that came to monopolize the discourse on religion. No doubt, the historical parameters of this overlap are key instances to query, because in this overlap also resides a schism—not the theological schism of the Christian Church (this is only a symptom), but a historical and perhaps even epistemological schism that has largely lapsed from the discourse and the scholarship.

6. This reality is rendered as a living being: Ἡ ἐπιστολὴ ἡμῶν ὑμεῖς ἐστε—"Our letter is you" (2 Corinthians 3:2). The "you" here is plural as well. Indeed, the plural subject both conducting and receiving the action, in the form of a pronoun without a name, is the characteristic mode by which Paul configures the Christian community against any previous identitary framework (Jews, Greeks, Romans) but also people (*laos*) in general as a political entity—indeed against any other communal name. Paul's Christian messianic community is anonymous in a constitutive sense; it is a pure pronoun linked to the verb of God. Giorgio Agamben also points this out in *The Kingdom and the Glory* (Stanford: Stanford University Press, 2011), 175.
7. There is another dimension here to be noted, even if I cannot pursue it in this context. Taubes's text is a testimonial of how, before its relatively recent academic fashion, the Paul phenomenon was an essentially German question, which in national-cultural terms (and, of course, "religious" terms, which, as Marx told us, are the very terms of Germany's secular history) is always also a Jewish question. An additional microdimension here is that Paul becomes also a specifically German Catholic question in a political-theological sense, which links Carl Schmitt and Martin Heidegger with the long trajectory of papal configuration of power. It is only apt then that Joseph Ratzinger as Pope Benedict XVI steps into the fold in such a timely manner.
8. Jacob Taubes, *The Political Theology of Paul*, trans. Dana Hollander (Stanford: Stanford University Press, 2004), 4. Henceforth cited in the text as T, followed by page number.
9. Jacques Derrida, *The Ear of the Other: Otobiography, Transference, Translation* (New York: Schocken, 1985), 1–38.
10. Incidentally, Agamben's choice to retranslate the use of "Christ" in Romans back into "Messiah" is hardly motivated by philological accuracy. In any language other than Hebrew and Greek, where the word's literal meaning ("the anointed one") remains present and intact, the words *Christ* and *Messiah* work as proper names, whose signification is surely not interchangeable. Very simply, the first has come and is present; the second is to come—not quite a petty theological difference. Agamben's retranslation obliterates the literal equivalence (and therefore Paul's negotiation) and simultaneously performs two authorial resignifications: (1) it erases from the name the notion of the *elect*; (2) it saturates the name with all the subsequent configurations of messianism as a modern discourse.
11. Giorgio Agamben, *The Time That Remains*, trans. Patricia Dailey (Stanford: Stanford University Press, 2005), 4. Henceforth cited in the text as A, followed by page number.
12. By the same token, Paul's Jewishness, like any social-imaginary attribute or identity, is subjected to the relativity of historical and geographical orbits. For instance, as Christianity becomes fully established in Seleucid Mesopotamia a couple of centuries later, there is a strong remembrance of "that pagan Paul." Brown, *The Making of Late Antiquity*, 72.
13. See David M. Reis, "The Areopagus as Echo Chamber: *Mimesis* and Intertextuality in *Acts* 17," *Journal of Higher Criticism* 9, no. 2 (Fall 2002): 259–77. Reis maps the range of Socratic tropes and also provides an extensive bibliography of the multitude of relevant writings.
14. Jean-Luc Marion offers a brilliant reading of this scene, rightly pointing out that this assessment of Athens being overwhelmed with idols occurs only in Paul's mind. He goes on to theorize that Paul offers his own idolatry—the "icon of the invisible God"—reiterating unbeknown to him the argument I conduct in the essay that follows, which examines how idolatry is inherent in all religions. See Jean-Luc Marion, *The Idol and the Distance*, trans. Thomas A. Carlson (New York: Fordham University Press, 2001), 19–26.

15. For a concise discussion of this particular configuration of divinity in ancient Greece, see Jean-Pierre Vernant, *Myth and Society in Ancient Greece* (Cambridge, MA: MIT Press, 1990), 101–19.
16. Hans Blumenberg, *Work on Myth* (Cambridge, MA: MIT Press, 1985), 22–25, 253–55.
17. See Alain Badiou, *Saint Paul: The Foundation of Universalism*, trans. Ray Brassier (Stanford: Stanford University Press, 2003), 17. Henceforth cited in the text as B, followed by page number.
18. See Cornelius Castoriadis, *The Imaginary Institution of Society*, trans. Kathleen Blamey (Cambridge, MA: MIT Press, 1987), 195–210.
19. Although we are speaking in Christian terms here because our subject is Paul, it is fair to note that no god has ever produced a gift without producing an exchange: the mere practice of devotion. Even the signification of *manna*, the quintessential figure of God's gratuity and graciousness, is linked to the economy of election and the covenant. Likewise, no eschatological/salvational discourse can trump the law of exchange: it exists on the promise of plenitude and finality of redemption, for which one exchanges the thankless task of trying to fight the untotalizable and contingent vicissitudes of life.
20. Marcel Mauss, *The Gift*, trans. W. D. Halls (New York: Norton, 1990), 36.
21. The notion *hēmitheos* (half-god), reserved for certain heroes fathered by gods (Hercules being the supreme example), is obviously not the same and cannot be considered as a source of conceptual derivation, because it pertains to a divine framework that is strictly polytheistic. Moreover, as the word itself suggests, *hēmitheos* designates a fragmented substance—a partial god—while *theanthropos*, as the epitome of the incarnation of the divine, invokes a unifying principle, whatever might be the theological arguments about consubstantiality. To put it dramatically, in assuming human flesh, God is indeed One: God overcomes the chasm of abstracted divinity and produces oneness where it is most lacking, in the human realm as such. In this respect, Christianity—though permeated by remnants of pagan practices—is, theologically, the quintessential monotheism.
22. Bruno Blumenfeld, whose work is a must read on the issue of Paul's historical relation to the Hellenistic world, is right to point out that Paul was hardly driven to topple the Roman imperial regime and that, on the contrary, he revered its laissez-faire treatment of the imperial fringes and foresaw the advantages of Roman political and juridical structures for the establishment and development of a new mode of social-political organization, signified by the early Christian communities. See Bruno Blumenfeld, *The Political Paul: Justice, Democracy, and Kingship in a Hellenistic Framework* (Sheffield: Sheffield Academic, 2001), 276–87. In this respect, Taubes and Badiou, each for reasons of his own, romanticize and exoticize Paul as a rebel against the Romans, even though the very history of Christianity and the ultimate political uses of Pauline theology simply discredit them. Along with them, yet another thinker of great erudition, Enrique Dussel, is distinguished for the same faltering. See, indicatively, Dussel, "The Liberatory Event in Paul of Tarsus," *Qui Parle* 18, no. 1 (Fall/Winter 2009): 111–80. Pauline writing is surely masterful in its seductiveness, but the fact that it still manages to pass for rebel writing while having spearheaded one of the greatest institutional achievements in human history, with such a bloody trail of power behind it, remains nonsensical to me.
23. For an elegant account of Agamben's negation of law and faith (as well as of their epistemological contours in Pauline thinking), see Lorenzo Chiesa, "Giorgio Agamben's Franciscan Ontology," *Cosmos and History: The Journal of Natural and Social*

Philosophy 5, no. 1 (2009): 105–17. Chiesa makes a convincing argument that, in *The Time That Remains*, Agamben thoroughly Christianizes the thinking that begins with *Homo Sacer* in a specifically Franciscan direction.

24. Georges Bataille, *The Accursed Share*, trans. Robert Hurley (Boston: Zone, 1988), 1:69.
25. Bataille, 1:70.
26. It's curious—or perhaps not—to see Jean-Luc Nancy entrapped like Agamben into ignoring Bataille (whom he also invokes) while discussing the workings of gift and grace in reference to James's Epistle—which he correctly diagnoses, in utter contrast to Paul's epistles, as containing/producing no theology per se. Like Agamben, Nancy is seduced by the presumption of gratuity in grace that will annul the tyranny of exchange. But when he concludes that "the receptivity must equal the donation in gratuity" he inevitably reiterates the framework of exchange, even in the presumption of a zero sum game, especially because he occludes the crux of James's practical purpose: to establish the real (not merely theological) terms of obedience to God—the *praxis* of obedience, or, more accurately, the *ergon* of obedience. Thus, Nancy's phrasing that epitomizes the self-determination of the gift—"to give oneself in turn to the gift"—should be at least amended, if not altogether rephrased, as "to give oneself *up* in *return for* the gift." See Nancy, "The Judeo-Christian (on Faith)," in *Dis-Enclosure: The Deconstruction of Christianity* (New York: Fordham University Press, 2008), 42–60.
27. Michel Foucault, *Fearless Speech* (New York: Semiotexte, 2001), 120.
28. Blumenfeld, *The Political Paul*, 93. Besides this brilliant critique, we should not forget that with this phrase Paul addresses a messianic community, a community that will come to exist at the very moment that it will cease to exist in a real worldly sense. To draw political conclusions from this phrasing, especially in modern terms, is just an absurd idea.
29. Agamben embarks on another trajectory in the Hebraic tradition that elicits from Paul's usage of *klētos* what he calls "the messianic vocation"—namely, the fact that all worldly and juridical duties specifically are conducted in the shadow of the messianic event and are thus always already annulled: "*The messianic vocation is the revocation of every vocation*," he indicatively notes (A, 23, his italics). But this hardly annuls the chasm.
30. On the extremely questionable grounds as to whether political theology is philosophy—but with an impetus quite unlike Badiou's—I have dedicated a few remarks in an essay on Carl Schmitt: Gourgouris, "The Concept of the Mythical," in *Does Literature Think?* (Stanford: Stanford University Press, 2003), 90–115. The matter is, of course, enormous and hardly evident.
31. The fanaticism with which early Christians gave themselves over to their martyrdom and exploited their persecution for their benefit is arguably a psychological symptom of welcoming the authority of this demand to give your life over to faith. In effect, the discourse of the desire for martyrdom is no different from the discourse of spirit possession. It is interesting that nowadays, when this symptom is proliferating in certain ranks of Islam, no one—whether against or in favor of such martyrdom in the name of Islam—seems to recall this Christian history of surrendering life to faith.
32. I find wonderfully provocative Blumenfeld's historically substantiated claim that Paul's rhetoric of "preference for death over life" was driven by the widely popular diffusion of such notions among itinerant Cynics in Asia Minor, who considered suicide the key to divine life. Blumenfeld is daring enough to speculate that Paul may have committed suicide in Rome. See Blumenfeld, *The Political Paul*, 22. Michel Foucault also

points to this association between Cynic renunciation of life or indifference to death and early Christian techniques of preaching and proselytizing. See Foucault, *Fearless Speech*, 116–20.

6. Every Religion Is Idolatry

1. I discuss this at length in Gourgouris, "Responding to the Deregulation of the Political," in *Lessons in Secular Criticism* (New York: Fordham University Press, 2013), 145–80. For an interesting handling of Paul Kahn's argument, see Jason Stevens, "The Cul-de-Sac of Schmittian Political Theology," *boundary 2* 40, no. 1 (Spring 2013): 83–135.
2. Giorgio Agamben, *The Kingdom and the Glory* (Stanford: Stanford University Press, 2011). Henceforth cited in the text. Regarding my discussion of Agamben throughout this text, I have learned a great deal from two erudite critiques, very much within the terms of *oikonomia* from Aristotle on to early patristic literature: Thanos Zartaloudis, *Giorgio Agamben: Power, Law and the Uses of Criticism* (London: Routledge, 2010); and Dotan Leshem, *The Origins of Neoliberalism: Modeling the Economy from Jesus to Foucault* (New York: Columbia University Press, 2016).
3. "Alle prägnanten Begriffe der modernen Staatslehre sind säkularisierte theologische Begriffe." But let us register the full quotation: "All significant concepts of the modern theory of the state are secularized theological concepts not only because of their historical development—in which they were transferred from theology to the theory of the state whereby, for example, the omnipotent God became the omnipotent lawgiver—but also because of their systematic structure, the recognition of which is necessary for a sociological consideration of these concepts." The second point about structures, and not ideologies or imaginaries, is often overlooked in favor of the simple analogical first point. Schmitt tried to refine his argument over the years—and this systematic affinity between the theological and the political was the primary ground, as it is more convincing than the analogical, but even this does not address the work done by the participle "secularized." See Carl Schmitt, *Political Theology*, trans. George Schwab (Cambridge, MA: MIT Press, 1988), 36. Henceforth cited in the text as PT, followed by page number.
4. For Agamben, secularization is a signature concept: "Signatures move and displace concepts and signs from one field to another (in this case from sacred to profane, and vice versa), without redefining them semantically. . . . Secularization operates in the conceptual system of modernity as a signature that refers it back to theology" (*The Kingdom and the Glory*, 4). But, of course, he gives little credence to the "vice versa." Theology is just as much a signature concept in relation to the secular, in the sense that political concepts—understandings of worldly power—needed to be theologized so as to produce consequently the abstracted notions of divinity that fuel the imaginary of the Abrahamic religious tradition.
5. Jacques Lezra, "The Instance of the Sovereign in the Unconscious: The Primal Scenes of Political Theology," in *Political Theology and Early Modernity*, ed. Graham Hammill and Julia Reinhard Lupton (Chicago: University of Chicago Press, 2012), 183–211. For an exhaustive account of the trajectory of political theology as an idea, on which I draw extensively, see Annika Thiem, "Political Theology," in *The Encyclopedia of Political Thought*, ed. Michael Gibbons (Oxford: Blackwell, 2013). For a thoughtful consideration of how the political theology and sovereignty discourses have emerged in

an Islamic context, see Andrew March, "Genealogies of Sovereignty in Islamic Political Theology," *Social Research* 80, no. 1 (Spring 2013): 293–320.

6. "The term 'political theology' really is one that I coined"—from Carl Schmitt's letter to Armin Mohler (April 14, 1952) on the subject of Jacob Taubes. Excerpt included in Jacob Taubes, *To Carl Schmitt: Letters and Reflections* (New York: Columbia University Press, 2013), 25.
7. In his critical reading of the debate between Carl Schmitt and the Catholic theologian Erik Peterson (discussed later), Jacob Taubes calls the trajectory from Eusebius to Augustine a "leap" (Taubes, *To Carl Schmitt*, 28). Strictly speaking, he is right, but in ways he does not account for and may not even fathom. As an "arch-Jew" educated within the "Protestant-Jewish consensus" (these are his self-descriptions), his political-theological enemy is Catholicism (the German variety all the more). He encounters—and is inordinately fascinated by—what Jacques Derrida later named *globalatinization*. He has no interest in—nor does he really understand—Christianity's encounter with things Hellenic, and even in his account of Paul, despite the insurmountable language issue, the reference frame is always Pauline Christianity as it feeds into and is retroactively configured by the imaginary of the Holy Roman Empire. Thus, the problematic relationship between Judaism and Hellenism, which leaves an indelible mark on Christianity, just isn't there for Taubes, so that it is easy for him to conclude that in the end "Judaism 'is' political theology" (22). In this latter sense, strangely enough, Taubes concurs with Peterson, even if by an altogether different sort of thinking: Taubes being in favor of political theology and Peterson being against it. In Peterson's case, the Judaism of political theology is driven by explicit anti-Judaism, so as not to say outright anti-Semitism, which I discuss later.
8. Gil Anidjar, *The Jew, the Arab: History of the Enemy* (Stanford: Stanford University Press, 2003) remains singularly instructive in this regard.
9. On the face of it, *Verfassungslehre* seems an aberrant text. Its bona fide impetus is a democratic constitutional theory, even if as a corrective of the Weimar situation—hence, here too the enemy is liberalism and the metaphysics of representative democracy. Despite such stunning statements such as "A democracy must not permit the inevitable *factual* difference between governing and being governed to become a qualitative distinction. . . . It is clear that all democratic thinking centers on ideas of *immanence* [and] the appeal to the will of God contains a moment of undemocratic transcendence. . . . Under democratic logic, only the will of the people must come into consideration because God cannot appear in the political realm other than as the god of a particular people" and so on, Schmitt ultimately understands the people as a unitary subject that authorizes a unitary figure of the State. Ultimately, a "democratic" Schmitt would argue for *dēmos monarchos*. See Carl Schmitt, *Constitutional Theory*, trans. Jeffrey Seitzer (Durham: Duke University Press, 2008), esp. 266–67. An exemplary discussion of this text can be found in Andreas Kalyvas, *Democracy and the Politics of the Extraordinary* (Cambridge: Cambridge University Press, 2009).
10. Carl Schmitt, *Political Theology II: The Myth of the Closure of Any Political Theology* (Cambridge: Polity, 2008). 49. Henceforth cited in the text as PT II, followed by page number.
11. Carl Schmitt, *The Nomos of the Earth* (New York: Telos, 2003), 70–71. Of course, to unravel the contortions that Schmitt goes to in order to make this argument will take us far afield. How one goes from the materiality of *nemein* (dividing, delineating, and the like) to "single divine *nomos*" cannot possibly be accounted for by the metaphoric weight of "walling space"—at least insofar as Schmitt *necessarily* considers it

the delineation of sacred space. This is utterly disputable both theoretically and historically—for example, the agora space, as the space of the political par excellence, lies outside the walled sacred space of the Acropolis, thereby explicitly separating the political from the sacred.

12. This is why "popular sovereignty" is an incoherent (or, at the very least, unstable) concept. See also Wendy Brown, *Walled States, Waning Sovereignty* (New York: Zone, 2014), 49–50.
13. "Monomythical" is a notion brilliantly theorized by Odo Marquard in *Farewell to Matters of Principle* (Oxford: Oxford University Press, 1989), 87–110. But to this string of terms we can just as well add what Bruno Latour has named "mononatural" in *Politics of Nature* (Cambridge, MA: Harvard University Press, 2004), 33, passim; what Peter Sloterdijk has named "monolatry" and "monohumanism" or, more precisely in reference to Latour, "monogeïsm" in *God's Zeal* (Cambridge: Polity, 2009), 24–29 and 145–46 respectively (henceforth cited in the text); what Edward Said has identified as "monocentrism" in *The World, the Text, and the Critic* (Cambridge, MA: Harvard University Press, 1983), 53; or what Jean-Luc Nancy has generally named "monovalence" in *Dis-Enclosure* (New York: Fordham University Press, 2008), 29–41. Details from these arguments and their different terms will occupy our attention in due time.
14. Jan Assmann, *Herrschaft und Heil: Politische Theologie in Altägypten, Israel und Europa* (Munich: Carl Hanser, 2000), 29. Henceforth cited in the text. Notice the shift from Schmitt's *Staatslehre* (theory of the state or doctrine of the state) to Assmann's *Staatsrecht* (law of the state or constitution of the state, but also public law). This is because, for Assmann, the theologization of the political entails taking over the entire realm of society's lawmaking capacity: law and theology become one and the political (self-)interrogation of the law (autonomy) is thereby barred.
15. A crucial work, in this regard, is Kathleen Davis, *Periodization and Sovereignty: How Ideas of Sovereignty and Secularization Govern the Politics of Time* (Philadelphia: University of Pennsylvania Press, 2008), which dismantles a great many assumptions about the relation between secularization and modernity. However, like many works of this kind, this book too does not dare to apply the same deconstructive logic to the historicity (and periodization) of the theological.
16. See Heinrich Meier, *The Lesson of Carl Schmitt* (Chicago: University of Chicago Press, 1998). Taubes insists on this as well, quoting in fact Schmitt's personal admission to him that he is a Christian and therefore locked into a de facto theological struggle with Judaism. See Taubes, *To Carl Schmitt*, 44, 54. Taking a direct cue from Schmitt's *Glossarium*, Peter Hohendal argues instead that there is a shift in the postwar work marked by "Catholic intensification" (*Verschärfung*)—Schmitt's words. See Hohendal, "Political Theology Revisited: Carl Schmitt's Postwar Reassessment," *Konturen* 1 (2008): 1–26. I will return to this point later in the discussion of Erik Peterson.
17. One might argue, retrospectively, that Schmitt diagnoses in Blumenberg's treatise an impulse similar to what propels Assmann: namely, political theology is always already a theologization of the worldly, a transposition that Schmitt, trying to explain Blumenberg's standpoint, beautifully characterizes as part of the "tragic mortgages from past epochs" (PT II, 117).
18. I elaborate on Schmitt's mythical proclivities, especially as this is articulated contra Georges Sorel, in "The Concept of the Mythical," in *Does Literature Think?* (Stanford: Stanford University Press, 2003), 90–115. It is worth recalling here Jacob Taubes's account of his own agonistic encounter with Schmitt—"the most violent discussions I ever had in the German language"—conducted precisely over Schmitt's mythical

proclivities: specifically, "historiography [being] forced into a mythical construction" (Taubes, *To Carl Schmitt*, 15). Of course, unlike Taubes, who objects to myth altogether, I take issue not with Schmitt's attraction to myth but with how Schmitt tries to domesticate myth via political theology. The third element in this discussion is Blumenberg, arguably the most erudite theoretician of myth, whom Taubes also challenges at about the same period. For an excellent discussion of this intersection and debate, see Brad Tabas, "Blumenberg, Politics, Anthropology," and Herbert Kopp-Oberstebrink, "Between Terror and Play: The Intellectual Encounter of Hans Blumenberg and Jacob Taubes," *Telos* 158 (Spring 2012): 135–53 and 119–34, respectively.

19. Sigmund Freud, *Moses and Monotheism*, in *The Origins of Religion*, Pelican Freud Library 13, trans. James Strachey (London: Penguin, 1985), 258. Henceforth cited in the text as MM, followed by page number. This is essentially the core argument in Regina Schwartz, *The Curse of Cain: The Violent Logic of Monotheism* (Chicago: University of Chicago Press, 1997) and partly in Peter Sloterdijk's *God's Zeal*.
20. Etienne Balibar, "Note sur l'origine et les usages du terme 'monothéisme,'" *Critique* 704–5 (2006): 19–45. Henceforth cited in the text; my translation.
21. Taubes uses this phrase from Psalms in a letter to Schmitt from 1979 with the hope of opening his eyes as to his erstwhile, now deceased friend's warning about where Schmitt was then headed as chief jurist for the Reich: "Astonishing is [Peterson's] reference to *Civitas Dei* III.30, which has nothing 'historical' but which in 1935 was shockingly contemporary: *caecus atque improvidus futurorum* [so blind and unable to see the future], a coded warning to you [Schmitt]—which you never received. You have no better friend than Peterson to put you on the path to the Christian Church. 'True are the wounds that the arrow of a friend inflicts' (in Hebrew abbreviated to *ne'emanim pizei obev*) it says somewhere in Psalms. . . . Peterson's arrow is no Parthian arrow, but a Christian one." Taubes, *To Carl Schmitt*, 28.
22. Michael Psellos, the greatest philosopher of the late Byzantine era (and in this sense, one might say, heir to Gregory Nazianzus, though not sanctified), was the first to reflect on Gregory's extraordinary skills, which he saw as divinely inspired: "That great man had received the first principles of philosophy from above, by uplifting his mind toward the incorporeal and divine forms. . . . One might then suppose that he also seized the beauty and power of his discourse in an ineffable way from some heavenly source and mixed it with his writings according to harmonies of a superior music. . . . This amazing man appears to have obtained what is beyond nature." "On the Style of Gregory the Theologian, §4:11–23," in *Michael Psellos: Rhetoric and Authorship in Byzantium*, by Stratis Papaioannou (Cambridge: Cambridge University Press, 2013).
23. Quoted throughout the text from the original Greek in my translation: http://users.uoa.gr/~nektar/orthodoxy/paterikon/grhgorios_8eologos_logoi.htm#29.
24. A possible counterargument could be that anarchy might be a cipher for democracy and polyarchy a cipher for aristocracy. Yet, strictly speaking, this cannot be the case in the Greek politico-philosophical sphere. Only Plato has charged democracy with anarchy and this, of course, as an enemy. But for the Church Fathers there is no substantial difference; polyarchy leads to anarchy. Gregory might be channeling here the position of Eusebius as it was articulated in his famous speech celebrating thirty years of rule under Emperor Constantine: ἀναρχία γαρ μάλλον καὶ στάσις ἡ ἐξ ἰσοτιμίας ἀντιπαρεξαγομένη πολυαρχία ("polyarchy produced by equality of power [means] anarchy and even more stasis") (*Oration in Praise of Constantine*, 3:6). In other words, polyarchy is the political rule of polytheism. The key concern is the common factor: the rule of the many, gods or humans alike. The aristocratic roots of democracy after

all cannot be disputed. While polyarchy is originally aristocratic, it is now inherent in democracy as literally the rule of the many, which for Gregory mirrors the rule of many gods (*polytheotēs*), the real enemy after all. In this context, democracy is polyarchy in governing principle and anarchy as political symptom.

25. See Nicole Loraux, *The Invention of Athens: The Funeral Oration in the Classical City* (New York: Zone, 2006). For an exceptional account of the full gamut of the notion of stasis, see Dimitris Vardoulakis, "Stasis: Beyond Political Theology?," in *Cultural Critique* 73 (Fall 2009), 125–147 and his subsequent elaboration in *Stasis Before the State: Nine Theses of Agonistic Democracy* (New York: Fordham University Press, 2017). Especially nuanced is also the treatment of stasis as a primal word (in Freud's sense) in Rebecca Comay, "Resistance and Repetition: Freud and Hegel," *Research in Phenomenology* 45 (2015): 237–66.
26. They do not, however, reside in the realm of friendship. If *philia* were to be invoked at all in terms of *stasis*, it would have to be restricted to its minor meaning of kinship. But *philia*, in its broadest most powerful sense, which outdoes the order of kinship, cannot submit itself to the order of stasis, and I disagree here with Vardoulakis's extensive (and brilliant, in its terms) reading of Aristotle's *Nicomachean Ethics* in this regard (Vardoulakis, "Stasis: Beyond Political Theology?," 137–40). The internal sphere within which *stasis* is enacted is not ontological, anthropological, or ethical, but political. *Stasis*, as strife, faction, or rebellion, is the semantic child of the polis. All other uses (including the one by Gregory Nazianzus discussed here) are mere translations of the notion: metaphorical invocations that are, at best, meant to politicize the semantic field. If within this translated context, these invocations are read literally as philosophical or, in this case, theological, they depoliticize the notion.
27. Marie-José Mondzain, *Image, Icon, Economy: The Byzantine Origins of the Contemporary Imaginary* (Stanford: Stanford University Press, 2005) is exemplary in pointing this out, while attempting to unfold the significance of iconic thought in the entire economy of Christianity. In this sense, it remains a singular antidote to Agamben's argument.
28. Crucial here is also the work of the other great Cappadocian theologian and Church Father, Gregory of Nyssa (335–95 CE), who engaged in the most extensive elaboration on the philosophical contours of *homoousios* and the distinction between essence (*ousia*) and hypostasis (which in Latin Christendom eventually came to signify "person"), so that the Trinity could be simultaneously one (in essence), even if three (in person/substance). A great resource to understanding Nyssa's complex work is Lucas Francisco Mateo-Seco and Gulio Maspero, eds., *The Brill Dictionary of Gregory Nyssa* (Leiden: Brill, 2010).
29. Thanos Zartaloudis, who has provided the most sophisticated analysis of Agamben's argument on the basis of *oikonomia*, sees this as a governmentality of nonpower (a neo-governmentality, as he calls it in light of the contemporary crisis of political legitimation). I would add that this "nonpower" that cannot be legitimated—which exceeds the necessity for legitimation—is precisely the real (and brutal) power of a cryptopolitics of sovereignty that flourishes in the depoliticization of society. In other words, the dangers of using Christological notions of *oikonomia* to explain contemporary "neoliberal" politics, as Agamben does, is to mistake the evident depoliticization of society for an alleged depoliticization of power. By all accounts, the latter is not the case, and it's frankly impossible to imagine it ever being so. See Zartaloudis, *Giorgio Agamben*, esp. 51–94.

30. Agamben goes on to add that the Cappadocian theologians are the ones who introduce to Christian theology the notion of hypostasis—from the verb *hyphistamai*, which means "to exist" but literally means "to stand under"—which takes over as the primary signification of essence from the prevalence of *ousia*, derivative of the verb *einai*, which means "to be." Essence thus turns into substance. But, interestingly, Agamben does not engage with the intersection of this new notion with the operative role that *stasis* plays in Trinitarian theology, despite the obvious etymological connection. In an admittedly free translation, we could say that substance is no longer a mere manifestation of singular being (essence), but the signification of otherness-in-being, of being that exists through discord with itself (*stasis*).
31. The subsequent history of Latin Christianity suggests that anti-Trinitarian movements were linked to more liberal sorts of politics, from the followers of Erasmus, to the Italian Humanists, to Unitarian and later Deist tendencies in England and its American colonies. The charge was consistently based on the idea that Trinitarian thinking was preposterous and an affront to both monotheism and humanism, in that it denigrated the human element of Jesus, which served as a model for all Christian mortals on earth. Of course, the fact that, against the consubstantial divinity of the Son, stood the divine "impregnation" of the Virgin by the Holy Spirit, which is as preposterous as any idea can get, was never addressed by these advocates of reason, nor were indeed their monotheistic obsessions in their configuration of humanism. But they did serve to obscure the extraordinary sophistication of the Trinitarian argument as a monarchical substantiation of the monotheistic imaginary, creating the false impression of a more robust and yet more liberal monotheism. For a concise history of these tendencies, see Michael Allen Gillespie, "The Anti-Trinitarian Origins of Liberalism" (Boston University Series on Religion and Politics, 2014), www.youtube.com/watch?v=L7QMQrIIOFM.
32. Erik Peterson, "Monotheism as a Political Problem," in *Theological Treatises* (Stanford: Stanford University Press, 2011), 95. Henceforth cited in the text.
33. My argument here is predicated on the thesis that monotheism is a much more complex proposition than merely unitary (or, even more, merely universal) logic. Hence, my assessment of the political significance of Gregory's gesture would be heretical in relation to most historians of the period. See, indicatively, Arnaldo Momigliano, "The Disadvantages of Monotheism for a Universal State," *Classical Philology* 81, no. 4 (October 1986): 285–97.
34. As Peter Brown has famously shown, the so-called decline of paganism was not a matter of collapse due the influx of some radically new ideas, but a slow internal process of transmutation. See Brown, *The Making of Late Antiquity* (Cambridge, MA: Harvard University Press, 1978), 49–50.
35. Despite the recent adorations of Paul, one might add. Here, all kinds of contradictions abound. For Badiou especially, who builds his argument on the antiphilosophical character of Paul, it would be inconceivable to think of Paul as antipolitical, or, in my terms, depoliticizing. And yet, Peterson's own prejudice makes this quite perceptible. In the end, if Pauline so-called antiphilosophy bears a politics, this would be the politics of theocracy, a politics that Paul explicitly represses but implicitly expounds.
36. Etienne Balibar, *Spinoza and Politics* (London: Verso, 1998), esp. 39–50.
37. Jean Luc Nancy, *Disenclosure: The Deconstruction of Christianity* (New York: Fordham University Press, 2008), 33. Henceforth cited in the text.
38. "This condition prohibits one from speaking of 'war of civilizations,' as if Western civilization confronts some other Arabic-Oriental one. This process has already begun

within the inner realm of Western civilization. After having created a situation within itself that destabilizes the different parts of old Europe, civilization tears itself apart. . . . [It] reveals its inability to expand as civilization. It expands (only) its own implosion." Jean-Luc Nancy, "The War of Monotheism: On the Inability to Expand: The West Battles Against Itself," *Cultural Critique* 57 (Spring 2004): 104–7.

39. Jacques Derrida, *Specters of Marx* (London: Routledge, 2006), 73.
40. In light of the section on Freud that follows, I add here Freud's own rather regretful articulation of what, unlike other places in history, the place of Palestine—his more generic choice of a name than Derrida's choice of Jerusalem—has bequeathed the world: "Palestine has produced nothing but religions, sacred frenzies, presumptuous attempts to conquer the outer world of appearances by the inner world of wishful thinking." The matter is not, of course, one of place, but one of what sort of dynamic is unleashed upon the world that the world (as inadequate as this singular notion might be) does not seem to be able to handle. See Freud's letter to Arnold Zweig, May 8, 1932, in Ernst Freud, ed., *The Letters of Sigmund Freud and Arnold Zweig* (New York: Harcourt, Brace and World, 1970), 40.
41. The theologian Christian Frevel has convincingly argued that the fact that monotheism is a modern concept does not bar us from using it to account for structures in antiquity that may have expressed it without naming it or even knowing it. It's a matter not of anachronism or historical transposition but of epistemological flexibility. As he takes monotheism to be a relational rather than an essentialist concept—and the contentious heterogeneity of its history testifies to that—Frevel finds it a heuristic category regardless of what may be questions of historical authenticity. See Christian Frevel, "Beyond Monotheism? Some Remarks and Questions on Conceptualizing 'Monotheism' in Biblical Studies," *Verbum et Ecclesia* 34, no. 2 (2013), www.ve.org.za/index.php/VE/article/viewFile/810/1839.
42. I deliberately mention that the Hindu action as the polytheistic mode of worship in this case is entirely subordinated to the monological, monovalent, monomythical nationalism that Hinduism singularly serves. Monotheism produces all kinds of psychohistorical symptoms even in domains that would not necessarily be identified with it, whether "polytheistic" practices or "secular" formations. The monomythical structure of the nation-form is one such psychohistorical symptom of monotheism in modernity, and it is remarkably consistent across multiple cultural traditions. An excellent meditation on this issue is Anustup Basu, "The 'Indian' Monotheism," *boundary 2* 39, no. 2 (Summer 2012), 111–41.
43. Jan Assmann, *The Price of Monotheism*, trans. Robert Savage (Stanford: Stanford University Press, 2010), 34. Henceforth cited in the text as PoM, followed by page number.
44. "That there is but a single God must be understood not as a philosophical speculation concerning substance or the supreme being, but on the basis of a structure of address. The One is that which inscribes no difference in the subjects to which it addresses itself. The One is only insofar as it is for all: such is the maxim of universality when it has its root in the event. Monotheism can be understood only by taking into consideration the whole of humanity. Unless addressed to all, the One crumbles and disappears." Alain Badiou, *Saint Paul: The Foundations of Universality* (Stanford: Stanford University Press, 2003), 76.
45. Hence, the extraordinary seductiveness of the myth of Exodus, not only for the Jews, but for an incredible range of oppressed peoples worldwide who drew their liberation myths from the biblical text (the most spectacular use of which is found in Jamaican

Rastafari religion). But it is also worth remembering here Edward Said's famous riposte to Michael Walzer's fetishism of the Exodus myth, which pointed out the book's deafening silence about the myth's celebration of the conquest of the indigenous peoples of Canaan. See Edward W. Said, "Michael Walzer's Exodus and Revolution: A Canaanite Reading," *Grand Street* 5, no. 2 (Winter 1986): 86–106.

46. The specific apostrophe has also been interpreted as evidence of Freud's Oedipal rebellion against his forefathers. The charge provides an added redoubling to the text's continuous attention to the repetition of the originary parricidal violence that lies beneath the process of institution, not just of a religion but of society as such. Its resonance with Freud's avowed ambivalence, in his preface to the Hebrew translation of *Totem and Taboo*, between resisting and belonging to the parameters of Jewish identity has been pointed out as well. See the insightful discussion in Barbara Johnson, *Moses and Multiculturalism* (Berkeley: University of California Press, 2010), 61ff.

47. This is in large part regarding the replay of Moses in Jesus and the slew of permutations it springs forth, including the replay of Paul in Freud. But it is ultimately a much grander and more ambitious argument about the chameleon-like "nature" of Christianity in the worldwide history of the last two millennia. "Is it not at all curious that Christ too was, as if by coincidence, a murdered leader who brought about the founding of 'two religions' (Judaism and Christianity, Catholicism and Protestantism), that this founder too was always already two (Jesus and Paul), and that behind Freud's Moses there was always Jesus of course but also Paul's Moses, ultimately a very Christian Moses?" Gil Anidjar, *Blood: A Critique of Christianity* (New York: Columbia University Press, 2014), 244.

48. Edward Said published his extended essay on Freud's *Moses and Monotheism* shortly before his death but he had at one time considered it part of his late-style project, which he left unfinished. See Edward Said, *Freud and the Non-European* (London: Verso, 2003).

49. I prefer to keep the more common translation of the multivalent verb *schaffen* as "make" rather than "create"—drawing from its old Saxon roots that yield the Middle English *schapen*, which is to say, *shape*—in order to emphasize the material work that goes into the fashioning of a certain culture: that the creation of a new form of culture is tantamount to the (re)making of a certain something of society into something else. The power of Freud's formulation is that no peoples exist as such. Or, more pointedly in this case, the Jews don't exist by an act of God, despite the myth of their divine election. Rather, like all peoples, they are made by the works of men and women; they are self-made, even if by the bizarre occasion of a foundational act that comes from a stranger, the work of one man (*ein Mann Moses*) who finds in them the opportunity to found a new people. Freud, of course, uses the same verb Luther does in his translation of the biblical phrase "God created man in his own image." But in this phrase too, by virtue of the mimetic qualifier, the verb denotes the vicissitudes of making. In this discussion, we are always talking of a certain poetics, of mythmaking as society's own *poiēsis*.

50. The complexity of making history, of history's *poiēsis*, which can only take place as the enactment of human networks (conscious or unconscious), is very much lost in the streamlining of the title's English translation, as Samuel Weber points out in his sumptuous meditation on this text: "In renaming *The Man Moses and Monotheistic Religion* to *Moses and Monotheism*, the English translator gave Freud's text the semblance of a unified work, but at the expense of obscuring its complexity as a heterogeneous network." See Samuel Weber, "Doing Away With Freud's Man Moses," in

Targets of Opportunity: On the Militarization of Thinking (New York: Fordham University Press, 2005), 71. Henceforth cited in the text.

51. Letter to Arnold Zweig, September 30, 1934. In Freud, *The Letters of Sigmund Freud and Arnold Zweig*, 91–93.
52. Ilse Grubrich-Simitis, *Early and Late Freud* (London: Routledge, 1997), 84. Henceforth cited in the text.
53. There is a famous phrase, about which innumerable commentaries have been written, that brings together in one gesture the form of Freud's own text with the form of the text of the historical fiction he is unraveling, down to the very plotline, the fictional character, and the historical readers across the ages: "In its implications the distortion of a text resembles a murder: the difficulty is not in perpetrating the deed, but in doing away with the traces" (MM, 283). Freud is not only a writer of a modernist (historical) novel; he is also the modernist reader of an archaic history. He fancies himself a detective (as archeologist or reader), but he is also privy to the scene of the crime as the criminal (the writer) who has fashioned the scene's many disguises.
54. See Michel de Certeau, "The Fiction of History: The Writing of Moses and Monotheism," in *The Writing of History* (New York: Columbia University Press, 1988), 308–54. I am using here the spelling present in the English translation. But the proper spelling should be *phantasy*, which I will use from now on. The French *fantaisie* in its classical meaning works appropriately to denote both the process of creative imagination and the objects it comes to produce, but it is marred by the contemporary connotations of whimsy or fancy, which tend toward triviality. In English, *fantasy* carries many of the same problems, chiefly the notion of unreality. What is essential here is to underline Freud's persistent attention to the phantasmatic capacity of the psyche: the fact that the psyche thinks in terms of phantasms and that, by extrapolation, the social imagination creates a whole range of institutions in the historical realm that are in reality fantasies, phantasms. For the complications of this notion in the various languages of psychoanalysis, see the entry "Phantasy (or Fantasy)," in *The Language of Psychoanalysis*, ed. Jean Laplanche and J.-B. Pontalis (New York: Norton, 1973), 314–19.
55. Grubrich-Simitis, *Early and Late Freud*, 60. "Traumatic conditions of extreme distress" refers obviously to the historical juncture, but Grubrich-Simitis's insightful argument is that the experience of Nazi barbarism triggers in Freud a return of repressed trauma that is linked to his own childhood, which goes beyond being Jewish as such: a personal traumatic distress whose deeply embedded displacement accounts for both his tendency to consider religion constitutively patriarchical and his eventual preference for the questionable phylogenetic explanation of religion over his more psychoanalytically refined argument of ontogenetic neurosis.
56. According to Freud, Moses creates God very much in his own likeness and image—at least, this is what the Hebrews perceive: "Probably they found it hard to separate the image of Moses from that of God, and their instinct was right insofar as Moses might have incorporated his own irascibility and implacability into the character of his God" (MM, 356). In turn, Grubrich-Simitis takes the play of likeness a step further: "The Moses representation surely belonged to the core of Freud's self" (71).
57. "Identity cannot be thought or worked through itself alone; it cannot constitute or even imagine itself without that radical originary break or flaw which will not be repressed, because Moses was Egyptian, and therefore always outside the identity inside which so many have stood, and suffered—and later, perhaps, even triumphed. The strength of this thought, I believe, is that it can be articulated in and speak to other besieged identities as well—not through dispensing palliatives such as tolerance

and compassion, but, rather, by attending to it as a troubling, disabling, destabilizing secular wound, from which there can be no recovery, no state of resolved or Stoic calm, and no utopian reconciliation even within itself." Said, *Freud and the Non-European*, 54.

58. For Jan Assmann, the Mosaic trauma is additionally to be located in the symptom of the Golden Calf, which is a reaction to Moses that "encodes a deeply traumatic experience connected with the prohibition on graven images. . . . The prohibition encodes an iconoclastic impulse which we might call a theoclastic thrust, . . . the destruction of the gods, who are excoriated as idols, the deicidal power of the Mosaic distinction." Correcting Freud, he goes on to add that "the trauma has nothing to do with parricide or the violent fate of the prophets, but with the trauma of deicide." See Jan Assmann, *Religion and Cultural Memory* (Stanford: Stanford University Press, 2006), 57–59. In other words, monotheism precipitates a cycle of killing god(s), as idolatry never stops lurking in its midst, ever fueling a traumatic iconoclasm. The details of the traumatic dialectics between idolatry and iconoclasm are discussed at the conclusion of this text.
59. To this we would have to add the meaning of *ghost*. Freud admits explicitly to being haunted by his own book's ghostly presence while struggling to complete it: "I determined to give it up, but it tormented me like an unredeemed ghost [*unerlöster Geist*]" (MM, 349). Presumably, the persistence to overcome his struggle to finish the book—the redemption from the ghost—would be itself a manifestation of *Geistigkeit*.
60. We might add that, as a configuration of Freud's atheism, *Geistigkeit* is enabled by the necessity to combat the rapacious institutions of the One as totalizing principle. As constitutive of society, formally speaking, *Geistigkeit* is thus presumed to be a principle of plurality that is an alternative to religion, irrelevant to ethnicity, and pertinent to the human condition as such. This viewpoint is certainly at work in Said's reading of *Moses and Monotheism*. The stranger-in-the-self argument disarticulates the identitary process, fissures the monological desire, and indeed complicates the *Geistigkeit* configuration as the unifying principle of the Jews. As a nonidentitary condition in Said's mind, *Geistigkeit* desacralizes itself and its own literal meaning, which is also to say, deethnicizes or denationalizes the process of attributing it to the Jews alone. Said, of course, had his own reasons for this sort of reading of Freud's intentions, which ultimately remains rather generous.
61. See Richard J. Bernstein, *Freud and the Legacy of Moses* (Cambridge: Cambridge University Press, 1998) for an extensive discussion of the various dimensions of *Geistigkeit* in this regard.
62. Jan Assmann has an interesting take on this very point, which Grubrich-Simitis misses, but it adds a crucial dimension to how we read Freud's *The Future of an Illusion*, which I don't have the space here to discuss properly: "The 'Mosaic prohibition' constructs an Archimedean point from which iconic religion can be unmasked as an illusion, and from which Freud can ultimately unmask religion itself as illusion" (PoM, 103). This may suggest that, in terms of equating "iconic religion" with religion per se, monotheism escapes the realm of religion as illusion (obsessional neurosis), even if Freud in fact constructs a laborious argument in order to chronicle its obsessions. The occasion marks one of Freud's own illusions, precipitated by his incapacity to perceive what remains cryptically iconic (idolatrous) in monotheism.
63. "The memory of the monotheistic truth requires that the polytheistic truth must be forgotten. The imperative 'Remember!' implies the opposite imperative 'Forget!' However, it is not possible to forget as easily as it is to remember. The imperative 'Forget!'

is paradoxical. This paradox contains the seeds of anxiety, guilt, and the trauma of monotheism." See Assmann, *Religion and Cultural Memory*, 57.

64. Cornelius Castoriadis, "Institution of Society and Religion," in *World in Fragments: Writings on Politics, Society, Psychoanalysis, and the Imagination*, ed. David Ames Curtis (Stanford: Stanford University Press, 1997), 325. Henceforth cited in the text as ISR. Translation modified when necessary.
65. It's interesting to think of Schmitt in this regard: "Even the journey into the desert or the climbing of the stylite's pillar can become a political demonstration, depending on the issue" (PT II, 84).
66. While still under the influence of Pierre Clastres, Marcel Gauchet argues how this existential split between society and itself at the very moment of its (self-)institution, which may be thought of as the moment of the emergence of religion, may also be thought of as the moment of the emergence of the State as social-imaginary form: "We may say that religion has been historically the condition of possibility for the State . . . [or] . . . the foundation of the State is itself the foundation of religion." See Gauchet, "La Dette du sens et les racines de l'État," in *La Condition politique* (Paris: Gallimard, 2005), 66–67.
67. Karl Marx, "Introduction to the Contribution to the Critique of Hegel's Philosophy of Right," in *Marx-Engels, Collected Works* (New York: International, 1975), 3:175. Italics in the original; translation slightly altered.
68. Although beyond the purview of this essay, there may be fertile ground to explore the connection of Castoriadis's term *socially effective religion* to what the young Hegel famously named "positive religion" in *The Positivity of Christian Religion* (1795). For Hegel "positive religion" happens when societies defer their self-authorization to a set of extrasocial (and, in that sense, supernatural) principles, which may be posited by society's intellect (*Geist*) but are nonetheless endowed with an authority of their own that exceeds this intellect, rendering them incomprehensible to reason and apprehensible by sheer obedience. For Hegel, Judeo-Christianity is expressly a mode of "positive religion." One might add that it becomes "socially effective" in the sense that obedience exceeds mere practices of worship and is posited as an elemental mode of societal organization. It is from this Hegel and against this Hegel that Marx will come to assert famously that "criticism of religion is the premise of all criticism"—the inaugural sentence of his "Introduction to the Contribution to the Critique of Hegel's Philosophy of Right" (1843).
69. In his brilliant study *No Religion Without Idolatry: Mendelssohn's Jewish Enlightenment* (Notre Dame: University of Notre Dame Press, 2012), Gideon Freudenthal focuses on what he sees, by way of Moses Mendelssohn, as the semiotic foundation of all religious practices, which makes idolatry unavoidable in all religion. The argument is similar to the one I am making here, except that for Freudenthal idolatry is the necessary other to religion, the mythical element without which religion cannot be constituted, while my reading of Castoriadis enables me to bring forth what is inherently idolatrous in religion as such, regardless of claims to the contrary, so that, rather than being two constitutively engaged but different elements, one is the basic operative and epistemic framework of the other, albeit concealed by the advent of monotheism.
70. Denis Diderot, *The Encyclopedia: Selections*, ed. and trans. Stephen J. Gendzier (New York: Harper, 1967), 139–40.
71. W. J. T. Mitchell, "Idolatry: Blake, Nietzsche, and Poussin," in *Idol Anxiety*, ed. Josh Ellenbogen and Aaron Tugendhaft (Stanford: Stanford University Press, 2011), 56–73. Henceforth cited in the text. Idol anxiety may be a perfect way to describe a whole

range of academic discourses on religion or so-called postsecularism these days that consider themselves radical. This collection of essays is a welcome exception.

72. Jan Assmann, "What's Wrong with Images?," in Ellenbogen and Tugendhaft, *Idol Anxiety*, 21–22. Henceforth cited parenthetically in the text.
73. The annihilation of Alexandria's Serapeum in 391 by Christian zealots during the reign of Theodosius I, after the imperial ban on pagan religious rites, signified the erasure of centuries of accumulated knowledge and precipitated what, from this standpoint, were rightly called the Dark Ages. For example, Anaximander's conception, in the sixth century BC, of the Earth as a sphere suspended in the void by an equilibrium of forces gave way to the conviction, for the subsequent millennium, that the Earth was flat and anyone who claimed otherwise was burned at the stake. The same annihilating desire arises with fury during the Reformation. The instances of decapitation and defacement of sculptural or mural depictions of the Gospel, as well as funereal sculptures of bishops, are still visible at the Dom Cathedral in Utrecht as relics of the Calvinist Reformation (1580). Given the total destruction of the Bamiyan Buddhas by the Taliban in Afghanistan (2001) or the arches of Palmyra by ISIS in Syria (2015), one wonders whether such traces of annihilating desire will continue to be visible at all. The annihilation is not just of the past but of the future.
74. Luce Irigaray, "La Transcendance de l'autre," in *Autour de l'idolâtrie: Figures actuelles de pouvoir et de domination*, ed. Bernard Van Meenen et al. (Brussels: Facultés Universitaires Saint-Louis, 2003), 45–46, my translation.
75. Xenophanes of Colophon, writing in the sixth century BC, had enough sense to argue that if bulls, horses, or lions had hands they would draw the form of their gods in their likeness, thereby affirming that anthropomorphic divinity exists only because it is a human creation. That he articulated this thought in order to criticize the anthropomorphic mythology of Homer and Hesiod, being thus the first to suggest that divinity may be precisely what cannot be conceptualized, is yet another tragic confirmation of the fact that humans cannot accept their capacity for radical creation.
76. I recall Marx again. His configuration of the realm of the profane is predicated on this strange phenomenon—the self-incapacitation of humanity by virtue of its awesome capacity to institute superhuman doubles of itself: "Man, who looked for a superhuman being in the fantastic reality of heaven and found nothing there but the reflection of himself, will no longer be disposed to find but the semblance of himself, only an inhuman being, where he seeks and must seek his true reality." See Marx, "Introduction to the Contribution to the Critique of Hegel's Philosophy of Right," 3:175.
77. This is what links the Renaissance with the Reformation to my mind—their antithesis is a dialectical continuation precisely in terms of humanism undoing itself in its name—but also what enables the critique of representation to emerge out of the practice of modernism, and so on. The exemplary treatment of this whole imaginary nexus remains Vassilis Lambropoulos, *The Rise of Eurocentrism: An Anatomy of Interpretation* (Princeton: Princeton University Press, 1993), which is a remarkable book in spite of its baroque structure and whose flight under the academic radar is testament both to its unorthodox brilliance and to the academy's almost requisite tendency to protect its keep.
78. And we would have to add, modernism itself. Andreas Huyssen, *Miniature Metropolis: Literature in the Age of Photography and Film* (Cambridge, MA: Harvard University Press, 2015) explores precisely this tendency in modernist thinking to configure language in terms of the image (Benjamin's *Denkbilder* is arguably the most famous articulation) in utterly condensed fashion, hence the miniature. This imagistic

condensation of language—we instantly think of Ezra Pound as well—in the German context takes place against the grain of an otherwise extensively cultivated *Bilderverbot* and can be said to carry a specifically post-Romantic (modernist) mediation of *Bildung*.

79. See Cornelius Castoriadis, "Radical Imagination and the Social Instituting Imaginary," in *The Castoriadis Reader*, ed. David Ames Curtis (Oxford: Blackwell, 1997), 321–22.
80. See an exceptional presentation of this process by Costas Douzinas in "The Legality of the Image," *Modern Law Review* 63, no. 6 (November 2000): 813–30.
81. This is perfectly corroborated by Emmanuel Lévinas at the very instant he abrogates the idolatrous significance of his utterance: "The Hebrew terms in the Old Testament that tend to get translated as God, *Deus*, or *Theos*, are proper names according the wishes of the Talmud. The name of God is always said to be a proper name in the Scriptures. The word God would be absent from the Hebrew language! A fine consequence of monotheism in which there exists neither a divine species nor a generic word to designate it. . . . The word designating the divinity is precisely the word Name, a generic term in relation to which the different names of God are individuals." In Lévinas, *Beyond the Verse: Talmudic Readings and Lectures*, trans. Gary D. Mole (London: Athlone, 1994), 119.
82. Marie-José Mondzain's otherwise exemplary meditation on what she calls "the Byzantine origins of the contemporary imaginary" misses this crucial fact. While, theologically speaking, she is correct to point out the distinction between idol and icon—"the image is invisible, the icon is visible; . . . the image is a mystery, the icon is an enigma; . . . the image is eternal similitude, the icon is temporal resemblance" (Mondzain, *Image, Icon, Economy*, 3)—once we understand that an idol reaches beyond the realm of the representation and is a matter of signification, the distinction lapses. Of course, in Byzantine historical reality the distinction is retained—through a most elaborate economy of its imaginary, as Mondzain demonstrates—precisely so as to conceal the idolatry that animates both iconic signification and the enormous theological literature produced on its behalf.
83. The most insightful account of this configuration is Rebecca Comay, "Materialist Mutations of the *Bilderverbot*," in *Sites of Vision: The Discursive Construction of Sight in Modern Philosophy*, ed. David Michael Levine (Cambridge, MA: MIT Press, 1999), 337–78.
84. The compass to Cattelan's history, which in the end animates this exhibit, is provided by Nancy Spector, chief curator of the Guggenheim Museum, in her *Maurizio Cattelan All* (New York: Guggenheim Museum, 2011). Spector sees the retrospective as an exercise in (self-)disrespect—"an installation that cunningly celebrates its futility"—with the artist hanging his work like laundry to dry.
85. See Talal Asad's "Free Speech, Blasphemy, and Secular Criticism" and Saba Mahmood's "Religious Reason and Secular Affect: An Incommensurable Divide?" in the volume *Is Critique Secular? Blasphemy, Injury, and Free Speech* (Berkeley: Townsend Humanities Center, 2009), 20–63 and 64–100, respectively. I address these arguments in detail in Gourgouris, "Detranscendentalizing the Secular," in *Lessons in Secular Criticism* (New York: Fordham University Press, 2013), 28–64.
86. An utterly prescient and one of the most instructive works on this issue is the collective publication of LABEL [Ligue pour l'Abolition des lois réprimant le Blasphème et le droit de s'Exprimer Librement], *Blasphèmes et libertés*, ed. Patrice Dartevelle, Philippe Denis, and Johannes Robyn (Paris: Cerf, 1993).

87. "Idolatry is a form of vandalism that often inspires a violent counter-reaction of antipathy to the idol," says the inimitable Judith Thurman, with her penchant for phrasing a complicated thought as if it's mere observation. The phrase occurs in her essay on the photography of Diane Arbus and is exemplary of how the visual is always psychically authorized, in the sense of how the subject objectifies itself in the process of apprehending (and thus creating) the object. In this case, Diane Arbus, an idol herself, suffers the counterreactive antipathy of idolatry. See Judith Thurman, *Cleopatra's Nose: 39 Varieties of Desire* (New York: Farrar, Straus and Giroux, 2007), 55.
88. See W. J. T. Mitchell, "On Critical Idolatry," *documenta 13*, June 12, 2012, http://d13.documenta.de/#/research/research/view/on-critical-idolatry.
89. For an insightful exploration of precisely these terms, see Mats Rosengren, *Cave Art: Perception and Knowledge* (London: Palgrave, 2012).
90. Jacques Rancière, *The Future of the Image*, trans. Gregory Elliott (London: Verso, 2007), 137–38.
91. No one has understood this better and articulated it more dramatically than Georges Didi-Huberman in his discussion of the clandestine photographic self-representation of annihilation from inside Auschwitz. See Didi-Huberman, *Images in Spite of All* (Chicago: University of Chicago Press, 2008).
92. Emanuele Coccia, *Sensible Life: The Micro-Ontology of the Image* (New York: Fordham University Press, 2016). My only objection to this unique argument is to its almost obsessive insistence on positing the mediatic space where images and sensible life coexist—make each other be, entwined in total codetermination—as an "outside": as the intermediate space between subject and object. But the very nature of *meson* (middle, medium) since Anaximander's fragment testifies to the impossibility of the "outside" as object (or subject, for that matter). The presumption that the form of the image as the medium of the sensible is quintessentially outside—outside the world, outside as such—is no different than the idolatrous ruse of unrepresentability.
93. Wole Soyinka, *Myth, Literature, and the African World* (Cambridge: Cambridge University Press, 1976), 41.

INDEX